# Law, Rights and Disability

D1635871

30107 004 897 077

*of related interest*

Care Homes Legal Handbook
*Jeremy Cooper*
ISBN 1 84310 064 9

Manual Handling in Health and Social Care
An A–Z of Law and Practice
*Michael Mandelstam*
ISBN 1 84310 041 X

Disabled Children and the Law
Research and Good Practice
*Janet Read and Luke Clements*
ISBN 1 85302 793 6

Community Care Practice and the Law
Second Edition
*Michael Mandelstam*
ISBN 1 85302 647 6

Children with Special Needs
Assessment, Law and Practice – Caught in the Act 4th edition
*John Friel*
ISBN 1 85302 460 0

Equipment for Older or Disabled People and the Law
*Michael Mandelstam*
ISBN 1 85302 352 3

Disability Politics and Community Care
*Mark Priestley*
ISBN 1 85302 652 2

Empowerment in Everyday Life
Learning Disability
*Edited by Paul Ramcharan, Gwyneth Roberts, Gordon Grant
and John Borland*
ISBN 1 85302 382 5

# Law, Rights
# and Disability

*Edited by Jeremy Cooper*

Jessica Kingsley Publishers
London and New York

All rights reserved. No part of this publication may be reproduced in any material form (including photocopying or storing it in any medium by electronic means and whether or not transiently or incidentally to some other use of this publication) without the written permission of the copyright owner except in accordance with the provisions of the Copyright, Designs and Patents Act 1988 or under the terms of a licence issued by the Copyright Licensing Agency Ltd, 90 Tottenham Court Road, London, England W1P 9HE. Applications for the copyright owner's written permission to reproduce any part of this publication should be addressed to the publisher.
Warning: The doing of an unauthorised act in relation to a copyright work may result in both a civil claim for damages and criminal prosecution.

The right of the contributors to be identified as authors of this work has been asserted by them in accordance with the Copyright, Designs and Patents Act 1988.

First published in the United Kingdom in 2000 by
Jessica Kingsley Publishers Ltd
116 Pentonville Road
London N1 9JB, England
and
29 West 35th Street, 10th fl.
New York, NY 10001–2299, USA


www.jkp.com


Copyright © 2000 Jessica Kingsley Publishers Ltd
Printed digitally since 2003


**Library of Congress Cataloging in Publication Data**
A CIP catalogue record for this book is available from the Library of Congress

**British Library Cataloguing in Publication Data**
A CIP catalogue record for this book is available from the British Library


ISBN 1 85302 836 3 ✓


Printed and bound in Great Britain by
Marston Lindsay Ross International Ltd,
Oxfordshire

# Contents

# Acknowledgements

I would like initially to acknowledge a debt to my friend and colleague, Stuart Vernon, with whom the idea for this book was conceived and developed, and who was responsible for finding and persuading several of the contributors to write chapters for this volume.

I would further like to thank Irene Clark, my invaluable assistant at Southampton Institute for her work on preparing the text. Many other people participated in the collective process that produced this volume, and I would therefore like to extend my thanks to all those who contributed various pieces of information to complete the complex jigsaw that constitutes the world of disability rights.

Some of these contributors are disabled, some are not, and this lack of distinction underpins an important theme of the book, that of collaboration and co-operation between people committed to the common goal, the elimination of discrimination.

BARCODE No. X 4897077

CLASS No. 344.0324 LAW

BIB CHECK   23 MAY 2003   PROC CHECK

6/03 apr

No.

LOAN CATEGORY N/L

# Preface

This book assesses the current state of development of the movement to enhance the position of disabled people in society, both in the UK and across the globe, in their struggle to move from a position of imprisonment to empowerment. Its focus is upon rights, upon the extent to which the law can assist in the strengthening of these rights, and upon the crucial role to be played by disabled people in fulfilling the promise of the worldwide rights movement. In particular the book examines the pivotal role played by the non-disabled 'caring professions' – lawyers, advisers, social workers and therapists, who have the power both to enhance the evolving emancipatory trends in attitudes to disabled people, and equally to ignore or reject these trends, thereby slamming the door upon such emancipation. This book confirms that the road towards emancipation and equality is a long road, a slow road, but that there is now hard evidence that the worldwide movement to strengthen the rights of disabled people, and to free them from the institutionalisation that has characterised so much of their recent history is gaining ground, as attitudes change and disabled people themselves gain the confidence to demand and articulate their requirement for equal treatment and respect.

Clare Picking begins the analysis of these issues in Chapter One by providing an overview of historical attitudes of non-disabled health and social care professionals to their relationship with their disabled clients, charting the beginnings of the movement from the medical model of disability to the social model of disability, a change which essentially provides the leitmotif for the entire volume. In this chapter, the relationship between disabled people and health and social care professionals is scrutinised from the position of disabled people themselves. The chapter provides a number of examples of good practice, emphasising that where this occurs it is invariably the result of a partnership approach, in which the disabled person works closely with the professional adviser, often assisted in this approach by disability groups, to ensure that the social issues associated with their disability drive any solution at which they may arrive. She concludes that the future role of health and social care professionals should be premised upon the understanding that they are a resource to be drawn upon, providing expertise and knowledge where useful, with an emphasis upon identification and removal of barriers, through partnership and co-operation with the disability community.

Lisa Waddington in Chapter Two confirms that the change in attitudes charted in Chapter One is a phenomenon that is widespread and growing. Concentrating upon the European Community, she demonstrates how changing assumptions about the nature of disability are now being reflected in the adoption of new national, and trans-European legislation. Using the field of employment as her case study, she provides a series of examples, together with an analysis and explanation of what lies behind these changing attitudes, pointing out that similar changes in attitudes are afoot in a number of other areas, including access to services, residential accommodation and education. The common theme of these changes is that of a civil rights approach to disability, which coincides with the development of a politically active disability movement in many parts of Europe. Of crucial continuing importance to this development is the increasing emphasis placed by the disability movement upon the potential of the institutions of the European Union in general, and of European law in particular, to take a central role in promoting disability rights. This potential is already being realised in the adoption of Article 13 of the revised European treaty, an Article which embraces the social model of disability and empowers the Community to 'take appropriate action to combat discrimination based on disability', including a new Directive.

Jeremy Cooper continues this theme in Chapters Three and Four, extending the analysis to review wider changes in international law and domestic law in a number of countries across the globe. Although international law is notoriously difficult to enforce, it nevertheless provides a common set of aspirations that bind countries together and that can be used by rights campaigners as the yardsticks against which progress in their country can be measured. He outlines the main international human rights covenants that include the rights of disabled people within their ambit, and examines the extent to which they provide enforcement machinery, or at the very least a forum in which to challenge the failures of respective governments to further the position of disabled people in their communities. Of particular recent importance has been the adoption by the United Nations in 1995 of the Standard Rules on the Equalisation of Opportunities for Persons with Disabilities, which offer a set of standards and a monitoring system that give governments a workable framework within which to develop their national disability policies for the future. Some countries have already adopted the Rules as part of their national legal system. In Chapter Four, Jeremy Cooper provides an overview of the global movement to embrace the rights of disabled people to equal rights and treatment within a social model of disability, through domestic legislation and other policy changes in over 35 countries. He concludes that there is real evidence of a burgeoning global movement, as significant as the civil rights movement of the 1960s, and the women's and gay rights movements of the 1970s and 1980s, manifested in a range of developments including the introduction of enforceable anti-discrimination legislation, in constitutional guarantees of equality, in specific entitlement programmes and in voluntary human rights manifestos.

The authors of Chapters Five, Six, Seven and Eight each provide a detailed expert exposition of the current law relating to disabled people in the UK with regard to the powers and duties of local authorities, with particular emphasis on community care (Belinda Schwehr, Chapter Five); the Disability Discrimination Act (Catherine Casserley, Chapter Six); housing and homelessness (Mary Holmes, Chapter Seven); and mental health (Kate Harrison, Chapter Eight). All four contributors also take a forward look at the likely impact of the new human rights legislation upon policies towards disabled people in their particular fields of analysis.

The optimism of the first eight chapters is tempered to some extent in Chapter Nine by a more sobering reflection on the extent to which old attitudes towards disabled children prevail, if only because children have less power to articulate protest, and to express a different perspective. Mairian Corker and John Davis draw upon empirical research carried out by themselves and others in recent years in Scotland to suggest that disabled children are still regarded as 'perpetual victims', through which people focus upon the disability not the child, and into whose lives the life-breathing forces of the social model have not yet emerged. They make a clear delineation between the rights approach as manifest in international instruments such as the United Nations Convention on the Rights of the Child, and the 'individualised and largely reactive practice of implementing the law', in which the duty to 'care' or to provide 'reasonable accommodation' can have the effect of suppressing any signs of prioritising the disabled child's human rights to be heard. This view contrasts with that of Suzy Braye, in Chapter Ten, who maintains that 'disabled children are children first and the legal framework for services to meet their social care needs is dominated by the Children Act 1989', although she readily concedes that the structures designed to allow for the law to implement such an approach are 'riddled with shortcomings and inconsistencies in both structure and implementation'. Of particular concern is her observation that there is evidence that the Act's principles 'are less likely to be observed in relation to disabled children than to others'. The chapter nevertheless provides a full and detailed account of the functions and the operation of the legislation to date in helping disabled children lead a full life alongside their non-disabled counterparts, and the role of carer support and inter-agency collaboration in striving to achieve this goal.

In Chapter Eleven, Michael Preston-Shoot brings us full circle and provides a comprehensive overview and analysis of the literature reporting on community care, and in particular on the experiences of disabled people and their carers in seeking to use the current systems of law and practice designed to support them. In the process of this overview, a critical analysis of the law, of policy guidelines, guidance and practice emerges, providing a firm basis for assessing both progress to date and the range of core issues that still need to be addressed. Returning to the findings and proposals contained in Chapter One, Michael Preston-Shoot asserts that 'one of several contradictions in community care policy centres on user opinion. Their opinion on need, and the services required to meet need, is subordinate to the view of the assessing practitioner'. He provides a substantial body of evidence suggesting that whilst the goal of partnership and user-based collaboration based upon the medical model is undoubtedly favoured by the disability community as a whole, there is still a long way to go before it is fully realised. The field is complex and contested, and 'accounts of practice given by users, carers and agencies show marked variations'. The final words of his chapter serve as a fitting ending to the book itself: 'The clear voices for change...call out not so much for modernisation of services, as for a fundamental reappraisal of what law, policy and practice are attempting to achieve.' It is to be hoped that this book will help in adding focus and clarity to our understanding of how far we have come, and how far we still have to go.

*Jeremy Cooper*

# CHAPTER ONE

# Working in Partnership with Disabled People

## New Perspectives for Professionals Within the Social Model of Disability

*Clare Picking*

In the past 30 years, the social model of disability has underpinned significant organisational development of disabled people, been adopted by disabled academics in the courses that they have managed to influence, provided a theoretical rationale for setting up services managed by disabled people (e.g. the Centres for Integrated/Independent Living), influenced government policy for direct payments to disabled people and strengthened the campaign for entrenched civil rights (Finkelstein 1999, p.860).

This chapter draws upon the views of disabled academics and activists and health and social care professionals to review the historical position of disabled people in society, their move from exclusion and powerlessness to the beginnings of empowerment and their freedom to make choices about how they wish to live.[1] The relationship between disabled people and health and social care professionals is scrutinised from the position of disabled people themselves. The chapter highlights suggestions of good practice and emphasises the need for professionals to adopt the social model of disability when working with disabled people to ensure they maximise their legal entitlements and empowerment as citizens.

English literature includes many references to disabled people, often using pejorative language. We read of people who were 'crippled', 'spastic' or 'the village idiot' and we are immediately intended to feel sorry for them. Literature tells us, however, that despite an apparent lack of equality with the rest of society, disabled people, particularly those with mental health problems or learning difficulties, historically lived in and were part of their communities and were cared for by their families. In 1601 the Poor Law changed this way of caring for disabled people by providing institutional care in the workhouse which was set up to give residential care and training to people who were blind, deaf or had an intellectual impairment and who could not earn a living for themselves. The 'asylum movement' which followed was intended to provide a therapeutic environment while still excluding people with mental health problems and certain conditions such as epilepsy from society, by situating large asylums on the outskirts of towns. These large hospitals with long corridors for easy surveillance, locked wards and uniformed staff were used more as prisons than homes. By the middle of the twentieth century they were deemed to be a failure and were gradually closed down, their residents beginning to return to live in the community.

After the second world war, improved health services started to develop for the whole population. The National Health Service was set up in 1948, followed by welfare services in hospitals which later also became community-based and were known after 1970 as 'social services'. Also in 1948 came the National Assistance Act, which defined disabled people for legal purposes as those people: 'over 18 years of age who are blind, deaf or dumb, have a mental disorder, or are substantially and permanently handicapped by illness, injury or congenital deformity or other such disability as may be prescribed'.[2]

Following these major statutory changes, rehabilitation teams run by doctors and new professions allied to medicine began to help people with physical and mental health disabilities to regain lost functions or to learn or adapt to new skills to enable them to live independently in their own homes. Disabled people became entitled to welfare benefits in their own right and certain types of employment, such as lift or car park attendants, were specially designated for them. Sheltered employment schemes were set up to develop training and employment prospects, linked to special resettlement officers based at the labour exchanges, subsequently unemployment offices, now known as job centres.

In 1970 the Chronically Sick and Disabled Persons Act was introduced. This Act for the first time obliged local authorities to keep a record of disabled people living in their community and to provide certain services to enable physically and sensorily disabled people to live in their own homes. In 1980 the World Health Organisation (WHO) devised the International Classification of Impairments, Disabilities and Handicaps (ICIDH) as follows:

**Impairment**: a permanent or transitory psychological, physiological or anatomical loss or abnormality of structure or function.

**Disability**: any restriction or prevention of the performance of an activity, resulting from an impairment, in the manner or within the range considered normal for a human being.

**Handicap**: a disability that constitutes a disadvantage for a given individual in that it limits or prevents the fulfilment of a role that is normal depending on age, sex, social and cultural factors for the individual (World Health Organisation 1980).

Further recognition of the significance of disability came when 1981 was designated the International Year of Disabled Persons by the United Nations.

It seemed on the surface that much had been done to integrate disabled people back into society and provide the assistance that they needed. However, by the 1980s some disabled people began thinking and writing in a way that questioned much of this progress. They pointed out that the legislation was vague, and they questioned why disabled people should still be seen as separate and different, not eligible for open employment and unable fully to participate in everyday life merely because of the obstacles presented by poor building and environment design.

Leading members of this group were academic activists, including Michael Oliver and Vic Finkelstein, who identified what they called the 'medical model' of disability, which they believed kept disabled people as an oppressed and powerless group. They argued that disabled people preferred to look at disability as a situation caused by the constraints placed on them by an unsympathetic society. Through what became known as the Union of the Physically Impaired Against Segregation (UPIAS) they pioneered what they called the 'social model' of disability which has become the central tenet of the self-organised disability movement (Shakespeare and Watson 1997). This group of people rejected the WHO definitions cited above, as they appeared to reinforce the medical model of disability. Instead they preferred definitions which placed responsibility for disabled people's 'problems' firmly with society, as follows:

**Impairment**: lacking part or all of a limb, or having a defective limb, organism or mechanism of the body.

**Disability**: the disadvantage or restriction of activity caused by a contemporary social organisation which takes no or little account of people who have physical impairments and thus excludes them from the mainstream of society (Oliver 1990, p.11).

Michael Oliver has since revised his views on the use of the term 'medical model' and now argues for use of the term 'individual model'. The two fundamental aspects of the individual model are:

1.  that it locates the 'problem' of disability within the individual, and

2.  it sees the causes of this problem as stemming from the functional limitations or psychological losses which are assumed to arise from disability (Oliver 1996, p.32).

He removes the strong 'medicalisation' approach of his previous descriptions (which implied that all disabled people have medical problems and doctors are the best people to help them), but continues to identify as crucial society's failure to provide appropriate services and to ensure that the needs of the disabled person are fully taken into account in its 'social organisation' in such areas as inaccessible public buildings, unusable transport systems, segregated education and excluding work arrangements (Oliver 1996).

Other writers, whilst agreeing that it is wrong to link disability entirely with illness and disease, stating that many disabled people are extremely fit and healthy, are nevertheless convinced that for some people symptoms do have a disabling effect and that certain medical aspects of disability should be retained within the social model (French 1993). Others state that the social model can be used effectively only once a person is medically stable (Craddock 1996).

Oliver also developed the 'personal tragedy' theory which implies that disability is some 'terrible chance event which occurs at random to unfortunate individuals' who have to adapt themselves to society. He points to the way charities approach fundraising, using strong images of pathos, to bear this out. The use of emotive language also demonstrates this theory when describing people as 'victims' or 'sufferers' of a particular condition (Oliver 1990).

## SOCIAL ROLE VALORISATION, EMPOWERMENT AND INDEPENDENT LIVING

Alongside the identification of the differing approaches to disability by disabled academic writers, other changes also started to take place which in turn helped to shape the way disabled people could start to make decisions for themselves. By the beginning of the 1960s, for instance, treatment and attitudes towards people with mental health problems began to be challenged and to evolve. Psychiatrists such as R.D. Laing described mental illness in terms of how society is constructed and the influence of family life on the individual (Laing 1959). New initiatives were introduced, such as voluntary hospital admissions together with improved drug therapies, the concept of therapeutic communities with no ward routines or staff uniforms and the development of day hospitals and support for patients to remain living at home instead of being admitted to hospital.

In the early 1970s the concept of 'normalisation', initiated in Scandinavia, was developed by Wolfensberger in the US and later introduced into Britain. This aimed at making available to people with learning difficulties 'patterns and rhythms of daily life as close as possible to the rest of society' (Wolfensberger 1972). The Program Analysis of Service Systems (PASS) training approach was then developed to extract from the normalisation principle a set of standards against which services could be judged. These were divided broadly into the impact of the service on the social image and competency of the service user (Wolfensberger and Thomas 1983). Wolfensberger further proposed to rename normalisation 'social role valorisation' which 'incorporated the creation, support and defence of valued social roles for people who are at risk of devaluation' (Brown and Smith 1992, p.5). In the 1980s, the King's Fund Centre in London published three papers (1980, 1984 and 1988) aimed at helping people with learning difficulties to plan their own lives. Based on the principles of normalisation and the idea of 'an ordinary life', they outlined reasonable expectations for people with learning difficulties in settings such as residential homes or day-care, including, for example, issues on decision-making and responsibility-taking. The concept behind these papers was that people with severe learning difficulties could and should live in ordinary homes, have ordinary jobs and have access to ordinary friends and social lives.

As ideas and services started to change, so the concept of empowerment has emerged; this means the process of supporting individuals, providing them with opportunities to take control for themselves, devolving decision-making to local levels and encouraging individual responsibility (Stewart 1994). Empowerment incorporates four main principles: entitlement, which comes from legislation, local contracts and charters; the social model, which means focusing on the social, economic and attitudinal barriers to a good quality of life; needs-led assessment, what people want to do in their daily lives; and promoting choice and control, which moves away from institutionalised provision (Morris 1997). A development from the change of emphasis on services arose through the growth of the Independent Living Movement, which started in the US. An English example of this new approach was developed in Derbyshire in 1985. Plans were made to build a new Young Disabled Unit, whereas local disabled people wanted improved community resources in order to stay out of such units. Seven areas were identified as needing to be addressed to enable a disabled person to participate in society on an equal basis: information, to enable choice; housing, which is accessible and well-located; technical equipment and counselling, to assist with making choices; transport and personal assistance when required; and access to all public buildings and amenities. A team of health professionals was set up to meet these needs and ensure that individuals were not admitted to hospital for non-medical reasons. They worked successfully across professional boundaries to overcome practical problems, and they adhered to the social rather than the medical model of disability, rejecting, for instance, any form of rehabilitation for the people they worked with (Silburn 1991).

Independent Living can now be said to be well-established with two defining concepts (Hasler, Campbell and Zarb 1999, p.5):

1. Choice over where to live, how to live, who provides assistance and

2. Control over who assists, how, when and what they do.

Independent living is built upon information, peer support, advocacy, accessible housing and transport, an accessible environment, technical assistance, income from benefits or wages and employment opportunities. Part of the information leading to choice is now successfully provided by Centres for Independent Living and resource centres which have been set up around the country by voluntary organisations and groups.

## LEGISLATIVE CHANGES

Notwithstanding the many signs of change in approach, the introduction of legislation became the only significant way that disabled people could establish their rights. Many disabled groups were nevertheless critical of any legislation which treated them as people with special needs, preferring instead legislation which outlawed and required removal of the environmental and social barriers which prevented them from participating on equal terms in everyday life (Davis 1996).

The Disabled Persons (Services, Consultation and Representation) Act 1986 strengthened the statutory responsibilities of local authorities to carry out assessments and provide services. This Act also introduced the concept of advocacy which, although never enacted, encouraged the practice of disabled individuals using their own 'authorised representative' at various stages in assessment and provision of services (Cooper 1994, p.88). The Children Act 1989 extended the Chronically Sick and Disabled Persons Act 1970 specifically to include children, thus eliminating age limits for assessment. The Local Government and Housing Act 1989 and the Housing Grants (Construction and Regeneration) Act 1996 both provided funding for private housing to be adapted for the needs of disabled occupants, while the Building Regulations (Access and Facilities for Disabled People – Approved Document M) provided minimum standard requirements for newly built public buildings (1991) and private housing (1999).

In 1990 the National Health Service and Community Care Act was introduced to provide state services supplemented by the private and voluntary sectors, requiring statutory authorities to act as enablers and purchasers, rather than sole providers. In this way the government hoped that the problems of professional dominance and dependency creation would be addressed (Oliver 1996). In addition, the Disability Living Allowance and Disability Working Allowance Act 1991 and the Disability Grants Act 1993, which established the Independent Living Fund, enabled monies to be paid directly to disabled people rather than through the filter of service providers (Drake 1999).

The Carers (Recognition and Services) Act 1995 introduced the requirement that local authorities take carers' needs into account when carrying out assessments and the Community Care (Direct Payments) Act 1996 enabled local authorities to give cash to disabled people to choose their own form of care (Cooper and Vernon 1996).

The most important piece of legislation, the Disability Discrimination Act 1996, recognised the progress made by the supporters of the social model by finally introducing the requirement that employers, businesses and services must ensure that all members of society have similar opportunities and are not excluded because of their disability (See Chapter Six, p.139).

More recently the proposed changes of the World Health Organisation definitions of disability to the 'Impairment, Activity Limitation and Participation Restrictions', while not carrying the full weight of legislation, have strengthened understanding of disability by synthesising the medical and social models of disability and offering a classification of all areas of human life (Bickenbach *et al.* 1999). Perhaps of even greater significance has been the increasingly high profile accorded in international law and policy to the 1993 United Nations Standard Rules on the Equalisation of Opportunities for Persons with Disabilities, discussed in Chapter Three.

## CHALLENGING THE ROLE OF HEALTH AND SOCIAL CARE PROFESSIONALS

The crucial intervention of disabled groups in this debate has been their critique of the way in which disabled people are treated by those very professionals who are supposedly there to 'help' them and who play such an important part in the process of empowerment. Identified for particular criticism is 'the scientific authority of medicine and the associated right to prescribe intervention' (Craddock 1996, p.76). In a similar critique health and social care professionals are seen as working largely within the medical model, having a need to be 'in charge', to 'maintain status' and to 'resist change' as well as 'militating against a wider and more creative view of meeting the client's needs' and 'seeing solutions, as well as client-professional relationships, only in this context' (Wright 1997, p.139).

The conflict between disabled people and professionals can be illustrated by the use of negative language. The idea of 'normality' is equated with health and the absence of impairment, implying that it has an opposite which is 'abnormality' and that this must apply to disabled people. The tendency to turn the noun into an adjective is still prevalent when referring to a disabled person as 'the stroke' or 'the spinal injury', instead of the person who has had a stroke or who has had a spinal injury (Northway 1997).

The value of rehabilitation itself has been placed in question. Oliver (1996) has described disability as a long-term situation which is not treatable medically and is not curable, yet the aim of rehabilitation is to restore the disabled person to 'normality', a fairly traditional definition of rehabilitation being 'the application of all measures aimed at reducing the impact of disabling and handicapping conditions and enabling disabled and handicapped people to achieve social integration' (Wilson and McLellan 1997, p.36). People with 'special needs' have been encouraged to achieve independence, starting with the personal activities of daily living, which may not be a particularly fulfilling goal, and then working towards independence in cultural and social aspects, which is often seen as the more fulfilling goal by disabled people themselves (Maclean 1995). Many professionals still think that independence means 'doing things for yourself', but for some disabled people the effort of achieving such physical independence 'traps them in a lifestyle of unceasing hard work'(Campbell 1994, p.89). Independence, they argue, is more a state of mind than a physical ability and an individual achieves self-determination, by having this control over their life, notwithstanding being highly dependent upon another person (Campbell 1994). This point can be illustrated across a series of themes.

### Assessment

Assessment is the key to identifying a person's needs and abilities. In hospital an assessment in preparation for a return to work or home life is based upon discussion, measurement and observation and involves all those professionals who work with the patient. Very often, however, patients fear that they must pass a test in order to be allowed home and sometimes conceal difficulties for fear this will go against them. A study in 1996 (Clark, Dyer and Hartman 1996) noted that in some instances the outcome of hospital home visits for older people was decided beforehand by the occupational therapist. In other words, therapists appeared to structure decisions in the direction they felt the outcome should be, mainly on issues of safety.

Patients sometimes also fear that their own priorities are not the same as those of the assessor. For example, in a questionnaire used to establish whether patients, carers and occupational therapists had similar concerns at point of discharge from a small community hospital, a significant difference between them was revealed on issues such as concern over social isolation, financial benefits and community services (Bore 1994). Similarly, functional assessments by occupational therapists do not always focus on what is important to the patient. Researchers in 1996 (Ward, Jagger and Harper 1996) found that areas of productivity and leisure were not included by any professions in a pre-discharge treatment programme for patients with hip fracture, although these were problem areas highlighted by the patients themselves.

Assessments for services in social services departments, defined mostly by the resources available, have traditionally been service-led rather than needs-led, which has meant that disabled people's needs have to fit into what is available for them. The outcomes of these assessments have often led to fragmented support by nursing and home care staff, with jobs or tasks divided according to job descriptions and only part of the care task provided by each. Clear boundaries are often not worked out by service providers so that, for instance, a disabled person may be 'denied access to a bath or shower because it is unclear whether it is for a medical or social reason' (Macfarlane 1996, p.7).

People need to know what assessments are for and to understand what role the assessor is taking. Smale and Tuson (1993) identify three models of assessment which can be used. In the procedural approach, the assessor helps the disabled person through a set procedure, matching needs with provision and the disabled person is a passive recipient; the questioning approach is one where the disabled person provides information and hears solutions to his or her needs, but does not act in partnership; the third model is the exchange approach which encourages the assessor to treat the relationship with disabled people, their carers and families more as a partnership in problem-solving and reaching a shared understanding of needs and solutions.

The role of social workers, some working as care managers following changes in legislation, could be used more effectively within the empowerment process. Adams (1996) states that this process is facilitated by means of self-advocacy or case advocacy, where the worker seeks to enhance the person's access to services by consciousness raising, by user-led practice and by reflective practice, which looks at current practice and reformulates goals and methods of working. The worker becomes an ally, someone who will listen carefully (not just problem-solve), assist in overcoming barriers, check entitlements and provide information. This can be especially informative and facilitative as a form of counselling to improve confidence. Managers need to recognise however that what they desire their workers to achieve (to empower other people) they must model in themselves and empower their own staff. This involves being available, listening carefully, being flexible about decision-making, but knowing the rules (Stevenson and Parsloe 1993). The idea of recording 'unmet need' has been criticised (Sim et al. 1998) as allowing the possibility for a gap to exist between professionally defined needs and those needs defined by disabled people themselves. There is a need to extend the definition of need beyond simple functional impairments to include structural definitions. But to be of any value at all, unmet need must nevertheless be recorded and managers have a key role in linking this information to strategic planning (Morris 1997).

Communication is a key factor in the assessment process. Where English is not the first language of the disabled person, it has been the custom to use members of the family as interpreters during assessment, or to seek the views of community leaders of relevant ethnic groups to explain various cultural practices. Community leaders of ethnic groups, however, do not necessarily represent a cross-section of views and since they are invariably male, this factor, plus the dependence on a family member to translate, means that Asian women, for instance, are frequently unable to express their needs directly (Cameron, Badger and Evers 1996). The challenges associated with communication during assessment do not just extend to language, but include people with dementia, learning disabilities or speech or sensory impairments. In these situations the consumers have often been identified as being the carers. Thus efforts have been made to involve carers in the assessment process to the exclusion of these disabled people who have sometimes been assumed to be incapable of such participation. The use of advocacy is much recommended in these situations and Goldsmith (1996) argues that listening to people with dementia is possible, using special skills and removing as many barriers to communication as possible.

### Equipment and adaptations

Results of a survey by SCOPE, the charity for people with cerebral palsy (SCOPE 1998) showed that equipment and adaptations can provide the pathway to ensuring an independent lifestyle, thereby marking the difference between active participation in society and exclusion from it. Equipment is often required to facilitate a speedy and safe discharge from hospital or may prevent a hospital admission; it may be a necessary part of continuing care or community care; it may be needed by carers and it plays a role in preventing accidents (Winchcombe 1998).

Crucial to disabled people and their equipment needs is the relationship they have with professionals, who are often seen as gate-openers and information providers (Marks 1998). Where provision is service-led with a traditional professional attitude this creates disempowerment. Where the service is needs-led, the user is empowered and self-determination is created. This term lends itself to the concept of control over one's own life (Campbell 1994). Some pieces of equipment for disability do not blend well into the domestic setting, are hard to accept and can lead to a feeling of loss of control over one's own environment. This is sometimes seen by professionals as a difficulty in accepting disability itself. Service users who are grateful for the products which enable greater independence rarely criticise those products, despite the lack of choice they are given. Gratitude is an expectation of people who are not disabled and, once expressed, they feel able to give more. The 'gratitude trap' further contributes to the lack of feedback or criticism (Barber 1996).

Provision of equipment should involve disabled people at the planning stage and information should be prepared which can assist in making choices, for example the choices of equipment catalogues (Marks 1998). The Disabled Living

Centres' Council has published guidance on good practice in disability equipment services (Winchcombe 1998) which states that this should include consultation with disabled service users; information on the services provided and ranges of products from all sources available; a choice of products with opportunities to consider alternatives to equipment and options available when setting up care packages; accessibility with widely known alternative ways into a flexible, responsive service, with opportunities for self-assessment; equity so that entitlement is related to personal need, and eligibility criteria are fairly applied; and the quality should be defined by users of the service. The role of the practitioner is crucial in providing information, advice, assessment and access to statutory equipment supply, but work practices must be reconsidered to give clear criteria and standards, good knowledge, efficient equipment delivery and technical support systems.

### Adapting the home or moving house

Appropriate accessible housing has been identified as a key component of independent living (Hasler, Campbell and Zarb 1999) and yet local authority housing departments appear not to have the necessary policies which coincide with the main themes of community care in areas such as independent living or user choice or involvement in decision-making (Nocon and Pleace 1997). A Living Options project in Shropshire in 1994 identified not only lack of funding and inappropriate housing stock as problems, but also attitudes of occupational therapists, grants officers, architects, builders and housing officers, and a failure to listen to disabled people or agree with their wishes. There was a strong desire to change current practice away from a professionally-driven and impairment-based model to better co-ordinated and efficient services which could accurately 'reflect the interdependency of housing and social support needs' (Nocon and Pleace 1997, p.121). Home improvement agencies were cited as a good example of this model.

### Care-giving and the role of carers

The nature of the care-giving relationship reflects and forms part of the practices that contribute to the way disability is defined in our society (Munford 1994). The way that care is given can affect how people feel about themselves; whether in fact they are a 'helped person' or a person requiring help (Thomas 1982, p.74). Relationships between people can change and it is important to retain choice in taking on a caring role. Relationships with paid professionals who are carers can be difficult and intimidating and lead to feelings of humiliation and loss of dignity on the part of the disabled person. Most care received by disabled people has not been their choice or under their control. It has been described as being oppressive, often custodial and provided in a controlling way (Macfarlane 1996).

Community health services can contribute to feelings of marginalisation by being inflexible over timings of staff visits or appointments and refusing to recognise the expertise of the disabled person concerning their own disability. This leads to unequal power relationships which can result in open hostility, people behaving in an antagonised way if challenged (Goodall 1992), or extreme forms of abuse (Northway 1997).

Since 1993 local authorities have taken over the funding responsibilities for residential and nursing care and the concept of 'community care' means that people can remain supported in their homes, if they so wish. Alongside this, however, the tightening of criteria has inevitably had an effect on people who provide care for their relatives, the unpaid carers. Legislation has now ensured that the carers of people already in receipt of services may have their own needs taken into account, but the assessment needs to be a sensitive process. This means that rather than providing a professionally-led approach, the assessor should act as a facilitator with the user and the carer at the centre of the process. There is a need for recognition of stress levels, limits on potential for employment, social contact and leisure, need for respite breaks, support, information and training. Where the disabled person and the carer have conflicting perceptions of need, workers should use their skills in enabling improved communication. Continuation of the caring role should not be taken for granted (Heron 1998).

### Day services

Oliver (1993, p.54) criticised those day services with 'institutionalised regimes' which fail to involve disabled people meaningfully in their running, in the 'transportation of users in specialised transport' and the 'rigidity of the routine activities' which all create dependency. Read (1996) describes the need for people who are mental health 'survivors' to have accessible local services to meet crisis needs: services which are near to their homes, open at flexible times and available when people feel especially lonely or isolated.

### Counselling and mental health services

Counselling has been identified as an area where therapists tend to make assumptions, for example that the onset of disability brings about emotional as well as physical changes and that the mind has to adjust in order for the individual to come to terms with the changed body image, and that through this process the disabled person can become psychologically whole again. This is particularly relevant to psychoanalysis and behaviourist therapies. Arguably, however, what is needed is counselling which seeks to help disabled people to take control over their lives (Lenny 1993).

Similarly social work education has been dominated by casework theories that have relied heavily on medical and psycho-social models of intervention with individuals. Social workers have unwittingly colluded with local authorities to ensure that disabled people are not empowered to receive services as of right. Claimants for practical help have been forced to become clients of casework and encouraged to conform to the medical model of disability which ignores disabling environments (Sapey and Hewitt 1991). People with mental health problems do not see themselves as having a disability and yet they are eligible for many of the services provided by health and social care professionals, especially if they have a combination of needs which include physical disability. Beresford, Gifford and Harrison (1996) have applied the concepts of the social model in this context, recognising that mental illness can 'stigmatise' and 'pathologise', emphasising 'abnormality' and 'inadequacy'. They suggest the need for a social response to distress and disablement which survivors experience, leading to survivor-led alternatives. Read (1996) emphasises the need to make choices about treatment, supported by information, especially about medication, accessible services, independent advocacy services, housing and employment schemes and training schemes.

Counselling, if based on the humanistic and person-centred approach, could also enable people to explore their own situations and the meaning these have for them to fulfill 'self-actualising tendencies'(Lenny 1993, p.237).

## ACHIEVING A NEW APPROACH

The changed position of disabled people, amounting to the beginnings of self-advocacy, has demanded a change in the way that health and social care professionals work. The move away from passivity which encourages self-determination challenges those situations previously controlled by professionals, so that important decisions can be made by disabled people themselves (Goodley 1997). This involves the recognition of the person's own set of priorities and their right to take risks.

A change in attitude by professional people towards disabled people themselves appears to be very important. Listening to what all disabled people say is part of a wider process of empowerment. This includes both formalised arrangements such as groups of people with similar concerns, and individuals when they are assessed or when their needs are discussed. Professionals should encourage regular communication, stimulate methods of self-expression, develop good listening, communication and observational skills and be able to interpret and assess. Empowerment for people with dementia or learning disabilities, for example, starts with offering and respecting choices such as what clothes to wear, what to eat, and where to sit, so that staff have to reverse roles, adapting to the minor role in all interactions, 'asking rather than telling'. This is time-consuming and it is tempting to make decisions for people, or use relatives to plan services, but the use of advocacy, 'the skilled outsider' is far preferable. Implicit in this approach is the concept of 'personhood' described by Kitwood (1997) which is based upon self-esteem, the place of an individual in a social group, the performance of roles and the integrity, continuity and stability of the sense of self. He describes this status or standing as being bestowed upon one human being by another and says that it implies recognition, respect and trust.

The use of appropriate language can convey positive attitudes and images (Phillips 1994) and promote the dignity of disabled people (Scullion 1997), but changing terminology is not in itself enough. It is easily possible to change terminology but not to change one's own attitude to the disabled person. It is still possible to 'give professional judgement a status that does not allow the disabled person's wishes to have any positive impact on the therapy they receive' (Gray and Robb 1997, p.470). Research has shown that the attitudes of health and social care professionals are not very different to those of the general public and that negative stereotyping is common (French 1994). To stereotype a disabled person is to place them in a disabled role, as a passive recipient of care, rather than taking an active part in decision-making. French (1994) describes how negative attitudes may influence self-image, encouraging feelings of inferiority, leading to feeling incapable of self-determination. Subsequently, both the attitudes of the public and the way services are delivered are influenced by this lack of self-worth. Health and social care professionals may adopt these attitudes unconsciously as the organisations they work for may require them to be 'in control' or place them in a position of conflicting demands, balancing resources against needs.

A study (Johnson 1993) into disabled people's perceptions of physiotherapy and attitudes of physiotherapists towards them revealed, in some cases, an 'insensitive and condescending approach'. Treatment was perceived as 'problem-centred' rather than 'client-centred' with little relevance to independent living, yet physiotherapists were seen as key members of teams of professionals which seek to enable independent living.

Occupational therapists have also been criticised for the way they approach problem-solving with disabled people by giving approval (or not) for funding of equipment and adaptations in a community setting or of home conditions to secure discharge from hospital (Abberley 1995). Abberley points out that use of performance criteria to measure successful occupational therapy can involve setting targets with or without the person's full knowledge or agreement. 'Realistic' targets ensure the disabled person does not fail to reach his or her goal and problem-solving can be used to overcome 'unrealistic' expectations. Reality is then defined in terms of what is in the power of the occupational therapist to deliver and success for patients depends on how realistic their expectations are, which in turn is based fundamentally on the occupational therapist's view of what is 'appropriate' (Abberley 1995).

A change of attitude can be achieved by working more closely with organisations of disabled people, not those set up for them. An example of involving users of services in an innovative way comes from the Bradford Home Treatment Service which has pioneered work in Yorkshire with people with mental health problems. This has been achieved by employing and attaching 'user-development workers' to a clinical team to contribute equally to discussions about issues such as progress of cases or how the budget is spent (James 2000). Other ways of achieving changes in attitude are by the development of greater interpersonal skills; helping people to 'minimise and manage problems caused by their disability to achieve maximum potential for mobility and independence' (Johnson 1993, p.519); evaluating whether the requirements of disabled people are matched by the aims of the profession (Johnson 1993); and a change from a custodial approach to care to one which recognises a responsibility to provide support and services in response to individual need (Seed 1994).

Understanding disability comes not only from talking and listening, but also with training. Research has demonstrated that among some health-care professional students the development of positive and negative attitudes to disability is influenced both by the way the issue is handled during training and by daily contact with disabled people (French 1994). Conversely, simulation exercises in disability awareness training appear to produce a negative response and do not contribute to improving understanding. Simulation focuses on difficulties and inadequacies, whereas disability equality training, given by trainers who are themselves disabled, can be more constructive. Role-play using disabled trainers, group discussion and looking at the way disability is portrayed in society are seen as helpful methods (French 1996). The need for disability studies to be included in the nursing curriculum has long been recognised (Goodall 1992) and disability equality training for staff of all disciplines should be arranged with at least one objective being to enable staff to train themselves not to need gratitude from disabled people when they carry out their work. Training in and awareness of the legal rights of disabled people is also important for all staff to undertake. Knowledge of the law leads to good practice, whereas ignorance of the law leads to defensiveness and a limited, cautious approach.

One of the most important changes for health and social care professionals will come with a shift from traditional approaches to the way treatment and services are delivered. A change in the view of rehabilitation is needed, for instance, so that it is seen as 'a process of active change by which a person who has become disabled acquires the knowledge and skills needed for optimal physical, psychological and social function' (Wilson and McLellan 1997, p.1) which implies that the purpose of rehabilitation is to assist disabled people in achieving the lifestyle of their choice. Client-centred practice, which places the patient at the centre of the process, has been used by occupational therapists in some settings for a few years. The example of the Canadian Occupational Performance Measure developed in 1980 can be used as an outcome measure of the person's self-evaluation of their occupational performance in areas of self-care, produc- tivity and leisure (Law *et al.* 1990). A 'top-down' approach to assessment is adopted, starting with inquiry into 'role-competency and meaningfulness' (Trombly 1993, p.253), so the roles most pertinent to the individual are the major focus of the assessment. Such an approach provides a complete framework upon which to build case management and is in line with the National Health Service and Community Care Act 1990 (Trombly 1993). Nurses who relin- quished the nurse-centred approach in favour of the client-centred approach would time visits to fit in with their patients' lives. Instead of 'doing' something for a patient because it is easier, they would encourage the patient to carry out personal care tasks for themselves if they wished (Goodall 1992). By this method, all health and social care professionals would become more flexible about appointment times and rotas for home-visiting which take into account people's needs. They would also be inclined to listen more closely to their patients, recognising their expertise concerning their own disability (Northway 1997). Medical need would reduce in importance over educational need for children. Instead of taking children from classes in order to see the doctor or physiotherapist, appointments would be made around class timetables (Oliver 1993).

Hospitals and health centres, dental and general practitioner surgeries can become environments which are accessible to all patients as standard practice. The good practice guide published by the Royal College of Physicians (1998) states that hospitals should be models of good practice and espouse the social model. In addition, it states that:

> patients have the right to be asked about their personal needs in advance of pre-arranged appointments or admissions;
>
> patients should be consulted directly about their treatment and arrangements made on their behalf;
>
> patients can expect that the disabilities they experience are not increased by inflexible regulations or routines;
>
> disabled people should be the tutors or trainers in any initiatives provided they have the right skills and, in line with the Disability Discrimination Act, that all unnecessary barriers to the hospital's services be removed (p.3).

For all professionals, the growth of evidence-based and reflective practices which involve self-evaluation and ensure that no intervention is carried out without some description of its value and worth is to be encouraged. Central to this concept is the consultation with those disabled people who are at the receiving end of the service. Reflection and self-evaluation are key components to empowerment of disabled service users in the context of professional work. Consultation with disabled people and research into aspects of disability are both vital contributions to developing the role of the health professional. Physiotherapists in 1996, carrying out research into services for patients who had survived a stroke, not only identified more accurately what services were needed, but concluded that the research itself contributed towards user empowerment (Thomas and Parry 1996). Researchers commented in 1997, that because there is no culture of post-qualification supervised practice in most of the health professions, they are never challenged to reflect upon the outcomes of therapy from a social perspective (Gray and Robb 1997).

## CONCLUSIONS

In summary, the future role of health and social care professionals should be such that, with the information they have to share, they can be seen as a resource to be drawn upon, as with architects or solicitors, offering knowledge and expertise. Thus the professional would become more of an intermediary or consultant, providing information upon which decisions can be based (Craddock 1996).

Finkelstein stated in 1991 that:

> the modern challenge is to provide alternatives to current practice so that workers and disabled people can share expertise in barrier identification and removal, both at the personal level (for the individual setting their own goals) and at the social level where public facilities need to be made truly public (p.35).

Co-operation, partnership and commonality of purpose still remain the best way forward today.

## REFERENCES

Abberley, P. (1995) 'Disabling ideology in health and welfare – the case of occupational therapy.' *Disability and Society 10*, 2, 221.

Adams, R. (1996) *Social Work and Empowerment*. Basingstoke: Macmillan.

Barber, J. (1996) 'The design of disability products: a psychological perspective.' *British Journal of Occupational Therapy 59*, 12, 561.

Beresford, P., Gifford, G. and Harrison, C. (1996) 'What has disability got to do with psychiatric survivors?'. In J. Read and J. Reynolds (eds) *Speaking Our Minds*. Milton Keynes: Open University.

Bickenbach, J., Sommath, J., Bradley, E. and Üstün, T. (1999) 'Models of disablement, universalism and the International Classification of Impairments, Disabilities and Handicaps.' *Social Science and Medicine 48*, 9, 1173.

Bore, J. (1994) 'Occupational therapist home visits: a satisfactory service?' *British Journal of Occupational Therapy 57*, 3, 85.

Brown, H. and Smith, H (1992) *Normalisation. A Reader for the Nineties.* London. New York: Tavistock/Routledge.

Bumphrey, E. (1995) (ed) *Community Practice. A Text for Occupational Therapists and Others Involved in Community Care.* London: Prentice Hall Harvester Wheatsheaf.

Cameron, E., Badger, F. and Evers, H. (1996) 'Ethnicity and care management'. In J. Phillips and B. Penhale (eds) *Reviewing Care Management for Older People.* London: Jessica Kingsley Publishers.

Campbell, J. (1994) 'Equipped for independence or self-determination?' *British Journal of Occupational Therapy 57*, 3, 89.

Clark, H., Dyer, S. and Hartman, L. (1996) *Going Home. Older People Leaving Hospital.* Bristol: The Policy Press.

Cooper, J. (1994) *The Legal Rights Manual.* Aldershot: Arena.

Cooper, J. and Vernon, S. (1996) *Disability and the Law.* London: Jessica Kingsley Publishers.

Craddock, J. (1996) 'Responses of the occupational therapy profession to the perspective of the disability movement, part 2.' *British Journal of Occupational Therapy 59*, 2, 73.

Davis, K. (1996) 'Disability and legislation: rights and equality.' In G. Hales (ed) *Beyond Disability: Towards an Enabling Society.* London: Sage Publications and the Open University.

Drake, R.F. (1999) *Understanding Disability Politics.* Basingstoke: Macmillan.

Finkelstein, V. (1991) 'Disability. An administrative challenge?' In M. Oliver (ed) *Social Work. Disabled People and Disabling Environments.* London: Jessica Kingsley Publishers.

Finkelstein, V. (1999) 'Extended Review: *Doing Disability Research,* Barnes, C. and Mercer, G. (eds)', *Disability and Society 14*, 6, 859.

French, S. (1993) 'Disability, impairment or something in between?' In J. Swain, V. Finkelstein and S. French (eds) *Disabling Barriers – Enabling Environments.* London: Sage Publications.

French, S. (1994) 'Attitudes of health professionals towards disabled people: a discussion and review of the literature.' *Physiotherapy 80*,10, 687.

French, S. (1996) 'Simulation exercises in disability awareness training: a critique.' In G. Hales (ed) *Beyond Disability: Towards an Enabling Society.* London: Sage Publications and the Open University.

Goldsmith, M. (1996) *Hearing the Voice of People with Dementia. Opportunities and Obstacles.* London: Jessica Kingsley Publishers.

Goodall, C. (1992) 'Preserving dignity for disabled people.' *Nursing Standard 6*, 35, 25.

Goodley, D. (1997) 'Locating self-advocacy in models of disability: understanding disability in the support of self-advocates with learning difficulties.' *Disability and Society 12*, 3, 367.

Gray, R and Robb, D. (1997) 'Clinical practice: the social impact of disability.' *British Journal of Therapy and Rehabilitation 4*, 9, 470.

Hales, G. (ed) (1996) *Beyond Disability: Towards an Enabling Society.* London: Sage Publications and the Open University.

Hasler, F, Campbell, J. and Zarb, G. (1999) *Direct Routes to Independence – A Guide to Local Authority Implementation and Management of Direct Payments.* London: Policy Studies Institute.

Heron, C. (1998) *Working with Carers.* London: Jessica Kingsley Publishers.

James, A. (2000) 'New mentality.' *The Guardian,* 26 January 2000, 6.

Johnson, R. (1993) 'Attitudes don't just hang in the air – disabled people's perceptions of physiotherapists.' *Physiotherapy 79*, 9, 619.

King's Fund Centre (1980) *An Ordinary Life: Comprehensive Locally Based Services for Mentally Handicapped People.* London: King's Fund Centre.

King's Fund Centre (1984) *An Ordinary Working Life. Vocational Services for People with Mental Handicap.* London: King's Fund Centre.

King's Fund Centre (1988) *Ties and Connections. An Ordinary Community Life for People with Learning Difficulties.* London: King's Fund Centre.

Kitwood, T. (1997) *Dementia Reconsidered.* Milton Keynes: Open University.

Laing, R. D. (1959) *The Divided Self.* London: Tavistock Publications.

Law, M., Baptiste, S., McColl, M., Opzoomer, A., Poltatajko, H. and Pollock, N. (1990) 'The Canadian Occupational Performance Measure: an outcome measure for occupational therapy.' *Canadian Journal of Occupational Therapy 57*, 2, 82.

Lenny, J. (1993) 'Do disabled people need counselling?' In J. Swain, V. Finkelstein and S. French (eds) *Disabling Barriers – Enabling Environments.* London: Sage Publications.

Macfarlane, A. (1996) 'Aspects of intervention: consultation, care, help and support.' In G. Hales (ed) *Beyond Disability: Towards an Enabling Society.* London: Sage Publications and the Open University.

Maclean, J. (1995) 'Achieving independence.' In E. Bumphrey (ed) *Community Practice. A Text for Occupational Therapists and Others Involved in Community Care.* London: Prentice Hall Harvester Wheatsheaf.

Marks, O. (1998) 'Equipment provision in the UK: equipped for equality?' *British Journal of Therapy and Rehabilitation 5*, 9, 446.

Morris, J. (1997) *Community Care: Working in Partnership with Service Users.* Birmingham: Venture Press.

Munford, R. (1994) 'The politics of care-giving'. In M.H. Rioux and M. Bach (eds) *Disability is not Measles: New Research Paradigms in Disability.* Ontario: Roeher Institute.

Nocon, A. and Pleace, N. (1997) 'Until disabled people get consulted...the role of the occupational therapist in meeting housing needs.' *British Journal of Occupational Therapy 1*, 60, 3.

Northway, R. (1997) 'Disability and oppression: some implications for nurses and nursing.' *Journal of Advanced Nursing 26*, 4, 736.

Oliver, M. (1990) *The Politics of Disablement.* Basingstoke: Macmillan.

Oliver, M. (ed) (1991) *Social Work. Disabled People and Disabling Environments.* London: Jessica Kingsley Publishers.

Oliver, M. (1993) 'Disability and dependency: a creation of industrial societies?' In J. Swain, V. Finkelstein and S. French (eds) *Disabling Barriers – Enabling Environments.* London: Sage Publications.

Oliver, M. (1996) *Understanding Disability: From Theory to Practice.* Basingstoke: Macmillan.

Phillips, J. (1994) 'Disability and language: does it matter?' *British Journal of Occupational Therapy 57*, 11, 445.

Phillips, J and Penhale, B. (1996) (eds) *Reviewing Care Management for Older People.* London: Jessica Kingsley Publishers.

Read, J. (1996) 'What we want from mental health services.' In J. Read and J. Reynolds (eds) *Speaking Our Minds.* Milton Keynes: Open University.

Read, J. and Reynolds, J. (1996) (eds) *Speaking Our Minds.* Milton Keynes: Open University.

Rioux, M.H. and Bach, M. (1994) (eds) *Disability is not Measles: New Research Paradigms in Disability.* Ontario: Roeher Institute.

Royal College of Physicians of London (1998) *Disabled People Using Hospitals: A Charter and Guidelines.* London: Royal College of Physicians.

Sapey, R. and Hewitt, N. (1991) 'The changing context of social work practice.' In M. Oliver (ed) *Social Work. Disabled People and Disabling Environments.* London: Jessica Kingsley Publishers.

Scullion, P. (1997) 'What's in a word: PAL for people with a disability.' *British Journal of Therapy and Rehabilitation 4,* 6, 292.

Seed, P. (1994) 'Changing services for people with learning disabilities.' In M. Titterton (ed) *Caring for People in the Community: the New Welfare.* London: Jessica Kingsley Publishers.

Shakespeare, T. and Watson, N. (1997) 'Defending the social model'. *Disability and Society 12,* 2, 293.

Silburn, L. (1991) 'A social model in a medical world: the development of the integrated living team as part of the strategy for younger physically disabled people in North Derbyshire.' In M. Oliver (ed) *Social Work. Disabled People and Disabling Environments.* London: Jessica Kingsley Publishers.

Sim, A.J., Milner, J., Love, J. and Lishman, J. (1998) 'Definitions of need: can disabled people and care professionals agree?' *Disability and Society 13,* 1, 53.

Smale, G. and Tuson, G. (1993) *Empowerment, Assessment, Care Management and the Skilled Worker.* NISW Practice and Development Series. London: HMSO.

Stevenson, O. and Parsloe, P. (1993) *Community Care and Empowerment.* York: Joseph Rowntree Foundation.

Stewart, A. (1994) 'Empowerment and enablement: occupational therapy 2001.' *British Journal of Occupational Therapy 57,* 7, 248.

Swain, J., Finkelstein, V. and French, S. (1993) (eds) *Disabling Barriers – Enabling Environments.* London: Sage Publications.

Thomas, C. and Parry, A. (1996) 'Research on users' views about stroke services: towards an empowerment research paradigm or more of the same?' *Physiotherapy 82,* 1, 6.

Thomas, D. (1982) *The Experience of Handicap.* London: Methuen.

Titterton, M. (1994) (ed) *Caring for People in the Community: The New Welfare.* London: Jessica Kingsley Publishers.

Trombly, C. (1993) 'Anticipating the future: assessment of occupational function.' *American Journal of Occupational Therapy 47,* 3, 253.

Ward, G.E., Jagger, C. and Harper, W.M.H. (1996) 'The Canadian occupational performance measure: what do users consider important?' *British Journal of Therapy and Rehabilitation 3,* 8, 448.

Wilson, B.A and McLellan, D.L. (1997) *Rehabilitation Studies Handbook.* Cambridge: Cambridge University Press.

Winchcombe, M. (1998) *Community Equipment Services: Why Should We Care? A Guide to Good Practice in Disability Equipment Services.* London: Disabled Living Centres Council.

Wolfensberger, W. (1972) 'The principle of normalization in human services.' In H. Brown and H. Smith (1992) *Normalisation. A Reader for the Nineties.* London. New York: Tavistock/Routledge.

UNIVERSITY OF CENTRAL LANCASHIRE LIBRARY

Wolfensberger, W. and Thomas, S. (1983) 'PASSING (Program Analysis of Service Systems Implementation of Normalization Goals) normalization criteria and ratings manual (second edition).' In H. Brown and H. Smith (1992) *Normalisation. A Reader for the Nineties.* London. New York: Tavistock/Routledge.

World Health Organisation (1980) *International Classification of Impairment, Disabilities and Handicaps: a Manual of Classification Relating to the Consequences of Disease.* Geneva: World Health Organisation.

Wright, R. (1997) 'Health needs assessment: a radical outlook for occupational therapists.' *British Journal of Occupational Therapy 60*, 3, 139.

## NOTES

1   I am particularly grateful to Judith Payling for providing valuable insights and commentary on an earlier version of this chapter.

2   National Assistance Act 1948, s.29(1).

CHAPTER TWO

# Changing Attitudes to the Rights of People with Disabilities in Europe[1]

*Lisa Waddington*

The last decade – perhaps even only the last five years – has seen notable changes in disability policy in Europe. Changed assumptions about the concept of disability have been reflected in the adoption of new national and pan-European legislation. As a consequence, policy which has sought to separate and segregate people with disabilities in 'special' schools, labour markets, residential accommodation and transport has, to some degree, and in some countries, been reconsidered. Attempts have been made to develop an integrated approach, opening up jobs, services and housing to all people irrespective of their ability or disability. A key element of this new approach has been the recognition that segregation and exclusion is not a necessary consequence of a physical or intellectual impairment, but the result of conscious policy choices based on false assumptions about the abilities of people with disabilities. The new approach recognises the role which discrimination – in the form of false assumptions and the failure to adapt inaccessible services and jobs – plays in disadvantaging people with disabilities and, conversely, how legislation seeks to combat elements of disability discrimination and creates equality of opportunity for people with disabilities. The new approach embraces a civil rights approach to disability.

This chapter will examine some of these developments and reflect on some of the attitudes and assumptions which lie behind disability policy in Europe. The area of employment will be used to illustrate changes in attitude, and the consequent changes in policy and legislation. It should be noted that the developments examined in employment policy have often been reflected in other areas, such as access to services, residential accommodation and education. The chapter will conclude with some reflections on developments which have led to this change in attitude and legislative approach.

## WHICH EUROPE?

The title of this chapter refers, somewhat obliquely, to changes in attitudes to the rights of people with disabilities in Europe. Europe is a large region, consisting of many different countries, and it seems appropriate to reflect on what is meant by 'Europe' in this context. The focus of this chapter will be on those European countries which make up the European Union,[2] and on the European Union itself, as a supra-national organisation with law-making powers. However, even within this relatively cohesive organisation there remain great differences in legal and philosophical approaches to disability policy. Furthermore, it should be borne in mind that, whilst the idea that people with disabilities frequently experience discrimination in many areas of life is gaining widespread acceptance within Europe, as evidenced by initiatives of the two major regional organisations (the European Union and the Council of Europe), this recognition is, as yet, only working through to affect policy and legislation in some European countries.

## THE OLD SCHOOL OF THOUGHT

I intend to use employment policy to illustrate the changes in attitude and consequent changes in policy which have occurred in some European countries. We can identify three general strands to the disability employment policies of most European countries:

1. the provision of support for workers with a disability and/or their employers, where workers with a disability obtain employment in the competitive labour market;

2. the reservation of a specific quota or percentage of jobs for workers with a disability;

3. the creation of a separate sheltered labour market exclusively for workers with a disability.

The first strand, whereby workers with a disability are given support and assistance so that they can obtain and maintain employment in a competitive environment, is usually targeted at workers with less severe disabilities and can be regarded as a long-standing attempt to secure the integration of such workers in the conventional labour market.

The second strand involves legislative intervention to promote the employment of people with disabilities through quotas. Early quota legislation was adopted following World War I and provided for employment quotas whereby employers were encouraged or obliged to employ a set percentage of disabled war veterans. The end of World War II saw the extension of these quota systems both in terms of the number of countries which chose to adopt them and in terms of the kind of disabled people protected, with the new quotas covering disabled civilians as well as ex-soldiers. With the exception of Scandinavia, the quota system became – and to a large extent still is – the standard response of practically all European countries, to the employment problems faced by people with disabilities seeking work in the conventional labour market (see Chapter Four). However, even though those people with disabilities who obtain work through a quota system work side by side with workers who have obtained employment in the conventional (usually competitive) manner, they remain part of a separate labour market, where a set percentage of jobs is reserved for those individuals classified as disabled, and where competition for jobs is theoretically restricted to this limited group.

The third strand which runs alongside the conventional labour market and the separate (quota) labour market, involves an alternative labour market which is both separate, in that it is confined to workers with a (severe) disability, and segregated, in that it is completely removed from the open labour market, with workers in the two labour markets usually having little contact with each other. This is the labour market based on 'sheltered employment', which is designed to provide work for those people with a disability who are regarded as 'unemployable' in the open labour market. The sheltered labour market has proved to be a popular element of disability employment policy in some Northern European countries, in particular the United Kingdom, the Netherlands, Ireland, Belgium, Germany and France, but has not been widely used in the southern part of Europe.

## EMPLOYMENT IN THE CONVENTIONAL (COMPETITIVE) LABOUR MARKET

Many European countries provide support to people with a disability and/or their employers, to enable the individual to secure and maintain employment. This support often takes the form of financial or personal support although legislation, imposing binding obligations on employers, often also has a part to play. The most common kinds of support and intervention which are provided are the following:

1. special assistance and advice targeted at people with a disability to help them obtain employment. This assistance may be provided from within the ordinary employment placement office, or from a separate specialist office;

2. rapid intervention to help prevent long-term unemployment of people with disabilities, for example offering of training or educational courses after only a relatively short period of unemployment;

3. loan or purchase of specialised equipment, for example adapted computer systems, furniture, protective equipment, to enable the individual with a disability to carry out a specific job;

4. provision of a job coach (on a temporary basis) to assist the individual with a disability to obtain the necessary skills;

5. grants to enable an employer to make physical adaptations to the workplace, such as the British Access to Work Scheme;

6. (temporary) subsidies or tax credits to employers who take on a worker with a disability;

7. additional legislative protection from dismissal for workers with a disability.

It is difficult to assess the effectiveness of these strategies. Some schemes providing financial assistance either to the worker or, in particular, the employer, have not been drawn on as much as was initially anticipated, possibly because employers are deterred by complicated application procedures. Legislative obligations on employers, such as restrictions in their ability to dismiss workers with a disability, may be a double-edged sword. Such provisions may well provide additional support for those workers with a disability already in employment; however, the existence of such rules may also discourage employers from taking on such workers in the first place. In any case, such schemes do little to address the problem of employers who simply do not wish to employ workers with a disability, either because they believe such workers are less effective or because they are concerned about the reliability of such workers. Instead, the schemes simply seek to make it easier for those employers who are already disposed to employing individuals with a disability to do so.

### Beliefs underlying support for employment in the conventional labour market

In recent years many European countries have sought to develop new tools to promote the employment of people with disabilities in the conventional labour market. This reflects the belief that employment in the open labour market is the preferred option for people with disabilities. It is also evidence that policy makers believe that (some) people with disabilities are able to compete and hold down jobs in the open labour market, albeit at times with additional public support. Finally, the instruments demonstrate that policy makers believe that the employment of people with disabilities can impose extra burdens on employers, in the form of the need to provide extra training, specialised equipment, an adapted workplace or some other cost, and that it is not appropriate for the employer to have to bear this cost. Instead the state should intervene and cover these extra costs. State support therefore usually attempts to make the employment of qualified people with disabilities no less attractive than the employment of qualified people without a disability, by removing any extra costs associated with the former. However, as noted above, administrative problems and the emphasis on the goodwill of employers (which does not always exist), has not made such an approach particularly successful.

## THE EMERGENCE AND DEVELOPMENT OF THE QUOTA SYSTEM IN EUROPE

As already noted, the first quota systems had their origins in the post-World War I period, and only covered disabled veterans. These quotas were based on the idea that society owed a duty to those who had been disabled while serving their country and by the end of 1923, Germany, Austria, Italy, Poland and France had all adopted such systems (Kulkarni, undated). In contrast, some countries, among them the UK, shied away from imposing an employment obligation on employers, and instead sought to encourage employers voluntarily to take on disabled veterans. The high unemployment levels among disabled veterans during the inter-war years, and the lack of success of the voluntary approach, led most European countries to turn to the obligation-based quota system in the post-World War II period. These second generation quotas were extended to cover the disabled civilian population. A consequence of this extension was that the concept of duty, which had existed when the systems were exclusively targeted at veterans, was lost, and the new quotas became part of overall social welfare policy.

The quota system has emerged as a key legislative tool in Europe to promote the employment of people with disabilities in conventional employment. Today, ten of the 15 Member States of the European Union have such a system,[3] and quotas can also be found in many European countries which are at present not members of the Union, such as Poland (Centre for Europe 1994; Third Report of the Federal Government 1994). All quota systems require employers to employ a set percentage of disabled workers, but within this general framework there is a great deal of scope for variety, and for this reason one cannot speak of a uniform European quota system. Instead European quota systems can be divided into three basic models. These are described in the following sections, and a brief assessment of their effectiveness is made.

### Legislative recommendation

Under this form of quota system employers are not obliged to employ a set percentage of disabled workers, but it is recommended that they do so. An example of such a system existed in the Netherlands. Under the 1986 Handicapped Workers Employment Act (WAGW)[4] public and private employers were required to facilitate the employment of disabled people, and a quota target of 3 to 5 per cent, to be achieved over three years, was set. All people receiving disability benefits or an invalidity pension were eligible for employment under the quota scheme. This quota was voluntary and the legislation did not provide for any sanctions in the event of employers failing to meet the quota. Instead, the government stated that it intended to introduce a legislative obligation, based on a quota of 3 to 7 per cent depending on the branch of industry or public sector concerned, if it became apparent that after the three-year period (that is, in 1989) employers were failing to meet the set quota. This obligation was to have been backed up by a fine of 10,000 florins per unoccupied position per year (Delsen and Klosse 1992).

By 1989 there had been little improvement in the employment situation of disabled people, and an official government report showed that only 2.2 per cent of workers with a contract of 15 days or more were disabled. The government did not respond to this by introducing a compulsory quota as it had threatened to do, but rather concluded that such a quota across all sectors of industry was not 'a practicable policy'.[5] The Dutch experience suggests that a voluntary quota, which imposes no legal obligation upon employers and provides for no sanctions, has little impact on the numbers of disabled people in open employment.

### Legislative obligation without sanction

Under this kind of system employers are obliged, through legislation, to employ a quota of disabled people, but this obligation is not backed up with any effective sanction. This model is typified by the quota system adopted in Britain after World War II. The quota, established in 1944 by the Disabled Persons (Employment) Act (DPEA)[6] (and abolished by the Disability Discrimination Act 1995), required all private employers with 20 or more employees to ensure that at least 3 per cent of their workforce was made up of registered disabled people. Public employers were not bound by this duty, but agreed to accept the same responsibilities as the private sector. It was not an offence for an employer to be below this quota, but an employer was not allowed to engage a non-registered person when below quota or where doing so would bring him or her below the quota, unless he or she had a permit granting exemption from this requirement. An employer who contravened the quota requirement was liable to a fine of not more than £500 or a term of imprisonment of not more than three months. In practice the British quota was not successful in promoting the employment of disabled people, and each year progressively fewer employers met their quota obligation so that in 1993 only 18.9 per cent of employers achieved the 3 per cent quota (compared with 30.4 per cent in 1984).[7]

There were a number of reasons for the failure of the British quota system, but it is submitted that the most important one was the unwillingness or inability of successive governments to enforce the quota by strictly policing the granting of exemption permits and prosecuting errant employers. The permission of the Secretary of State was needed before any prosecution under the Act could be commenced, and governments of both parties were consistently unwilling to sanction prosecution, and instead chose to issue bulk exemption permits to employers allowing them to recruit non-registered workers. As a result most employers, where they were even aware of the Act (and many were not), regarded compliance with the DPEA as obtaining an exemption permit before hiring non-registered workers, rather than achieving the 3 per cent quota. Consequently fewer and fewer eligible disabled people chose to register, thereby reducing the number of individuals qualifying for preferential treatment under the DPEA. From 1979 it became statistically impossible for all employers to meet their 3 per cent target and by the early 1990s, the Employment Service estimated that only a third of those eligible to register actually did so, meaning that only 1 per cent of the workforce was registered as disabled.

Evidence from Britain clearly shows that it is insufficient simply to legislate to impose an obligation on employers to employ disabled people. Such quota systems do little more than rely on the goodwill of employers, and do not greatly increase the chances of the targeted individuals in the open labour market. The quota was finally abolished in Britain on 2 December 1996, when the employment provisions of the new disability anti-discrimination law, the Disability Discrimination Act 1995, came into force (see Chapter Six).

### Legislative obligation with sanction (levy-grant system)

This is the form of quota which has attracted most interest from those countries which have sought to introduce or modify a quota system in the 1980s and 1990s. This approach involves setting a quota and requiring that all targeted employers who do not meet their obligation pay a fine or levy which usually goes into a fund to support the employment of people with disabilities. Germany provides one of the earliest examples of such a system, and its quota has since served as a model for other countries.

The present German quota system was established by the Severely Handi-capped Persons Act (*Schwerbehindertergesetz – SchwbG*) in 1974.[8] The *SchwbG* sets a quota of 6 per cent for all public and private employers with 16 or more employees. In calculating the quota, certain workers are counted as occupying two or three quota places. This applies to those individuals whom the

Employment Office feels are particularly difficult to employ because of their degree of disability, and to disabled people receiving vocational training within the firm. All severely disabled people whose disability amounts to at least a 50 per cent reduction in working capacity are covered by the *SchwbG*. In addition the employment office can extend the protection of the law to those with a work-related disability of 30–50 per cent if it is satisfied that the individuals concerned experience difficulty in obtaining or maintaining employment as a result of their disability.

Employers who do not meet their quota obligation are obliged to pay a levy of 200DM per month for every unfilled quota place. This money is used exclusively to promote the rehabilitation and employment of severely disabled people and can, for example, be used to provide grants to employers who exceed their quota obligations to help them meet any extra costs, such as adaptations to buildings or the provision of special training. The law is based on the principle that all employers above a certain size should contribute to the economic integration of severely disabled workers. Ideally this integration should occur through the actual provision of employment for such workers, but where this is not the case, a contribution should be made via the levy procedure.

The German quota system has undoubtedly made a greater contribution to promoting the employment of disabled people than the two systems previously described. However, in recent years the German quota has become progressively less effective. Since 1982, when the average quota achieved was 5.9 per cent, the situation has steadily worsened, and in 1992 the average percentage of severely disabled workers employed within firms had fallen to 4.3 per cent. The German quota has proved itself incapable of maintaining the targeted level of employment for severely disabled people during a period of economic recession. The economic difficulties, combined with the relatively low levy, seem to make payment a more attractive option than the unknown risks of hiring a severely disabled worker.

### Beliefs underlying the quota system

European quota systems clearly aim to promote the employment of people with disabilities, and are based on the belief that, without some form of legislative intervention, disabled people would not make up the relevant (quota) percentage of the employed workforce. It is submitted that in addition quotas are based on two related assumptions: first, that employers will not hire large numbers of disabled people unless they are required to do so and second, that a large number of people with disabilities are unable to compete with their non-disabled counterparts for jobs on an equal basis, and win them on their merits. In short the assumption is that most workers with a disability are less valuable economically and less productive, and that, if such workers are to be integrated in the open labour market, employers need to be obliged to hire them. Numerous employers have taken their cue from the legislation and accept these assumptions. This is reflected in the fact that many employers resist the idea of, and obligations under, quota systems, and frequently 'buy' themselves out of their obligation where this is an option, preferring to employ a largely non-disabled workforce.

The history of the European quota systems demonstrates that an employment system which is based on the idea that the protected group of workers is 'inferior' cannot achieve permanent and significant successes, since employers will attempt to evade their obligations to employ such workers. In addition those workers who obtain employment through the quota scheme, and perhaps even those workers with a disability who obtain employment on their merits in open competition, risk being stigmatised by the existence of the scheme, as the perception may exist that such individuals are less good workers and have only obtained employment as a result of the affirmative action programme.

Nevertheless, it should be noted that quota schemes remain in force in most European countries and are an important element of government policies which seek to promote the employment of people with disabilities. In addition, such schemes are frequently popular with people with disabilities, who often identify the problem with such schemes as weak enforcement and lack of sanctions for employers who do not meet their obligation, rather than with the schemes per se. Organisations representing people with disabilities in the UK, whilst generally welcoming the adoption of disability anti-discrimination legislation, opposed the repeal of the quota law during the period c. 1993–1995, when it became apparent that the then Conservative governement might repeal the quota legislation as the 'price' for adopting the Disability Discrimination Act. Instead they argued that both the new anti-discrimination law and the quota law should be strictly enforced.

## THE EMERGENCE AND DEVELOPMENT OF SHELTERED WORKSHOPS IN EUROPE

Another important element of employment programmes for people with disabilities, at least in Northern European countries, has been the creation of a completely separate labour market designed for those people with a disability regarded as unable to function in the conventional labour market. The 1989 European Labour Force Survey found that approximately 350,000 people worked in sheltered employment with three member states (Germany, France and the Netherlands) accounting for about 80 per cent of these workers.[9] In the years following World War II, the International Labour Organisation (ILO) and a number of other international and regional organisations adopted instruments promoting the development of sheltered employment (Chapter Three, p.73). ILO Recommendation No. 99 of 1955, on the adaptation and vocational rehabilitation of disabled people, refers to sheltered employment as one of the measures to be used to allow people with disabilities to obtain or retain suitable employment. According to the Recommendation, sheltered employment should be provided for 'disabled persons who cannot be made fit for ordinary competitive employment.'[10] The object of employment in sheltered workshops is to 'provide, under effective medical and vocational supervision, not only useful and remunerative work but opportunities for vocational adjustment and advancement with, whenever possible, transfer to open employment.'[11] Similar definitions of both the target group and the objectives of such employment can be found in current national legislation, as well as in texts of the Council of Europe[12] and European Community.[13]

Whilst the stated object of all such programmes is to provide both useful remunerative work and training and prepare the worker for employment in the open labour market, there has been a notable lack of success with regard to the latter objective. In most countries operating such programmes, less than 5 per cent of workers are able to make the move from the sheltered to the open labour market per year. Indeed, at a time when public spending is frequently decreasing, there may actually be disincentives for individual sheltered workshops to promote the transfer of their more able workers. Sheltered programmes are often expected to cover an increasing amount of their own costs, through the sale of goods and services which they produce. Given that scenario, the workshops are understandably reluctant to lose their most productive workers and may seek to exclude potential workers who are expected to have a low productivity.

In recent years, and particularly since the late 1980s, some countries have been attempting to move away from the classical form of sheltered employment, with workers with a disability working in a factory-like setting and having little contact with the outside world, and to develop more open forms of employment, where the worker has the opportunity to interact with people from outside the enclosed, sheltered environment. These new initiatives, sometimes referred to as semi-sheltered employment, nevertheless provide a considerable degree of protection for the worker and do not amount to employment in the open labour market. Examples of this new approach include the creation of small groups of workers who, under the guidance of one or more qualified individuals, provide services, such as agricultural or catering services, to firms, or the placing of individuals, accompanied by a person who provides permanent training and support, with ordinary employers. In both cases the individuals with a disability remain employed under the sheltered employment scheme.

### Beliefs underlying sheltered employment schemes

Under sheltered employment schemes it is recognised that individuals with (more severe) disabilities are capable of work of economic value – for the goods and services produced by sheltered workshops are sold in the open market – but that these workers are not yet able to hold down jobs in the open labour market. This reduced ability was seen, until recently, as justifying the separation and segregation of such workers from the rest of the workforce. This segregation may well be one of the reasons why the objective of preparing workers for employment in a competitive environment was – and is – only infrequently achieved. Recently efforts have been made to reduce the barriers between open and sheltered employment; however, this is proving to be time-consuming and expensive, and the vast majority of people employed under sheltered employment schemes still work in a segregated and separate environment.

## APPROACHES TO AND BELIEFS UNDERLYING AREAS OTHER THAN EMPLOYMENT

The developments and attitudes examined above have also been reflected in other areas of policy, such as education, housing and access to transport. In all of these areas people with disabilities have been able to participate in mainstream services if they could meet the requirements of those services, for example, the ability to learn in a large group while not disrupting lessons; the ability to enter, move around and utilise ordinary housing while not disturbing neighbours excessively; the ability to board a mode of transport and understand how a system works. In addition, public assistance was sometimes provided to enable individuals to function in the mainstream environment, for example, additional classroom help or extra lessons.

For that group who could not make use of ordinary facilities which were largely designed without people with disabilities in mind, alternative 'separate and segregated' services were provided. With regard to education, this took the form of 'special' schools attended only by children with disabilities. Educational expectations and standards at such schools were usually lower than at conventional schools, even for those children who did not have a learning disability. With regard to housing, this took the form of large institutions housing hundreds of people with disabilities, with individuals often sleeping in huge dormitory-like rooms. Over the last decades these institutions have tended to close down, or at least been broken up into smaller units. With regard to transport, separation and segregation took the form of door-to-door transport for people with disabilities. This transport often had to be ordered hours or days in advance, was restricted to a certain number of journeys per week and was at times unreliable. In many respects the situation remains the same today.

## RECENT DEVELOPMENTS: A REASSESSMENT OF THE NOTION OF DISABILITY AND MOVES TO COMBAT DISCRIMINATION

An important reassessment of disability policy has been occurring in a number of European countries over the past decade. The reassessment has involved both the development of a new concept of disability and consequent changes in legislation and policy. The policies described in the previous section were developed at a time when the medical model of disability was dominant and, more important, accepted by policy-makers. This model holds that limitations or difficulties linked to a disability primarily result from the physical or mental impairment which an individual has, and are largely unconnected to the surrounding environment. This model has provided a theoretical justification for the separation and segregation of the people with disabilities. The model also justifies only a limited public intervention to encourage the integration of people with disabilities in the open labour market and the ordinary education system. Since the problem is located primarily in the individual and in his or her physical or intellectual condition, it is individuals who must adapt if they wish to participate in mainstream society. If individuals cannot meet the expectations and norms of mainstream society, then they are offered – and confined to – an alternative, separate and often segregated, labour market, education system or residential accommodation.

However, as explained in Chapter One, in recent years this approach has been questioned – first by groups representing the interests of people with a disability and, later, by some policy makers. The medical model of disability has increasingly been rejected in favour of a social model which embraces a civil rights approach (see Chapter One). This latter model holds that the disadvantages associated with disability stem primarily from the failure of the social environment to adjust to the needs and aspirations of people with disabilities, rather than from the inability of individuals to adapt to society and the environment. The argument here is that it is discrimination – in the physical and attitudinal environment, prejudice, stigmatisation, segregation and a general history of disadvantage, which we have come to associate with disability – which is the major problem for people with a disability. This can be seen as a fundamental reconceptualisation of disability and, since it focuses on deficiencies in society and the environment instead of those in the individual, it has different policy implications from the medical model. Under the social model, disability is seen as representing a dynamic relationship between individuals with a disability and their surroundings, so that the emphasis is switched from the individual to the broader social, cultural, economic and political environment. This has the advantage of not focusing on the alleged inabilities or limitations of an individual, and has the potential to allow for the consideration of the capabilities of those concerned. The model also allows for the recognition of discrimination in its many forms as one of the most important barriers to the economic and social integration of people with disabilities, and justifies public intervention designed to combat this discrimination and guarantee rights – related to participation in society – for people with disabilities.

At the pan-European level probably the most important manifestation of this change in attitude has been an amendment to the Treaty of the European Community allowing for legislative action to combat disability discrimination (see p.49). However, the adoption of these measures, and the subsequent adoption of a directive addressing, inter alia, disability employment discrimination, was a reflection of the changes in attitude and policy that were already occurring in a number of member states of the European Community. Recent years have therefore seen the adoption of national legislation designed to combat disability discrimination, in the labour market and beyond, in many European countries and beyond (see Chapter Four). The acceptance of the social model of disability, and the recognition of the need to take legislative action to combat disability discrimination and protect social and civil rights has however not resulted in one common response which can be found in all European countries, but in a number of different responses using a variety of legal tools and approaches. France was, for example, one of the first European countries to extend the protection of the law to victims of disability discrimination by making such discrimination a criminal offence. More recently the constitutions in Germany and Finland have been amended, and in both cases the equal protection clause now explicitly names disabled people as a protected group. Meanwhile legislators in the UK and other countries[14] have recently adopted laws addressing disability discrimination, and, at time of writing, a proposal for such legislation may be presented to the Dutch Parliament.[15] These responses reveal at least three different approaches to combating disability (employment) discrimination in Europe through legislation. Whilst Germany and Finland have opted, in the first instance, for constitutional law, Britain, Sweden and Ireland have favoured civil law, and France has resorted to criminal law. These developments are examined in further detail below, and attention is paid in particular to the impact of the relevant legislative provision and concept of disability discrimination as defined, if at all, in the legislation.

### Constitutional law: the Federal Republic of Germany and Finland

Prior to 1994 the German Basic Law (*Grundgesetz*) or Constitution contained no provision specifically favouring people with disabilities, and no reference to disability was found in Article 3 which covers equality. On 27 October 1994 the

Basic Law was amended, and the following text was added to Article 3: 'No one may be disadvantaged on the basis of his disability'.[16]

The Constitution has subsequently been amended a number of times, and the complete text of Article 3 now reads:

1. All humans are equal before the law.

2. Men and women are equal. The state supports the effective realisation of equality of women and men and works towards abolishing present disadvantages.

3. No one may be disadvantaged or favoured because of his sex, his parentage, his race, his language, his homeland and origin, his faith, or his religious or political opinions. No one may be disadvantaged because of his disability.[17]

At the public level the new provision binds the legislature, the executive and the administration and applies to the Federal Government, the *Länder* and *Gemeinden* (regions and localities), as well as to all public servants acting in an official capacity. There is an obligation to ensure that new statutes, regulations and administrative norms do not discriminate against people with a disability, and to amend existing provisions which have that effect, and for the courts to interpret instruments and hand down rulings which do not discriminate solely on the grounds of disability. This could mean that controversial rulings, such as the Flensburg decision[18] in which a district court held that the value of a holiday had been reduced because the plaintiffs had to share hotel meal times with a group of disabled people, might now be unconstitutional. The provision has already had consequences at the level of the *Länder*, where legislators have inserted clauses into new public transport acts to ensure that the needs of people with mobility disabilities are taken into account in the purchasing of vehicles and constructing of facilities.[19] However this is one of the rare examples of constitutional change provoking legislative change, and up until now the new non-discrimination clause has had little practical effect.

Nevertheless, given the extent to which constitutional norms penetrate the German legal system, this amendment clearly contains the potential to lead to improvements in the situation of people with a disability. However, there are a number of major problems with the German approach and the constitutional amendment on its own is insufficient to make major inroads into the problem of disability discrimination. The new provision is a simple statement which fails to define the key concepts of 'disadvantaged' and 'disability'. If the principle of disability non-discrimination is truly to become part of the German legal culture, the constitution arguably needs to be backed up by a thorough anti-discrimination law which clearly defines both the group of beneficiaries and the nature of the prohibited act. This is currently being lobbied for by people with a disability in Germany who, through their Forum of Disabled Lawyers and Judges, have produced a draft proposal which includes definitions of the concepts of 'handicap' and 'discrimination'.

In Finland, extensive legislative reform in the early 1990s involved the rewriting of the Chapter of the Constitution dealing with fundamental rights. As of August 1995, the constitution provides that:

(1) All persons shall be equal before the law;

(2) No one shall, without acceptable grounds, be afforded a different status on account of sex, age, origin, language, religion, conviction, opinion, state of health, disability or any other reason related to the person.[20]

The Finnish constitution has recently undergone a thorough revision and updating, and a new constitution came into force on 1 March 2000. However, other than re-numbering, no substantive changes were made to this section of the constitution.[21]

### Civil law: the UK

The 1980s saw numerous parliamentary attempts to secure the adoption of some form of disability anti-discrimination legislation in Britain. These proposals all took the form of private member's bills, and universally failed to secure the support of Conservative governments. In 1994, in a very controversial move, the then Minister for Disabled People, with the support of his back-bench colleagues, 'talked out' a widely supported bill. As a result of the uproar which followed this unco-operative stance, the government agreed to introduce and support a disability discrimination bill.[22] Although widely criticised, not least of all for its enforcement mechanism, the bill passed all three readings in both houses of parliament, and received the royal assent on 8 November 1995.

The Disability Discrimination Act 1995 addresses disability discrimination in the areas of employment, education and transport, as well as a number of other fields such as the provision of goods, facilities and services and premises. It is discussed in detail in Chapter Six. For our purposes, the concepts which are of vital importance for an understanding of the legislation, and which heavily influence its effectiveness, are 'disability' and 'discrimination'. The Disability Discrimination Act 1995 is more thorough than its German and French counterparts. It attempts to address the problem of defining disability and discrimination and recognises that some balance must be sought between the interests of employers and the interests of disabled people. However, given the lack of clarity of so many of the Act's key terms, ranging from 'impairment' to 'justified' unfavourable treatment, it is questionable whether the Act can achieve that balance.

### Criminal law: France

In July 1990 the French Parliament adopted Law No. 90–602 concerning the protection of persons against discrimination on grounds of their state of health or their 'handicap'.[23] This law amended the Penal Code, and made it a criminal offence for providers of goods or services to refuse to supply to an individual or association on the grounds of state of health or handicap, or for an employer to refuse to hire or to dismiss an individual on these grounds. The Penal Code also covers discrimination based on origin, sex, customs, marital status, ethnic group, nationality, race or religion.

Article 225–1 of the New Penal Code defines discrimination as: 'all distinctions made between physical persons on account of their origin, sex, family situation, state of health, handicap, customs, political opinions, trade union activities, their membership or non-membership, true or assumed, of an ethnic group, nation, race or religion' [author's translation].[24]

Although the Code contains this very broad definition of discrimination, which also extends protection to legal persons, it makes clear that not all forms of discrimination are punishable under the criminal law. Article 225–2 specifies that discriminatory behaviour, as defined in Article 225–1, may result in a prison sentence of two years and a fine of 200,000 FF when it consists of:

1. refusing to provide a good or service;

2. hindering the normal exercise of any economic activity;

3. refusing to employ a person, or sanctioning or dismissing a person;

4. subjecting the provision of a good or service to a condition based on one of the grounds referred to in Article 225.1;

5. subjecting an offer of employment to a condition based on one of the grounds referred to in Article 225.1.

The Code clearly aims to cover all economic transactions, including those related to employment, and to exclude personal relationships from its scope. However, the Code goes on to state that discrimination based upon state of health or handicap is permitted in certain cases, even where it involves the provision of a good or service or employment. Article 225–3 states that Article 225–2 does not apply to:

1. Discrimination based on state of health, which consists of operations which aim to prevent or cover the risk of death, risks posed to the

physical integrity of a person or risks of incapacity for work or invalidity.

2. Discrimination based on state of health or handicap, which consists of a refusal to employ or register based on medically proven lack of aptitude either in the framework of Title IV of Book II of the Labour Code[25] or in the framework of the legislation relating to the statutory provisions applying to the civil service [author's translation].

Presumably the intention behind this latter provision was to ensure that employers are not liable for refusing to employ an individual who is unable to perform the job at issue. On the other hand, the Code makes no clear provision for determining when discrimination on the grounds of disability has actually occurred. More particularly the Code fails to specify whether there is any obligation on employers to alter the working environment where this would allow the individual to perform a particular job. In the absence of a clear statement to this effect, it seems unlikely that such a requirement can be read into the law, meaning that it is not a criminal offence to refuse to hire, or to dismiss someone whose disability requires even a minor adjustment or accommodation.

Commentators have criticised the French approach to employment discrimination, and have argued that it fails to protect minorities adequately (see Gitter 1994; Forbes and Mead 1992). The French law fails to define the concept of 'handicap' and the precise scope of the protected group. Furthermore, the French Penal Code does not deal adequately with the intricacies of disability discrimination, generally treating it in the same way as all other sorts of discrimination, and neglects the important issue of reasonable adjustment or accommodation. This fact, and the legislative neglect of indirect discrimination,[26] means that employers have a great deal of freedom when it comes to making unfavourable employment decisions concerning disabled people under the Penal Code. The balance between the interests of disabled people and the interests of employers, which other jurisdictions have sought to establish, does not seem to have greatly concerned French legislators in this case. Therefore, of all the disability anti-discrimination laws, in Europe or elsewhere, French law[27] seems to provide the least protection to disabled people and the least effective remedies where discrimination is established.

## EUROPEAN COMMUNITY RESPONSE

After a drawn-out round of negotiations lasting two years, at the 1996 inter-governmental conference held to revise the European Treaties a new Article was included in the Treaty on the European Community giving the Community the ability to take action to combat discrimination on a number of grounds, including disability. The new provision is found in Article 13 of the revised Treaty and reads:

> Without prejudice to the other provisions of this Treaty and within the limits of the powers conferred by it upon the Community, the Council, acting unanimously on a proposal from the Commission and after consulting the European Parliament, may take appropriate action to combat discrimination based on sex, racial or ethnic origin, religion or belief, disability, age or sexual orientation.

The Article only allows the Community to take action to combat discrimination on the named grounds and does not amount to such action itself. Furthermore, action can only be taken in those areas which fall 'within the limits of the powers' conferred by the Treaty, and must be backed by unanimous support from all member states (through their participation in the Council of Ministers of the European Union).

The inclusion of Article 13 in the Treaty is significant in that the new provision embraces the social model of disability[28] and recognises the existence of disability discrimination within the European Community. The Article also acknowledges that the Community has some competence to address this issue. Acting on this competence, on 25 November 1999 the Commission proposed its long-awaited 'non-discrimination' package, which included a proposal for a framework Directive for Equal Treatment in Employment and Occupation[29] covering all grounds referred to in Article 1, with the exception of sex, which is already the subject of a number of equal treatment Directives in the area of employment.[30] (For further information see Bell 2000 and Waddington 2000.)

On 17 October 2000 the Social Policy Council reached a political agreement to adopt this Directive. Formal adoption was expected to occur in November 2000, once authentic versions of the Directive had been prepared in all official languages.[31] The Directive covers employment and occupation, including conditions for access to employment and promotion, vocational guidance and training, employment conditions and membership of workers' and employers' organisations (Article 3). Direct and indirect discrimination are expressly added, as is harassment (Article 3). With regard to people with disabilities, the Directive establishes an obligation to provide reasonable accommodation. This requires employers to take appropriate measures to enable a person with a disability to have access to, participate in, or advance in employment, or to provide training for such a person, unless such measures would impose a disproportionate burden on the employer (Article 5). One should note that an implementation period of six years is provided for with regard to the disability discrimination (Article 17). [32]

In addition to providing the legal basis for specific directives, Article 13 may well influence the action of the Community institutions when adopting policy and legislative action based on other Treaty articles; that is, the influence of the

Article also depends on the extent to which non-discrimination and equal opportunity become tools used when drafting and interpreting Community legislation and policy (for a detailed examination of the significance and likely impact of Article 13 see Waddington 1999).

The implementation of the non-discrimination principle through binding Community law would influence national policy and legislation in all member states, including those which have thus far failed to adopt disability non-discrimination legislation, and in this way Article 13 may have a very significant impact indeed.

## BELIEFS UNDERLYING ANTI-DISCRIMINATION LAWS

It has already been noted that the development of anti-discrimination laws in Europe was prompted by a reconceptualisation of disability by policy makers, and specifically by a move away from the medical concept of disability towards the social concept which embraced a civil rights approach. However, the tools which European policy makers have chosen to use to combat disability discrimination vary in their legislative effect, degree of detail and, to a certain degree, in the extent to which they embrace the social model of disability.

The approach followed by the UK, Sweden and Ireland, involving the adoption of fairly detailed civil law which is designed to combat disability discrimination, perhaps involves the greatest recognition of the complexities of disability discrimination. Most significantly these statutes, unlike for example the constitutional provisions and the French Penal Code, provide a definition of disability and a definition of disability discrimination which embraces not only direct and indirect discrimination, but also discrimination in the form of failing to make an accommodation or adjustment to allow the participation of a person with a disability. In addition, these laws impose significant obligations on employers and service providers and are not designed only to impact on the state (as in the case of the German constitutional provision) or only apply in the case of intentional discrimination (as in the case of the French Penal Code). In that sense, one can regard such laws as the most detailed elaboration of the social model of disability. Constitutional provisions, whilst achieving a far lesser degree of detail and specification, and having a lesser impact on relations between private parties, are nevertheless important in that they recognise the right to equality and freedom from discrimination as being a fundamental right and worthy of a high degree of protection.

The French criminal law is, in contrast, probably the most confused translation of the social model of disability into legislation. It imposes obligations on private parties, but only covers cases in which the employer or service provider intended to discriminate. However, the social model recognises that most forms of discrimination and disadvantage are not the result of intentional exclusion but result from attitudes and an infrastructure which simply take little account of the needs of people with disabilities. The social model therefore requires not only action to combat intentional discrimination but also, and perhaps even more, action to combat unintentional indirect discrimination and discrimination in the form of failure to make an accommodation or adjustment to meet the needs of people with disabilities, neither of which is covered by the French Penal Code.

Notwithstanding the above observations, we can nevertheless identify some general beliefs behind the adoption of anti-discrimination provisions in Europe. It has been argued earlier with regard to employment that important elements of European disability employment policies are based on the belief that workers with a disability are not able effectively to compete for jobs in the open labour market because they are less productive than workers without a disability, and therefore that employers must be obliged to employ such workers through quota systems. Anti-discrimination legislation, in contrast to these assumptions, is based on the belief that workers with a disability are as good as their non-disabled counterparts and that given the appropriate non-discriminatory environment they are able to compete successfully for jobs on their merits. Anti-discrimination legislation is also based on the belief that children with a disability are entitled and able to receive education at a conventional school, and that people with disabilities are entitled and able to live among the rest of society and account should be taken of their needs. The starting points for the adoption of the 'old' and 'new' legislation and policy are therefore very much opposed.

## REASONS BEHIND THE CHANGE OF APPROACH

As already noted, the revision of the approach to disability and the adoption of anti-discrimination laws and provisions has occurred over a relatively short period in Europe. It is submitted that there are a number of reasons for this rapid change.

### An idea whose time had come

The acceptance of the social model of disability and the adoption of disability anti-discrimination legislation is by no means a recent phenomenon confined to Europe – indeed, in some respects Europe is lagging behind other countries. The European developments noted in this chapter have been preceded by a revision of the concept of disability and consequently policy in North America and Australia and, indeed, the United Nations. Furthermore, changes in Europe have been mirrored more or less simultaneously by changes in countries in Africa, Asia and South America among others. It seems that a revision in the approach to disability was long overdue, and is occurring with surprising speed across the globe. These matters will all be addressed in detail in Chapters Three and Four.

### Role of disability non-governmental organisations

The last few years have seen the development of a politically active disability movement in many parts of Europe. Whilst in some countries, such as the UK, politically sophisticated organisations representing the interests of people with disabilities have been active for some time, in others the development of such a movement is a relatively recent phenomenon. The growth of the disability movement has been prompted, to a significant degree, by developments at the European Community level. The Community has provided funding for activities organised by non-governmental organisations which focus on disability and for the establishment of what has become an independent European Disability Forum made up of numerous national and pan-European Community disability non-governmental organisations. A key part of the work of the European disability movement has been the campaign for the inclusion of a non-discrimination article which specifically mentioned disability at the previous revision of the treaty on the European Community (see above, p.49). This initiative brought together many national disability organisations which campaigned at both the European and national level and served to heighten awareness and educate disability organisations in Europe about non-discrimination legislation. Lessons learnt in the European context have been and are, in some cases at least, also proving to be of use in similar national campaigns which are slowly reaping rewards.

## CONCLUSION

Recent years have seen important and noticeable changes in the approach to disability policy in many European countries. Underlying this change is a view of disability based on a social model, and a key element of the new approach is the adoption of anti-discrimination legislation.

European countries, with their different legal systems and traditions, have chosen to address disability discrimination through a variety of legislative tools, including constitutional provisions, civil law and criminal law. Thus far the civil law provisions have achieved the greatest detail and dealt in the most sophisticated manner with the problem of disability discrimination. Such statutes cover not only direct and indirect discrimination, but also discrimination in the form of failure to make an adjustment or accommodation to meet the needs of an individual with a disability. The adoption of such a law in Sweden is important in that it demonstrates that such an approach is not only of relevance to common law countries in Europe (ie the UK and Ireland).

Anti-discrimination legislation can, and usually does, apply across many areas, including employment, access to goods and services and transport. The legislation is based on a principle which is of universal relevance and applicability. Earlier legislation, which provided either for only limited support to allow participation in mainstream society or, frequently, for segregation or separation of people with disabilities, applied to specific areas such as employment or education. The non-discrimination principle may, because it is of general relevance, bring more cohesion to disability policy.

One can question whether legislation and policy adopted in an earlier period, and based on the medical model of disability, can or should co-exist with the new approach, from either a philosophical or practical point of view. The question has been raised, for instance, with regard to employment quotas. The answer depends, to a large extent, on the legislation or policy at issue. For example, intervention designed to facilitate the employment of people with disabilities in the open labour market through the provision of financial or technical support for employers seems compatible with the new approach. Such support will assist the employer to make adjustments or accommodation to meet the needs of workers with a disability, and in fact complements the non-discriminatory approach.

Quota systems would seem to be less compatible with the non-discriminatory approach. However, it is submitted that the real test should be whether quotas, or any other legislation or policy, actually work or could be made to work, in the sense that the legislation or policy contributes to the well-being of people with a disability. The analysis in this chapter suggests that quota systems which are based on a recommendation or which are not enforced serve little useful purpose. Quota systems which are enforced through a fine or a levy may in fact not be much more effective in securing employment for people with a disability. However they are undoubtedly effective in securing substantial funds to promote the employment of people with a disability. No doubt, for many policy makers, this reason alone will be sufficient justification for the retention of such quotas.

It is submitted that the influence of the social model of disability and the adoption of disability anti-discrimination legislation is likely to continue in Europe. The role of the European Community, which has adopted this approach and which has now adopted binding anti-discrimination disability legislation, will be vital in this respect. It should be recalled that the European Community and Union are expected to expand in the coming years with the accession of a number of countries in Eastern Europe. A European Union of 30 or more countries in the next decade is not an unlikely prospect. In addition, the experience of those European countries which have already adopted national anti-discrimination provisions is likely to influence those countries which have yet to do so.

# REFERENCES

Bell, M. (2000) 'Article 13 EC: the European Commission's anti-discrimination proposals.' *Industrial Law Journal 29*, 1, 79.

Centre for Europe (1994) 'Law on Employment and Vocational Rehabilitation of Disabled People.' *Disability: Problems and Solutions*, Warsaw University: Information and Documentation Unit of the Council of Europe.

Delsen, L and Klosse, S. (1992) 'Integration of the disabled in the work process: the Dutch policy.' *The Geneva Papers on Risk and Insurance 17*, 62, 119.

Forbes, I. and Mead, G. (1992) *Measure for Measure, A Comparative Analysis of Measures to Combat Racial Discrimination in the Member States of the European Community.* Southampton: Equal Opportunities Studies Group, University of Southampton. Research Series No.1, Employment Department.

Gitter, D. (1994) 'French criminalization of racial employment discrimination compared to the imposition of civil penalties in the United States.' *Comparative Labor Law Journal 15*, 485.

Kulkarni, M. (undated) *Quota Systems and the Employment of the Handicapped. Experiences in Three Countries.* Michigan: University Center for Institutional Rehailitation, Michigan State University.

Lunt, N. and Thornton, P. (1993) *Employment Policies for Disabled People.* Department of Employment.

Third Report of the Federal Government (1994) *The Situation of the Disabled and the Development of Rehabilitation.* Bonn: Bundesministerium für Arbeit und Sozialordnung.

Waddington, L. (1999) 'Testing the Limits of the EC Treaty Article on Non-Discrimination', *Industrial Law Journal*, 28, 2, 133.

Waddington, L. (2000) 'Article 13 EC: setting priorities in the proposal for a horizontal employment directive.' *Industrial Law Journal 29*, 1, 2.

# NOTES

1    This chapter is based on a paper presented to a seminar at the University of California at Berkeley on 22 November 1999. The author is grateful to the Human Rights Research School of Maastricht University for providing financial support and to Professor Theresia Degener, Visiting Professor at Berkeley 1999–2000, and the Law School at Berkeley for facilitating the visit. As the book went to press on 31st October 2000 it has not been possible to include information on developments since that date.

2    The following 15 countries are currently members of the European Union: France, Germany, Italy, Belgium, Netherlands, Luxembourg (founder members, 1957), the UK, Ireland, Denmark (1973), Spain, Portugal (1983), Greece (1986), Austria, Sweden and Finland (1996).

3    Portugal, the UK and the three Scandinavian member states do not have a quota system. Denmark, Sweden and Finland object on the grounds that the registration necessarily associated with the quota system is unacceptable.

4    *Wet arbeid gehandicapte werknemers*, law of 16 May 1986, Stb. 300, amended by the law of 26 April 1995, Stb. 1995, 250. This Act replaced an earlier Act (*Wet plaatsing minder-valide arbeidskrachten* of 1947) which imposed an obligation on employers to employ a set quota of 'less able-bodied' workers. This obligation was not backed up with an effective sanction.

5    Report to the International Labour Organisation for the period 1 July 1990 to 30 June 1992, referred to in Lunt and Thornton 1993. In 1994, however, the Dutch government

accepted, in theory at least, that it has an obligation to meet a 3 per cent quota. Aart Hendriks and Maathijs Vermaat, '*Het Nederlandse gehandicaptenbeleid: een doekje voor het bloeden*' ('The Dutch Disability Policy: a cloth to mop up the blood.'), *Nederlandse Juristen Blad* (1995), f.n. 36.

6    7 & 8 Geo 6 c. 10

7    This is based on information provided by the Disability Branch 1 of the British Employment Service.

8    *Bundesgesetzblatt I S. 1421, ber. S. 1550*. The *SchwbG* has been amended a number of times since 1974.

9    There were at that time 12 Member States; subsequently Austria, Finland and Sweden joined the European Community.

10   Article 32(1)

11   Article 33

12   See, for example, *A Coherent Policy for the Rehabilitation of Disabled People.* Resolution AP (84) 3 adopted by the Committee of Ministers on 17 September 1984. Strasbourg, Council of Europe, 1984, 21.

13   See, for example, *Council Recommendations on the Employment of Disabled People in the Community,* 86/379/EEC.

14   Including Ireland and Sweden. For a global overview of these developments see Chapter Four.

15   The draft bill on the 'Prohibition on Making an Unjustifiable Distinction on the Grounds of Handicap or Chronic Disease'.

16   Original: '*Niemand darf wegen seiner Behinderung benachteiligt werden*'. *Gesetz zur Änderung des Grundgesetzes, Bundesgesetzblatt, Jahrgang 1994, Teil I, 3146.*

17   Source: Würzburg University International Constitutional Law homepage, at www.uni-wuerzburg.de/law/

18   AG Flensburg, *Neue Juristische Wochenschrift* 1993, 272.

19   *Invisible Citizens, Disabled Person's Status in the European Treaties.* Report for the European Day of Disabled Persons, European Parliament, 1995, doc.nr. D/1995/7560/2, p.66.

20   Source: Würzburg University International Constitutional Law homepage, www.uni-wuerzburg.de/law/

21   The relevant article will now be contained in Chapter 2, 'Basic rights' in Section 6, 'Equality'.

22   It was clear from the beginning that the government sponsored bill was going to be much less 'radical' than most of the private member's bills which had been introduced in the late 1980s. Most of these bills had been closely modelled on the Americans with Disabilities Act of 1990.

23   *Loi 90–602 du 12 juillet 1990 relative à la protection des personnes contre les discriminations en raison de leur état de santé ou de leur handicap.* ('Law of 12 July 1990 on the protection of persons against discrimination on the grounds of their health or handicap.') *Journal Officiel de la République Française,* 13 July 1990, 8272.

24   The original version can be found in the most recent edition of the *Code Pénal,* Codes Dalloz.

25   This Title only deals with procedural aspects of the work of doctors in the workplace.

26   French law fails to proscribe indirect discrimination because the legislature did not wish to criminalise what is generally considered to be an unintentional wrong.

27   However, it should also be noted that whilst this is the only law specifically addressing disability employment discrimination, disabled individuals can also rely, in certain cases,

on provisions of the civil law contained in the Labour Code. In cases of wrongful dismissal motivated by discrimination plaintiffs can rely on the wrongful discharge statute. Although this does not specifically cover discriminatory dismissals on the basis of disability, it does provide for remedies, including damages and/or re-instatement, where the dismissal is not made for a '*cause réelle et sérieuse*' ('a genuine and serious cause'). The Labour Code also places an obligation on employers to reassign workers who have been disabled as a result of a work-related accident or illness to another job within the enterprise where, as a result of the injury, the original position can no longer be maintained. There is no such statutory obligation with regard to other workers who become disabled. However, French courts have increasingly been willing to find that employers are obliged to offer such workers alternative employment, or to make other accommodations to meet the needs of disabled employees.

28  This model had in fact already been accepted by the key Community institutions – see Commission Communication and the Council Resolution of 20 December 1996 on equality of opportunity for people with disabilities at COM(96) 406 final, 30 July 1996 and OJ C 12/1 13 January 1997 respectively.

29  COM (1999) 565 final.

30  The provisions concerning discrimination on the grounds of race were subsequently also excluded from the framework Directive, as a specific Article 13 Race Directive was adopted in June 1999.

31  At the time of writing no official version of the Directive was available. However a draft version of the Directive was issued in English on 20 October 2000 (Interinstitutional File 1999/0225 (CNS)) and the information included in this chapter is based on this text. It is expected that the final version of the Directive will strongly resemble this draft text.

32  In contrast the provisions concerning religion or belief and sexual orientation are only subject to a three year implementation period. Age is also subject to a six year implementation period.

CHAPTER THREE

# Improving the Civil Rights of People with Disabilities Through International Law

*Jeremy Cooper*

In a keynote speech in 1997, the United Nations High Commissioner for Human Rights urged that the international human rights debate should give more priority to the rights and empowerment of people with disabilities.[1] Two years later, an editorial in the house journal of Disability Awareness in Action offered evidence that two million disabled people 'still suffer human rights abuses of a truly shocking nature'.[2] This chapter will review the framework of rights development for disabled people over the past 20 years, from an international perspective, in an effort to audit aspirations against reality.

## INTERNATIONAL LAW

Human rights are both universal and particular to specific minorities. People with disabilities frequently share a common experience of isolation, exclusion and discrimination. In addition they often suffer from an inferior quality of life, either because they are not afforded the same benefits that a universal human right affords to those without their disabilities, or because specific rights which are given to them, as a minority, are not enforced. Numerous human rights declarations, conventions, covenants and protocols have been painstakingly drawn up in various international arenas since 1945, but very few of these have been specific to disabled people. Disabled people, despite being arguably 'the largest minority in the world' (Degener and Koster-Dreese 1995, p.9; Despouy 1991, p1; in fact there are more than 500 million disabled people, of whom two thirds live in developing countries) are a group of people whose human rights have not been well developed or protected. There are some promising signs, however, that this is finally beginning to change.

International lawyers concede that the framework of international law has not yet found a solution to the problem of the enforcement of the standards of behaviour set out in the key international documents. In the majority of cases, the protection of human rights through international obligations is only binding on states that have signed the relevant international convention, which can only be a voluntary act. Thereafter, any enforcement of the terms of the agreement is ultimately a question of political will on the part of the relevant states, as a reflection of the wider social and political values operating within that state. Notwithstanding these cautionary caveats, international human rights law still provides the best framework that we have, in which to debate the basic minimum standards of behaviour expected of the nation state towards an individual, and of individuals towards one another. (See Cooper and Whittle 1998 for a more detailed analysis of the interrelationship of law and enforcement procedures in this complex area.)

## GENERATIONS OF RIGHTS

Underlying all forms of the legal expression of disability human rights is a fundamental distinction between rights that are legally enforceable entitlements, and those that are not (Bickenbach 2000).

This section outlines the broad human rights framework through which the machinery of persuasion or enforcement currently strives to operate across the globe. Human rights are generally divided into three categories, normally called 'generations of rights'.

### Civil and political rights

The first generation of human rights includes the right to life, the right to freedom of opinion, the right to a fair trial and the right to protection from torture, slavery and violence. Considered to be fundamental rights, they are also the bundle of rights that are normally described as our basic civil liberties, without which the human condition becomes intolerable.

### Economic, social and cultural rights

The second generation of human rights reflects the higher aspirations of humankind to a quality of life that justifies the suspension of other personal liberties by handing over to the state the monopoly on the regulation of coercive force and the power to make laws. This generation of human rights is less clearly defined than the first generation, but includes the right to work in just and favourable conditions, the right to social protection, the right to an adequate standard of living, the right to the highest possible standards of physical and mental health that a given society can afford, the right to education, the right to enjoy the benefits of cultural freedom and scientific progress and *the right to enjoy all such rights free of discrimination* (my italics).[3] This series of rights is deliberately defined as a 'second generation' of rights because on the deepest level of core human values it could be argued that they are less 'fundamental' to the survival of a civilised society. Conversely, however, it can be argued that the contract by which the individual grants power and authority to the state is implicitly brought into question if the state is unable to provide the basic framework at least to develop these rights.[4]

### Development rights

The third generation of human rights is still contested and controversial, and is rooted in the law and development movement. Whilst no mention was made of development rights in the Universal Declaration of Human Rights of 1948, they have played an ever increasing part in human rights debate in the past 20 years. Contained in this group of rights is the right to peace and security, the right to economic autonomy and the right to development itself. The movement to establish development rights alongside the first and second generation of human rights remains strong and buoyant, and continues to grow apace.

## THE WORK OF THE UNITED NATIONS[5]

The starting point for any analysis of international human rights law in the contemporary world must be the United Nations. The Universal Declaration of Human Rights (UNDHR) which was adopted by the General Assembly of the United Nations on 10 December 1948 remains the touchstone for human rights development policy. The UNDHR is not legally binding on any state or person, but it possesses enormous symbolic force as an agreed statement of the 'common standard of achievement for all peoples of all nations'.[6] Most of the constitutions of the world drafted since 1948 contain the tenets of the UNDHR as central to their existence. The rights and freedoms contained in the UNDHR have been articulated with even greater precision in subsequent international covenants – which are treaties and which therefore have binding legal force in respect of those countries which voluntarily sign the covenant.

The two principal covenants covering international human rights were both drawn up in 1966 and both came into force in 1976.

## The International Covenant on Civil and Political Rights (ICCPR)

This Covenant is directed towards the upholding of first generation rights and imposes obligations upon 'contracting states' (that is, those states which formally ratify the Covenant, which is a voluntary act) to uphold the right to life, liberty, security, equality before the courts, peaceful assembly, marriage and having a family, freedom of association, conscience, thought and religion. Perhaps the most important clause in the Covenant for people with disabilities is contained in Article 26, which guarantees equality of treatment without unfair discrimination:

> All persons are equal before the law and are entitled without any discrimination to the equal protection of the law. In this respect, the law shall prohibit any discrimination and guarantee to all persons equal and effective protection against discrimination on any ground such as race, colour, sex, religion, political or other opinion, national or social origin, property, birth, or other status.

This Article effectively prohibits discrimination on any ground unless a 'reasonable and objective justification can be established by the defendant contracting state'.[7]

When we examine the specific rights that the ICCPR sets out to protect and guarantee, a number appear to be of actual or potential relevance to people with disabilities, of which the following are a summary (Quinn 1995):

> No one shall be subjected to torture or to cruel, inhuman or degrading treatment or punishment (Article 7)

> No one shall be subjected without his free consent to medical or scientific experimentation (Article 7)

> Everyone has a right not to be subjected to arbitrary and unnecessary arrest and any other kind of institutional abuse (Article 9)

> No one shall be subjected to arbitrary or unlawful interference with his privacy, family, home or correspondence, nor to unlawful attacks on his honour and reputation (Article 17)

> States must recognise the right of men and women of marriageable age to marry and to found a family (Article 23)

> States must recognise the right of everyone to take part in the conduct of public affairs, directly or through freely chosen representatives, to vote, and to have access, on general terms of equality, to public service in their country (Article 25).

## The International Covenant on Economic, Social and Cultural Rights (ICESCR)

Alston and Quinn (1987) believe international jurisprudence effectively imposes immediate obligations on states to adopt strategies that will lead to the full realisation of economic, social and cultural rights, as set out in this Covenant. Whilst this may be true as an abstract statement of international law, the reality is more pedestrian. This Covenant is directed towards second generation rights and obliges 'contracting states' to take steps to the maximum of their available resources, progressively to achieve the full realisation of the rights recognised in the Covenant.[8] These include such things as medical services, employment rights, social security, family protection, child protection, physical and mental health, education and the enjoyment of a common cultural heritage. The Covenant expresses the expectation 'that all such rights will be exercised without discrimination of any kind as to race, colour, sex, language, religion, political or other opinion, national or social origin, property, birth or other status'.[9] According to the General Committee set up to monitor the implementation of the Covenant (see below, p.64), this includes 'disability based discrimination':

> The Covenant does not refer explicitly to persons with disabilities. Nevertheless the UNDHR recognises that all human beings are born free and equal in dignity and rights and, since the Covenant's provisions apply fully to all members of society, persons with disabilities are clearly entitled to the full range of rights recognised in the Covenant.

For the purposes of the Covenant, the General Committee defines 'disability-based discrimination', to include:

> any distinction, exclusion, restriction or preference, or denial of reasonable accommodation based on disability which has the effect of nullifying or impairing the recognition, enjoyment or exercise of economic, social and cultural rights.

> In addition, in so far as special treatment is necessary [contracting states] are required to take appropriate measures, to the maximum of their available resources, to enable such persons to seek to overcome any disadvantages, in terms of their enjoyment of the rights specified in the Covenant, flowing from their disability.

The General Committee is further of the opinion that: 'In order to remedy past and present discrimination, and to deter future discrimination, comprehensive anti-discrimination legislation in relation to disability would seem to be indispensable in virtually all State parties (i.e. contracting states)'.[10]

Although the General Comment is not binding, and governments are legally entitled to ignore its contents (Alston 1995), it nevertheless provides a powerful and unambiguous statement of principle from the key body charged with interpreting the intention of the Covenant.

Of equal importance is Article 3, whereby all the contracting states undertake to ensure the equal right of men and women to the enjoyment of all the economic, social and cultural rights set out in the Covenant. It follows that if disabled citizens of a contracting state are prevented from enjoying the same economic, social and cultural rights as able-bodied citizens, that state is de facto in breach of the Covenant. Articles which may be of particular significance to people with disabilities include the following:

> The right of everyone to just and favourable conditions of work, ensuring a decent living for themselves and their families, and equal opportunity to be promoted to an appropriate higher level (Article 7)

> The right of everyone to the enjoyment of the highest attainable standard of physical and mental health (Article 12)

> Higher education shall be made equally accessible to all, on the basis of capacity, by every appropriate means (Article 13)

> The right of everyone…to take part in cultural life (Article 15).

## Implementation of the Covenants

Common to both Covenants is a provision that all contracting states must submit periodic reports regarding the implementation of the provisions of the Covenants to the United Nations. In the case of the ICCPR, the report is to the Human Rights Committee of the United Nations, which is an independent committee of 18 elected representatives, of 'high moral character and recognised competence in the field of human rights',[11] who study the reports and transmit through the Secretary General of the United Nations such General Comments as they may consider appropriate to the state parties. In the case of the ICESCR, the periodic reports are submitted to the Committee on Economic, Social and Cultural Rights,[12] with a similar mix of human rights experts as those appointed to the Human Rights Committee, who make similar General Comments in the light of the reports they receive.

The procedures for generating and acting upon the general comments are evolving quite rapidly. In particular, the Committee on Economic, Social and Cultural Rights 'has transformed the supervision system beyond recognition' (Craven 1995, p.102).

> The Committee's work has been marked by a series of procedural reforms, undertaken swiftly and with relative ease, that places it in the position of having one of the most developed and potentially effective reporting mechanisms of all

the human rights supervisory bodies. Notably the Committee has undertaken to receive both written and oral information from non-governmental organisations, has adopted the procedure of making State-specific concluding observations following its consideration of State reports, conducts general discussions with experts from other fields and organisations, and drafts general comments to further an understanding of the normative content of the rights in the Covenant and the reporting obligations (Craven 1995, pp.102–3).

Overall it is agreed that the committees should play a facilitative role in assisting contracting states in the development and realisation of human rights. Disability groups should note in particular the developing view that states should be encouraged to make it possible for national organisations to participate in the implementation of the rights (Craven 1995).

If a contracting state is not able to guarantee the upholding of all the rights set out in the relevant Covenant at the time of signature, it must undertake the following:

To take the necessary steps...to adopt such legislative or other measures as may be necessary to give effect to the rights recognised in the present Covenant (ICCPR, Article 2) AND

To ensure that any person whose rights or freedoms [as recognised in the Covenant] are violated shall have an effective remedy (ICCPR, Article 2)

To take steps *to the maximum of its available resources* [my italics], with a view to achieving progressively the full realization of the rights recognised in the present Covenant (ICESCR, Article 2).

In addition to the above procedures, the United Nations has a further power to investigate any complaints that suggest the existence of a consistent pattern of gross and reliably attested violations involving many people over a long period.[13] It can also from time to time carry out thematic investigations of alleged human rights violations in a country or countries through its own specially appointed working groups or individual rapporteurs. The United Nations also has residual powers to appoint Special Rapporteurs on generic issues. This option was taken up with respect to disability in 1984, when Leandro Despouy was appointed Special Rapporteur on Human Rights and Disability by the Sub-Commission on Prevention of Discrimination and Protection of Disability, and again by the appointment of Bengt Lindqvist a decade later (see p.71).

### *Optional protocols*

### *ICCPR*

Where a state party signs the Optional Protocol to the ICCPR, it thereby recognises the competence of the Human Rights Committee to receive and consider communications from any individual who is subject to the jurisdiction of the state in question. Once the Human Rights Committee has received a complaint under this Protocol, it will first ascertain that the complaint is not already being investigated under another form of international investigation and that all domestic complaints procedures have been exhausted. Having consulted all parties in question it will then consider the complaint in closed session and forward its findings to the complainant and to the state in question. At the time of writing however, the British government has not yet agreed to sign the Optional Protocol, a matter causing concern to human rights groups in the UK. (For further discussion of these issues see Wadham and Leach 1995; Foley 1995.)

### *ICESCR*

There is currently no equivalent Optional Protocol allowing groups and individuals to petition the Committee directly with regard to alleged violations of the ICESCR. Such an option does however remain under serious consideration, and there is general agreement that such an Optional Protocol would be a beneficial development.[14] At the time of going to press, a Draft Optional Protocol to the ICESCR is under consideration within the Committee.[15]

## INTERNATIONAL CONVENTIONS

A number of international Conventions – which like Covenants are treaties binding those states which sign up to them – have been concluded under the auspices of the United Nations since 1966. Each has its own reporting systems to help strengthen and consolidate its programme of human rights protection. Of particular note in this regard are the Convention on the Elimination of All Forms of Racial Discrimination (1963), the Convention on the Elimination of All Forms of Discrimination Against Women (1979) and the Convention on the Rights of the Child (1989). Whilst none of these Conventions deals primarily or specifically with discrimination against people with disabilities, each contains Articles and provisions that can be implicitly extended to this group. For example, in the UK the Invalid Care Allowance, paid to people caring full-time for disabled relatives or friends, was held in its original form to breach the Convention on the Elimination of All Forms of Discrimination Against Women because it excluded from its ambit married women who were caring for a disabled relative (Smith 1986).

The enforcement procedure attached to the Convention on the Elimination of All Forms of Racial Discrimination is of particular interest, as it allows, in addition to the normal reporting procedures, for an optional system of individual petition whereby an individual, or group, can go directly to the relevant Enforcement Committee (in this case a body of 18 independent experts), alleging that their rights guaranteed by the Convention have been violated. This right of individual petition must however be accepted by the relevant State party for it to be taken up by an individual or group.[16] UNICEF has published a very useful Implementation Handbook for the Convention on the Rights of the Child, which explains and analyses each provision, and its interpretation by experts across the world, and also provides illustrative examples of the Convention's implementation from a number of different countries (UNICEF 1998).

The Standard Rules on the Equalisation of Opportunities for Persons with Disabilities adopted by the United Nations General Assembly in 1993[17] are perhaps the most promising and significant international expression of standards that can be used by disability rights campaigners to further their cause by putting moral pressure on governments to conform to internationally agreed norms. They are dealt with below in more detail (see p.71).

In December 1999, Rehabilitation International, a federation of national and international organisations working for the prevention of disability, the availability of rehabilitation and the equalization of opportunity for people with disabilities, presented to the United Nations its Charter for the Third Millennium, proposing, *inter alia*, the creation of a new United Nations Convention on the rights of people with disabilities. Earlier attempts to establish a Convention had only been backed by a limited number of member states and had been unsuccessful. Rehabilitation International has researched the current level of support and found a much more positive climate, reflecting a wider knowledge of the presence of people with disabilities in society and the need to adopt an inclusive approach to human rights. Rehabilitation International has also called for accessibility standards in development assistance. Parallel to this development, the Irish government has submitted to the United Nations General Assembly a draft resolution on the human rights of persons with disabilities.[18] Either a simple majority, or for more important matters, a two-thirds majority, is normally required to adopt a Resolution in the General Assembly.

## DECLARATIONS

Another form of United Nations activity in its work to strengthen the civil rights of citizens across the globe is the use of the Declaration. This is a device whereby member states of the United Nations General Assembly seek to 'register a consensus of opinion, or a direction in which sentiment is moving' (Nicholas

1975, p.117), and probably represents the Bagehot conception of 'the highest truth that people will bear' (Bagehot 1867). Declarations are not accompanied by any enforcement machinery. As instruments of principle, however, they are highly valued and effective tools for argument and persuasion. It has been noted by more than one commentator in the past that Declarations have often led to treaties.[19]

Of special interest to people with disabilities are the Declaration on Social Progress and Development which was proclaimed by the General Assembly of the United Nations on 11 December 1969;[20] the Declaration of the Rights of Mentally Retarded Persons which was proclaimed by the General Assembly of the United Nations on 20 December 1971;[21] and the Declaration on the Rights of Disabled Persons which was proclaimed by the General Assembly of the United Nations on 9 December 1975.[22]

## Declaration on Social Progress and Development

This important Declaration specifically proclaims in Article 11(c) the necessity of protecting the rights and assuring the welfare of children, the aged and the disabled, and the protection of the physically and mentally disadvantaged.

## Declaration of the Rights of Mentally Retarded Persons

This declaration makes a number of important statements regarding 'mentally retarded persons' (that is, people with learning difficulties):

> The mentally retarded person has, to the maximum degree of feasibility, the same rights as other human beings;
>
> In particular,
>
> a right to proper medical care and physical therapy and to such education, training, rehabilitation and guidance as will enable him or her to develop his ability and maximum potential;
>
> a right to economic security and to a decent standard of living;
>
> a right to perform productive work or to engage in any other meaningful occupation to the fullest possible extent of his capabilities;
>
> wherever possible, he or she shall live with his or her own family or with foster parents and participate in different forms of community life;
>
> the family with which he or she lives should receive assistance;
>
> if care in an institution becomes necessary, it should be provided in surroundings and circumstances as close as possible to those of normal life;

the right to a qualified guardian when this is required to protect his or her personal well being and interests;

the right to protection from exploitation, abuse and degrading treatment;

if prosecuted for any offence the right to due process of law with full recognition being given to his or her degree of mental responsibility;

if restriction of freedom becomes necessary, the procedures used must contain proper legal safeguards against every form of abuse, must be based upon an evaluation of the social capability of the person by qualified experts, and must be subject to periodic review and to the right of appeal to higher authorities.

### *Declaration on the Rights of Disabled Persons*

This is a very important point of reference for people with disabilities who are seeking a statement of the general principles of decency and protection that international law expects of national states in the policies and attitudes they adopt towards their citizens with mental or physical disabilities. What is astonishing is that this particular Declaration appears to have been so little used by disability rights campaigners, both in the UK and abroad. After the normal caveat regarding 'limited resources,'[23] the Declaration calls for national and international action to ensure that it will be used as a common basis and frame of reference for the protection of the rights it goes on to proclaim. It sets out in 12 powerful paragraphs a statement of the rights of disabled people defining what should be the norms of a civilised society going into the 21st century. Not only does the Declaration set out the norms, it also clearly links disability with the first and second generation rights guaranteed in the two human rights Covenants.

Thus the Declaration states that disabled people:

have the inherent right to respect for their human dignity, defined as first and foremost the right to enjoy a decent life, as normal and full as possible;

have the same civil and political rights as other human beings;

are entitled to the measures designed to enable them to become as self-reliant as possible;

have the right to medical, psychological and functional treatment, including prosthetic and orthotic appliances, to medical and social rehabilitation, education, vocational training and rehabilitation, aid, counselling, placement services and other services which will enable them to develop their capabilities and skills to the maximum and will hasten the process of their social integration or reintegration;

have the right to economic and social security and to a decent level of living;

have the right, according to their capabilities, to secure and retain employment or to engage in a useful, productive and remunerative occupation, and to join trade unions;

are entitled to have their special needs taken into consideration at all stages of economic and social planning;

have the right to live with their families or with foster parents and to participate in all social, creative or recreational activities. No disabled person shall be subjected, as far as his or her residence is concerned, to differential treatment other than that required by his or her condition or by the improvement that he or she may derive therefrom. If the stay of a disabled person in a specialised establishment is indispensable, the environment and living conditions therein shall be as close as possible to the normal life of a person of his or her age;

shall be protected against all exploitation, all regulations and all treatment of a discriminatory, abusive or degrading nature;

shall be able to avail themselves of qualified legal aid when such aid proves indispensable for the protection of their persons and property. If judicial proceedings are instituted against them, the legal procedure applied shall take their physical and mental condition fully into account;

shall (together with their families and communities) be fully informed by all appropriate means, of the rights contained in this Declaration.

## INTERNATIONAL YEARS AND DAYS[24]

International years provide for a sustained programme of action directed towards longer-term outcomes. They also have the particular advantage of directly enabling the participation of disabled people in activities and campaigns that raise awareness and influence policy. 1981 was the International Year of Disabled Persons, which was followed by a decade of activities directed towards disabled people. One of the long-term outcomes of this designation was the World Programme of Action concerning Disabled Persons, adopted by the General Assembly of the United Nations in 1982.[25] Another awareness raising mechanism utilised by the United Nations and other international organisations is the use of the international day. At the end of the United Nations Decade of Disabled Persons (1983–1992) the General Assembly proclaimed that 3 December should be observed each year as the International Day of Disabled Persons, to be organised by the UN Commission for Social Development. Proclamation of the Day has three purposes:[26]

To commemorate the anniversary of the adoption by the General Assembly of the World Programme of Action concerning disabled persons;

To ensure continued promotion of disability issues beyond the United Nations Decade of Disabled Persons and to further the integration into society of persons with disabilities;

To promote increased awareness among the population regarding gains to be derived by individuals and society from the integration of disabled persons in every aspect of social, economic and political life.

The day continues to be an annual focal point for campaigning and unifying activity among disabled groups and their supporters every year across the entire globe.

## The Standard Rules

One of the most important outcomes of all this activity has been the adoption by the United Nations of the Standard Rules on the Equalisation of Opportunities for Persons with Disabilities. The Rules were initially intended to be a manifesto of moral and political values, rather than a statement of legal rights and protections (Michailakis 1999). Commenting on the status of the Rules, the pressure group Disability Awareness in Action has however observed as follows (DAA 1995):

Although States cannot legally be forced to carry them out, the Rules should become an accepted standard internationally when they are used by a large number of States. They offer an international instrument with a monitoring system to help make sure the Rules are effective. There is more detailed guidance than ever before to what is needed. They require a strong political and practical commitment by States to take action for equalisation of opportunities for disabled people.

It is possible to go further still and argue that if the Rules are applied by a large number of states with the intention of respecting them as rules in international law, they can become part of what is generally described as international customary law, that is, general principles of law recognised by civilised nations. In February 1998, the Greek government took the radical step of actually incorporating the Standard Rules into Greek national law.

The international monitoring of the implementation of the Rules is co-ordinated through the United Nations Commission for Social Development, under the auspices of the United Nations Economic and Social Council (ECOSOC). A Special Rapporteur, advised by an international Panel of Experts, has been appointed to give advice to individual countries, organise regional workshops, conduct global surveys and provide regular global monitoring reports. In the first four years of office, the Special Rapporteur produced two overview reports to the Commission, two global surveys,[27] and five reports. A third global survey is underway. The current mandate for the Special Rapporteur expired in August 2000 but the Panel of Experts is of the view that the initiative should continue, ensuring in the process the increased involvement of international disability non-governmental organisations (NGOs), with a concentration on social development and human rights. The Special Rapporteur is of the view that the effect of the Standard Rules across the globe has been largely positive:

> The adoption of the Standard Rules and the activities with the monitoring mechanism have created a momentum, which it is very important to keep alive. In our second survey, 85% of responding Governments stated that the Rules have led to rethinking or strengthening of their disability policies. A considerable number of Governments have adopted new legislation, made plans of action or otherwise initiated a further development of their policies, based on the Standard Rules.[28]

The Rules are grounded in the belief that equal participation of disabled people in society is only possible where the following four pre-conditions are met:

Rule 1: States should take action to raise awareness in society about persons with disabilities, their rights, their needs, their potential and their contribution.

Rule 2: States should ensure the provision of effective medical care to persons with disabilities.

Rule 3: States should ensure the provision of rehabilitation services to persons with disabilities in order for them to reach and sustain their optimum level of independence and functioning.

Rule 4: States should ensure the development and supply of support services, including assistive devices for persons with disabilities, to assist them to increase their level of independence in their daily living and to exercise their rights.

The Rules go on to identify eight target areas of life in which principles of equality regarding those with disabilities ought to be concentrated. The eight areas are Accessibility, Education, Employment, Income Maintenance and Social Security, Family Life and Personal Integrity, Culture, Recreation and Sports, and Religion.

Finally, the Rules outline a variety of processes through which such equality can be achieved, including legislation, policy making and planning, the dissemination of more detailed information and research, personnel training, national monitoring systems, greater recognition of the role of disabled people's organisations, and greater international co-operation.

## UNITED NATIONS AGENCIES

The most important UN agencies for these purposes are probably the ILO, UNESCO and the WHO.

### The International Labour Organisation (ILO)[29]

In 1991, The UN Special Rapporteur on Disability wrote of the ILO in the following terms (Despouy 1991):

> Since its establishment over 70 years ago, the ILO has never ceased to advocate that disabled persons, whatever the cause or nature of their disability, should be afforded every opportunity for vocational rehabilitation, including vocational guidance, training or readaptation as well as opportunities for employment, whether open or under sheltered conditions (p.11, para.50).

Thus whilst the term 'human rights' does not appear in the ILO constitution, it has nevertheless been one of the few specialised UN organisations which has adopted a specific profile on human rights within the sphere of its activity, primarily labour and employment. This profile has been manifest in particular through its Conventions.

### Convention 111 concerning discrimination in respect of employment and occupation

This Convention was adopted by the ILO in 1958, and came into force in 1960. Under this Convention a ratifying country undertakes to declare and pursue a national policy designed to promote, by methods appropriate to national conditions and practice, equality of opportunity and treatment in respect of employment and occupation, with a view to eliminating any discrimination in respect thereof.[30]

The UK has not ratified this Convention.

### Convention 142 concerning vocational guidance and vocational training in the development of human resources

This Convention was adopted by the ILO in 1975 and came into force in 1977. Under this Convention a ratifying country agrees to establish and develop open, flexible and complementary systems of general, technical and vocational education, educational and vocational guidance and vocational training, whether these activities take place within the formal education system or outside it.[31]

The UK has ratified this Convention.

## Convention 159 concerning vocational rehabilitation and employment (disabled persons) and recommendation no. 168

This Convention was adopted by the ILO in 1983 and came into force in 1985. Under this Convention a ratifying country agrees to adopt a national policy on vocational rehabilitation and employment of disabled people, not only in specialised institutions and sheltered workshops but alongside non-disabled people in mainstream training centres and in open employment, to put such a policy into action and regularly to review and monitor its implementation (for an account of the history of this Convention and Recommendation and a discussion on ways in which it might be implemented, see ILO 1992).

This Convention was of particular importance during the UN Decade of Disabled Persons (see above, p.70). A number of projects were set up at this time under the auspices of the ILO, aimed at the 'deinstitutionalisation, mainstreaming and normalisation of disabled persons within the labour market' (Degener 1995, p.21) particularly in Africa and Indonesia (Momm and Konig 1989; Stace 1987).

The UK has not ratified this Convention.

### The United Nations Educational, Scientific and Cultural Organisation (UNESCO)

The primary concern of UNESCO is the promotion and protection of cultural rights. According to its Constitution,[32] the purpose of UNESCO is:

> To contribute to peace and security by promoting collaboration among the nations through education, science and culture in order to further universal respect for justice, for the rule of law and for the human rights and fundamental freedoms which are affirmed for the peoples of the world, without distinction of race, sex, language or religion, by the Charter of the United Nations.

## Convention against discrimination in education

This Convention was adopted in 1960 by the General Conference of UNESCO and came into force in 1962.

The Convention reformulates the UNDHR statement that 'discrimination in education is a violation of the right of every person to education' and declares that:

> discrimination in education includes depriving any person or group of persons of access to education of any type or at any level... or limiting any person or group of persons to education of an inferior standard... or inflicting on any person or group of persons conditions which are incompatible with the dignity of man.[33]

It has been ratified by the UK.

### The World Health Organisation (WHO)[34]

Although the WHO has been criticised for failing to define health as an international human right (Leary 1993), it is nevertheless appropriate to include it in a review of the various international bodies that can play a part in engaging the international community in a rights-based discourse concerning disability. As the primary role of the WHO is the exchange of information and knowledge with regard to health matters (public and private), it will come as no surprise that the WHO is associated primarily with the 'medical model' definition of disability (see Chapter One). As a consequence, the resolutions and reports of the policy making organs of the WHO have in recent years referred to only two solutions to disability: rehabilitation or prevention.[35] More promising, however, was the publication in 1990 of a report sponsored by WHO-Europe, on health and social legislation for disabled persons in 25 European countries, which presents a far more progressive picture in those countries of a shift of emphasis away from the 'medical model' towards human rights issues (Pinet 1990). In addition, at the time of going to press the WHO is currently in the process of revising the ICIDH[36] to incorporate the 'social model of disability', which is a very significant step (see Chapter One and Bickenbach and Somnath 1999). Finally, reference should be made to the WHO Declaration of Alma Ata in 1978 which recognised the right to health for all and the importance of promoting community-based projects.

## REGIONAL NETWORKS

An increasing source of influence on the international scene is the phenomenon of the regional network, either within or across continents (for example the European Union and the Council of Europe, see Chapter Two), that seeks to agree a set of norms that it will strive to uphold within the region, although there is no basis in law for enforcing these norms. One such example is the Organisation of American States (OAS),[37] whose General Assembly adopted in June 1999 the Inter-American Convention on the Elimination of All Forms of Discrimination against people with disabilities. Under the terms of the Inter-American Convention, countries that are parties to the treaty agree to adopt legislative, social, educational or labour-related measures that will fully integrate people with disabilities into society. They also make a commitment to ensuring that new buildings facilitate access and that existing structures are made as accessible as possible. The Inter-American Convention calls for rehabilitation, education, job training and other measures to ensure the optimal level of independence and quality of life for persons with disabilities. It also stresses the need for public awareness campaigns to help eliminate prejudices and stereotypes.

The Convention defines a disability as 'a physical, mental, or sensory impairment, whether permanent or temporary, that limits the capacity to perform one or more essential activities of daily life, and which can be caused or aggravated by the economic and social environment'.

The other more recently formed regional grouping is in the continent of Africa. In 1986, the African Charter on Human and People's Rights came into force, under the auspices of the Organisation of African Unity (OAU). Around 50 African states have signed up as parties to the Charter. A leading work on international human rights describes this as: 'The newest, the least developed or effective, the most distinctive and the most controversial of the regional human rights regimes' (Steiner and Alston 1996, p.689).

The sole implementing organ of the African Charter is the African Commission on Human and People's Rights, which has few powers and has been 'hesitant in exercising or creatively implementing and developing them' (Steiner and Alston 1996, p.689). Other examples of pan-African co-operation are cited in Chapter Four.

## REFERENCES

Albrecht, G. Seelman, K. and Bury, M. (2000) (eds) *Handbook of Disability Studies.* Beverly Hills: Sage.

Alston, P. (1995) 'Disability and the ICESCR.' In T. Degener and Y. Koster-Dreese, (1995) (eds) *Human Rights and Disabled Persons: Essays and Relevant Human Rights Instruments. International Studies in Human Rights, Volume 40.* Dordrecht: Martinus Nijhoff.

Alston, P. and Quinn, G. (1987) 'The nature and scope of states parties: obligations under the international covenant, social and cultural rights.' *Human Rights Quarterly 9,* 156.

Bagehot, W. (1867) *The English Constitution.* Reproduced by Fontana Library, London in 1963 with Introduction by R.H.S. Crossman. London: Fontana Library.

Bickenbach, J., Somnath, J., Bradley, E. and Üstün, T.(1999) 'Models of disablement, universalism and the ICIDH.' *Social Science and Medicine 48,* 9, 1173.

Bickenbach, J. (2000) 'Disability human rights, law and policy.' In G. Albrecht, K. Seelman and M. Bury (2000) (eds) *Handbook of Disability Studies.* Beverly Hills: Sage.

Cooper, J. and Dhavan, R. (1986) (eds) *Public Interest Law.* Oxford: Basil Blackwell.

Cooper, J. and Whittle, R. (1998) 'Enforcing the rights and freedoms of disabled people: the role of transnational law: Part I.' *Mountbatten Journal of Legal Studies 2,* 2, 3.

Craven, M. (1995) *The International Covenant on Economic, Social and Cultural Rights: A Perspective on its Development.* Oxford: Clarendon Press.

DAA (1995) *Information Kit on the United Nations Standard Rules on the Equalisation of Opportunities for Persons with Disabilities.* London: Disability Awareness in Action.

Degener, T. (1995) 'Disabled persons and human rights: the legal framework.' In T. Degener and Y. Koster-Dreese (1995) (eds) *Human Rights and Disabled Persons: Essays and Relevant Human Rights Instruments. International Studies in Human Rights, Volume 40.* Dordrecht: Martinus Nijhoff.

Degener, T. and Koster-Dreese, Y. (1995) (eds) *Human Rights and Disabled Persons: Essays and Relevant Human Rights Instruments. International Studies in Human Rights, Volume 40.* Dordrecht: Martinus Nijhoff.

Despouy, L. (1991) 'Human rights and disability.' UN Document E/CN.4/Sub 2/1991/31, later published as (1993) *Human Rights and Disabled Persons, Human Rights Study Series 6.* New York: United Nations Press.

Foley, C. (1995) *Human Rights, Human Wrongs, the Alternative Report on the United Nations Human Rights Committee.* London: River Orams Press.

ILO (1992) *Job Creation for Disabled People: A Guide for Workers' Organisations.* Geneva: ILO.

Jones, M. and Marks, L. (1999) (eds) *Disability, Divers-Ability and Legal Change.* The Hague: Kluwer.

Leary, V. (1993) 'Implications of a right to health.' In K. Mahoney and P. Mahoney (1993) (eds) *Human Rights in the Twenty-First Century.* Dordrecht: Kluwer.

Lindqvist, B. (1998) *Report of Special Rapporteur to the 54th Session of the Commission on Himan Rights.* New York: United Nations.

Mahoney, K. and Mahoney, P. (1993) (eds) *Human Rights in the Twenty-First Century.* Dordrecht: Kluwer.

Michailakis, D. (1999) 'The Standard Rules: a weak instrument and a strong commitment.' In M. Jones and L. Marks (1999) (eds) *Disability, Divers-ability and Legal Change.* The Hague: Kluwer.

Momm, W. and Konig, A. (1989) 'Community integration for disabled people: a new approach to their vocational training and employment.' *International Labour Review 128,* 4, 497.

Newman, F. (1985) Introduction. In T. Degener and Y. Koster-Drese (1995) (eds) *Human Rights and Disabled Persons: Essays and Relevant Human Rights Instruments. International Studies in Human Rights, Volume 40.* Dordrecht: Martinus Nijhoff.

Nicholas, H. (1975) *The United Nations as a Political Institution.* Fifth Edition. Oxford: Oxford Paperbacks.

Pinet, G. (1990) *Is the Law Fair to the Disabled?* Copenhagen: WHO Regional Publications, European Series No. 29.

Quinn, G. (1995) 'The international covenant on civil and political rights and disability: a conceptual framework.' In T. Degener and Y. Koster-Dreese (1995) (eds) *Human Rights and Disabled Persons: Essays and Relevant Human Rights Instruments. International Studies in Human Rights, Volume 40.* Dordrecht: Martinus Nijhoff.

Smith, R. (1986) 'How good are test cases?' In J. Cooper and R. Dhavan (1986) (eds) *Public Interest Law.* Oxford: Basil Blackwell.

Stace, S. (1987) 'Vocational rehabilitation for women with disabilities.' *International Labour Review 126,* 3, 301.

Steiner, H. and Alston, P. (1996) *International Human Rights in Context: Law, Politics, Morals.* Oxford: Clarendon.

UNICEF (1998) *Implementation Handbook for the Convention on the Rights of the Child.* New York: UNICEF.

Wadham, J. and Leach, P. (1995) 'Protecting human rights in the United Kingdom.' *New Law Journal 146,* 1133.

## NOTES

1   From Romanes Lecture delivered by Mary Robinson at Oxford University, 11 November 1997.

2   *Disability Tribune*, November 1999, 1.

3   ICESCR Article 2 (2).

4   It is interesting to note in this context that the US Declaration of Independence specifically states: 'that all men are created equal [and] are endowed by their creator with certain unalienable rights...and that wherever any form of government becomes destructive of these ends, it is the right of the people to alter or abolish it'.

5   This chapter only provides a general overview of the relevant work of international organisations with regard to disabilities. The best source of detailed information is the UN website (www.un.org/esa/socdev/disother.htm).

6   Statement of Eleanor Roosevelt as Chairman of the UN Committee on Human Rights, New York Inauguration of United Nations Assembly, 1948.

7   See *Communication No. 516/1992 Simunek v The Czech Republic*, views adopted 1995; *Communication No. 395/1990 Spenger v The Netherlands*, views adopted 1992; *Communication No. 182/1984, Zwaan de Vries v The Netherlands*, views adopted 1987; *Communication No. 172/1984, Broeks v The Netherlands*, views adopted 1987; *Communication No. 180/1984, Danning v. The Netherlands*, views adopted 1987.

8   ICESCR Article 2(1).

9   ICESCR Article 2(2).

10  All General committee quotes are from *General Comment No. 5, 1994, E/C12/1994/WP13*, 1 December 1994.

11  ICCPR, Article 38(1), (2).

12  This is a direct organ of the United Nations, the Economic and Social Council (ECOSOC).

13  UN Resolution 1503 1970.

14  See *Konate, E/C.12/1991/SR.13* at 10, para. 51; *Bonoan-Dandan, E/C.12/1991/SR.14*, qt 14, para. 67; and Craven 1995.

15  *Committee on Economic, Social and Cultural Rights, report of the 14th/15th session, Official Records, 1997, Supplement No.2, E/1997/22, Annex IV, 91.*

16  For an example of a successful use of individual petition under this Convention see *Yilmaz-Dogan v The Netherlands C.E.R.D. Report, G.A.O.R., 43rd Session, Supp.18,p.59* (1988).

17  *Resolution 48/96* 20 December 1993.

18  Resolutions normally take the form of a UN Resolution. As we go to press, the UN Commission on Human Rights had agreed the text of this draft resolution.

19  Newman (1985), for example, has noted the preambulary paragraphs in the two Covenants, and the United Nations' Racial, Women's, Children's and Torture Treaties, as examples of this process. He also suggests that 'experience in monitoring the UN's 1993 Equalisation Rules for the Disabled may well lead to a consensus that additional treaty law is needed' (p.5).

20  Resolution 2542 (XXIV).

21  Resolution 2856 (XXVI).

22  Resolution 3447 (XXX).

23  As with all the second generation declarations, a recognition that these rights require resources as well as commitment is always contained in the preamble, thus in this case we

find the phrase, 'aware that certain countries, at their present stage of development, can devote only limited efforts to this end'.

24    See also Chapter Four, on Africa.

25    For more information, see the UN website at www.un.org

26    *Resolution 1992/47/3; Resolution 48/97; Resolution 1993/29; Resolution 48/97.*

27    The most important of these was published as a book, Government Action on Disability Policy.

28    Report of Special Rapporteur, Bengt Lindqvist, to 54th Session of the Commission on Human Rights, Geneva, 31 March 1998. His report in February 2000 to the 38th Session of the Commission for Social Development was however more conditional in a number of areas.

29    For further information consult website: www.ilo.ch

30    Article 2.

31    Article 2.

32    Article 1.

33    Article 1.

34    For further information see website: www.who.ch

35    *WHO Resolution WHA 42.28, 19.5.89; WHO Report EB89/15, 9.12.91; WHO Resolution EB89.R7, 27.1.92; Report A45/6, 10.4.92; WHO Resolution WHA45.10, 11.5.92.*

36    International Classification of Impairments, Activities and Participation (ICIDH-2) can be found on the website www.who.int/icidh/

37    For further information on the OAS see the website: www.oas.org

# CHAPTER FOUR

# Improving the Civil Rights of People with Disabilities Through Domestic Law

## A Global Overview

*Jeremy Cooper*

Whilst international law can define broad principles of justice to which governments should aspire, it is national (that is, domestic) laws that are the most likely source of real change for disabled people at a micro level. Bickenbach (2000) identifies, within domestic legal systems, four basic kinds of legal expression of human rights for people with disabilities:

1. Enforceable, anti-discrimination legislation;
2. Constitutional guarantees of equality;
3. Specific entitlement programmes;
4. Voluntary human rights manifestos.

There is increasing evidence that all four of these approaches are starting to emerge in various stages of development around the world, as we begin a new millennium. In this chapter, developments in national laws and policies concerning disability rights in a number of countries across the globe are explored.[1]

## AFRICA

It is hard to give an overview of the situation regarding the rights of disabled people in Africa, so diverse are its social, political and economic cultures. The information that is available suggests some limited progress. This progress may be accelerated by the declaration, in Mexico City in December 1998, at the Fifth World Assembly of the Disabled Peoples' International (DPI), of the African

Decade of Disabled Persons which was formally adopted in Africa as part of the Cape Town Declaration in January 1999.[2] This Declaration demands that disability issues should be prioritised and allocated specific funding in government budgets; that enforceable and implementable disability legislation and policies should be evaluated and monitored; that self-representation of people with disabilities should be promoted in all structures of government; and, most important of all, that the UN Standard Rules should be incorporated into national legislation across the region.[3] The Declaration calls upon governments throughout Africa publicly to record their realisation of the demands of disabled people for equal rights and equal treatment, so there is now significant activity across Africa to promote the implementation at state level of the Standard Rules.[4]

In individual African countries a number of developments have been reported. In Libya, the People's General Congress Law No. 3 on Disabled Persons 1981 states that: 'Every disabled person is entitled to housing, care services at home, prostheses and appliances, education, rehabilitation, employment, exemption from income tax, accessible public transport, buildings and resorts, and exemption from custom duties on imported appliances.'

In Madagascar, a project called 'Laws for Disabled People' was initiated by a group of disabled people, the Ikoriantsoa Foundation, in the 1990s. The project has conducted a survey of the socio-economic situation of disabled people in Madagascar, and on the basis of this survey organised a national forum which drew up a legislative plan to address disability issues. In February 1998, the plan was officially adopted by the government and promulgated as law by the President of the Republic. The operational plan is now being developed.[5] Namibia has used the UN Standard Rules to formulate national policy on disability, adopted by its Parliament in 1997.[6] In Nigeria, at a televised press conference in 1998 in Lagos State, the National League of Nigerians with Disabilities called for human rights legislation to be introduced specifically to protect disabled people, to be formulated by a proposed National Commission on Disability. Much of the promise of the Cape Town Declaration is reflected in draft legislation currently being developed in South Africa, initially known as the Promotion of Equality and Prevention of Unfair Discrimination Bill 1999.

A Disabled Women's Development Programme was also set up in 1998 with the aim of countering negative attitudes to disabled women.[7] In July 1999 in Cameroon the Yaounde Declaration was promulgated, pledging the Central African Sub-Region States to adopt a convention on the implementation of the UN Standard Rules and ratifying the creation of the African Rehabilitation Institute. Uganda has recently adopted a new Constitution, which takes a strongly progressive line with regard to the rights of disabled people.[8] For example, it states that:

Society and the State shall recognise the right of persons with disabilities to respect and human dignity.

Persons with disabilities have a right to respect and human dignity and the State and Society shall take appropriate measures to ensure that they realise their full mental and physical potential.[9]

Parliament shall enact laws for the protection of persons with disabilities.[10]

As a direct consequence, of these changes, thousands of disabled Ugandans now have positions of power and responsibility in the public services. Steps have also been taken in the areas of education and access to public buildings to operate the philosophy of the UN Standard Rules. In 1996, Zambia passed a Persons with Disabilities Act, which also incorporated aspects of the UN Standard Rules. In Zimbabwe, the Zimbabwe Disabled Persons Act provides for the rehabilitation and welfare of disabled persons and has the stated aim of achieving equal opportunities for disabled people to receive all community and other services. The Act has created a National Disability Board, with a full time Director for Disabled Persons' Affairs, who works with government ministries to put the Act into practice. The high-powered board is also charged with drawing up policies to effect equalisation of opportunities, independent living, freedom from discrimination, employment, income generation, the provision of orthopaedic appliances and improvements to the social and economic status of disabled people. Penalties for discrimination in breach of the Act include a fine of up to $4000, and/or a year in prison. According to Disability Awareness in Action, Zimbabwe has a big programme of public awareness-raising on disability issues, mainly by disabled people's organisations and the government.[11]

## AUSTRALIA[12]

### Federal law

Under Australian federal law, the Federal (Commonwealth) Government only has power to legislate within the Constitution on a limited range of matters. One such power is called the external affairs power, whereby the Commonwealth Government can impose legislation upon states if they deem it necessary to ensure that Australia is complying with her obligations under international treaty law. These powers have been used, for example, to ensure state adherence to the International Convention on the Elimination of All Forms of Racial Discrimination, the International Convention on Civil and Political Rights, and most important of all, the ILO Discrimination (Employment and Occupation) Convention. The culmination of this activity was the introduction in 1993 of the Disability Discrimination Act 1992, one of the most comprehensive rights-based pieces of anti-discrimination that the world has yet seen, and a major reform in the law prohibiting discrimination against people with disabilities (Jones and Marks 2000; Jones and Marks 1999; McDonagh 1993).

Since 1993, the Disability Discrimination Act has been in operation throughout Australia. It is a comprehensive piece of anti-discrimination legislation covering people with all impairments or a history of impairments. By choosing to deal with disability in legislation separate from other instruments dealing with discrimination the Act was sending out a clear message to disabled people that discrimination on the grounds of disability raises a whole set of discrete issues that are different from those associated with, for example, race or gender.

The Act created a new body, the Human Rights and Equal Opportunity Commission (HREOC), with responsibility for overseeing the operation of the anti-discrimination machinery. The Commission was headed by a Disability Discrimination Commissioner. Although the Commission promised much, the first Commissioner, Elizabeth Hastings, resigned in 1997, in the wake of the announcement by the Federal Government of substantial cuts in their funding of the HREOC. Since her resignation, she has been replaced by Acting Commissioners. At the time of her departure, Ms Hastings was reported as saying:[13]

> There has been much activity occurring over the past four and a half years, in all the areas covered by the DDA, but the right to belong in, contribute to and benefit from our society without discrimination is not one that can yet be taken for granted by people who have disabilities.

The functions of the Commission are considerable,[14] and include:

> To enquire into alleged infringements of the anti-discrimination provisions of the Act, and to endeavour by conciliation to effect a settlement;

> To report to the Minister on matters relating to the development of disability standards, and to prepare and publish guidelines for the avoidance of discrimination on the grounds of disability;

> To undertake research and educational programmes, and other programmes, on behalf of the Commonwealth (of Australia) for the purpose of promoting the objects of the Act;

> To examine actual and proposed enactments in order to ascertain whether they might be inconsistent with the aims of the Act, and report to the Minister accordingly;

> (With leave of the Court) to intervene in any legal proceedings that involve issues of discrimination on the grounds of disability.

In defining 'discrimination', the Act described two types of disability discrimination, 'direct discrimination' and 'indirect discrimination'.

Direct discrimination is said to occur when:

Because of the aggrieved person's disability, the discriminator treats or proposes to treat the aggrieved person less favourably than, in circumstances that are the same or not materially different, the discriminator treats or would treat a person without the disability.[15]

Indirect discrimination is said to occur when:

The discriminator requires the aggrieved person to comply with a requirement or condition:

(A) with which a substantially higher proportion of persons without the disability comply, or are able to comply;

and (B) which is not reasonable having regard to the circumstances of the case;

and (C) with which the aggrieved person does not or is not able to comply.[16]

The Act applies in a wide variety of settings as follows:

Employment: This extends to partnerships, contract work, trade or professional bodies, trade unions and employment agencies, and covers application and interview arrangements, transfer, promotion, training and dismissal.[17]

Education: This extends to admission of students, denial of benefits, expulsion of students and subjection of the student to any detriment.[18]

Access to Premises: This includes any refusal of access to public premises, or terms imposed upon access to facilities that are available on such premises, once access is obtained.[19]

Provision of goods, services and facilities: Discrimination is prohibited with respect to refusal to provide goods, services or facilities to a disabled person.[20]

Accommodation: This includes, with relation to both residential and business accommodation, any form of discrimination for example in relation to allocation procedures, refusal of permission to make necessary alterations and adaptations, and denial of access of benefits normally associated with such accommodation.[21]

Clubs and sports: Discrimination is forbidden with regard to membership application and criteria for clubs, and to benefits provided by such clubs, similarly to access to any sporting activity, or its coaching or administration.[22]

At the end of 1999, the Australian Attorney General introduced into the Australian Parliament important new legislation, the Human Rights Legislation Amendment Bill (No 1) 1999. He stated that the passage of the legislation would constitute an important step in providing human rights complainants, including people with disabilities, with an effective and cost-efficient process for making complaints under anti-discrimination legislation. The new Bill is designed to speed up the process of complaining under the Act, to ensure that human rights litigants are given fair and equitable access to justice should they choose to pursue a human rights complaint in the Federal Court, when conciliation in the Human Rights and Equal Opportunity Commission (HREOC) has failed. The Bill includes provisions designed to ensure that conciliation conferences in the HREOC are conducted fairly, taking into account the special needs of parties to the complaint, particularly those with a disability. In addition, a person with a disability unable fully to participate in a conciliation conference can now nominate someone to appear on his or her behalf. Some disability groups have raised concerns about the fees which apply to cases in the Federal Court. To meet these concerns, the Bill includes a special arrangement whereby complainants suffering financial hardship can apply to the Attorney General for financial assistance to pursue discrimination complaints. In introducing the legislation, the Attorney General maintained that the government was supported by both the HREOC and the Law Council of Australia.

Finally, the Bill amends the Disability Discrimination Act to enable the Attorney General to make standards under the Act in relation to the access to, and use of premises by, people with disabilities.

### State laws

Since the introduction of the Disability Discrimination Act, state laws regarding discrimination against disabled people have become less important. Nevertheless, in a variety of ways, state law in Australia provides further layers of protection to the rights of disabled citizens, and also in some cases introduces the related concept of affirmative action programmes. The civil rights of physically disabled citizens not to suffer discrimination are protected by law in four of the seven Australian States: New South Wales, Victoria, South Australia and Western Australia. With the exception of South Australia, this protection is extended to include discrimination on grounds of intellectual impairment. In Victoria and Western Australia, mental disorder is also included. There are two important pieces of legislation in the state of Victoria: the Intellectually Disabled Persons' Services Act 1986 (IDPSA) and the Disability Services Act 1991 (DSA). (For a more detailed discussion of the first of these two statutes see Carney 1988; Preston and Gregson 1987.) The IDPSA sets standards regarding provision of services, and admission and treatment of mentally disabled people in residential institutions. It also establishes a code of conduct, or set of principles, based upon concepts of equity, integration, participation and civil rights. The DSA regulates the funding of disability services for both physically and mentally disabled people, based upon a set of articulated principles set out in the Act and defined as follows:

> Persons with disabilities are individuals who have the inherent right to respect for their human worth and dignity, have the same basic human rights as other members of Australian society and have the same rights to realise their individual capacities for physical, social, emotional and intellectual development, to access to services which will support their attaining a reasonable quality of life, to participate in decisions which affect their lives, to receive services in a manner which least restricts their rights and opportunities, to pursue grievances in relation to services.

## AUSTRIA

In 1997 the government of Austria amended its constitution in order that the equal position of disabled people in society would be formally recognised. It is not clear, however, that the Austrian Government is making any further changes in law or policy to back up this change in the constitution.

## BULGARIA

In 1997, the Bulgarian Council of Ministers set up a Rehabilitation and Social Integration Fund with the purpose of implementing a national policy on the social integration of disabled people. What is of special interest in the Bulgarian approach to policy towards disabled people is the extent to which it is grounded in the principles of the Standard Rules, with their emphasis upon human rights, and the social model of disability.

## CANADA

Canada was the first country in the world to include a full equality clause in its constitution that unequivocally included disability in its wording. For a full account of the campaign that led to this outcome see Lepofsky and Bickenbach 1985. The Canadian Charter of Rights and Freedoms[23] states as follows: 'Every individual is equal before and under the law and has the right to the equal protection and equal benefit of the law without discrimination and, in particular, without discrimination based on race, national or ethnic origin, colour, religion, sex, age or mental or physical disability.'

It should be noted that the Charter demonstrates a highly assertive and positive approach to the problem of inequality by adding the words, 'equal protection and equal benefit', a protection that is reinforced by a further section of the Charter that seeks to protect affirmative action programmes from being outlawed as 'discriminatory':[24] 'Subsection 1 does not preclude any law, program or activity that has as its object the amelioration of conditions of disadvantaged individuals or groups including those that are disadvantaged because of race, national or ethnic origin, colour, religion, sex, age or mental or physical disability.'

Several Supreme Court decisions have used the Charter to set out a series of powerful protections for people with disabilities (Rioux and Frazee 1999). The significant limitation on the Charter provision is, however, that it only applies to federal and provincial government legislation and activity. It does not apply to discrimination by private citizens.[25] Its impact on the lives of many Canadians with disabilities has, however, been considerable:

> The introduction of the Charter has had important implications for people with disabilities. All federal and provincial legislation is now subject to Charter scrutiny, and can be challenged on the basis that it discriminates against people with disabilities. Discrimination in the provision of housing, education, conditions of employment, as well as differences of treatment in criminal and civil law can now be challenged as violating the equality guarantees (Kimber 1993, p.192).

The Canadian Human Rights Act[26] has reinforced these sentiments in detail, and at the same time created a special Human Rights Commission for dealing with complaints about discrimination:

> Every individual has an equal opportunity with other individuals to make for himself or herself the life that he or she is able and wishes to have…without being hindered in or prevented from doing so by discriminatory practices based on race, national or ethnic origin, colour, religion, age, sex, marital status, family status, disability or conviction for an offence for which a pardon has been granted.

Shortly thereafter a Federal Task Force on Disability Issues was established to hold public consultations with Canadians with disabilities to seek their advice and guidance on future government action. The subsequent report, 'Equal Citizenship for Canadians with Disabilities: the Will to Act', formed a blueprint for further reforms. In 1998, the Human Rights Act was amended to include a 'duty of accommodation' designed to ensure that federal employers and service providers are supportive of, and accessible to, people with disabilities. In addition the Canadian Evidence Act has been amended to provide for alternative means of communicating in court, the Criminal Code has been modified to make jury service possible for disabled people,[27] new agreements have been negotiated with the provinces under the Employability Assistance for People with Disabilities initiative helping disabled people to find and keep jobs, and tax assistance measures for disability and medical expenses have been increased, better to recognise the extra costs faced by people with disabilities.[28]

In addition to the above federal law provisions which can be used to declare unconstitutional any provincial law that runs contrary to these guarantees, all of the ten provinces have themselves enacted their own human rights protections for disabled people under provincial legislation. The first province to do so was New Brunswick, which in 1976 introduced its first human rights legislation, and specifically included disabled people within its remit. Then, in 1980 Ontario passed a law stating that every child in the province was worthy of an education appropriate to its needs, regardless of impairment. This was followed by the introduction of the Ontarians with Disabilities Bill. The Ontario Human Rights Commission's annual report for 1998–1999 observed that although the Ontarians with Disabilities Act received its first reading in November 1998, it was not passed when the House prorogued in December 1998. It went on to state that in 1998–1999, 'discrimination against people with disabilities remained one of the largest areas of complaints filed with the Commission, representing 25% of all grounds cited'.

The Commission recommended that the government 'implement both regulatory and non-regulatory approaches to removing barriers. Also, barriers should be defined more broadly than those related to physical impediments'.

The agency with the lead role in Canada in developing government sponsored initiatives to help people with disabilities is the Human Resources Development Canada (HRDC).[29]

## CHINA

It is estimated that there are over 60 million disabled people in the People's Republic of China. Whilst little is known about the rights and treatment of disabled people within the People's Republic, it is interesting to note that disabled people have a specific legal identity as a separate group with a right to free legal assistance in the current skeleton legal aid network in China (Cooper 1999). One promising public statement recently emerged from the Vice Premier Li Lanqing who announced in 1998:[30] 'In addition to enhancing public respect for the human rights and personal dignity of disabled people, we should also provide them with an equal opportunity to participate in the community and help them become more economically self-reliant.'

A further clue to developing policy in China is to be found in the words of Deng Pufang, Chairman of the China Federation for Disabled Persons: 'Without co-ordinated efforts from all sectors of society, a marked improvement in the lives of disabled people would not have been possible.'

## COSTA RICA

Since May 1996 Costa Rica has enacted an Equal Opportunities Law for people with Disabilities, based on the UN Standard Rules, with its own monitoring Commission.

## FRANCE

Since July 1990 it has been unlawful under the French Penal Code[31] (and therefore a criminal offence) to discriminate against a person on the grounds of health or impairment, where this is unjustified, in providing goods, services or employment. Furthermore, an employer cannot refuse to recruit a person, nor dismiss an employee, nor take action short of dismissal on grounds of health or disability, unless the employee's inability to continue has been certified by a doctor. Offenders can be punished by imprisonment, a fine, or a combination of both. France also operates a quota scheme across both public and private sector employment for undertakings employing at least 20 staff.[32] Since 1991 the quota has been set at 6 per cent of full-time or part-time positions (from an original figure of 3 per cent in 1988). There are, however, a number of ways in which an employer can be exempted from these provisions, most of which have financial implications.

For more detail on the current situation in France see Chapter Two, p.48.

## GERMANY

Germany presents a different approach to the question of civil rights protection from that in any of the above examples, and also from that which currently operates in the UK. (See generally Brooke-Ross 1984; Brooke-Ross and Zacher 1983; Jochheim 1985; Rasnic 1992; Youngs 1994; and Chapter Two, p.45–47.)

A number of rights are drafted directly into the Constitution, which is binding on all the states of Germany (known as *Länder* (plural) or *Land* (singular)). As a direct consequence, any law passed by a state that contravenes any Article of the Constitution will be without legal force and can be ruled as such either by the court structure within the *Land* in question (the county court or *Landgericht*; the appeal court or *Oberlandesgericht)* by the appeal court which overarches all the *Länder (the Bundesgerichtshof)* or by the constitutional court itself (the *Bundesverfassungsgericht*).

Whilst there was no Article in the original post-war Constitution of Germany dealing explicitly with discrimination on grounds of disability, or the rights of disabled people, Article 1 of the Constitution is clearly relevant to this issue and has great potential as a guardian clause that can be used pro-actively on behalf of this constituency.

### The Basic Rights

> The dignity of the human being inviolable, it is the duty of all State authority to
> have regard to it and to protect it. (Article 1, Basic Laws)

The Basic Law in Germany is a collection of fundamental norms setting out conditions under which the State derives authority, including the Basic Rights of defence against the State. Although in principle, the Basic Rights of the German Constitution only bind the 'organs of state' (that is, they do not operate on transactions between private organisations and individuals) in one case in the Mannheim Court,[33] involving an attempt by a private school to expel an epileptic child on the basis that other children and their parents were upset by their being in the presence of such a child, the court held that the act violated Article 1 and was therefore unenforceable.[34]

More recently the German Constitution has been amended, with a new equal protection clause, including the phrase 'no one may be disadvantaged on account of his disability'.[35] For the detail and a discussion on this clause, see Chapter Two, p.46.

Prior to insertion of this provision in the Basic Law, the rights to human dignity and corporeal integrity (Articles 1 and 2 of the Basic Law) had already been used in favour of the disabled and a comprehensive protection of the disabled under the ordinary law had already been developed on the basis of the social state principle[36](which did not, however, give rise to claims for positive steps by the state).

Germany also has a quota system for employment similar to that operating in France. This is discussed in detail in Chapter Two (p.39–40). German unfair dismissal laws are also very protective of employees who are or who become disabled in the course of their employment (Doyle 1995). There was a potential conflict between the above duty to employ disabled persons and Article 33, paragraph two of the Basic Law as to the basis on which public servants should be selected; the Federal Constitutional Court has ruled that quotas for disabled employees in the public service were constitutional.[37]

Finally, it should be noted that the ban on discrimination against disabled people finds expression in the interpretation of the new regime of the abortion legislation (1995). The disablement of the foetus is omitted as an independent ground for abortion. But medically attested serious impairment of the physical or psychological condition of the mother is a possible ground – and this can include cases where knowledge of the disablement of the foetus leads or can lead to impairment of the health of the mother – although this would have to be confined to serious cases.[38]

## GREECE

In February 1998, Greece adopted the Standard Rules as part of Greek national law. As part of the accompanying campaign to raise public awareness of the implications of this important decision, a law has also been adopted that mandates TV and radio stations to allocate time for awareness-raising messages. The National Council of Disabled People in Greece is also playing a key role in the development of a national action plan to incorporate the Standard Rules across Greek society. New draft laws on employment and social care are using the Rules as part of their drafting framework.

## GUATEMALA

In 1997, the National Council for Disabled People was created in the Republic of Guatemala, and signed by Congress. Fifty per cent of the representatives on the Council are disabled people.[39]

## HONG KONG

Through legislation first proposed in 1994, the Hong Kong government has established an Equal Opportunities Commission from which disabled citizens can seek redress when they consider themselves to have been harassed or discriminated against because of their disability. Disability in this respect includes those diagnosed HIV positive or with AIDS. The relevant legislation bears striking similarity to that of the UK and Australia (Chapter Six), but it is wider (Petersen 1999). The new law (Ordinance) renders unlawful, discrimination against people on the ground of their or their associates' disability in respect of their employment, accommodation, education, access to partnerships, membership of trade unions and clubs, access to premises, educational establishments, sporting activities and the provision of goods, services and facilities. It makes wide ranging provision against harassment and vilification of persons with a disability and their associates. The Commission has the power not only to instigate formal investigations into allegations of discrimination, it can also assist individual cases.[40]

## HUNGARY

Following a lengthy campaign by the National Association of Disabled Persons' Associations of Hungary (MEOSZ), the Hungarian Parliament passed, in March 1998, the Disabled Peoples' Rights and Equal Opportunities Act. It is very far-reaching, and creates a model of good practice that could well be followed in other jurisdictions. The Act sets out a deadlined agenda for a number of key achievements including accessibility of mass transport (2010), integrated education (2005), and accessibility of all public buildings (2005). There is a committee set up to co-ordinate the Act's implementation, which includes leaders of disabled people's groups. It is possible to use the court system to address violation of disabled citizens' rights under the Act. The Act also covers such matters as employment opportunities, access to sporting facilities and cultural programmes and the 'right to rehabilitation'. Despite the strength of these provisions, Hungary retains a range of totalitarian institutions for mental patients that have been severely criticized.

## INDIA

In May 1995, the Government of India published a draft Bill relating to the improvement of the quality of life of disabled people in India, the Persons with Disabilities (Equal Opportunities, Protection of Rights and Full Participation) Bill 1995. Under the Bill it was proposed to set up a Central Co-ordination Committee for the promotion of opportunities, the protection of rights, and the encouragement of full participation in society of disabled people. Under the Bill, 'disability' meant[41] any of: 'Blindness, low vision, leprosy-cured, hearing impairment, locomotor disability, mental retardation, or mental illness.'

The Bill was passed by Parliament in December 1995, and became law as the Indian Disability Act in February 1996. Under this new legislation, the Central Co-ordination Committee is supposed to monitor the activities of a national network of local committees, which will be charged with policy implementation over a wide range of issues including promoting the integration of disabled people, reviewing with donor agencies funding policies from the perspective of disabled people and developing affirmative action policies in employment, vocational training, and care and protection systems. The legislation also contains a non-discrimination clause specifically aimed at disability abuse (for example, using a disabled person against their will for begging, or obtaining benefits meant for disabled people) with punishment by fine or imprisonment in some cases for up to two years.[42] The passage of the legislation into a reality is proving extremely problematic.

## IRELAND

The Irish Commission on the Status of People with Disabilities was established in December 1993 with the purpose of presenting the Irish government with proposals that would give disabled people the same opportunities to participate as all other people in Irish life. Chaired by a judge, 60 per cent of its membership were disabled people, their advocates, or family members, the remaining membership being drawn from statutory and voluntary agencies. The

Commission adopted a deliberately high profile, organising a series of large public meetings across the country, and receiving over 3000 pages of written submissions.[43] Among the many issues that it addressed were education, housing, employment and transport needs, and the possibility of introducing comprehensive anti-discrimination measures to include disability.[44] The Commission published its findings in 1996, which led to the passing of the Employment Equality Act in 1998.[45] The Employment Equality Act prohibits both direct and indirect discrimination in employment on nine grounds, which include disability. All aspects of employment are covered: access to employment, vocational training and conditions of employment (including pay, work experience, promotion and dismissal). Although the original Employment Equality Act passed all stages in both Houses on 26 March 1997, in May 1997 the Supreme Court held that some aspects of the Act were unconstitutional, including some of the provisions relating to disability. These provisions would have obliged employers to bear the cost of special treatment or facilities for people with disabilities unless the employers could show that this caused them undue hardship. The Supreme Court considered this to be an unjust attack on employers' property rights, contrary to Article 43 of the Constitution. The legislation was revised to require employers only to make 'reasonable accommodation' to meet the needs of disabled employees (actual or potential) where 'nominal costs' were involved. The legislation is in some ways conservative, and cautious. The definition of disability is heavily within the 'medical model' (see Chapter One, pp.13–14), although it is a very broad and comprehensive definition and there is no requirement that the disability is shown to affect a person's daily life, nor is there any bottom limit on the number of employees necessary for the Act to have effect. Sections 34–35 allow discrimination against people with a disability where it can be shown that there is clear actuarial or other evidence that significantly increased costs would arise if the discrimination were not permitted, and furthermore permit the payment of differential wages to people whose disability reduces their work rate.

At the meetings of the 54th United Nations Human Rights Commission, Ireland presented a long and comprehensive resolution on the advancement of the rights of people with disabilities, that formed the basis of a subsequent draft Resolution of the UN that is still under consideration. [Chapter Three, p. 67, fn.18]

## ISRAEL

Israel has recently passed a law on 'Equal Rights for Persons with Disabilities', [5758-1998] which is very far-ranging in its remit, and is based upon the principle that 'discrimination on the basis of disability is prohibited'. It is one of the most comprehensive pieces of legislation in the world with respect to upholding the rights of disabled people to the same opportunities as able-bodied people across a range of life activities including employment, public services, transport, health services, family life and respect for privacy. As in the German law, personal dignity is the framing concept that underpins the legislation.

## ITALY

Two sets of laws designed to strengthen the rights of disabled people were passed in Italy in the 1990s, relating to general assistance, social integration and employment protection.[46]

## JAPAN

In 1994, the Japanese government published its 'Disabled Persons' Fundamental Law' which was supposed to lay out the basic principles it believed should govern all state and private sector dealings with disabled people. Article 3, for example, states: 'The dignity of all disabled persons shall be respected and they shall have the right to be treated in such a manner. All disabled persons shall, as members of society, be provided with opportunities fully to participate in social, economic, cultural and other areas of activity.'

When the Japanese government published its blueprint for support for disabled people, however, the most old-fashioned model of state attitudes towards disabled people emerged: specialist caring for disabled people in institutions.[47] There was to be no input from disabled people themselves into the planning, or the delivery of any new system. Outraged by such an approach, the Disabled People's International Japan submitted a counterplan, based upon the principle of self-help with disabled groups taking the lead in the provision of appropriate community welfare services. A protracted struggle lies ahead, which at the same time might create a model of resistance that could well be followed in other countries.[48]

## NEPAL

Legislation passed in Nepal in 1982 (the Disabled Protection and Welfare Act 1982) as part of its commitment to the International Year of Disabled Persons deals comprehensively with the political and socio-economic needs of disabled people, and as such is one of the more advanced statements of law, that are in line with the general philosophy of the ICESCR. The preamble of the Act states: 'To enable disabled people to participate as active and productive citizens, provisions will be made to protect their welfare through prevention of impairment, health education, training facilities and employment opportunities and by defining a fundamental right to equality.' (For greater detail and commentary on this and other recent developments in the Asian Pacific Rim and Asia generally see ESCAP 1993.)

In 1998 the Nepal Federation of the Deaf and Hard of Hearing hosted an Asia Regional Workshop on the UN Standard Rules, which was attended by a large number of delegates from several Asian countries. An ongoing strategy for implementation of the rules was agreed at the workshop.

## THE NETHERLANDS

For many years, disabled people's organisations have lobbied consecutive governments to introduce an additional clause into Article 1 of the Dutch Constitution stating: 'All persons in The Netherlands shall be treated equally in equal circumstances. Discrimination on the grounds of religion, belief, political opinion, race or sex or any other grounds shall not be permitted'. Unfortunately this has proved, for the most part, merely symbolic politics, although the wheels have started grinding in part with the introduction in 1998 of a draft Bill, entitled the Prohibition on Making an Unjustifiable Distinction on the Grounds of Handicap or Chronic Disease Bill (Hendriks 1999).

## NEW ZEALAND

In 1993 the New Zealand Human Rights Act, which includes provisions relating to unlawful discrimination, was extended to include, among other groups, disabled people. The ambit of the protection is broader than the UK's Disability Discrimination Act, extending for example to educational institutions. People who believe they have suffered discrimination appeal in the first instance to the Human Rights Commission who will seek to resolve the matter. If an agreement between the parties cannot be reached, the matter can proceed to the Complaints Review Tribunal for a hearing. At the time the legislation was introduced, the government gave itself until the year 2000 to ensure that all legislation, policies, practices and procedures complied with the Act (known as Project Consistency 2000). In practice, it is still some way from achieving that target, and has obtained parliamentary approval, agreed with the Human Rights Commission, to extend this period for a further two years to 1 January 2002.[49] The Commission has established a rigorous monitoring and reporting mechanism designed to maximise the chances of achieving compliance by this date[50] (Bell 1998).

More troubling to the disability community is the passage through parliament at the time of going to press of the Intellectual Disability (Compulsory Care) Bill, which seeks to set up a system of compulsory care for people with intellectual disabilities, including children and young people, when a specialist assessor determines that they are a danger to themselves or to others. A powerful umbrella organisation of disabled people in New Zealand, lobbying the government on all these issues, is the Disabled People's Assembly (New Zealand).[51]

## PERU

On January 6th 1999 there was published in Peru the 'People with Disability General Law', [Law No. 27050].[52] The law represents the achievement of an historic objective in Peru, by integrating all disability issues under one generic roof, designed to provide a legal framework for the protection of the health, work, education, rehabilitation of all Peruvians with disabilities so as ultimately to achieve full social, economic and cultural integration, in line with the aspirations of the 1993 Peruvian Constitution. The Law also set up a Council to develop further disability policies (Consejo Nacional de Integracion de la Persona con Discapacidad (CONDIS) (National Council for People with Disability Integration)) and a specialised Ombudsman service for the defence and promotion of people with disability rights. Similar services have been set up in other Latin American countries, including Argentina.

## THE PHILIPPINES

Since 1990 the Organisation of Disabled Persons in the Philippines has served as the primary national organisation for disabled people, co-ordinating campaigns and monitoring the enforcement of the Philippines' imaginative and progressive legislation for disabled people. The two major legal instruments that contain the guarantees of the rights of disabled people in specific situations are the Philippine Constitution 1987 and the '"Magna Carta" for Disabled Persons 1992'.[53] The Constitution contains a number of clear provisions with regard to disabled people, as follows ( 1995):

The right of disabled persons to vote without the assistance of other persons.

The selection of a sectorial representative for disabled persons.

A comprehensive approach to health development which makes available essential goods, health and other social services to all people, with priority given to the needs of the underprivileged including disabled persons.

The right to participate in all levels of social, political and economic decision-making.

The protection of rights of all citizens to quality education at all levels. This provides impetus to education programmes for special groups and for free public education for disabled students at elementary and secondary level.

The provision for vocational skills training for disabled persons along with adults and seniors of school-aged youth (p.41).

As part of the process of securing these rights the Constitution also orders the state to establish a special agency for disabled persons for their integration into the mainstream of society. This has duly happened, with the creation of the National Commission Concerning Disabled Persons, described as 'an all encompassing consultative forum advising and co-ordinating all matters pertaining to the welfare of disabled people' (DAA 1995, p.40).

The 'Magna Carta' for Disabled Persons was enacted as a further piece of legislation designed to amplify and extend the implementation of the provisions set out in the constitution. The Act provides for the rehabilitation, self-development and self-reliance of disabled people and their integration into mainstream society. Furthermore, it is to serve as a framework for future legislation, aimed at the realisation of 'full participation and equalisation of opportunity'. Contained in this Act are a number of detailed provisions including the prohibition of discrimination against disabled people in specific settings; use of public facilities, transportation services, and employment; and the setting up of rehabilitation and self-reliance projects for disabled people. Finally it should be noted that the Philippine Government has recently passed further laws protecting disabled people in particular situations – for example the Accessibility Law requires installation of special parking places, ramps on doorways and stairs, bars in public toilets, and other aids and adaptations to help disabled people.

## SCANDINAVIA

With their long and proud tradition of advanced social welfare programmes it is not surprising that the countries of Scandinavia have a fairly advanced rights-based legislative programme designed to integrate people with disabilities into normal society.[54] Denmark has a long history of social legislation that includes provision of the rights of disabled persons, based upon principles of equality and participation by all who wish to participate in public life. The implementation of these measures has largely been devolved to local authorities. In Finland, the Standard Rules were adopted by the Government as early as 1993, and on the basis of these rules, Finland set out its own disability policy programme in 1995. In the same year the Constitution Act of Finland was amended to include a new provision on the equal treatment for persons with disabilities, according to which no one shall be assigned a different status on the basis of their health or disability. There is a National Council on Disability linked to the Ministry of Social Affairs and Health, working as a co-operative body between the relevant authority and disability organisations. The Act on Services and Assistance for Disabled People aims to promote independent living and equal opportunities for persons with disabilities on the Scandinavian welfare model that seeks to ensure for all inhabitants the services they need, irrespective of their financial or social status. Finland has also produced a 'tool box' of guidance for local authorities on how they can implement the Standard Rules at the local level.[55] In Sweden, organisations of disabled people receive grants, and are treated as public sector partners in the decision making process. The guiding principle throughout all these processes in one of integration, seeking to make normal society as available as possible to the disabled by a process of adaptation and access. The Social Services Act, the Act Providing for Adaptation of Public Transport to the Needs of Disabled People, the New Syllabus for the Compulsory School, and the Building Code all contain examples of the practical operation of this principle. In addition, the Swedish Co-operative Body of Organisations of Disabled People (HSO) has initiated a project encouraging local authorities with responsibility for many social policy issues to draw up policies for disabled people in conformity with the UN Standard Rules.[56] Finally, in 1999 Sweden introduced a new law against discrimination in the workplace based upon disability.

Sweden has, however, been severely criticised by the Special Rapporteur on the Standard Rules following a recent audit he carried out at the behest of the Swedish Government. He highlighted unclear and complicated systems of rules, poor working conditions, lack of resources, and changing values caused by the economic crisis as key factors leading to his conclusion that 'there are considerable deficiencies in attitudes to disabled people [in Sweden]'.[57]

In Norway, an extensive Plan of Action for Disabled People containing over 50 measures has been in place since 1990, and involves a highly imaginative programme of co-ordinated activities across a number of government ministries including such measures as improving access to public buildings, development grants for new technology in industry facilitating disabled employment opportunities, and a big 'books-on-tape' campaign across a number of sectors. The Norwegian activities extend beyond their national frontiers to include assisting groups of disabled individuals in developing countries.

## THAILAND

As in Nepal, the United Nations Decade and Year of the Disabled were used by the Thai government as the catalysts for the introduction in 1992 of the Welfare and Rehabilitation Law for the Disabled. In the field of employment a system of tax incentives has been introduced to try to encourage employers to accept disabled people on their staff, together with penalties for those who do not, paid into the National Rehabilitation Fund. The incentives are real, allowing an employer to deduct from their income for tax purposes double the amount of money they pay in wages to the disabled employee. A similar incentive has been set up for the owners of buildings, vehicles or other public services who improve their facility to make it more accessible to disabled people (ESCAP 1993). Another important development in Thailand, signalled through the 1992 Law, was the creation of the Commission for Rehabilitation of Disabled Persons, which runs a national registration scheme for disabled people that triggers entitlement to special medical and educational services and to advice about employment and legal advice.

## USA

The landmark legislation of the USA in the field of disability protection, the Americans with Disabilities Act (herein after referred to as the ADA) came into effect in 1990.[58] The ADA affects discrimination in both the private and the public sector. The Act covers four main areas: employment, public accommodations, public transport services and telecommunications. For the purposes of this Act, an individual is considered to have a disability and therefore come under the protection of the Act if he or she has a physical or mental impairment that 'substantially limits' (Zappa 1991) a 'major life activity', and either has a record of such impairment or is regarded as having such an impairment (Feldblum 1991). Protection also extends to those who have a known relationship or an association with such a disabled individual. The list of what constitutes a 'major life activity' is extensive and includes seeing, hearing, speaking, walking, breathing, performing manual tasks, learning, caring for oneself and working. A further interesting feature of this protected class is that it extends to those who are seen or treated as handicapped by others, even though they are not. Case law initially identified a wide range of health conditions which are considered as disabilities: impairments in vision and hearing; mental illnesses and learning disabilities; diseases such as epilepsy, multiple sclerosis, cerebral palsy, diabetes and heart disease; carrier states, including hepatitis; and psychological and behavioural conditions such as alcohol and drug dependency.

Despite this, in 110 ADA cases decided in 1995 and 1996 in which the definition of disability was raised, judges found that the individual met the statutory definition in only six cases. An American Bar Association study in 1998 suggested that of 1200 cases filed under Title 1 of the ADA since 1992, employers won 92 per cent, while employees won only 8 per cent. Courts deciding ADA cases have arrived at a restricted definition of disability through two principal methods. First, many courts analyse whether a plaintiff is substantially limited in the major life activity of working, even when the plaintiff's impairment logically can be better understood as a limitation in some other life activity. Once the argument focuses on limitations in working, courts often conclude that the impairment is not sufficiently limiting because there is a range of jobs that the individual can still perform. For example, in *Ellison v Software Spectrum*[59] Phyllis Ellison was diagnosed as having breast cancer, had a lumpectomy and received radiation treatment. During a reorganisation of Ms Ellison's division at work, her job was eliminated. The court held that Ms Ellison was not disabled even though she experienced 'nausea, fatigue, swelling, inflammation, and pain' because she was still able to work.

Even when an individual's claim that their impairment limits a major life activity other than working is accepted, there is a second method by which the US courts have restricted coverage under the ADA. Accepting that the disability limits a major life activity, the courts have asked whether the limitation is 'substantial'. For example, in *Dutcher v Ingalls Shipbuilding*[60] the court concluded that a woman who had sustained serious injury to her right arm in a gun accident was not disabled under the ADA. The court said that, although she had difficulty picking things up from the floor and holding things high or tight for long periods of time and was limited in repetitive rotational movements, she could still take care of the normal daily activities such as eating, driving a car and carrying shopping bags.

A final way in which the courts have restricted the protection available under the ADA is to look at the mitigating effects of treatment. While the US Equal Employment Opportunities Commission has said that the mitigating effects of treatment should not be taken into account, courts have ruled that a person receiving treatment for a condition may not be regarded as disabled under the legislation, because as a result of medication, their condition is under control.

Most worrying of all, the Supreme Court has, in a series of key decisions in the summer of 1999, ruled that physical impairments that can be treated are not protected from discrimination. In a key judgement, the Court held that: 'Congress never intended the law to cover American workers who can correct their impairments by wearing glasses or hearing aids or taking medication. Instead the law covers the 43 million people with more serious disabilities who need its protection to bring them into the economic and social mainstream'. [60A]

### Employment

The aim of this section is the development of a capacity for independent living as well as social integration through employment.[61] An employer with 15 or more employees cannot discriminate against a 'qualified individual' with a disability. A 'qualified individual' is someone who meets legitimate skill, experience, education and other requirements, and who can perform the essential functions of the job, with 'reasonable accommodation' (Cooper 1991; Stine 1992) by the employer, for example making existing facilities accessible to disabled employees, adapting or acquiring new equipment or machinery, special training materials, readers, interpreters and so forth.[62] Essentially what is expected by the legislation under this concept of 'reasonable accommodation' is that which is 'readily achievable' – that is, easily accomplishable and able to be carried out without too much expense or difficulty. The size and nature of the business is taken into account when deciding what should be achieved. Employers are not expected to invest in changes that would cause them 'undue hardship' (see Tucker 1992), for example if the 'accommodation' required might 'fundamentally alter the nature or operation of a business.'[63] Thus, a night club owner employing a visually impaired waiter could not be expected to increase the light power in the club to enable the waiter to see better, as in the long-term this would act to the detriment of the employer and other employees.[64] If outside funding is unavailable and the cost of making the job accessible to the disabled employee could cause undue hardship to the employer, the disabled individual must be allowed (though not required) to pay the proportion of the cost causing the 'undue hardship'. Financial assistance is available to employers in the form of tax credits and deductions should they need to carry out any such adaptations. The relevant ADA regulation in this regard explicitly defines the process of determining reasonable accommodation as 'an informal, interactive problem-solving technique involving both the employer and the qualified individual with a disability'.[65] Preliminary research suggests that where applied, the process of making 'reasonable accommodation' is in fact reaping positive financial benefits for employers (Light 1995): 'For every dollar a company spends in making an 'accommodation', they get back 35 dollars in terms of increased productivity, reduced employee turnover, lowered training costs, and savings in insurance compensation costs'. Notwithstanding this positive affirmation, a 1998 Louis Harris and Associates poll commissioned by the National Organisation on Disability found that 71 per cent of persons of working age (18 to 64) with disabilities were not employed, as compared with 21 per cent of Americans without disabilities. In a comparable poll carried out in 1986, four years before the ADA came into effect, 67 per cent of people with disabilities were not employed, compared with 10 per cent of all Americans.

### Public services

No qualified individual with a disability shall by reason of such disability be excluded from participation in or be denied the benefits of the services, programmes or activities of a public entity or be subjected to discrimination by any such entity. Public services, for these purposes, include those who provide services or goods to the public, even though the service is privately run – for example shops, cinemas, schools, restaurants and so forth (Burgdorf 1991; Jones 1992).

The legislation deals with the question of affirmative obligations with regard to existing obligations on the following way: 'Public entities shall make reasonable modifications in policies, practices or procedures when the modifications are necessary to avoid discrimination on the basis of disability, unless the public entity can demonstrate that the modifications would fundamentally alter the nature of the service or activity'. [66]

Thus, where existing physical facilities are concerned: 'A practical entity shall operate each service, program or activity, so that [such service]...when viewed in its entirety, is readily accessible to and usable by individuals with disabilities'. [67] Alterations to existing facilities must 'to the maximum extent feasible, be altered in such a manner that the altered portion of the facility is readily accessible to and usable by individuals with disabilities'. [68]

The exceptions to this overall provision are as follows:

affirmative action that would threaten the significance of an historic property. [69]

action that the service could demonstrate would result in a fundamental alteration in the nature of the service, or in undue financial administrative burdens. [70]

More positive however is the section relating to the construction of new facilities by public entities: 'Every new building must be designed and constructed in such manner that the facility is readily accessible to and usable by individuals with disabilities, if the construction was commenced after January 26th, 1992'. [71]

## Public transport services

In framing the terms of the public transport provisions, Congress favoured the integrationalist approach, that is, the adaptation of regular transport for disabled users rather than the provision of special transport. Under the public transport provisions, all public transport services must now be guaranteed accessible to disabled passengers, although there are limited exceptions such as where it is not technically possible, or adaptation will impose upon the provider an 'undue financial burden'. The provisions are stringent and comprehensive. Thus, for example, every new bus must have a wheelchair lift installed (Quinn 1993), and every second-hand bus purchased must demonstrate 'good faith efforts' to ensure that the bus is accessible to disabled people. All 'key' rail stations [72] must be readily accessible and usable by individuals with disabilities.

## Telecommunications[73]

By virtue of this section all telecommunications equipment must be altered to enable hearing and speech impaired people to use, at no extra cost to the disabled user (the extra cost in reality being born by an increase in the cost of calls for all users) (Scott 1994). The aim of these changes is to attempt to reduce the sense of isolation experienced by the hearing impaired, an isolation that could be dramatically reduced by the use of technologies through telecommunication.

## REFERENCES

Bayefsky, A. and Eberts, M. (1985) (eds) *Equality Rights and the Canadian Charter of Rights and Freedoms.* Toronto: Carswell.

Bell, S. (1998) 'Rationing the right to health.' *Journal of Law and Medicine 6* (1), 83.

Bickenbach, J. (2000) 'Disability human rights, law and policy.' In G. Albrecht, K. Seelman and M. Bury (2000) (eds) *Handbook of Disability Studies.* Beverly Hills: Sage.

Brooke-Ross, R. (1984) 'The disabled in the Federal Republic of Germany.' *Social Policy and Administration 18*, 172.

Brooke-Ross, R. and Zacher, H. (1983) *Social Legislation in the Federal Republic of Germany.* London: Bedford Square Press.

Burgdorf, R. (1991) 'Equal members of the community: the public accommodations provisions of the ADA.' *Temple Law Review 64*, 551.

Carney, T. (1988) 'The Mental Health, Intellectual Disability, Services and Guardianship Acts: how do they rate?' *Legal Services Bulletin* (June) 128.

Cooper, J. (1991) 'Overcoming barriers to employment: the meaning of reasonable accommodation and undue hardship in the Americans with Disabilities Act.' *University of Pennsylvania Law Review 139*, 1431.

Cooper. J. (1999) 'Lawyers in China and the rule of law.' *International Journal of the Legal Profession 6*, 1, 71.

DAA (1995) *Overcoming Obstacles to the Integration of Disabled People.* Unesco sponsored report as a contribution to the World Summit on Social Development, Copenghagen. March 1995. London: Disability Awareness in Action.

Davenport, G. (1992) 'The ADA: an appraisal of the major employment-related compliance and litigation issues.' *Alabama Law Review 43*, 307.

Doyle, B. (1993) 'Employment rights, equal opportunities and disabled persons: the ingredients of reform.' *Industrial Law Journal 22*, 2, 89–103.

Doyle, B. (1995) *Disability, Discrimination and Equal Opportunities. A Comparative Study of the Employment Rights of Disabled Persons.* London: Mansell.

ESCAP (1993) *Asian and Pacific Decade of Disabled Persons 1993–2002: The Starting Point.* New York: ESCAP.

Feldblum, C. (1991) 'The ADA definition of disability.' *The Labour Lawyer 7*, 11.

Gostin, L. and Beyer, H. (1993) *Implementing the Americans with Disabilities Act: Rights and Responsibilities of All Americans.* Baltimore: Paul Brookes.

Government of Canada (1999) *Future Directions to Address Disability Issues for the Government of Canada: Working Together for Full Citizenship.* Ottawa: Government of Canada.

Habeck, R., Galvin, D., Frey, W., Chaddeston, L. and Tate, D. (1985) *Economics and Employment of People with Disabilities: International Policies and Practices.* East Lansing, MI: University Centre for International Rehabilitation, Michigan State University.

Hendriks, A. (1999) 'From social (in)security to equal opportunities – a report from the Netherlands.' In M. Jones and L. Marks (1999) (eds) *Disability, Divers-ability and Legal Change.* The Hague: Kluwer.

Jochheim, K. (1985) 'Quota system policy in the Federal Republic of Germany.' In R. Habeck *et al* (1985) *Economics and Employment of People with Disabilities: International Policies and Practices.* East Lansing, MI: University Centre for International Rehabilitation, Michigan State University.

Jones, M. (1992) 'Real estate impact of the ADA.' *Real Estate Law Journal 21,* 3.

Jones, M. and Marks, L. (1999) (eds) *Disability, Divers-Ability and Legal Change.* The Hague: Kluwer.

Jones, M. and Marks, L. (2000) (eds) *Explorations on Law and Disability in Australia.* Annandale: The Federation Press.

Kemp, E. and Bell, C. (1991) 'A labour lawyer's guide to the ADA of 1990.' *Nova Scotia Law Review 15,* 31.

Kimber, C. (1993) 'Discrimination law in Canada.' In G. Quinn, M. McDonagh and C. Kimber (1993) (eds) *Disability Discrimination Law in the United States, Australia and Canada.* Dublin: Oak Tree Press.

Lepofsky, M. and Bickenbach, J. (1985) 'Equality rights and the physically handicapped.' In M. Bayefsky and M. Eberts (1985) (eds) *Equality Rights and the Canadian Charter of Rights and Freedoms.* Toronto: Carswell.

Light, R. (1995) *We Have Become People: A Report on the Results of Federal Disability Legislation in the United States.* London: Disability Awareness in Action.

Mayerson, A. (1991) 'Title 1 Employment provisions of the ADA.' *Temple Law Review 61,* 499.

McDonagh, M. (1993) 'Disability discrimination law in Australia.' In G. Quinn, M. McDonagh and C. Kimber (1993) (eds) *Disability Discrimination Law in the United States, Australia and Canada.* Dublin: Oak Tree Press.

Mikochik, S. (1991) 'The Constitution and the ADA: some first impressions.' *Temple Law Review 64,* 619.

Petersen, C. (1999) 'Equal opportunities: a new field of kaw for Hong Kong.' In R. Wacks (1999) (ed) *The New Legal Order in Hong Kong.* Hong Kong: HKU Press.

Petter, A. (1989) 'Canada's Charter flight: soaring backwards into the future.' *Journal of Law and Society 16,* 151.

Powell, C. (1991) 'The ADA: the effect of Title 1 on employer/employee relations.' *Law and Psychology Review 15,* 313.

Preston, M. And Gregson, F. (1987) 'New deal for intellectually disabled.' *Law Institute – Journal* (August) 800.

Quinn, G. (1993) 'Disability discrimination law in the United States.' In G. Quinn, M. McDonagh and C. Kimber (1993) (eds) *Disability Discrimination Law in the United States, Australia and Canada.* Dublin: Oak Tree Press.

Quinn, G., McDonagh, M. and Kimber, C. (1993) (eds) *Disability Discrimination Law in the United States, Australia and Canada.* Dublin: Oak Tree Press.

Rasnic, C. (1992) 'A comparative analysis of federal statutes for the disabled worker in the Federal Republic of Germany and the United States.' *Arizona Journal of Comparative and International Law 9,* 283.

Rioux, M. and Frazee, C. (1999) 'The Canadian framework for disability equality rights.' In M. Jones and L. Marks (eds) (1999) *Disability, Divers-ability and Legal Change.* The Hague: Kluwer.

Scott, V. (1994) *Lessons from America: a study of the Americans with Disabilities Act.* London: RADAR.

Stine, M. (1992), 'Reasonable accommodation and undue hardship under the ADA of the 1990s.' *Dakota Law Review 37,* 97.

Strauss, K. and Richardson, R. (1991) 'Breaking down the telephone barrier: relay services on the line.' *Temple Law Review 64,* 583.

Tucker, B. (1992) 'The ADA: an overview.' *University of New Mexico Law Review 13,* 34.

Wacks, R. (ed) (1999) *The New Legal Order in Hong Kong.* Hong Kong: HKU Press.

Weirich, C. (1991) 'Reasonable accommodation under the Americans with Disabilities Act.' *The Labour Lawyer 7*, 27.

Youngs, R. (1994) *Sources of German Law*. London: Cavendish.

Zappa, J. (1991) 'The ADA 1990: improving judicial determinations of whether an individual is "substantially limited."' *Minnesota Law Review 75*, 1303.

## NOTES

1      The UK is not included in this chapter as developments in this country are dealt with substantively in the book as a whole.

2      This took place at the African Seminar on Development and Co-operation, Disability and Human Rights, 28–30 January 1999, as reported in the *Official Publication of DPI*, Spring 1999, 6, 1.

3      F. Pale, in *Insight*, September 1998 (newsletter of the Botswana Council for the Disabled).

4      For example, in January 1998 the African Rehabilitation Institute held a regional conference with disability NGOs to promote the Rules, followed by a regional workshop for delegates from six African countries, to develop a common approach to the involvement of disabled people's organisations in developing an implementation programme.

5      *Disability Awareness in Action 66*, 1998, 9.

6      *Disability Awareness in Action 64*, 1998, 7.

7      *Disability Awareness in Action 61*, 1998, 3.

8      Ugandan Constitution: Social and Economic Objective XVII.

9      Ugandan Constitution: Protection and Promotion of Fundamental and Other Human Rights and Freedoms: Chapter Four, para.35(1).

10      *Ibid*, para.35(2).

11      *Disability Awareness in Action 64*, 1998, 7.

12      For a very recent account of some of the developments in Australia see Jones and Marks 1999, and Jones and Marks 2000.

13      This quotation in *AAD Outlook* was reported in *Disability Awareness in Action, 58*, 1998, 3. For a detailed assessment of the first five years by Ms Hastings herself, see *Foundations: Reflections on the First Five Years of the DDA in Australia, December 1997*, available on the website www.hreoc.gov.ac/disability-rights

14      Disability Discrimination Act 1992, No. 135, s.67(1)

15      DDA s.5(1)

16      DDA s.6

17      DDA Part 2, Division 1

18      DDA s.22

19      DDA s.23

20      DDA s.24

21      DDA s.25

22      DDA ss.27–8

23      The Charter is the supreme law of Canada, and any statute that is inconsistent with it is invalid. Constitution Act 1982, s.52 *Law Society for Upper Canada v Skapinker*, 1984, 9 DLR (4th) 161.

24      Charter s.15(2)

25      Charter s.32. See also *Retail, Wholesale and Department Store Union v Dolphin Delivery Ltd* (1986) 33 DLR (4th) 174. For a critique of this narrow range of the Charter see Petter 1989.

26      R.S. 1985, c.H–6

27    *Disability Awareness in Action 58*, 1998, 9.

28    Government of Canada (1999) p.5.

29    Website: www.hrcd-drhc.gc.ca

30    Both this and the following statement from Deng Pufang were recorded in the official government newspaper, the China Daily, and quoted in *Disability Awareness in Action 68*, 1998, 1.

31    Amendments to Articles 187 and 416 Penal Code. Law No. 90.602 12 July 1990. See *Journal Officiel de la Republique Française*, 13 July 1990 at 8272.

32    Law No. 87.517 10 July 1987

33    LG Mannheim: NJW 1982, 1335. *Acceptance by a kindergarten of a child suffering from epilepsy.*

34    In a later case based upon the Schools Act of Lower Saxony, the courts upheld the law which gave children who needed special support because of a disability a right to remain in communal schooling (rather than a 'special school') unless this need could not be satisfied in the communal schools or where the circumstances did not allow it. The court approved the constitutionality of this Act, but said that a heavier burden rested on the party who sought to establish that an exception applied. *Decision of the 1st Senate of the Federal Constitutional Court, 30 July 1996*, cited in *Das Grundgesetz*, Kommentar, Munich: C.H. Becksche Verlagsbuchhandlung.

35    Basic Law, Article 3, Para. 3. Although disability must not be a basis for inequality of treatment, discrimination between disabled persons may, however, be permissible. Although disability is not defined, it should in principle include the mentally as well as the physically disabled. The Federal Constitutional Court described disabled people as those who suffer from an impairment of function which is not merely transitory and which is based on an irregular physical, mental or psychological condition (*BVerfGE 57*, 153, 160). It would seem therefore that the chronically ill are covered by the definition.

36    The social state principle recognises the fundamental importance of human dignity as the guiding concept for all state action, together with an associated duty on the part of the state to ensure conditions enabling each individual to lead his or her life.

37    *BVerfGE 57*, 139, 159

38    218a para. 2 StGB

39    Information provided to *Disability Awareness in Action 59*, 1998, 7.

40    For more detailed information consult the website www.eoc.org.hk

41    Quoted in *Disability Awareness in Action 33*, 1995, 2.

42    *Disability Awareness in Action 28*, 1995, 8–9

43    See *Disability Awareness in Action 28*, 1995, 8–9 for a short summary of some of the main concerns expressed in the submissions.

44    For more information, contact the Commission on the Status of People with Disabilities, Department of Equality and Law Reform, 43–49 Mespil Road, Dublin, 4, Ireland.

45    This came into effect on 18 October 1999. I am grateful to Anne Maria Kennedy for supplying much of the information contained in this section.

46    Law 104, 5 February 1992: *Legge Quadro Per l'Assistenza, l'Integratione Sociale e I diritti delle Persone Handicappate* (Legal framework for the assistance, social integration and rights of handicapped persons); Law 68, 12 March 1999: *Norme per il Diritto al Lavoro dei Disabili* (Rules for the right to work of disabled persons).

47    This was a classic example of Bickenbach's fourth model of state approaches to disability human rights; see above, p.81.

48    *Disability Awareness in Action 61*, 1998, 3.

49    Human Rights Amendment Act 1999. For further information consult the website www.hrc.co.nz

50   *Able Update 9 (1)* 1999 7–8. A new left-leaning government in New Zealand appears to be more in sympathy with the concerns of disability rights groups than its predecessor.

51   Website: www.dpa.org.nz

52   For futher information please contact Dr. Ricardo Zevallo, Commissioner from the Office of the Ombudsman in Peru. Tel: (511) 4264626 or email rzevallos@ombudsman.gob.pe

53   Republic Act No. 7277 24 March 1992.

54   A copy of the Plan of Action, which is being monitored by the Norwegian Ministry of Health and Social Services, can be obtained from the Publications Division, PO Box 8169, Dept 0032, Oslo 1, Norway.

55   *Disability Awareness in Action 60*, 1998, 7.

56   Note that in 1999 Hampshire County Council in the UK became the first local government in the world specifically to adopt the UN Standard Rules as part of its overall planning policy.

57   *Disability Awareness in Action 72*, 1999, 6–7. For more information on the situation in Sweden contact paul.lappalainen@stockholm.mail.telia.com

58   A great deal has been written both in this country and elsewhere about the history, impact and philosophy of this legislation. A good overview which both analyses the Act and also looks at it from a British perspective is Doyle 1993. For a full and comprehensive study of the ADA see Gostin and Beyer 1993. For an assessment of the constitutional authority for such legislation see Mikochik 1991. The best source for updated information on US Disability Law is the *Physical and Mental Disability Law Reporter*, which is an ABA periodical publication.

59   85 F.3d 187 (5th Cir. 1996)

60   83 F.3d 723 (5th Cir. 1995)

60[a]   *Sutton v. United Airlines Inc.*, 119 S.Ct 2139 (1999).

61   Quinn 1993. For a detailed assessment of the philosophy of the sections of the ADA that deal with employment rights for disabled people see: Davenport 1992; Kemp and Bell 1991; Mayerson 1991; Powell 1991.

62   42 USC p. 12111 (9) For detailed commentary on these provisions see Weirich 1991.

63   See *Alexander v Choate*, 469 U.S. 287.

64   This example is taken from the *EEOC Interpretive Guidance to the ADA* 29 CFR 1630.2(p), App. at 414.

65   29 CFR para. 1630

66   28 CFR 35.130 (b) (7)

67   28 CFR 35.150 (a)

68   28 CFR 35.151 (b)

69   28 CFR 35.130 (a) (2)

70   28 CFR 130 (a) (3)

71   28 CFR 35. 151 (b)

72   These are defined as those which after public consultation are identified by the network concerned, taking account of a number of factors including the particular importance of end stations, stations serving major activity centres, major interchange stations, and stations where passenger boardings exceed the average by more than 15 per cent: 49 CFR 37,.47–51.

73   See generally on this issue Strauss and Richardson 1991.

# CHAPTER FIVE

# The Legal Regulation of the Powers and Duties of Local Authorities with regard to Disabled People

*Belinda Schwehr*

The contribution of legal analysis and case law to social care for disabled people is a controversial topic. It was fashionable in academic circles in the 1980s for criticism to focus on the peripheral nature of judicial reviews, which were not only infrequent but also largely limited to establishing a narrow point of law on special facts. Once, however, the legislation from several different eras was overlaid by the 1990 National Health Service and Community Care Act (NHSCCA) and 'care management' became the order of the day, the stage was set for a host of fundamental questions to be litigated in time-honoured adversarial style. The determination of a hard-core group of lawyers to exploit the inherent ambiguity of much discretionary wording in the overlapping statutory provisions has led to better liaison between professionals and pressure groups and equipped clients and advice agencies to change the non-legalistic culture which had pervaded the 1980s. This sea change has radical implications for the assessment process as it affects different client groups and the culture of negotiation of care plans and budget management. It also affects the scope for professionalism among social services staff. This chapter will explore the influence of this flood of legal proceedings on social care for people with disabilities, in particular as it relates to budget management and adult protection. It will also look at the Human Rights Act 1998, in an attempt to predict its likely impact on social services.

## ESTABLISHING ELIGIBILITY FOR SERVICE

Several important cases have explored the extent to which a local authority's resources or lack of them may be taken into account when it is called upon to exercise certain service-related functions imposed upon it by law. All these cases have turned upon whether the functions in question are 'duties' or 'powers'. The line between these two functions is neither well-defined nor easily predicted. In the key 1997 case of *R. v Gloucestershire CC ex p. Barry*,[1] the House of Lords finally determined that resources (and conversely lack of resources) are legally relevant to the assessment of the needs of disabled persons.

This case established that:

1. 'needs' must be identified against eligibility criteria set with regard to the authority's budget;

2. the duty to make arrangements for services only arises when the authority is satisfied that its making the arrangements is 'necessary' to meet the identified need;

3. criteria for 'satisfaction' of that necessity may be altered, depending on the resources available;

4. once the duty to make arrangements has arisen, a lack of resources is irrelevant to performance of the duty.

The worst effect of this litigation has been the setting by local authorities of eligibility criteria so high that money is only earmarked for those users at most severe risk of harm. Preventative services have been largely abandoned, and the government has had to offer financial incentives and new money for preventative projects. On a more positive note, however, eligibility criteria are now a legitimate tool for rationing finite resources, and provide a means, in theory, to treat with reasonable consistency everyone within an authority's boundaries, which was by no means a certainty before the *Gloucestershire* case. Authorities are now setting eligibility criteria in Local Community Care Plans with greater care, and on the basis of fuller research and consultation. 'Unmet need' can now be openly acknowledged as existing in fact, as it is unlawful to fail to meet that need in only one situation; namely, where need has been acknowledged, and the authority has agreed to provide something to meet that need, but has then run out of money. As a matter of law, unmet need outside the authority's eligibility criteria can now lawfully exist. If this clarification encourages recording of actual unmet need, without fear of inviting legal action via judicial review, then the planning process will eventually benefit.

Many campaigning groups have criticised the decision in the *Gloucestershire* case, arguing that as there could never be a set of eligibility criteria that were so extreme as to deserve the label 'unreasonable,'[2] 'unreasonableness' as a deterrent to authorities over-tightening their criteria is of little value. And it is true that there has been no decided case in which eligibility criteria have been quashed on this ground, although there is one case[3] where an authority's own application of its criteria to an individual was quashed as 'plainly wrong'. This does suggest that arbitrary refusal to acknowledge that someone meets the test the authority has itself set may be a fruitful source of legal challenge in the future.

'Unreasonableness' has tended to be the basis for challenges to assessment outcomes, rather than to eligibility criteria. In *Haringey (No.1)* (1997)[4] Mr Norton's care package had been cut upon reassessment from 24 hour care to five hours a day. He challenged this cut, as it seemed like a blatant case of 'unreasonableness'. There was however evidence that his original care package had been unnecessarily generous, having been set at a time when there was no budgetary crisis and before the relative nature of the word 'necessary'[5] had been appreciated. The care manager had committed the care provision in the knowledge that a carer was willing to move in and provide 24 hour care for very little money; so the assessor's identification of need had been understandably inexact. Against that background, the Court reluctantly held that this was not a case in which the proposed changes could possibly be described as plainly 'unreasonable'. But the Court did not stop there; it looked at the care manager's thought process and held that it was unlawful for the authority to tell managers they were obliged to assess 'personal care needs', but not bound to assess 'social' or 'exceptional' needs.[6] Excluding these whole areas of need was a mistake of law, because the list of potential services set out in the legislation[7] provides an overall indication of areas of need which the statute requires to be considered, even if the need does not then meet the 'necessity for intervention' test. This mistake in approach to assessment also explains why it was not automatically unreasonable for the care manager to conclude that five hours of care a day was sufficient, as the five hours were intended for 'personal care needs' only.

It is interesting to note that authorities are still wary of removing services from those who previously qualified, probably on the basis that people are much more likely to complain or litigate in such circumstances. But having different versions of criteria and applying them only to new users itself sets up a different kind of inequity which may lead to political, if not legal challenge – for example, where neighbours with similar needs receive different care packages, simply because one of them deteriorated earlier at a time when more money was available. In my experience, most authorities have 'priority groupings' posing as eligibility criteria, without any clear trigger for recognising when intervention is 'necessary'. Alternatively they adopt a matrix with a clear point at which it is indicated they will see their intervention as 'necessary.' The care planning stage is then determined by the availability of budget or staff hours at that precise moment rather than by the professional's assessment of what could feasibly meet need. Neither of these approaches is supported by careful analysis of the *Gloucestershire* case, for neither of the reasoned majority judgments in the Lords suggested that it is lawful to take the precise state of the budget into account at the moment of individual assessment. Rather they emphasised the need for eligibility criteria to be raised or lowered at committee level, taking resources into account if necessary, before any re-assessment of need may lawfully occur and affect the service package. The factual basis for the first instance decision in the case was that Mr Barry's services had been cut by Gloucestershire Social Services without any re-assessment, purely because funds were running out. Given that the first instance Court was prepared to hold such action unlawful, it did not need to focus on the relevance of resources at any particular stage of the assessment process. But since the first instance decision meant that the users would be re-assessed, with reference to a shortage of resources, they were allowed to appeal on this issue, despite having won the case overall. So the case was not about Mr Barry's individual assessment – it was about the process, and the setting of criteria.

The issue became more complex in the Court of Appeal, as some of the judges focused on resources at the stage of identifying need, others on the question of their relevance at the stage of deciding whether intervention was 'necessary'. The majority opinions in the House of Lords (the highest court in the United Kingdom hierarchy for matters of national law. The Lords can decide cases by a majority, as happened in this case (three to two)), dealt with the question of resources by reference to prior eligibility criteria for types of need and degrees of need, set according to the budget. It is not clear that tailoring eligibility or the actual contents of a care package to what is available on the day of an individual's assessment is authorised by the decision in *Gloucestershire*. The Lords focused on the distinct stages of identifying needs, and then making a provision decision (in the sense of deciding whether a care package is necessary), and regarded those two stages together as the assessment, which should both be done against published criteria. Lord Nicholls said that it was important to bear in mind that the relevant law contemplates three separate stages: the identification of need, the question of necessity for provision, and then the making of arrangements pursuant to the duty at the end of s.2 (see note 6). At that point, resources are no longer relevant. Overall, then, it is highly arguable that once a local authority's eligibility criteria have been published, they must be applied consistently unless changed formally and re-published. This would be also a fruitful line of argument to help pin down the meaning of Health Authorities' eligibility criteria (for example, for free NHS nursing care after hospital discharge), which are also applied with alarming flexibility.

The ongoing saga of Mr Norton and Haringey London Borough Council (LBC) raises a slightly different set of issues. Taken back to court a second time by Mr Norton,[8] Haringey LBC managed to increase Mr Norton's care package in terms of hours while keeping it under its cost-cap, which was the equivalent cost to the authority of providing residential or nursing care. The majority of authorities now seem to be doing this. Mr Norton again challenged the decision.

Haringey offered another £40 a week for the user's care plan just before trial, so although the judge discussed cost-capping in a neutral fashion, he was not obliged (and did not choose) to decide the case on the basis of the alleged illegality of referring to a resources-based policy at the point of formulating the response to the assessment. The additional £40 per week made it impossible for him to find that the provision decision was unreasonable (see *Wednesbury*, note 2). Local authorities still attempt to justify cost-capping of domiciliary care by reference to a different principle, established in the *Lancashire* case[9] – that it is lawful to adopt the cheaper of two alternative means of meeting need. There is no legal difficulty in the authority choosing residential care, after valid assessment and if it is appropriate in social work terms, and if account has been taken of the client's and carer's views, in order to meet need. The legal difficulty arises, however, when authorities are faced with a refusal to accept the offer and are tempted to defer to the client's (more costly) wishes for fear of liability or media attention. Despite it being lawful to regard the authority as discharged from a duty in the face of persistent and unequivocal refusal to accept a reasonable offer[10] authorities still prefer to negotiate with users to give them something, whilst at the same time claiming that it is legitimate to offer what is already known to be less than is feasibly required to meet their assessed needs. In law, this is a weak position. In *Gloucestershire*, McCowan LJ considered the resources question in relation to the question, whether it was necessary that the authority should step in and provide services. In the Court of Appeal and the House of Lords, the declarations allowing resources to be taken into account appear to have been limited to the question of whether services were necessary.

In light of the above, it is highly probable that it is unlawful to cap domiciliary packages to any particular level. What is reasonable is not the test of what is lawful in public law, and some statutory power must still be found to justify the expenditure of any public money. To cost-cap domiciliary care arguably downgrades the duty which a disabled person, who has successfully passed through the eligibility criteria, will already have triggered – the duty to make arrangements to meet the assessed need. It bypasses the professional evaluation of the care manager. Recent cases concerning education[11] and disabled facilities grants[12] indicate that the courts will not allow that to happen. The critical point is that the reduced cost domiciliary care package is not an adequate alternative to residential care; the only legitimate choice is between residential (or nursing) care and a home-based package that will actually be adequate to meet need. Neither the *Gloucestershire* case, nor the Government's guidance,[13] support the view that once the duty stage has been reached, shortage of resources is relevant.[14] On the contrary, counsel for the Secretary of State in the Court of Appeal conceded that resources would be irrelevant once the authority has decided that it is necessary to provide services in order to meet someone's need. Furthermore, McCowan LJ stated that once an authority is under the duty, 'resources do not come into it'.[15]

Swinton Thomas LJ in the Court of Appeal characterised the duty, once triggered, as a duty to meet the assessed needs of the individual. It was conceded in the Lords that there should be flexibility in the making of arrangements, provided always that the need is met. Lord Nicholls said that the duty gave rise to a right to have assessed needs met, so far as it is necessary for the authority to meet them.[16] Lord Clyde said a shortage of resources will not excuse failure in that regard and would not be relevant to the question of whether or not the duty should be performed. He thought that the criteria as to the severity of need required to trigger necessity could be matched against resources, but did not mention level or frequency of particular services.

However, in favour of cost-capping being legal, there are the following points: in *Gloucestershire*, Hirst LJ dealt with the question of resources in relation to both assessment and the arrangements required to meet them. There is nothing to suggest whether he was envisaging an actual discretion as to amount of service, despite the duty to meet need, or merely legitimating the choice of the cheaper of adequate alternatives to meet need. Lord Lloyd in the Lords assumed that resources can operate to impose a cash limit on what is provided.[17] Gloucestershire's own criteria had contained recommended levels of service for different degrees of disability and isolation, and were not criticised in that regard. However, Lord Lloyd believed that they had been set without regard to resources, and only with regard to civilised society's expectations of a decent quality of life for disabled persons as interpreted by the Committee, which is unlikely to be so, given that levels of service are easy to cost and work backwards from. Lord Nicholls specifically said 'a person's need for a particular type or level of service cannot be decided in a vacuum from which all considerations of cost have been expelled'.[18] He went on to envisage the care manager using criteria to decide at what level a person has a need for assistance, even after they had satisfied the necessity point for eligibility for a service package.[19] He emphasised that the extent to which quality of life would be improved 'by the provision of this or that service at this or that level' was part of the assessment of need and necessity.[20] Thus the legal question seems to turn upon the extent to which levels (not just types) of service provision may or may not lawfully appear as part of the criteria for identifying need or necessity. Lord Nicholls clearly envisaged that the criteria for the identification of need would themselves refer to levels of service response. Lord Clyde did not. Lord Hoffman managed to agree with both of them.

Logically, eligibility criteria can either be about incapacities in the ordinary business of life, which could actually be helped by a service within the scope of the legislation (such as help with meal preparation, washing, toileting, dressing and so forth), or they could be expressed in terms of 'a need for a hot meal once a day', 'a bath once a week', 'incontinence care twice a day' or 'assistance with dressing and undressing morning and night', all based on the Social Services Members' view of what civilised society requires. In the latter case, anyone meeting those criteria would automatically qualify for a specific service (because they would have triggered the deemed 'necessity' point) and the actual level or frequency of service response stage would already have been determined.

In fact this makes little sense in real life because it would prevent people who, for example, only needed help with, say, a bath a bit less than once a week, or people who were incontinent in the night only, even though they plainly needed help in the mornings, from ever qualifying. It makes much more sense, in social work terms, for the eligibility criteria for identifying 'need' to be expressed in terms of incapacities, and the necessity point set by reference to a scoring system involving a comparison of range and severity of needs (and risk), against degrees of dependency (taking into account existing human or financial resources that the user is willing and able to put towards meeting their own need). The expertise of the care manager would then be utilised in putting together a package of service which the client would be consulted about and which would actually meet those assessed needs which would otherwise go unmet. That way, the resources outflow is theoretically controlled by way of changes to the criteria, but not by way of pressuring the care managers to offer less than is feasibly required to meet eligible, acknowledged needs.

## LINKING RESOURCES TO ASSESSMENT

Attempts have been made to apply the principles developed in the *Gloucestershire* case to the duty of assessment. That duty is triggered whenever it appears to a local authority that someone for whom they may provide community care services may be in need of such services.[21] In *Bristol CC ex p. Penfold*,[22] a middle-aged single parent with relatively minor anxiety problems who wished to be able to live with her daughter had sought rehousing through the housing authority and had turned down offers of premises, such that any relevant housing function had been lawfully discharged. She then applied for a community care assessment, maintaining that she was entitled to be considered for accommodation under s.21 of the National Assistance Act (NAA) 1948 because she was in need of care and attention not otherwise available to her for some other circumstance than the normal range of situations regarded as triggering the s.21 duty (this function is the basis for virtually all local authority residential accommodation provision, and is geared mainly to the aged, ill or disabled, none of which Mrs Penfold appeared to be). The authority tried to contend that because its policies on 'need' for s.21[23] could not conceivably lead to a decision to provide such accommodation to her, there was no duty to assess her.

The Court held that the duty was triggered by the appearance of need for any service which could be provided, not one which was, as a matter of local policy and practice, actually likely to be provided. The judge also held that it was appropriate to regard the provision of bare housing, without other services, as a community care service within s.21 whenever it was a means of meeting care needs which would otherwise have to be met by some other sort of social services package (as opposed to the housing authority being liable where there is simply a 'purely' homeless person having a 'normal' housing need). The right to refuse assessment would only arise in a case where no reasonable authority could possibly think that the applicant appeared to be even possibly in need of any community care service which could legally be provided under any of the relevant legislation. Since the functions all have different triggers (some require ordinary residence, others do not), this is a challenge even for a community care lawyer. It is plain that a care manager cannot do it unassisted, much less an administrator without a social care or nursing background. Hence 'screening-out' policies are likely to attract legal challenge. The policy behind this decision is that 'unmeetable' need must be recorded if it is ever to be fed into the planning process; thus there is still a purpose to assessment, even if the outcome is negative, and regardless of how light a touch is thought appropriate in terms of investigation.

## RESOURCES AND RESIDENTIAL ACCOMMODATION

In the case of *R v Sefton MBC ex p. Help the Aged*,[24] the Court of Appeal clarified that authorities are not entitled, because of their own finances, to defer compliance with their duty to accommodate certain persons (including disabled persons)[25] pending the claimant's resources falling below a threshold set by the authority itself. The duty is to accommodate people who 'are in need of care and attention which is not otherwise available to them'. The Court partly applied the *Gloucestershire* approach, in the sense that it held that the authority may develop eligibility criteria for identifying 'need', subject to unreasonableness, based on its own resources. This does not allow for much room for manoeuvre, of course, because this client group is at high risk of harm if nothing is done for them. However, the case established that unless the authority concludes that the care thus identified as needed is 'otherwise available', the authority then owes an absolute duty under the legislation to provide the accommodation, regardless of its own resources, at least in cases where the client falls within the terms of Directions issued by the government.[26] Here, *Gloucestershire* was distinguished; no duty to arrange a service under the Chronically Sick and Disabled Persons Act (CSDPA) 1970 arises, even though a need is identified, until an authority decides it is 'necessary' to make arrangements to meet that need.

This decision obviously calls into question the legality of any budget-driven residential care waiting list. Liverpool County Council apparently settled a Mrs Winter's case regarding a waiting list in 1998 and later that year, some 18 authorities were identified by the *Sunday Times* (26 July 1998) as having waiting lists.

Nevertheless, the most common practices for managing budgets in this service area include the following.

### Probably unlawful

> One in, one out policies (death required before a place is freed);
>
> A limited quota of new placements per month, or a limited sum of money released from a budget for new placements per month.

These policies would appear to be unlawful because treating resources as relevant to when the duty is discharged is tantamount to regarding the duty as a discretion.

> Those who are in NHS beds awaiting discharge, although the set date has already passed, being made to wait, on the basis that they have 'care and attention' 'otherwise available'.

It is unlikely that any Court would regard the care and attention received as a bed-blocking trespasser, as amounting to the care and attention supposedly provided under s.21 NAA.

> Encouraging people to stay in hospital awaiting a place in the home of their choice.

This is likely to be unlawful because there is no right to choose a place in a particular home if it is not currently available.[27]

### Probably lawful

> Those whose carers are agreeable to carrying on for a bit longer being made to wait, perhaps with a little more help at home, although the client's assessment has, for all other purposes, been completed.

This would seem to be lawful, but inviting a crisis, since carers can lawfully 'down tools' if they do it on reasonable notice.

> Informal agreement negotiated with hospital Trusts not to set discharge dates until Social Services resources become available.

Such agreements, based more often on ignorance (by Trusts) of social services legal developments, than on goodwill, avoid a waiting list even arising, since such patients (apparently at least) still have medical needs, which must logically trump social care needs.

In my view, a waiting list caused or exacerbated by financial rationing is clearly incompatible with the outcome of *Sefton* (see note 24), identifying, as it did, the notion of a duty. That is not to say that any kind of waiting list would have to be unlawful: there might be no place available in any given area within an appropriate distance of the user's community and visitors; or no suitably specialist provision available for a particular client. In those circumstances it would be unlikely that a Court would hold an authority to be in breach of the general public law duty to implement any decision within a reasonable time. Need would have to be met in the meantime, however, if the client counted as 'disabled', because of the CSDPA.

In the recent case of *Wigan MBC ex p. Tammadge*[28] the Court confirmed that resources are irrelevant to the implementation of the duty to accommodate once an assessment has been completed. However, the case does not formally determine the waiting list question because the real issue in the case was whether or not an assessment had, in legal terms, actually been finally completed, not the authority's stance after that point.

## SUMMARY ON LEGALITY OF RATIONING RESOURCES

The trend away from a lack of resources being relevant to the (failure to) discharge statutory functions in community care has several implications.

Decision-makers need to know under which statute and at which stage of the process the particular decision is being made, because the case law always focuses on the particular wording of the statute to determine whether there is a duty or a discretion. Decades of non-legalistic thinking in social work need to be reconsidered, because it is as illegal to give services to someone who does not qualify as it is to deny them to someone who does. Far from being stigmatising, identification as 'disabled' ensures entitlement to a service once criteria have been met regardless of a shortage of resources (at least, pending re-assessment against tighter criteria).

Using vigorous budget-keeping as the prime indicator of managerial skill is shortsighted: the starting point for lawful practice should be managerial commitment to guaranteeing that statutory duties are funded, even if that means virement of money across teams, localities, service sectors, client groups and even directorates within an authority. In the *Tandy* case (see note 11), the Lords made this point clear – the duty is a corporate one, imposed on the authority, and this means that it is not legally possible to say 'the money has run out' until there are no discretionary projects still receiving funding from an authority.

## PROTECTING VULNERABLE ADULTS

The terms 'impairment', 'handicap', 'disorder' and 'disability'[29] appear in statutory provisions, and people adjudged to fit within these descriptions are capable, in law, of qualifying for services if they also meet the particular authority's eligibility criteria. 'Mental incapacity', as such, does not trigger entitlement to any particular service under statute. Incapacity, whether through learning difficulties, brain injury or dementia, does, however, have significance for day-to-day management of assessment. In *North Yorkshire CC ex. p. Hargreaves*,[30] a care manager was criticised for allowing herself to be persuaded (wrongly) by a brother taking a caring role, that his sister, the client, could not contribute to the assessment, which was therefore quashed. Thus, every day, care managers will be obliged to take pragmatic decisions about the capacity of their clients regarding daily living decisions, in order to determine how far to try to obtain the client's own views.

Furthermore, if consent from an individual client cannot be obtained, then to proceed with a move to residential care or arranging home care services might constitute trespasses against the completely incapacitated client. Relatives, parents and next of kin currently have no legal right to make decisions for the adult client, and so the local authority's acting upon such 'decisions' from them also risks legal challenge. Relying on the consent of a principal carer may be enough for all practical purposes, and acceptable in ethical terms when the carer is doing a good job (because of what the Courts have said about the doctrine of necessity and the general law of negligence) and is in agreement with the authority, but it surely cannot be regarded as good enough if abuse or even a conflict of financial interest is perceived to exist between client and carer.

Different types of decision making call for differing degrees of mental capacity. For example, consent to medical treatment or managing one's finances may require more capacity than signing a valid tenancy agreement; and that last decision could require more capacity than is necessary for a decision whether to move to residential care or which, out of two places, to live in. Decisions as to with whom to spend time, of course, may be regarded by some as straightforward, and by others as extremely sensitive and complicated.[31] Whilst the statutory framework lays down procedures governing the taking over of financial management, it says nothing comprehensive about welfare-related decision-making power.

## GUARDIANSHIP

Powers of guardianship are currently given by the Mental Health Act 1983 (MHA), ss.7–10. The local Social Services Authority may accept an application for guardianship and confer on the Authority or persons specified in the application, to the exclusion of any other person, by way of the powers contained in s.8:

(a) the power to require the patient to reside at a place specified by the Authority or person named as guardian;

(b) the power to require the patient to attend places at times so specified for the purpose of medical treatment, occupation, education or training;

(c) the power to require access to the patient to be given, at any place where the patient is residing, to any registered medical practitioner, approved social worker or other person so specified.

According to the last and current Codes of Practice[32] guardianship enables the establishment of an authoritative framework for working with a patient with a minimum of constraint to achieve as independent a life as possible within the community. Where it is used it must surely be part of the patient's overall care and treatment plan – that is, used constructively in tandem with the local authority's powers to assess the need for community care services.[33] A patient under guardianship is not liable to be detained at all, and thus the provisions of MHA 1983 s.56(1) regarding deemed consent to medical treatment do not apply, regardless of the scope of the definition of the treatment. Close physical restriction would also be outside the framework, given the more draconian express powers which exist under other provisions.

A guardianship application may only be made in respect of a client on the grounds that they are suffering from a limited type of mental disorder, being mental illness, severe mental impairment or psychopathic disorder, and their mental disorder is believed by professionals to be of the nature or degree which warrants their reception into guardianship, and it is necessary in the interests of the welfare of the patient or for the protection of other persons that the person should be so received. At its most constructive, all factors which might affect the well-being of the patient might be covered by the phrase 'interests of the welfare of the patient', including their need to be protected from exploitation (subject to case law discussed below). This wording is surely wide enough to encompass the need to prevent the person's welfare being prejudiced at some time in the future. In these circumstances the recommending doctors would need to be satisfied that there is a real risk of such an eventuality occurring, for example an attempt by a relative to remove a mentally incompetent resident from a care setting to accommodation where his or her welfare may be seriously prejudiced. A guardianship application must be founded on the written recommendations in the prescribed form of two registered medical practitioners. A patient's nearest relative can object and defeat an application. A recent case[34] established that 'seriously irresponsible conduct' (the test of severe mental impairment) means more than merely being incapable of attaining normal standards of self-care if left to oneself. This judgment does make it harder to protect people with moderate, rather than severe learning impairment, through guardianship. It meant, in that case, that the 'nearest relative's' objection was not unreasonable, so his displacement and the guardianship were all inappropriate.

There is no requirement that the patient consent to the guardianship. The last Code of Practice implied that co-operation of the prospective patient was required, but that was always logically inconsistent with guardianship having to be thought of as both warranted and necessary (for the welfare of the patient) in the first place (and only appropriate, if 'compulsory powers' were needed). Perhaps tellingly, the paragraph relating to recognition of the authority of the guardian has now been changed. It reads: 'Key elements of the plan should include: *depending on the patient's level of 'capacity'*, his or her recognition of the 'authority' of, and willingness to work 'with', the guardian' [emphasis added by author].[34a]

## THE EXTENT OF THE POWER

Whilst providing the guardian with a power to 'return' the patient, it is correct to state that the MHA gives no specific power to enable a person to take and convey a patient under guardianship to a specified place from which they have not absconded (although s.25A (supervised discharge) does give such a power). The definition of 'absent without leave'[35] refers to returning the person, and it could be argued that that word and use of the verb ('absents' himself) imply that the person must already have been at the place at which he is required to reside. Thus, the traditional approach holds that it would be a trespass to the person (and it used to say in the Code that guardianship should therefore not be used) physically to take an unwilling person from their home into residential care. That statement was probably limited to those patients not lacking capacity regarding that particular issue, as it was also said (somewhat inconsistently) that it could be appropriately used as 'a means of providing a framework for deciding the care of a person assessed as needing residential care but lacking the mental capacity to decide whether or not to enter such care'.[36]

It is interesting to note that the amendments to the Code of Practice omit one of the previous paragraphs stating that guardianship should not be used solely for the purpose of transferring an unwilling person into care, whilst leaving in the paragraph which states that the s.8 power (see above, pp.119–120) does not authorise the removal of a patient against his or her will. But in the light of the decision in the case of *L v Bournewood MH Trust*,[37] passive acquiescence does not amount to consent, so if the traditional analysis is correct, it would still be a trespass to move someone who was merely acquiescent.

It is likely, however, that the judiciary would not, if it were ever tested in the Courts, limit the construction of the Act so as to defeat guardianship's benign use in this way. If the person has no other appropriate means of support, a decision for a move to residential care without any means of implementing it will not be worth taking from the viewpoint of either the patient, the guardian or society. Since guardianship is only available in certain cases of mental illness or impairment where it is considered to be necessary and appropriate, it must generally, in practice, depend upon a judgement as to the person's capacity to look after him or herself (short of their needing to be formally detained). If that is so, then it surely must implicitly confer a general power to make welfare-related decisions and implement them? The recent case of *R v Kent CC ex p. Marston*[38] suggested that guardianship confers implied power on the guardian to act to promote the welfare of individuals (the man in this case happened, clearly, to lack capacity). This must cover physically removing them without their or their carer's consent (for example, from situations of suspected abuse) to the place where the guardian requires them to reside. At the very least, there is no decided case precluding the argument that s.7, which contains the statutory pre-conditions for amenability to the regime of guardianship, implicitly allows the guardian so to act, where to do so is in the best interests of the patient.

It was even said in *Marston* that the s.8 express powers can override the 'perceived wishes' of the patient. Yet a qualification of the best interests doctrine for guardians is the fact that the court said that the implied duty to act for the welfare of the individual would not allow 'totalitarian' conduct by the authority. Whether forcing someone into residential accommodation against their capacitated wishes would amount to totalitarianism might depend on whether the Courts thought that European human rights principles (see below, p.127) allow interference with people's private lives for legitimate social aims even when the person still enjoys some capacity, although not full capacity. It also remains to be tested whether the guardianship power can be used to preclude a patient from seeing someone with whom the patient has an existing relationship without breaching human rights to respect for private or family life.

Subject to this area of uncertainty, if guardianship were given some real meaning in the way suggested in this chapter, the 'authoritative framework' could come to be seen as an essential prerequisite to lawful involvement of care managers in the lives of incapacitated adults, and as a current adult protection power, rather than as a rarely-used and time-consuming function of little utility.

## DECLARATORY RELIEF

It is now possible for local authorities to be awarded declaratory relief (used to clarify the legal rights of the parties) by the Courts, in any dispute about daily living arrangements for an incapacitated client, on the precedent of *Re S*,[39] a case involving a rich Norwegian who suffered a deep incapacitating stroke while in this country. His co-habitee (mistress) arranged to hospitalise him privately (and paid for the treatment through a power of attorney she had been given previously), and she visited daily. Without her knowledge, his adult son arrived in England and obtained his father's discharge from the consultant. As the son was preparing to fly his father back to Norway, the co-habitee obtained an interim injunction preventing the patient's removal. The Court was later asked by the man's wife what legal rights the co-habitee had at stake, to justify declaratory relief, but the co-habitee asked the same question of the wife. The Court agreed that the only legal rights at stake were the man's – which were to be cared for as he would have chosen. Since he could not express his wishes, the Court would hear evidence and make the decision in his best interests.

This jurisdiction, an extension of the means used to decide difficult life and death decisions in medical treatment cases,[40] may be of use where guardianship is not obtainable because of local psychiatric reluctance to categorise people with learning disabilities, or dementia sufferers, as sufficiently mentally impaired or mentally ill to get through the statutory gateway. However, in the case of *Cambridgeshire CC v R*,[41] the judge was of the opinion that declaratory relief was not available to the local authority as the protector of the individual when moderate learning disability would, in her view, have justified guardianship and enabled the authority (either through the s.8 powers or by arrangement with the proprietor of the home where the patient was residing) to prevent undesirable persons from entering the home. However, since this case, local authorities have regularly sought declaratory relief in the Family Division, according to counsel with whom the author has discussed the issue, notwithstanding their absence from the law reports because of their sensitive and confidential nature. It should be noted that without evidence of incapacity, no applicant would be entitled to declaratory relief under this jurisdiction. The very recent Court of Appeal decision in *Re F* (see note 33) established that the Court could make a declaration justifying restraint or even detention of a person, in their own best interests, using this jurisdiction, at the suit of a local authority.

## IS THE PERSON INCAPACITATED?

Before declaratory relief is available, it must first be established that the person lacks capacity to understand the nature, purpose and effects of the particular proposal. Capacity to consent involves comprehending and retaining the relevant information, believing it and weighing it in the balance to arrive at a choice. Given the scope for abuse, and since a person is to be considered competent in the absence of evidence to the contrary, the disputants' agreement that the person is incapacitated should not be sufficient to give the Court jurisdiction, but I believe that it has been accepted as such, on more than one occasion. Its weakness is that it can only be used to decide 'single issue' disputes, not ongoing matters of care and 'control'.

## CARERS AND 'BEST INTERESTS'

The Government's paper 'Who Decides?'[42] and the Law Commission's 1995 paper on Mental Incapacity[43] both proceeded on the footing that there was no common law 'best interests' power for carers or relatives. Otherwise there would have been no need for the proposed 'continuing power of attorney' which would have given attorneys power to make welfare-related decisions, notwithstanding the supervening incapacity of the donor of the power. Indeed, the *Bournewood* decision does not clarify the extent to which relatives or carers can rely on the doctrine of necessity to justify their day-to-day handling of an incapacitated person. However, the above developments in the declaratory relief jurisdiction and related fields have arguably led to the 'discovery' of that common law power at least for full time carers.

The common law doctrine of necessity provides a defence to conduct which is tortious, such as medical intervention without the consent of the patient. If the situation allows, the High Court is an impartial tribunal which can give reassurance in advance by way of declaratory relief that the best interests of the person require the intervention. In *Re F*[44] in 1989, the Lords made it clear that the Court cannot give consent in place of the person, but merely clarifies whether certain actions are or were in his or her best interests, and hence lawful. In *Re F*, Lords Brandon and Bridge discussed how the doctrine of necessity can justify surgery, without the consent of the patient, by medical professionals. Lord Griffiths included 'people charged with the care of the mentally incompetent' in the categories of persons who can rely on the doctrine. Lord Goff held that justifiable 'treatment' can extend to every part of a person's caring for another's welfare. This approach was *obiter* in relation to non-professional, non-medical intervention. Lord Jauncey agreed with both Lords Brandon and Goff, but appeared only to be contemplating medical treatment.

In *Re C*,[45] the Court accepted that arranging an incapacitated person's association with someone else could be in their best interests. The Court treated Lord Goff's speech in *Re F* as creating a jurisdiction governing the management of adults with limited mental capacity, including everything done by a carer referable to the preservation of life, health or well-being, or the prevention of deterioration in physical or mental health. In *Re S* (see note 39), it is important to note that neither disputant was currently caring for the incapacitated stroke victim, but both had views about what was best for him. The Court stressed that neither mistress, wife nor son had any legal right or duty to care for the future welfare of the patient, and that it was the legal right of the patient to the exclusion of all others to choose where he lived, and the nature and extent of his medical and other care, which gave the Court its jurisdiction. It is arguable that if the mistress had been a full-time carer, she would have had a higher right than the wife, but still subject to the court's regulation. In a recent case, *Re D-R*,[46] a father wanted to see his severely impaired adult daughter after a break in contact of over two years. This was denied by the Court, on 'best interests' principles. In the most recent case (*Re F*) questions of permitting supervised access only were regarded as legitimate for the Court to decide. This approach is at least consistent with the principle that questions of association are part of the 'treatment' of incapacitated persons.

It is therefore suggested that the case law supports the proposition that since existing carers, while they undertake the caring role, can rely on necessity as a doctrine which operates to make their day-to-day choices presumptively lawful, at least until challenged as negligent or 'not in the best interests' of the person. It is as if the standard of care applicable to the duty owed to incapacitated adults is not merely to avoid harm, but to avoid anything not in their best interests. Clearly, by analogy with the medical cases, it does not, however, give carers a power to consent on behalf of the individual to otherwise tortious action, so it does not solve the apparent want of legal authority for the authority's intervening to move a person to residential care.

## THE LOCAL AUTHORITY AND 'BEST INTERESTS'

So can a local authority which is proposing to care or already caring for a client also rely on necessity to protect its actions from claims of trespass by disgruntled relatives, for instance? Given the lack of clarity in the law, local authorities regularly fail to intervene in situations where a relative or carer purports to block a care manager's suggestions as to an appropriate service response. Furthermore, an incapacitated person may have no one willing to participate in care decisions at all, yet still be incapable of consenting in law to intervention which amounts to a trespass.

It is possible that the doctrine of necessity (albeit translated into an implied statutory power spelled out of the local authority's functions of assessment and provision for people's care) legitimates intervention for acquiescent clients lacking capacity. It is suggested that the Courts might be pragmatic enough to hold that it does, so transportation of persons to residential care would become lawful, if in the best interests of the person, even without guardianship, and would overcome an enormous area of concern to care managers. At the very least, it is likely that the Courts would grant standing to an authority seeking clarification by way of declaratory relief in such circumstances, so long as the proposed client was made a party to the proceedings, as well as the carer unwilling to give up the primary decision-making role.

Where the individual is apparently strongly opposed to the authority's proposal, the first question must be: does the person lack capacity to decide the particular issue in question? If not, then it would be a potential breach of human rights to force a physical interference on their bodies (for example, by transporting them) or their homes (for example, by enabling service providers to gain access). The only powers available to social services in such cases are those under s.47 of the National Assistance Act 1948, enabling actual removal and detention of persons who are not necessarily incapacitated but who are presenting a health risk by the way they are living; and the power under s.135 of the Mental Health Act 1983 to remove someone believed to be mentally disordered from their home for assessment, with the help of a police constable under a magistrate's court warrant. It is noteworthy that one of the exceptions to Article 5 of the European Convention on Human Rights ('the right to liberty') is based on control of the spread of infectious diseases. Thus the s.47 power might well survive scrutiny under the Human Rights Act 1998. Interference with privacy and home life may also be justified by reference to legitimate social aims and the protection of health, or the rights and freedoms of others, under ECHR Article 8.

If an Authority is already undertaking a caring role in relation to an incapacitated person, it is suggested that it will have a higher right to make decisions based on best interests than a relative who suddenly appears on the scene. It will at least be in no worse position, in terms of the legal framework, than if there were no one else involved in the situation at all. If neither an authority nor an existing carer has been involved prior to the need to take technically tortious action arising, but someone other than a bystander (for example, a relative) is now on the scene and disagreeing with the proposals, then declaratory relief is appropriate, in my view, and both sides will have standing. The relative is not elevated above any other interested party in relation to welfare decisions, even if they hold appointeeship or power of attorney or are the person's receiver: those jurisdictions are based on management of property and financial affairs and limited thereto.

Where there is a someone already involved substantially in caring for an incapacitated person who blocks the authority's proposal, but on objectively reasonable grounds, Lord Goff might well say that the individual has a higher right to make decisions, as the current de facto carer, but only until challenged by way of declaratory relief proceedings. It is likely that the authority would have standing if it wanted to arrange services in substitution for, or in addition to, what the person was getting from the current carer.

Where there is a carer or a third party linked in some way with the incapacitated person who is suspected of abusing the person (physically, sexually, emotionally or financially) then this analysis would suggest that it is essential for the authority to apply for declaratory relief quickly, for an isolated issue, or consider guardianship for an ongoing and flexible statutory power to intervene. Sedley LJ confirmed in *ReF* that this may be a positive duty imposed on the Courts and local authorities by the advent of human rights principles.

## CONCLUSIONS ON LAW AND THE PROTECTION OF VULNERABLE ADULTS

This analysis shows that it is essential for medical professionals and social services staff to document the reasons for believing that incapacity as to any particular question has arisen. Local authorities must appreciate that they have the power to seek declaratory relief, without having to take out guardianship proceedings. It is one thing for the Court to give doctors a right to intervene regarding matters within their own sphere of competence; but quite another to accord de facto carers a common law presumptive right to take decisions about day-to-day welfare if safeguards are not laid down by statute, or if no independent agency is willing to police those decisions.

Finally, this chapter looks at the likely impact of the incorporation of the European Convention on Human Rights (ECHR) into the law of the UK from October 2000.

## THE HUMAN RIGHTS ACT 1998

Section 1 of the Human Rights Act 1998 sets out the particular rights and freedoms (the 'Convention rights') to which the Act gives further effect, in particular Articles 2–12 and 14 of the European Convention on Human Rights and Articles 1–3 of the First Protocol.

Section 3(1) provides that 'so far as it is possible to do so, primary legislation and secondary legislation must be read and given effect in a way which is compatible with Convention rights'. This section probably enables Courts to go beyond the current practice of only construing genuinely ambiguous provisions in accordance with the ECHR, because the provision is analogous to the Courts' approach to EU Directives (where they will actually strain to construe UK legislation consistently with EU law) and also because the provision is stronger than the wording in the 1993 New Zealand human rights instrument, under which innovative interpretation is already the norm.

Section 6 makes it 'unlawful for a public authority to act in a way which is incompatible with one or more of the Convention rights'.

However, the section does not apply where the incompatible conduct is clearly required by primary legislation or by secondary legislation made under incompatible legislation.[47] In such a case, the High Court may only issue a declaration of incompatibility between UK law and the Act. Discretionary decisions of administrative bodies will have to be assessed in accordance with the principles of proportionality and non-discrimination in order to ascertain whether there has been a breach of any Convention right made part of UK law. This is because the Act requires all Courts and Tribunals to take account of European Commission and Court jurisprudence, and these principles are fundamental to the approach there.

Claims of unlawful action via judicial review proceedings, or reliance on Convention rights in other legal proceedings, are restricted to 'victims' – a concept from ECHR law which has been directly imported into the domestic regime.[48] In ECHR terms, a victim is 'any person, non-governmental organisation or group of individuals *directly affected* by the act in question'.

Associated case law reveals that the concept of being 'directly affected' covers people who are closely and personally related to those who are directly affected, and also people who are potentially affected by a proposed action.

## HOW CAN CLAIMS BE MADE?

The Act enables private individuals and other entities qualifying as 'victims' to argue Convention points either:

> as applicants for judicial review, against a public body, or as 'a person affected' by somebody else's challenge where the challenge involves a Convention right, either on its own, or together with the other traditional grounds for judicial review;

> as applicants in specially constituted proceedings against bodies not amenable to judicial review, or as appellants in any ordinary civil or criminal case, where the court or tribunal at first instance is said itself to have violated a Convention right (for example, Article 6 – fair trial), or the prosecution was based on investigation or procedure contrary to a Convention right;

> as parties in domestic Courts where EU law is being considered, where the parties claim that the relevant EU law would be interpreted by the European Court of Justice (and should be by the domestic Court) in line with fundamental obligations found in the Convention;

> as 'defendants' or 'respondents' to any civil or criminal proceedings instituted by any public body against them, in which a Convention point can be taken.

It will not be possible for anyone to bring 'the state' to Court, as can be done in Strasbourg, to allege that it has not legislated to secure a Convention right between individuals, because Article 1 of the ECHR has not been included in the Act's scheduled rights.

## ARE THESE RIGHTS UNLIMITED?

Complainants and their advisers will of course have to remember that most of the rights and freedoms contained in the Articles 'incorporated' into the Act contain express restrictions which require any Court adjudicating upon the action or decision to balance the interests of society against the interests of the complainant. The rights can be seen as those which are absolute (for example, no torture), those which are limited (for example, Article 6, limited in certain defined circumstances expressly set out) and those which are qualified (Articles 8–11, qualified according to the balance to be struck between individuals' and the wider public's competing interests). In relation to limited and qualified rights, states have been given fairly wide 'margins of appreciation' (that is, the benefit of the doubt) in the past by the ECHR which fears losing the support of member states. Thus, so long as an interference with the right is lawful, serves a legitimate purpose, is necessary in a democratic society, and is not discriminatory, the action will generally be upheld. Exploring these concepts in the domestic context will require judges to go further than their existing strictly supervisory jurisdiction and this is why it is said that *Wednesbury* unreasonableness (see note 2) will no longer be the test of what is lawful in judicial review. Whilst the Court itself will have to say whether the judges themselves think that the action or decision was proportionate to the problem sought to be addressed, it is still envisaged that the Courts will remit the matter back to the local authority or other public body to make the decision again. Hence public bodies are not simply going to be overridden by Courts acting as appeal courts in all cases. It is also thought highly probable that Courts are going to be anxious to continue to give full weight to the policy choice of Parliament to leave decision making to the discretion of public bodies because of the extreme sensitivity of the function concerned (such as child protection work) or the range of issues which have to be taken into consideration, inevitably beyond a judge's experience and understanding. It is for that reason that commentators are saying that even though the concept of a 'margin of appreciation' may not protect public bodies from human rights challenges in the UK courts, the Courts' traditional reluctance to interfere with otherwise legal, discretionary, non-justiciable (such as resource allocation) or expert 'clinical' decisions, subject only to unreasonableness or unfairness, will continue to provide a buffer against too many speculative claims.

# GENERAL HUMAN RIGHTS ISSUES IN WELFARE LAW

### Government guidance

To what extent should guidance from central government now be read in conformity with the Convention (wherever possible without straining the use of language overmuch)? Action may be required under statute to be taken 'under' guidance (for example, s.7 of the Local Authority Social Services Act 1970 imposes this duty); but what if it appears to breach a human right, for example, accepting a relative's consent to an act which would otherwise be a trespass? Will the section 6 (2) defence, which gives public authorities an excuse for acting incompatibly with human rights provisions when they are forced to do so by clear wording in a statute, apply? In fact it has already been accepted by the courts that if guidance (even guidance given some additional weight by express statutory provision) is wrong in law, then that is a very good and lawful reason for failing to follow it.[49]

### Immunity from suit

Will virtual immunity from suit for damages for negligent exercises of statutory functions be found to be inconsistent with Article 6, that is, the right to a fair determination of civil rights? The European Court case of *Osman*[50] and the Commission's approach in *X v Bedfordshire County Council*[51] suggest that this area will have to be reviewed by the Court, because they imply that access to a court is limited in practice by policy-based judgements favouring broad immunity for local authorities in negligence liability. That means public sector negligence now may well become actionable once again.

### Best value and fiduciary duties

Will the current fiduciary duty to consider the most cost-effective means of meeting people's needs have to be loosened in the light of rights to respect for home, family life and privacy under Article 8, and the general doctrine of proportionality? At the moment it is appropriate to choose the cheapest means of meeting a need so long as one has taken into account the possibility that some other way might provide better (or 'best') value. The Act implies that enabling people to stay together in a family unit and have services at home, or have a more limited number of carers providing personal care, will become more important, and at the very least, shift the balance of decision making away from general policies to closer consideration of individual cases.

## Positive actions

To what extent will positive action be required, or be able to be justified by a local authority's referring to someone else's human rights which they were protecting by interfering elsewhere? Even though the local authority cannot be a 'victim' for Human Rights Act purposes, there is nothing to prevent its pointing to some legitimate social aim which it felt under an obligation to pursue which necessarily involved interfering with some other human right. The s.3 interpretative duty could be said to justify reading implied and incidental powers more widely so as to extend the powers given by Parliament for innovative, pro-active actions. It is not a power of general competence for all public bodies, but it does liberalise to some extent the traditional approach to construing statutory frameworks and *vires*. But to what extent would a shortage of resources be a good excuse for failing to do something in this regard? If budget allocation decisions have to be 'proportionate', will judges feel better able to intervene to require financial adjustments?

## Relationships with contractors and partners

Contracting officers may have to take on board that if the private sector is contracted to contribute towards the provision of a service on behalf of the authority, or to provide a service under typical statutory duties to 'make arrangements' for the provision of a service, the content of the service might be challengeable on human rights grounds (Article 3 and Article 8 principles covering, respectively, the prohibition of inhuman or degrading treatment and the right to respect for private and family life and the home). Thus conditions and standard setting will become more important. Companies will also be entitled to claim a breach of their human rights, since a registration may count as a 'possession' for the purposes of Article 1 of the First Protocol (the right to peaceful enjoyment of possessions and due process in the regulation thereof) and continued presence on an approved list of contractors is likely to count as a civil right for the purposes of Article 6 (due process in the determination of one's civil rights). Thus tendering, contracting, monitoring, inspection and registration regimes need to be overhauled so as to conform.

## Decision making processes

Commentators frequently raise the concern that there is a chance at least that the general range of public bodies' functions will be found to be in the public law sphere and hence somehow outside the definition of 'determination of civil rights or obligations' for Article 6 procedural fairness purposes. But ECHR jurisprudence already establishes that the term 'civil rights' goes beyond private law relationships and covers other areas left in this country to the purely public law jurisdiction of judicial review. Planning, professional regulation, disputes between public sector landlords and tenants, compulsory purchase, licensing and functions to do with social welfare have all given rise to the conclusion that civil rights were in play in European cases. Assuming that administrative decisions in the social services field do give rise to the kind of civil right covered by Article 6, do all these processes need to be overhauled, or will access to judicial review be enough?[52] Where an applicant has not benefited from a fair and public hearing before the deciding authority, the Court may be required to provide a hearing on the merits itself. The Court might however simply find that the decision maker has not acted consistently with Article 6 and remit the matter to the same original body, in order that it might increase procedural fairness the next time. Of course that would be problematic if the decision in question was one in respect of which the decision making authority could never claim to be independent and im-partial, in the sense required by European law, and that will always be so, when the first level decision maker is an officer or member of a local authority. In this area, the judicial review court might have to descend more fully into the merits arena, in order to provide a proper Article 6 guarantee. The only other option would appear to be a declaration of incompatibility and the consequential proliferation of many new Tribunals.

### Potential areas of HRA impact within social services in the UK

Although it is early days, it is likely that the issues set out below are those that will be most susceptible to the influence of the new Human Rights Act. The likely key Articles will be 2–6, 8 and 14.

### Obligations to the destitute

Will NAA s.21, which defines the functions of local authories in providing accommodation, have to be read more widely, now it must be construed consistently with the right to life? Judicial commitment to human rights provided a basis for the first s.21 decisions on asylum seekers, even before the Convention rights were incorporated into UK law.[53] New legislation requires the 'solely destitute' as excluded from provision under this section – can this be lawful?

### Removal of residential care homes' registrations

Issues arise regarding procedural fairness (Article 6) if this is done on an ex parte emergency basis; further, the registration may be seen as a property right, under the First Protocol. In addition, will someone say that closure foreseeably led to increased premature mortality amongst the residents, inconsistently with the virtually unqualified right to life under Article 2?

## Right to respect for privacy, family and the home

What does the right to respect for one's home, family life and private life mean, if one is in residential care? Can the other residents be one's 'family'?

## Inhuman treatment standards

Is it inhuman or degrading to be tagged electronically if one has dementia and has lost the capacity to consent to being tagged? What about restraint and bed guards, and locks beyond the capability of residents? ECHR courts have given medical professionals a very wide margin of appreciation when considering apparently 'therapeutic' regimes. Interference is allowed under Article 8(2) for the protection of health. On the other hand, the ECHR court has more recently said that whether treatment or punishment is degrading depends on its nature and context.[53] There is no justification available for a breach. Might aspects of the regime in a residential home amount to inhuman treatment under Article 3? Can things like room size, an authority's insistence that 'standard' accommodation means sharing a room, and the provision of only communal meals in a home be consistent with Article 8 rights?

## Fair decisions

How can an authority make an Article 6 compliant 'deprivation of assets' decision when it has a financial interest in the outcome? Would the High Court's review of the reasonableness of the finding that a client in residential accommodation had deliberately deprived himself of income or capital, satisfy the Article 6 guarantees of an impartial Tribunal with full jurisdiction? Do decisions on care packages amount to determinations of civil rights? And if so, what does Article 6 require of this area of decision making – recourse to a Tribunal which does not yet exist, or merely to judicial review?

## Section 47 of the NAA

Detention of those of unsound mind is allowed under UK and ECHR law, but what of detention under the insanitariness provisions of the National Assistance Act 1948? This allows for compulsory removal from a private residence and detention of someone who need not even suffer from mental incapacity. Detention may be lawful under domestic law but unless the occupier is an alcoholic, drug addict, a vagrant, a threat in terms of the spread of infectious diseases, or a person of unsound mind, that is not good enough under the Convention's Article 5. In a Dutch case[55] it was held that the deprivation of liberty could not be justified simply because someone's views or behaviour deviated from the norms prevailing in a particular society.

## Discrimination

Age cut-offs for certain services or lower cost ceilings for the over–65s could potentially constitute discrimination in the amount of respect accorded to the private or family lives of the elderly.

## Limits to the best interests doctrine?

If self-determination is a right which gives way, in UK law, to necessity and statutory powers, where the person's or society's best interests require, is that consistent with European jurisprudence? There must be a line over which the means for 'protection' of people lacking capacity become unlawful because they are excessive, or amount to 'totalitarian' conduct (the word used in *Marston*); or inhuman or degrading treatment (the words used in the ECHR and the HRA) or an unjustified interference with the person's rights to liberty or association with others. In *Re F* Sedly LJ discussed the effect of the HRA on this area of law and suggested it was in accordance with Article 8 for a court to sanction restraint or detention in order to protect someone's best interests.

As for guardianship, requiring a person to live somewhere, or access to another to be given by the patient under s.8 MHA powers, is a plain interference with the patient's right to respect for their private life. Stopping someone from being visited by a member of their family under the best interests implied power or physically taking someone to residential care seems equally clear-cut. Indeed, the power to obtain the patient's forcible return to the chosen residence might be seen to amount to detention, although not in the ordinary physical sense of the word. Yet if detention can be justified as part of someone's best interests, it must surely become arguable that it might be justified within the regime of guardianship.

The right merely to 'respect' under Article 8 and the express qualifications to that right give rise to a potential justification for interfering with the human rights of those lacking mental capacity. Those exceptions to the right relate to legitimate social aims necessary in a democratic society, so long as they are in accordance with the law. The right to liberty is expressly qualified in the case of persons of unsound mind. My prediction is that the most common forms of interference under guardianship would be upheld as compatible with human rights, always assuming that the person was incapacitated as to the particular issue which was the subject of the interference.

Support for that prediction can be found in *Marston*. The Court of Appeal (in dismissing an application for leave to appeal) rejected the suggestion that the blocking of access to the patient (in fact it was a refusal to facilitate access between him and his foster brother) raised a human rights issue. Perhaps that is because the best interests power is predicated upon exactly the same principles as justification for interference with the rights in Article 8.

The Court's finding that any 'totalitarian conduct' would be outside the 'best interests' power must, in context, be limited to mean conduct that could not reasonably be thought to be required for the best interests of the person; or conduct towards those rare patients under guardianship who are not actually incapacitated with regard to the issue in question. It is crucial to note that access to guardianship is not dependent upon a finding of incapacity as to any particular issue. Whilst *Marston* suggested that the 'perceived wishes' of the individual could be overridden in relation to the s.8 powers, the Court was probably assuming that the person concerned lacked capacity as to seeing his foster brother again. It is probable that in future, a person's human rights will trump the best interests power (whether common law or statutory in origin), and will prevent any interference in those areas of daily life over which a person still enjoys capacity.

It is quite clear that the Human Rights Act will both lengthen and enrich negotiations and litigation between public authorities and disabled service users. Social Services can expect to be one of the main targets for far-reaching claims. This will make an awareness of law and legal reasoning even more important in this fascinating field. It will be a brave official in the Legal Services Commission who turns down an application for financial assistance to bring a human rights challenge.

## CONCLUSIONS

As can be seen from this review of recent legal developments, it is no longer realistic for local authorities to make practice and policy decisions without paying proper regard to the respect paid by Courts to the professionalism of care management staff, and the enormous significance of judicial review law, the risk of litigation and their own public body status. Service users and their advisers would also do well to become comfortable in the use of more legalistic language and principles when debating the extent of rights to community care.

## NOTES

1    [1997] 2 All ER 1 and (1997) 1 CCLR 1–114.

2    As defined in the leading case of *Associated Provincial Picture Houses Ltd v Wednesbury Corporation* [1948] 1 KB 223. The principle established in this case has become the defining concept used by judges to invalidate the exercise of discretion in certain

circumstances. The 'Wednesbury test' requires evidence of wholly unreasonable conduct or reasoning before the Courts will intervene.

3    *R v Ealing LBC ex p. C* (unreported, CA, November 1999).

4    *R v Haringey LBC ex p. Norton* (judgement given 15 July 1998, CO/555/97).

5    It was not until the *Gloucestershire* case in 1997, that it was finally decided that 'necessity' was a relative concept, taking its shape from the elected members' views as to what civilised society requires by way of a 'reasonable quality of life'.

6    See s.2(c) of the CSDPA 1970.

7    The CSDPA was the relevant statute, because the client was physically disabled, through multiple sclerosis, and the authority wanted to support him via domiciliary care.

8    *R v Haringey LBC ex p. Norton (no. 2)* (1998) 1 CCLR 168.

9    *R v Lancashire County Council ex p. Ingham* [1996] 4 All ER 422.

10   See *R v Kensington & Chelsea LBC, ex p. Muriqi Kujtim* [1999] 4 All ER 161.

11   *R v East Sussex County Council, ex p. Tandy* [1998] 2 WLR 884.

12   *R v Birmingham City Council, ex p. Taj Mohammed* [1998] 3 All ER 788.

13   Care Management and Assessment: Practitioners' Guide; Managers' Guide, London: HMSO; SSI, SSWG 1991a; 1991b.

14   (1997) 1 CCLR, 1–114, at 15.

15   (1997) 1 CCLR, 1–114, at 16H.

16   (1997) 1 CCLR, 1–114, at 50H.

17   (1997) 1 CCLR, 1–114, at 44F.

18   (1997) 1 CCLR, 1–114, at 49F.

19   (1997) 1 CCLR, 1–114, at 49F.

20   (1997) 1 CCLR, 1–114, at 49K.

21   National Health Service and Community Care Act 1990, s.47.

22   *R v Bristol City Council, ex p. Penfold* (1998) 1 CCLR 315.

23   These policies can be framed, legally, following the *Sefton* and *Gloucestershire* decisions, by reference to resources, or lack of resources.

24   (1997) 1 CCLR 57.

25   This duty arises under s.21 National Assistance Act 1948 when read with Local Authority Circular 93/10.

26   LAC 93/10.

27   See Choice of Accommodation Directions 1992, as amended.

28   (1998) 1 CCLR 581.

29   'Impairment': Mental Health Act 1983, s.1; 'handicap': National Health Services Act 1977,s.8; 'disorder': National Assistance Act 1948, s.29; 'disability': National Assistance Act, 1948, s.21.

30   *R v North Yorkshire CC ex p. Hargreaves* [1994] 26 BMLR 21.

31   In 'Making Decisions' (October 1999) (see note 42 below) the government has signalled its intention to widen the jurisdiction of the Court of Protection to appoint managers for incapacitated persons. Such managers will be able to make health, welfare and financial decisions for patients within certain confines.

32   Code of Practice under s.118 MHA 1983, the latest having been issued in 1999. Note this does not have statutory force.

33   In this case under the National Health Service and Community Care Act 1990, s.47.

34   *Re F (a child) (Care Order: Sexual Abuse)* [2000] 1 FCR 11.

34[A]  MHA Code of Practice, 1/4/99.

35   MHA s.18(6)

36   The old Code of Practice, now para. 13.10(b)

37   (1998) 1 CCLR 390.

38   5 September 1997, unreported.

39   [1995] 1 FLR 1075.

40   As for example in the leading case of *Airedale NHS Trust v Bland* [1993] AC 789.

41   [1995] 1 FLR 50.

42   'Who decides? Making decisions on behalf of mentally incapacitated adults.' (1997) London: HMSO (Cmnd. 3803).

43   Law Commission Report No. 231 (1995).

44   [1989] 2 WLR 1025.

45   [1993] 1 FLR 940.

46   [1999] 1 FLR.

47   HRA s.6 (2)(a) and (b)

48   HRA ss.7(7) and 7(3)

49   This may be highly relevant to the Code of Practice under the Mental Health Act, and s.7 LASSA guidance such as CRAG, and Policy Guidance from the Department of Health – about model eligibility criteria, for instance.

50   (1999) Crim. LR 82.

51   *Z and Others v United Kingdom.* Application No 29392/95 (1999). Unreported.

52   As statutory appeal on a point of law has already been held to be in the context of the planning appeal system, *Bryan v UK,* 21 EHRR 342 (1996 Series A No 335-A).

53   *R v Westminster LBC ex p A* (1997) 30 HLR 10.

54   *Tyrer v United Kingdom* (1978) 2 EHRR 1.

55   *Winterwerp v Netherlands* (1979) 2 EHRR 387.

# CHAPTER SIX

# The Disability Discrimination Act

## An Overview

*Catherine Casserley*

The Disability Discrimination Act 1995 is not the fully comprehensive civil rights legislation that disabled people campaigned for, but it does represent a significant milestone. The Act covers employment, trade organisations, goods facilities services and premises, education and transport. The educational provisions provide merely for publication of details about arrangements made for disabled students at schools, and of disability statements to be provided by colleges, although this will change shortly.[1] The transport provisions provide for accessibility regulations to be made for new build trains, buses and coaches (public service vehicles).[2] The Regulations relating to trains came into force on 1 January 1999, whilst the PSV regulations were brought out in July 2000.[3] There is also provision for licensed taxis to be made fully accessible and for it to be an offence for a taxi driver to refuse to carry a wheelchair user, or someone with a guide or hearing dog,[4] although there is no date as yet for implementation of these provisions.

This chapter looks at the basic provisions of the Act in the spheres of employment (excluding trade organisations) and goods, facilities, services and premises and at the cases brought under the Act since its implementation in December 1996.

## DISABILITY

The definition of disability was one of the aspects of the Act that disabled lobbyists were particularly concerned about, as it draws quite heavily on the 'medical model' of disability (see Chapter One, p.13) It is also this area that has given rise to most of the cases so far taken to the Employment Appeal Tribunal (EAT).

The Act defines disability in section 1 as: 'a physical or mental impairment which has a substantial and long-term adverse effect on the ability to carry out normal day-to-day activities'. Any mental impairment must be a clinically well-recognised mental illness.[5] Certain conditions are excluded from the definition of disability, such as addiction to alcohol, nicotine or any other substance,[6] whilst a severe facial disfigurement is to be effectively treated as a disability.[7] Regulations[8] and Guidance[9] supplement the definition of disability. The Guidance is admissible in evidence in any proceedings before a tribunal, county court or sheriff court, and it shall be taken into account in determining any question arising in proceedings where it appears relevant.[10] The Employment Appeal Tribunal has repeatedly emphasised the importance, particularly at this early stage in the Act's life, of taking the Guidance and Codes into account.[11] 'Substantial' is stated in the Guidance to be 'more than minor or trivial',[12] whilst Schedule 1(2) (a), (b) and (c) state that an impairment is long-term if it has lasted for at least 12 months, it is likely to last for 12 months or it is likely to last for the rest of the life of the person affected.

'Ability to carry out normal day-to-day activities' is defined in Schedule 1, paragraph 4. An impairment is to be treated as affecting the ability of the person concerned to carry out normal day-to-day activities if it affects one of the following:

    mobility

    manual dexterity

    physical co-ordination

    continence

    ability to lift, carry or otherwise move everyday objects

    speech, hearing or eyesight

    memory or ability to concentrate, learn or understand

    perception of the risk of physical danger.

The Guidance gives detailed examples of what it would be reasonable and unreasonable to regard as 'substantial adverse effects' in relation to each of the above eight normal day-to-day activities.[13] Where an impairment is corrected by medical treatment, medication, prosthesis, auxiliary devices or other aids, but would otherwise meet the definition of disability, the Act states that it is still to be treated as an impairment – that is, the effect of any medical treatment is to be disregarded. This disregard does not apply to spectacles, however.[14] In addition, past disabilities, recurring conditions and progressive conditions, such as HIV (so long as they have some effect, and it is likely that they will have a substantial effect in the future) will be covered.[15]

The meaning of disability is one of the areas that Employment Tribunals seemed initially to have had most difficulty with when interpreting the Act. The

Employment Appeal Tribunal in *Goodwin v The Patent Office* provided guidance on how to approach the issue of disability.[16] G, who was a paranoid schizophrenic, was dismissed from his employment as a patent examiner at the Patent Office following complaints from work colleagues about his odd behaviour. He complained to the Tribunal that his employers had discriminated against him by dismissing him for a reason relating to his disability. The Tribunal heard evidence from a doctor that G had a mental illness. He experienced thought broadcasting, auditory hallucinations and paranoia. His ability to sustain concentration for any period was impaired because of these symptoms. The Tribunal held that whilst he had a mental impairment, and the impairment adversely affected his ability to concentrate, the effect upon him was not substantial because he could care for himself at home without assistance and he could get to work and carry out that work to a satisfactory standard. There was therefore no disability. G appealed.

The EAT held that the evidence should have led the Tribunal inevitably to the conclusion that G was unable to carry on a normal day-to-day conversation with his colleagues and that he had a disability within the meaning of the Act. The EAT laid down four areas that tribunals must consider when faced with an issue relating to the definition of disability:

1.  Does the applicant have an impairment which is either mental or physical? Where there is doubt as to whether a mental illness falls within the definition, it would be advisable to ascertain whether the illness is mentioned in the World Health Organisation's International classification of diseases [see Chapter Three, p.75].

2.  Does the impairment affect the applicant's ability to carry out normal day-to-day activities in one of the respects set out in Schedule 1 para 4(1) and does it have an adverse affect? The fact that a person can carry out such activities does not mean that his ability to carry them out has not been impaired. The focus of the Act is on the things that the applicant either cannot do or can only do with difficulty, rather than on the things that the person can do.

3.  Is the adverse effect substantial? The Tribunal should examine how an applicant's abilities have actually been affected while on medication and then consider the deduced effects and whether the actual and deduced effects on ability to carry out normal day-to-day activities is clearly more than trivial.

4.  Is the adverse effect long-term?

In the case of *Kapadia v London Borough of Lambeth*,[17] the Employment Appeal Tribunal held that an employment tribunal had erred in disregarding the deduced effects of the applicant's impairment. Mr Kapadia was diagnosed as having reactive depression and was medically retired from his job with Lambeth Council. He applied to the Employment Tribunal on the basis of disability discrimination. The respondents contended that he was not disabled within the meaning of the Act, although they called no witnesses. Mr Kapadia gave evidence, along with his GP and his consultant. The Tribunal held that Mr Kapadia had a mental impairment which have an adverse effect on his ability to carry out day-to-day activities, but the effect was not substantial. On appeal, the EAT made a declaration that Mr Kapadia was disabled; they said that whilst they did not preclude the possibility that a tribunal might for good reason reject uncontradicted medical evidence, in this case the majority simply disregarded the medical evidence in favour of a judgement made apparently solely on the basis of how the appellant appeared to the lay members when giving his evidence, and this was unacceptable. They further held that in the absence of any medical evidence to the contrary, they were quite satisfied that the counselling sessions with a consultant clinical psychologist constituted treatment within the meaning of paragraph 6, Schedule 1, and so could be disregarded. They rejected the respondents' suggestion that the counselling sessions did not amount to treatment because they prevented the patient from needing drug treatment for his condition and thus were directed towards the reduction of the appellant's symptoms and not to correcting his mental impairment. The Court of Appeal upheld the EAT's decision (see [2000] IRLR 699).

In *Greenwood v British Airways plc*,[18] Mr Greenwood claimed disability discrimination as he had been refused promotion due to his past sick record of periods of depression. At the time of the refusal of promotion, he was fit and well, although two months later the depression recurred. He claimed discrimination on the basis of a past disability or alternatively on grounds of a current, recurrent, disability. The Employment Tribunal held that he was not disabled, but the EAT said that in considering whether the effect was likely to recur, the Employment Tribunal should not have looked at the situation solely at the time of the discrimination but over the total period for which the effect existed, including recurrence after the discrimination.

Whilst medical evidence may be necessary, it is ultimately a question of fact as to whether or not someone's day-to-day activities are substantially adversely affected.[19] Medical evidence does tend to be used in cases where disability is at issue, and the Tribunal can now pay for a medical report and the attendance of a medical expert where necessary. The potentially wide definition of disability has led to a variety of conditions being held to be disabilities: for example, ME;[20] a condition involving pain from kidney stones and an undiagnosed cause;[21] and sciatica and a club foot.[22]

## EMPLOYMENT

The employment provisions of the Act were implemented on 2 December 1996, and between then and the end of October 1999, ACAS records 5841 complaints as registered in the Employment Tribunals. The employment provisions are also supplemented by Regulations[23] and by the Code of Practice for the Elimination of Discrimination in the Field of Employment against Disabled Persons or Persons who have had a Disability.[24] The employment provisions do not apply to any employers with fewer than 15 employees.[25] The figure was originally 20, but this has, following a review,[26] been reduced to 15. The original figure of 20 reflected the exemption given to such companies from the quota scheme which had previously operated, whereby employers had to employ a certain number of disabled people.

The Act is silent on the issue of whether associated companies can be counted together in determining whether or not the employee threshold is met, but the EAT has held that there is nothing in the DDA which enlarges the meaning of 'employer' so as to include 'associated employers'.[27] However, the Code of Practice does make it clear that independent franchise holders are exempt, if on an individual basis they do not meet the employee threshold, regardless of how many employees the franchise network has as a whole.[28] Certain employments are also excluded – statutory office holders, such as police officers; prison officers (except custody officers); fire fighting members of the fire brigade; members of naval, military or air forces of the Crown; members of Ministry of Defence police, British Transport police, Royal Parks constabulary or the UK Atomic Energy Authority Constabulary. The Scottish EAT has recently confirmed that serving police officers are not covered by the Act.[29] The term 'employment' is given the same broad meaning as in other anti-discrimination statutes, including employment under a contract of service or apprenticeship and also a contract personally to do any work.[30] The employment covered has to be at an establishment in Great Britain (including Northern Ireland).[31] In addition, contract workers are also protected from discrimination against them by a principal.[32] The issue of contract workers was considered in the case of *Abbey Life Assurance Ltd. v Tansell*.[33] Mr Tansell offered computer skills and services through Intelligents Ltd., a company in which he was sole shareholder and one of four directors. He placed his name with several agencies, including MHC. MHC entered into an agreement with Abbey Life Assurance to supply personnel to them. A contract was then entered into between MHC and Intelligents to supply Mr Tansell's services to Abbey Life, which contract had the effect of putting him under the control of Abbey Life. Fees were paid to MHC, who in turn paid Intelligents.

Mr Tansell brought a claim of disability discrimination against both MHC and Abbey Life on the grounds that he had been withdrawn from the site by MHC because Abbey Life rejected his services by reason of his disability. At a preliminary hearing to determine whether or not he was a contract worker, the employment tribunal took the view that the DDA[34] requires a direct contractual relationship between the employer and the principal. On that basis the applicant was not a contract worker for Abbey Life. The tribunal found, though, that he was a contract worker for MHC. MHC appealed and Mr Tansell cross appealed.

The Employment Appeal Tribunal held that where there is an unbroken chain of contracts between an individual and the end user, the end user is the principal (within the meaning of s.12(6)). Such a construction gave effect to the general principle that the statute should be construed purposively and with a bias towards conferring statutory protection rather than excluding it. It was clear that the end user should be the target about whom complaint is made. The cross appeal was thus allowed, as well as the employment agency's appeal against the finding that the first respondent was a contract worker for them. Abbey Life was given leave to appeal to the Court of Appeal. The Court of Appeal upheld the decision of the EAT, stating, 'it is more probable that Parliament intended to confer than to deny protection from discrimination in cases where the supply of the employee was made by his company to the principal through an employment agency rather than direct to the principal'.

## DISCRIMINATION

Under the provisions of the Act,[35] it is unlawful for an employer to discriminate against a disabled person:

> in the arrangements made to determine to whom he should offer employment;

> in the terms on which he offers employment; or

> by refusing to offer or deliberately not offering employment.

It is also unlawful for an employer to discriminate against a disabled person whom he employs:

> in the terms of employment he affords him;

> in the opportunities afforded to him for promotion, a transfer, training or receiving any other benefit;

by refusing to afford him, or deliberately not affording to him, any such opportunity;

by dismissing him, or subjecting him to any other detriment.[36]

The definition of 'discrimination' has a different emphasis to that in either race or sex legislation. The Act states[37] that an employer discriminates against a disabled person if:

a) for a reason which relates to the disabled person's disability, he treats him less favourably than he treats others to whom that reason does not or would not apply; and

b) he cannot show that the treatment in question is justified.

The interpretation of 'less favourable treatment' and in particular the issue of the comparator – to whom one compares the disabled person for the purposes of less favourable treatment – has given rise to much confusion. This was largely rectified by the Court of Appeal in the case of *Clark v TDG Ltd* (trading as Novacold).[38] Mr Clark had an accident at work and subsequently had a back problem for which he had 16 weeks off work. He was dismissed when his employer received a report from an orthopaedic consultant that he was unable to state when it would be possible for Mr Clark to return to work. The Employment Tribunal rejected his complaint of disability discrimination, on the basis that he was not treated less favourably than Novacold would have treated others absent from work for reasons other than disablement. They went on to say that if, contrary to their view, there had been less favourable treatment, it would not have been justified. The Employment Appeal Tribunal upheld the decision of the Employment Tribunal, albeit they said with some reluctance.

The Court of Appeal allowed the appeal. They held that in deciding whether the reason for less favourable treatment does not or would not apply to others, it is simply a case of identifying others to whom the reason for treatment does not or would not apply. The test of less favourable treatment is based on the reason for the treatment of the disabled person and not on the fact of his disability – it does not turn on a like for like comparison of the treatment of the disabled person and of others in similar circumstances. The statutory focus of the DDA is narrower than that in sex and race legislation. The persons who are performing the main functions of their jobs are 'others' to whom the reason for the dismissal of the disabled person (that is, inability to perform those functions) would not apply. The Court of Appeal further held that, although the meaning of s.5(1) was ambiguous, they thought it more probable that Parliament meant 'that reason' in s.5 to refer only to the facts constituting the reason for the treatment and not to include within that reason the added requirement of a causal link between the reason and the disabled person. In the present case, there was less favourable treatment. The only outstanding issue was that of justification, which was remitted to the Tribunal for consideration.

The question had arisen prior to this decision as to whether an employer has to know of a person's disability as a prerequisite of a finding of 'less favourable treatment', as it does not explicitly state this in the Act. The Code of Practice states[39] that an employer must do all they could reasonably be expected to do to find out whether or not someone is disabled. In the case of *O'Neill v Symm*,[40] where a woman with ME was dismissed from her employment, the EAT stated that knowledge of the disability, or at least the material features of it as set out in Schedule 1 to the Act, is relevant to whether the reason for the employer's action relates to the disabled person's disability. The word reason as a matter of causation involves knowledge of the matter that is material. What is material to discrimination on the ground of disability is disability, and not merely one or other equivocal symptoms. It is arguable, however, that this decision sits rather uneasily with that of *Clark v Novacold*, above. In addition, in the subsequent decision of *Heinz and Co. Ltd. v Kendrick*,[41] the EAT stated that: 'There is, in our judgement, no need to imply into the statute a requirement not expressly present, namely that the employer should know of the disability as such, or as to whether its material features fell within or without Schedule 1 of the 1995 Act'. This issue was further examined in the case of *London Borough of Hammersmith and Fulham v Farnsworth*,[42] which again held that the employer's knowledge of the applicant's disability was irrelevant for whether they treated her less favourably for a reason that related to her disability within the meaning of s.5(1)(a); and that the approach the EAT in *O'Neill v Synom and Co.* that actual knowledge is required is no longer good law in light of the decision of the Court of Appeal in *Clark v TDG Ltd* T/a Novacold.

## REASONABLE ADJUSTMENTS

An employer also discriminates if:

1. he fails to comply with a section 6 duty imposed on him in relation to the disabled person; and

2. he cannot show that his failure to comply with that duty is justified. (DDA s.5(2))

The duty to make reasonable adjustments is one of the most important and potentially far-reaching aspects of the Act. Section 6 (1) (a) and (b) states that where any arrangements made by or on behalf of an employer or any physical feature of premises occupied by the employer place the disabled person concerned at a substantial disadvantage in comparison with persons who are not disabled, it is the duty of the employer to take such steps as it is reasonable in all the circumstances of the case to prevent the arrangements or feature having that effect. These duties apply to arrangements for determining to whom employment should be offered, and to any term, condition or arrangements on which employment, promotion, a transfer, training or any other benefit is offered or afforded. Examples are given in s.6 (3) of steps which an employer may have to take in relation to a disabled person in order to comply with the duty:

making adjustments to premises

allocating some of the disabled person's duties to another person

transferring him to fill an existing vacancy

altering his working hours

assigning him to a different place of work

allowing him to be absent during working hours for rehabilitation, assessment or treatment

giving him, or arranging for him to be given, training

acquiring or modifying equipment

modifying instructions or reference manuals

modifying procedures for testing or assessment

providing a reader or interpreter

providing supervision

Where premises occupied by employers are leased, the Act implies into the lease a term so that the occupier can make alterations to comply with the duty to make reasonable adjustments.[43]

In determining whether or not it is reasonable for an employer to take steps to comply with the s.6 duty, regard shall be had to:

the extent to which taking the step would prevent the effect in question

the extent to which it is practicable for the employer to take the step

the financial and other costs which would be incurred by the employer in taking the step and the extent to which it would disrupt any of his activities

the extent of the employer's financial and other resources

the availability to the employer of financial or other assistance with respect to taking the step.[44]

An employer will only have these duties under the Act if he knows, in the case of an applicant, that the disabled person is or may be an applicant for employment and, in any case, that the person has a disability and is likely to be put at a substantial disadvantage, as outlined above.[45] The EAT case of *Ridout v TC Group*[46] concerned a woman who applied for a job and was shortlisted for interview. She had epilepsy, controlled by Epilim, which she disclosed on her CV. The prospective employers did not contact her about interview arrangements and when she arrived at the interview, she found that the room had bright fluorescent lighting without diffusers or baffles. She was wearing sunglasses around her neck. When she entered the room, she made some comments to the effect that she might be disadvantaged by the lighting. The employers however, as was held by the Employment Tribunal, believed this to be an explanation relating to her sunglasses. Ms Ridout completed the interview without using the sunglasses and did not tell the employers that she felt unwell or disadvantaged. The Employment Tribunal dismissed a complaint of disability discrimination on the basis of failing to make a reasonable adjustment in respect of the physical arrangements for the interview.

The EAT held that the Employment Tribunal had not erred in law in finding no unlawful discrimination. They were entitled to find that the employers were not in breach of their obligations to make a reasonable adjustment to the physical features of premises when they interviewed Ms Ridout in a room with bright lights. The duty to make reasonable adjustments requires a tribunal to measure the extent of the duty, if any, against the actual or assumed knowledge of the employer both as to the disability and its likelihood of causing the individual a substantial disadvantage. Tribunals should be careful not to impose upon disabled people a duty to give a long detailed explanation as to the effects of their disability merely to cause the employer to make adjustments which the employers probably should have made in the first place. On the other hand, it is equally undesirable that an employer should be required to ask a number of questions as to whether a person with a disability feels disadvantaged merely to protect themselves from any liability. In the present case, the EAT said that the appellant had a very rare form of epilepsy and the Tribunal was entitled to conclude that no reasonable employer could be expected to know, without being told in terms by the appellant, that the arrangements which were made for the interview might disadvantage her. Whether the employer should have taken any other steps as a result of what was said at the interview was a matter of fact and evidence for the Tribunal.

How far employers should go in making adjustments is a question of fact to be determined by the Tribunal in individual cases. The Code of Practice gives detailed guidance on this, and the EAT looked at the extent of an employer's duty in this regard in the case of *Kenny v Hampshire Constabulary*.[47] Mr Kenny was a graduate with a qualification in information technology. He applied for the post of analyst/programmer with Hampshire Constabulary and was offered the job, subject to his employer being able to make arrangements for his needs. He had cerebral palsy and needed assistance with urinating. An application for a support worker was made under the Access to Work scheme. There was some delay in the application being assessed, and the employers subsequently withdrew the job offer on the grounds that they needed to fill the vacancy urgently. An Employment Tribunal dismissed a claim of disability discrimination, holding that whilst the reason for withdrawal of the offer was for a reason relating to disability, and whilst a support person as required falls within the remit of s.6(1), the employers were justified in withdrawing the offer. The applicant appealed, with the employer cross appealing. The EAT held that the Employment Tribunal had correctly found that the employer had not discriminated, contrary to s.5(2), by withdrawing the job offer. The EAT stated that there had not been a failure to make a reasonable adjustment: the arrangements which were necessary to enable the applicant to work with the respondent did not fall within the duty to make a reasonable adjustment under s.6. An employer's duty under s.6 is restricted to 'job-related' matters. Not every failure to make an arrangement which deprives an employee of a chance to be employed is unlawful.

The EAT has laid down guidelines for Employment Tribunals in dealing with reasonable adjustment cases. In *Morse v Wiltshire County Council,*[48] the EAT stated the following:

The duty to consider reasonable adjustments clearly applies to cases of redundancy;

Tribunals must go through a series of sequential steps when considering an allegation of discrimination under the 'reasonable adjustment' provisions;

They have to consider whether any duty is imposed on the employer to make adjustments i.e. whether or not employees are put at a substantial disadvantage, by arrangements made by the employer;

They must then decide whether, if such a duty is imposed, the employer has taken such steps as were reasonable, in all the circumstances of the case, in order to prevent the relevant arrangements or features having the effect of placing the disabled person concerned at a substantial disadvantage in comparison with persons who were not disabled;

Finally, if the Tribunal has found that the employer has failed to comply with a s.6 duty, it must then decide whether the employer had shown that his failure was justified;

It is for the Tribunal to decide what is 'reasonable' or not, looking at the matter objectively. The Tribunal can substitute its own judgement for that of the employer – it does not have to look at whether or not a reasonable employer could have acted as the employer did.

The importance of following the principles laid down in the *Morse* case was stressed in *Stevens v JPM International Ltd.*[49] Mrs Stevens was dismissed on grounds of ill health and absence. The Employment Tribunal rejected her complaint of disability discrimination. The EAT allowed an appeal against this decision, stating that whilst the *Morse* decision does not have to be observed in every case, it is an important decision and in this case, it should have been followed. They did not think that even taking into account Mrs Stevens' disability, looking at the question of justification would have been futile. The Tribunal should have considered:

> Whether the employers had made unjustified assumptions about the appellant's lack of capacity to fulfil the requirements of the job;

> Whether the requirements of the job could be adjusted to accommodate her abilities;

> Whether there was proper medical evidence which was accessible to them, which would have enabled them to conclude that she was not going to be fit to undertake a trial as a receptionist in the foreseeable future.

In the case of *London Borough of Hillingdon v Ms A.F. Morgan*,[50] Mrs Morgan, a Service Information Officer with Hillingdon LB, had returned to work after being on sick leave with ME. She found returning to work stressful, and left. The doctors were of the view that she should have a gradual return to work. Thereafter, the council attempted to meet her needs through its redeployment process. Working from home was suggested, but met with a negative response from the council. The Employment Tribunal upheld a claim of disability discrimination, both in terms of less favourable treatment and a failure to make reasonable adjustments. The local authority appealed, on the basis that there was no obligation to provide work at home for the applicant; and no obligation to offer the applicant the alternative job irrespective of merit. The EAT upheld the Employment Tribunal's decision. It made the following points:

> The employers in this case treated Mrs Morgan as they would have treated any other person who fell for redeployment within their redeployment scheme. To that extent, they have failed in their duty.

> Since the coming into force of the DDA, it was their duty to deal with people who became disabled at work in accordance with the statutory requirements as amplified by the Code of Practice.

If they had approached the matter in that way, they would not have simply regarded this as another redeployment case where they had to see if there was a job available and if not to offer one which was below the level at which she had been working. The Act requires more. They are required to see if they can make reasonable adjustments so as to enable a person who is disabled to be retained in their employment.

Mrs Morgan was not simply to be treated as a potential redeployee. She needed specific measures to be considered and taken.

> It is not for the Employment Tribunal to identify or select the job that they think she could have done. It was not their responsibility to identify the particular post.

> For the foreseeable future, all DDA cases should refer to the relevant Codes of Practice which have been looked at during the course of the hearing and findings made in relation to them [this is particularly where there have been breaches of the Code].

The Court of Appeal in *Clark v Novacold* (see p.146) also held that the duty to make reasonable adjustments does not apply to the dismissal itself of a disabled person, although it would clearly apply to pre-dismissal situations.

## JUSTIFICATION

Unlike the sex and race discrimination legislation, potentially direct disability discrimination can be lawful if it is justified. Both less favourable treatment and a failure to make reasonable adjustments can be justified if the reason for it is 'both material to the circumstances of the particular case and substantial'.[51]

In the case of *Baynton v Saurus General Engineers*,[52] the EAT looked at the question of 'justification' in disability discrimination cases. Mr Baynton had been dismissed after being off sick, and his job given to someone from a related firm who would otherwise have been made redundant. Mr Baynton failed in his claim before the Employment Tribunal and appealed to the EAT. The EAT stated that it is now accepted that the word 'justifiable' used in the Sex Discrimination Act requires an objective balance between the discriminatory effect of the condition and the reasonable needs of the party who applies the condition.[53] The EAT went on to to say that the statutory test in s.5(3) is unique. 'Material to the circumstances of the case' must include the circumstances of both the employer and the employee. Thus the Tribunal should have considered the effect of the failure of the respondent to warn Mr Baynton that he was at risk of dismissal, or to find out the up-to-date medical position before dismissing him. Had they taken those steps, they would have found out that Mr Baynton was due to see his consultant, and bearing in mind that the appellant was not at that time in receipt of sick pay, the Tribunal would have to balance the desirability of awaiting the outcome of that consultation with the need to save another employee from redundancy in the related company. In the case of *Heinz Co. Ltd. v Kenrick*,[54] however, the EAT held that the threshold for justification of disability is very low. While it held that the balancing exercise in Baynton (see p.151) is not precluded, it was said that section

5(3) provides that treatment *is* (as opposed to 'can be') justified if the reason for it is both material to the particular case and substantial. '...if the reason for the treatment relates to the individual circumstances in question and is not just trivial or minor then justification has to be held to exist in the category of case which we are dealing with, namely that in which no s.6 duty falls upon the employer.'

In a further comment on the issues of justification, the EAT in the case of *London Borough of Hammersmith and Fulham v Farnsworth* [2000] IRLR 691, held that knowledge, or lack of knowledge of an applicant's disability is not a necessary ingredient for the purposes of the test of justification in s.5 (1)(b) and s.5(3) (save to the extent that s.5(3) is affected by s.5 (5)).

## PROOF OF DISCRIMINATION

As with any claim of discrimination proof can be particularly hard to obtain, and in many cases, particularly those involving recruitment, the Tribunals will have to rely upon inferences drawn from the circumstances of the case.

In the case of *Kirker v British Sugar*,[55] the Employment Appeal Tribunal held that the Tribunal was entitled to look at both pre-DDA implementation events and at the scoring of the applicant in a redundancy exercise, which it considered objectively unjustified, to draw the inference of disability discrimination in the employer's assessment.

*Roberts v Warrington Borough Council*[56] concerned a Mr Roberts' application for a job with Warrington Council. Mr Roberts had a hearing impairment. He was invited for interview, at which he had an interpreter and he was given 30 minutes for the interview instead of the usual 15. He did not get the job, and brought a claim of disability discrimination against the council. The Tribunal dismissed his claim, although they stated that they had no doubt as to Mr Roberts' length of experience and capabilities. They held that the choice of employee was supported by the requirements of the particular task. They further said that the majority of the Tribunal was satisfied that there was no deliberate act on the part of the Tribunal not to employ the applicant. Mr Roberts appealed the decision.

The EAT allowed the appeal. They said that the Tribunal should have gone through the *King v Great Britain China Centre*[57] formula and that the Tribunal should have used the *King* case to flush out what the stated reason was and then consider whether that was the real reason, and what inferences could be drawn from it. On the basis that the EAT did not know why Mr Roberts was not appointed the appeal was allowed. The EAT also stated that: 'The disabled (sic) had been largely ignored until the Disability Discrimination Act. Although there were quota systems, these were rarely enforced. This Act challenges us all to examine why it is that we are not appointing someone'.

## REMEDIES

A complaint of disability discrimination under the employment provisions of the Act must be brought to the Employment Tribunal,[58] within three months of the act of discrimination. The Tribunal has jurisdiction to hear a claim out of time if it considers it 'just and equitable' to do so. In disability cases, it is possible to argue that the effects of someone's disability have caused problems in their being able to access legal advice or the Tribunal mechanisms.[59] If the claim of disability discrimination is successful, the Tribunal can award compensation, including that for injury to feelings, as well as making recommendations as to the employer's conduct, and a declaration as to the rights of the complainant (s.8). In considering remedies, the EAT has laid down guidance for dealing with DDA claims, recognising the particular issues that may arise in dealing with medical evidence in respect of future loss of earnings.[60] Damages for injury to feelings in disability cases are currently lower than those awarded in race and sex discrimination cases, according to the Equal Opportunities Review of compensation awarded in 1999.[61] The highest awards for injury to feelings so far appear to be:

> *Bridges v Sita (GB Ltd.)*, where £15,000 was awarded for injury to feelings, on the basis that the applicant was confronted by the respondent's decision to dismiss him in what he found to be a particularly hurtful and inexplicable manner. The Tribunal found that these circumstances had 'a serious and lasting impact upon the Applicant'.[62]

> *Ninseema v London Borough of Waltham Forest*, which also made an award of £15,000 for injury to feelings, where the applicant resigned following the respondent's failure to make reasonable adjustments.[63]

> *Harling v CL Plastics Limited*,[64] where the tribunal awarded £25,000 for injury to feelings. The applicants had been verbally and physically persecuted over a period of 18 months because of his disability. The tribunal took £15,000 as the starting point, and awarded aggravated damages, to bring the total to £25,000.

> In *Forder v Southern Water*, the Tribunal awarded £7500 for injury to feelings, including £2500 aggravated damages.[65] In considering the injury to feelings award, the Tribunal considered, among other things, the size of the organisation and its failure to take account of the DDA.

The highest total award so far was made in the case of *Kirker v British Sugar*.[66] Mr Kirker, who is visually impaired, was made redundant by British Sugar, and an Employment Tribunal held that he had been discriminated against for a reason relating to his disability. In considering his future loss of earnings, the Tribunal considered a report by the Royal National Institute for the Blind on the lack of employment prospects for visually impaired people. The Tribunal reached the conclusion that Mr Kirker was unlikely to obtain other employment, and that he would have stayed with British Sugar, and awarded him £102,717 in damages. This was subsequently taxed, however, and the Tribunal then re-opened the case to determine how much the award should have been gross. The parties subsequently settled between them for a total of £167,000.[67]

## GOODS, FACILITIES AND SERVICES

The basic, non-discrimination component of the goods, facilities and services provisions of the Act came into force on 2 December 1996. The definition of 'provider of services' is contained in section 19(2) of the Act: 'a person is a provider of services if s/he is concerned with the provision in the United Kingdom of services to the public or a section of them, regardless of whether payment is made'.

The list of examples of service providers contained in s.19(3) includes hotels and boarding houses; facilities by way of banking, access to loans credit or finance; facilities for entertainment; the services of any profession or trade, or any local or other public authority. The Code of Practice Rights of Access to Goods Facilities Services and Premises was reissued in June 1999 and it provides guidance on the interpretation of the Act. It is admissible in evidence in any proceedings under the Act and, where a provision of it appears to be relevant to a question under consideration by the court, it shall be taken into account in determining that question.[68] The Code contains an expanded list of the sorts of service providers covered by the Act, including courts, the emergency services and telecommunications and broadcasting organisations.[69]

By virtue of section 19(5), and the Disability Discrimination (Services and Premises) Regulations 1996[70], a number of potential service providers are excluded from the remit of sections 19, 20 and 21: these include educational and ancillary services, and 'any service so far as it consists of the use of any means of transport'. It is likely, however, that education will be covered by the Act in the future, as the Government issued a consultation document, entitled 'SEN and Disability Rights in Education Bill'. It is proposed that the recommendations of the Disability Rights Taskforce, contained in its report 'From Exclusion to Inclusion' (published by the DfEE in December 1999) are followed in relation to education. Specifically, the government is proposing to end the exclusion of education from coverage by the DDA's access to service provisions, and particular provision will be made with regard to education for disabled students aged both below and above 16. The Bill proposes that it will be unlawful for education providers to discriminate against a disabled child in defined circumstances.

These rights will be enforced through the SEN (Special Educational Needs) Tribunal, although there will be no power to award compensation. There will be a duty of education providers to plan systematically to increase the accessibility of schools for disabled children.[71]

Section 19 of the Act makes it unlawful for a provider of services to discriminate against a disabled person:

by refusing or deliberately not providing a service provided to the public;

by failing to comply with a section 21 (reasonable adjustment) duty so that it is impossible or unreasonably difficult for the disabled person to make use of the service;

in the standard or manner of service provided to the disabled person;

in the terms on which the service is provided.

Of the relatively few cases taken under these provisions so far,[72] most have involved refusal of service. One of the few that have reached court is the case of *Martin Blankley and Ors. v Imelda Lydon.*[73] This case involved the refusal of service to a group of people with learning difficulties. They had arranged to go to a public house on Boxing Day, but when they arrived, they were asked to leave by the landlady as she said that she could not cope with them. At the hearing, the district judge found that the plaintiffs had been discriminated against for a reason relating to disability, and awarded damages for injury to feelings of £800 each, a total of £8000. An application to set aside the judgement was dismissed.

Examples of cases taken involving service on different terms which have settled include the case of *Hitchin and Bass Taverns Ltd. and Ray Banks.*[74] Mr Hitchin, a blind guide dog owner, issued proceedings for a refusal to serve and service on different terms/different standard/manner. The defendants denied any breach of the DDA, stating that Mr Hitchin's guide dog had been behaving in an unruly manner. The case was settled on the day of the court hearing with payment of £1500 compensation, an apology and a statement by the landlord that he had been mistaken as to the conduct of the guide dog. A number of other cases have involved refusal of access to buildings to guide dog owners (see Casserley 2000 for more details).

## DISCRIMINATION

Discrimination is given essentially the same definition in this part of the DDA as in the employment provisions: a service provider discriminates against a disabled person if, for a reason related to the disabled person's disability, they treat a disabled person less favourably than they treat or would treat others to whom that reason does not or would not apply; and if the service provider cannot show that the treatment is justified.[75] The service provider also discriminates if he or she fails to comply with a section 21 duty (to make 'reasonable adjustments') imposed upon him or her in relation to the disabled person; and if he or she cannot show that the failure to comply with that duty is justified.[76] The issue of the 'comparator' is likely to be dealt with in goods and services cases with reference to *Clark v. Novacold* (see above, p.146). It is also worth noting in this respect, however, the case of *R v Powys CC ex.p. Hambridge (no.2)*, which concerned the charging structure for home care in Powys which was banded according to income. The effect of this banding was that Mrs Hambridge, who was in receipt of disability living allowance, paid more for her care than those who were only in receipt of Income Support and placed in Band A. Mrs Hambridge sought a judicial review of the banding structure on the grounds that, among other things, the council had discriminated against her in breach of the DDA 1995, s.19. The Court, however, decided that Powys CC had not discriminated against Mrs Hambridge. It held that she was required to pay more than people in Band A because she had more money than these people. The reason for her having the extra money (her receipt of disability living allowance on account of her disability), was not part of the reason for the difference in entitlement. The Court took *Clark v Novacold* into consideration in reaching this outcome. It is, however, questionable as to whether it was properly applied, although the decision in Powys has been upheld on appeal.[77]

## REASONABLE ADJUSTMENTS

This section of the Act is perhaps the most radical, in that it involves service providers having to alter the way in which they deliver their services, goods or facilities to ensure that disabled people can have access to them. The duty to make what are known as 'reasonable adjustments' is owed to disabled people at large, in that it does not rely upon an individual disabled person approaching the service provider about their service; and it is anticipatory – service providers should think ahead about the needs of their disabled customers.[78] No adjustment is required, however, where it would fundamentally alter the nature of the service in question, or the nature of the trade, profession or business.[79]

Most of the duty to make reasonable adjustments[80] came into force in October 1999. The remaining parts will be implemented in 2004. By virtue of section 21 of the Act, service providers must take reasonable steps to change practices, policies or procedures, that make it impossible or unreasonably difficult for disabled people to make use of a service provided to other members of the public. The example given of this in the Code of Practice is that of a 'no dogs' policy in a store which should be waived to allow guide/hearing/assistance dogs onto the premises.[81] Reasonable steps must also be taken to remove, alter or provide a way round a physical feature[82] – such as steps or a doorway – or to provide a reasonable means of avoiding it where the feature makes it impossible or unreasonably difficult for a disabled person to use a service. The only obligation that came into force in October 1999 was to provide the service by a reasonable alternative means; the other obligations do not come into effect until 2004.

Service providers also have to take reasonable steps to provide auxiliary aids or services where they would enable disabled people to make use of a service provided to members of the public or facilitate its use. The examples given of auxiliary aids and services in the Act are information on tape or the provision of a sign language interpreter.[83] The Code of Practice gives detailed guidance on different types of auxiliary aids and services, including accessible websites and subtitles.[84] Whilst this section of the Act indicates that auxiliary aids or services must be provided only where they would enable or facilitate the use of a service (as opposed to where it would otherwise be impossible or unreasonable to use the service), it is worth noting that failure to provide such aids or services may only be actionable where their absence has made it impossible or unreasonably difficult to use the service.[85] The Act does not define 'reasonable', nor 'impossible or unreasonably difficult'. The Code, however, does give guidance on what factors may be taken into account in determining these issues.[86]

## JUSTIFICATION

'Justification' involves both a subjective and an objective test: the service provider must be of the opinion that one or more of the 'justifications' are satisfied, and it must be reasonable in all the circumstances of the case for that opinion to be held by them.[87] The exhaustive list of 'justifications', contained largely in s.20 of the Act, states:

the treatment is necessary in order not to endanger the health or safety of any person (and this may include the disabled person);

the disabled person is incapable of entering into an enforceable agreement or of giving an informed consent, and for that reason the treatment is reasonable in that case;

in a case where a refusal of service is alleged, the treatment is necessary because the provider of service would otherwise be unable to provide the service to members of the public;

where service of different standard or terms is alleged, the treatment is necessary for the service provider to be able to provide the service to the disabled person or other members of the public;

where service on different terms is alleged, the difference in the terms on which the service is provided to the disabled person and those on which it is provided to other members of the public reflects the greater costs to the provider of services in providing the service to the disabled person – this is not applicable where the greater cost is as a result of meeting a s.21 obligation; [88]

where the discrimination occurs in relation to insurance, the treatment is based on information, e.g. actuarial or statistical data, relevant to the assessment of risk, is from a source on which it is reasonable to rely and it is reasonable; [89]

in certain circumstances where the discrimination relates to guarantees, deposits in respect of goods, facilities and premises. [90]

'Health and safety' grounds are often used to discriminate against disabled people – for example, the claim that a wheelchair is a fire hazard. The Code of Practice makes it clear that dubious health and safety grounds cannot provide a justification for discrimination, and specifically states that fire regulations should not be used as an excuse to place unnecessary restrictions on disabled people. [91] The only case to deal with this issue so far has been that of *Damon Rose v Bouchet*. [92] Damon Rose was a blind guide dog user, who tried to get accommodation for the Edinburgh Festival. Mr Bouchet refused him accommodation on the basis that there was not an adequate handrail to his premises and he thought that the steps would therefore be dangerous for a blind person. He confirmed this view with his wife. Mr Rose brought a claim under Part III of the DDA on the grounds that Mr Bouchet had either refused him a service or had refused him premises for a reason relating to his disability. Mr Bouchet defended the proceedings on the basis that the treatment was justified on the grounds of health and safety (a justification available in 'premises' cases, as well as in 'goods, facilities and services' cases). The Sheriff dismissed the claim, holding that Mr Bouchet was justified in his refusal of premises. Mr Rose appealed, and the Sheriff Principal dismissed the appeal. He held that the test of justification in s.24 is in part objective and in part subjective – it is significantly different from the justification contained in the employment provisions of the Act. In this case, the Sheriff's decision was not open to challenge merely because he had neglected to make reference to the Code of Practice. It is worth noting that the Code of Practice on Rights of Access, Services and Premises has now been considerably strengthened in relation to the information to be taken into account in considering 'all the circumstances' of the justification test, including asking the disabled person for their opinion before reaching a decision on such a justification. [93]

## PREMISES

The sale or rent of premises is dealt with separately, in sections 22 to 24 of the Act. It is unlawful for a person with power to dispose of any premises to discriminate against a disabled person:

> in the terms on which they offer to dispose of the premises to the disabled person;

> by refusing to dispose of those premises to the person;

> in their treatment of the disabled person in relation to any list of persons in need of premises of that description – this clearly applies to waiting lists.

This section does not apply to resident landlords unless they employ an estate agent to find a tenant or they advertise such a vacancy and, in certain circumstances, small dwellings are exempted.[94]

It is unlawful for a person managing premises to discriminate against a disabled person occupying those premises:

> in the way they permit the disabled person to make use of any benefits or facilities;

> by refusing or deliberately omitting to permit the disabled person to make use of any benefits or facilities; or

> by evicting the disabled person or subjecting him to any other detriment.

Whilst the basic definition of discrimination (less favourable treatment) is the same as in the rest of the goods and services provisions,[95] the justifications are slightly different.[96] The justifications consist of, as above, health and safety and incapacity to enter into a contract, as well as two other ones: where discrimination is in the way the disabled person has been permitted to use a benefit or facility, that this is necessary for the disabled person or other occupiers to make use of a benefit or facility; and, where the discrimination is in refusing to permit the use of a benefit or facility, this is necessary in order for other occupiers to make use of the benefit or facility.

## REMEDIES

Cases under the goods, facilities, services and premises provisions can be brought to the county court in England, Northern Ireland and Wales, or the Sheriff's court in Scotland. Courts can award any of the remedies available in the High Court,[97] such as injunctions, declarations and damages in tort as well as what is likely to be the only form of damages in such cases – compensation for injury to feelings.

Some of the few goods, facilities and services cases litigated so far have involved no dispute of fact or liability, but have involved arguments as to whether or not a declaration of discrimination should be granted, as this is a discretionary remedy. In the case of *Ginley v Virgin Cinemas Ltd.*[98] the District Judge granted a declaration to a visually impaired guide dog owner who had been refused access to a cinema because of his guide dog. The District Judge stated:

> Discrimination against disabled people is prevalent, otherwise the Act would not have been passed. The purpose of the Act is not only to give individual claimants remedies, but also to eliminate discrimination... Discrimination occurs not only as the result of a conscious intention to discriminate – very often it is the result of the actions of well motivated people, as it was in this case...The purpose of the Act would not be served by refusing a declaration in circumstances such as this. That might be seen as sweeping discrimination under the carpet.

In the case of *Gurney v British Telecommunications plc,*[99] where the defendant cancelled the claimant's request to transfer his telephone service to another provider because they did not provide Braille bills (and thus refused service for a reason relating to disability) the District Judge adopted the reasoning of District Judge Madge in the *Ginley* case.

## DISABILITY RIGHTS COMMISSION

The Act did not initially provide for any form of enforcement body, such as exist under the Race Relations Act 1976 and the Sex Discrimination Act 1975 (CRE and EOC), and this has been criticised as a major flaw in the Act. In 1999, however the Labour Government passed the Disability Rights Commission Act. This establishes a Disability Rights Commission which will be able to promote disability equality and to take up cases under the DDA. It began its work in April 2000.

## REFERENCES

Casserley, C. (2000) 'DDA successes – an update.' *New Beacon 984.*

## NOTES

1    See ss.29–31 of the DDA (all statute references are to the Disability Discrimination Act (DDA), unless otherwise stated). See also pp.154–155.

2    ss.40–47

3    Rail Vehicle Accessibility Regulations 1998, SI 1998/2456; Public Service Accessibility Regulations 2000, SI 2000, 1970

4    ss.32–39 A consultation on the implementation of s.37 was issued in July 2000 and it is proposed to bring this section into force on 1/3/2001.

5    Schedule 1 para (1) (1), SI 1996/1970

6    Disability Discrimination (Meaning of Disability) Regulations 1996(2) and (3)(1), SI 1996/1455

7    Schedule 1 para 3

8  Disability Discrimination (Meaning of Disability) Regulations 1996, SI 1996/1455.

9  *Guidance on Matters to be taken into account in determining questions relating to the definition of disability* (hereafter referred to as Guidance), 1996, London: HMSO.

10  s.53(5), (6)

11  See *Goodwin v the Patent Office*, EAT [1999] IRLR 4

12  Guidance, Part II, para. A1

13  Guidance, Part II, paras. C5–C21

14  Schedule 1, para. 6

15  Schedule 1, paras. 2 & 8, Schedule 2

16  Supra f.n. 11

17  IDS Brief, 645, 11

18  (1999) 625 IRLB 3, EAT

19  *Vicary v British Telecommunications plc* [1999] IRLR 680.

20  *O'Neill v Symm and Co Ltd.* [1998] IRLR 232.

21  *Howden v Capital Copiers (Edinburgh) Ltd.* (1997) 598 IDS Brief.

22  *Tarling v Wisdom Toothbrushes Ltd. T/a Wisdom* (1997) IDS Brief 15.

23  The Disability Discrimination (Employment) Regulations 1996, SI 1996 1456.

24  1996, London: HMSO.

25  s.7(1) and Disability Discrimination (Exception for Small Employers) Order 1998, SI 1998/2616.

26  This was carried out in accordance with s.7(2) and (4) of the Act.

27  *Hardie v CD Northern Ltd.* [2000] IRLR 87.

28  Code of Practice (Employment) para. 2.6 (above, note 24)

29  *Person v Central Scotland Police* [1999] 619 IRLR 18.

30  s.68(1)

31  s.4 (6) and s.68(2)–(5), as amended by Equal Opportunities (Employment Legislation) (Territorial Limits) Regs. 1999 SI 1999/3163

32  s.12. For the purposes of the DDA, a 'principal' is a person ('A') who makes work available for doing by individuals who are employed by another person who supplies them under a contract made with A.

33  [2000] IRLR 387

34  s.12

35  s.4(1)

36  s.4(2)

37  s.5(1)

38  [1999] IRLR 318

39  Code of Practice, Employment, para 4. 57.

40  [1998] IRLR 232

41  [2000] IRLR 144

42  [2000] IRLR 691

43  s.16

44  s.6(4)

45  s.6(6)

46  [1998] IRLR 628

47    [1999] IRLR 76

48    [1998] IRLR 352

49    Employment Appeal Tribunal Appeal No: EAT/910/98.

50    Employment Appeal Tribunal Appeal No: EAT/1493/98.

51    s.5(3)–(4)

52    [1999] IRLR 604

53    *Hampson v Department of Education and Science* [1989] IRLR 69 (CA)

54    [2000] IRLR 144

55    [1998] IRLR 624

56    Appeal No. EAT/497/98

57    [1991] IRLR 513. This case held that a Tribunal can, where a finding of a difference of treatment may point to racial discrimination, look to the employer for an explanation. If no explanation is put forward, or the Tribunal considers it to be inadequate or unsatisfactory, it can infer that a discrimination was on racial grounds. See also *Zafar v Glasgow City Council* [1988] ICR 125 (another race case).

58    s.8, Schedule 3 Part 1, para. 3

59    For example, see the case of *Etherington v ATS Midlands Ltd.*, Nottingham ET, Case No. 2602204.

60    See *Buxton v Equinox Design Ltd.* [1999] IRLR 158.

61    EOR No. 93 September/October 2000.

62    Case No. 2301175199, London South, 25/11/99.

63    Case No. 3201853/98/5 London Stratford.

64    Case No 1804928/99

65    18 May 1998, Case No. 3101262, Southampton ET.

66    [1998] IRLR 624.

67    See EOR Discrimination Law Digest No. 41, Autumn 1999.

68    s.53(5) and (6)

69    Code of Practice, Rights of Access para. 2. 13.

70    SI 1999/1836. No.9

71    With regard to post-16 education, it is proposed that it will be unlawful for education providers, in relation to the provision of education and services provided primarily for students (to include things such as student letting and accommodation services), to discriminate against a disabled person by failing to make a reasonable adjustment, where any arrangements, including physical features of premises, place him at a substantial disadvantage in comparison to persons who are not disabled; or unjustifiably treating him less favourably, for a reason which relates to his disability, than the provider treats others to whom that reason does not apply. It is proposed that these duties will be enforceable in the county or sheriff's court, where compensation may be claimed. Other providers of education services to the public will fall within the existing Part III, as will organisations such as youth and community services provided by education authorities or voluntary groups, which presently fall under the education exclusion.

72    In 'Monitoring the Disability Discrimination Act (DDA) 1995', Institute of Employment Studies, May 1999, it was stated that only nine cases had been lodged under Part III (ss.19–28) between 2 December 1996 and late August 1998.

73    20 January, Nottingham County Court.

74    Preston County Court, Case no: PR 808374, order made on 30 September 1999.

75  s.20 (1)

76  s.20 (2)

77  (1999), 2 CCLR 460

78  Code of Practice, Rights of Access etc. para. 4.7–4.8

79  s.21(6)

80  s.21

81  Code of Practice, Rights of Access para. 5.4. Of the few cases pursued under these parts of the Act so far, most appear to have involved refusal of access to guide dog owners.

82  'Physical features' are defined in The Disability Discrimination (Services and Premises) Regulations 1999, SI No. 1191.

83  s.21(4)

84  Code of Practice Rights of Access Goods Facilities Services and Premises, Chapter 5.

85  s.19 (1) (b)

86  Code of Practice, paras. 4.10, 4.11, 4.16, 4.17. Note also that no auxiliary aids or services are required before 2004 which involve making a permanent alteration to, or would have a permanent effect on, the physical fabric of the premises (Disability Discrimination (Services and Premises) Regulations 1999, SI 1999 /1191).

87  s.20 (3) (a) and (b)

88  s.20 (4)

89  Disability Discrimination (Services and Premises) Regulations 1996 SI1996/1836.

90  Disability Discrimination (Services and Premises) Regulations 1996 SI1999/1836.

91  Code of Practice, Rights of Access para. 6.11.

92  [1999] IRLR 436

93  See particularly para. 6.7

94  s.22 (2) and s.23

95  s.24 (1)

96  s.24 (3)

97  s.25(2) and (5)

98  D.J. Madge, West London County Court, Case No. WL 901352.

99  D.J. Gill, Milton Keynes County Court, Case no. MK 907665.

# CHAPTER SEVEN

# Disability, Housing and Homelessness

*Mary Holmes*

In order for disabled people to be in a position to achieve independent living and a decent quality of life, it is vital that they are provided with suitable housing. People with disabilities experience the same housing problems as able-bodied people, for example problems of housing acquisition, homelessness, security of tenure, disrepair, harassment, or anti-social neighbours.[1] Specific housing needs, however, also arise out of disability. It is possible to find property either to buy or to rent in the private sector that is suitable for the needs of a disabled person and, of course, some disabilities do not require property to be specially adapted. However, where the mobility of the disabled person is affected, it may be crucial that both access to the property and the internal arrangements are adapted to the particular needs of the occupant. This chapter will focus on matters that have dimensions that are particularly relevant to the needs of disabled people.[2] It will consider, in particular:

> the powers and duties of local housing authorities to allocate housing, and to meet the needs of homeless people;

> the adaptation of existing accommodation, including disabled facilities grants, home repair assistance and the impact of new building regulations;

> financial assistance through housing benefit and council tax benefit.

The use of social services to provide for housing needs under their statutory responsibilities towards disabled people has been addressed in Chapter Five.

## POWERS AND DUTIES OF THE LOCAL HOUSING AUTHORITY TO ALLOCATE HOUSING

Each local authority is required by the Housing Act 1996[3] to ensure that there is a housing advisory service which can give advice about, *inter alia*, local housing opportunities, including private sector options, housing registers, local authority allocations policy, landlords and letting agents.[4] This will include accommodation belonging to the local authority itself and other social housing landlords. All local authorities are required to maintain a housing register.[5] The register is used to allocate housing to 'qualifying persons'[6] who satisfy the local authority's particular criteria for the selection of new tenants or for nomination by the local authority to social landlords (for example, housing associations) for new tenancies. Otherwise a local housing authority can allocate accommodation in such a manner as it considers appropriate[7] according to its allocation scheme.[8] Within that scheme local authorities are required[9] to give 'reasonable preference'[10] to, *inter alia*, people living in unsatisfactory housing conditions, households consisting of or including someone with a particular need for settled accommodation, usually taken to mean long-term accommodation on medical or welfare grounds, and households whose social or economic circumstances are such that they have difficulty in securing settled accommodation. Someone who is living in inaccessible housing or housing which is unsafe because of disability should be considered as living in unsatisfactory conditions. The Code of Guidance on the Allocation of Accommodation and Homelessness[11] contains advice as to how the local authority might exercise its powers of allocation and expands on these criteria by suggesting that 'reasonable preference' should include households who need social housing 'to give or receive care, or because their personal circumstances make stability particularly important. Such households may include someone with a physical or learning disability; or someone who is elderly or mentally ill; or a person with a progressive condition such as Multiple Sclerosis; or a person with addictive behaviour or behavioural difficulties.'[12] A disabled child may be a person with a need for settled accommodation on medical or welfare grounds, in which case the views of the social services authority should be sought.[13]

The local authority is also required to give greater priority or 'additional preference'[14] to those who cannot reasonably be expected to find settled accommodation for themselves in the foreseeable future. Such applicants might be particularly vulnerable, for example, as a result of old age, physical or mental illness, and/or because of a learning or physical disability; who may, nevertheless, be able to live independently with the necessary support but who could not be expected to secure accommodation on their own initiative. Additional preference should also be considered in cases where, for example, a carer lives with a disabled person and provides virtually around the clock care or where all members of the household are elderly or infirm.[15]

Whereas the local authority may adopt any reasonable procedures[16] in its approach to allocation of housing, the policy should be flexible as opposed to formulaic[17] and will include a scheme for determining priority and assessing severity of need; this may be, for example, by points earned according to identifiable criteria or quota-based. Points for priority housing can also include assessment of current housing conditions and sharing with family. Households including dependent children and pregnant women attract priority points, as do households with no wage earner or where the head of the household is in part time or low paid work and those households which have been identified as being homeless. (Homelessness and the local authority duties in respect of the homeless are defined in Part VII of the Housing Act 1996 and are considered below, p167.) The Code contains some indicators of the reasonable preference criteria that relate to disability which, while not intending to be exhaustive, include mental illness or disorder; physical or learning disability; chronic or progressive medical conditions (for example MS, HIV or AIDS); infirmity due to old age; the need to give or receive care; need for adapted housing and/or extra facilities, bedroom or bathroom and the need, on medical grounds, for improved heating, sheltered housing, ground floor accommodation or to be near friends or relatives or a medical facility.[18] Each local authority will have its own scheme for identifying priority and the indicators contained in the Code are only illustrative of what could be taken into account; local factors may also influence the way in which priority is identified. The extent to which a local authority gives a particular weighting to the various indicators is for it to decide; it must, however, publish its allocation policy[19] and provide a summary free to anyone who asks.

A recent initiative has encouraged local authorities to establish disability housing registers (DHRs) of either purpose-built property or property adapted for the specific needs of disabled people. The National Disabled Persons Housing Service has published a guide for the compilation of a DHR with examples of how the registers operate in some local authority areas. There is not, however, a mandatory requirement to establish such registers and provision for identifying suitable property and matching it with those with specific needs will vary from area to area; some local authorities have excellent provision and some have none at all.[20]

When an applicant for housing is placed on the housing register they should receive information which indicates, in general terms, the applicant's position on the register and length of time that they will have to wait to be housed.[21] Each authority determines its own offer policy.[22] It may set aside a quota of anticipated allocations for groups of applicants with special characteristics or those referred by social services, welfare or other specialised agencies, although it should not confine its offers to those with special medical or welfare needs from a quota.[23] It is also possible that applicants who owe rent may find that they are not offered accommodation until that debt is discharged[24] or, at least, they will be accorded less priority than someone who has a similar housing need but no rent arrears.[25]

Where an applicant receives care from a carer who does not need to live with the applicant, local authorities should take account of the applicant's need, where appropriate, for a spare bedroom for the carer to ensure that carers are able to fulfil their responsibilities, for example, occasionally staying overnight to take the applicant to the hospital the next day or to cover at weekends where the social service department only provides care during the week.[26] In such circumstances it is important that applicants make clear their needs when applying for housing in order that the authority can take proper note of those needs, particularly where the authority is very short of accommodation.

A disabled applicant for social housing is very likely to be a 'qualifying person' if all that is taken into account are those criteria that relate to reasonable and additional preference identified in s.167. However, local authorities are also permitted to identify classes of either qualifying or non-qualifying persons.[27] The risk that they run in so doing is that they may, by excluding a class, also exclude someone whose individual characteristics would otherwise make them appropriate for social housing. Commonly some residence period is required and those who currently own their own homes are usually non-qualifying persons,[28] as may be those who have been evicted for breach of a tenancy agreement or anti-social behaviour. Additionally the local authority must exclude anyone subject to immigration control,[29] unless they are persons from abroad who are specifically identified as qualifying persons by regulations.[30]

Applicants are also entitled to see the entry on the housing register relating to themselves and to receive a copy of that entry free of charge.[31] The information that is required[32] to be contained in the register is limited and does not include reference to the priority needs that an applicant might have, such as those that arise out of disability. Any challenge to assessment of priority should include a request for clarification of reasons; it will be important to ensure that all necessary supporting information from the applicant's doctor, social services or other professional has been received and considered by the local authority. Where, however, the local authority decides not to put an applicant on the register or to remove him from the register they are obliged to notify him in writing of that decision, the reasons for it and that he has 21 days in which to request a review of the decision.[33] There is no further right of appeal from a review (as there is with homelessness decisions); any further challenge would need to be by way of judicial review, although lobbying the assistance of a local councillor may be a speedier way to resolve the matter.

## Transfers

Transfers to more suitable accommodation because of a change in circumstances, such as an acquired disability, are not covered by the 1996 Act. The Housing Act 1985 contains a requirement that local authorities shall publish their rules relating to transfers;[34] otherwise the law relating to transfer is found in the cases and the judicial insistence that discretionary policies be administered fairly.[35] Transfer schemes will normally enable a tenant with a medical or similar need to be reallocated suitable property. This may, however, only be achievable with the intervention of social services. The joint circular on Housing and Community Care[36] recommends that a composite assessment of all the needs of a family or household is made where, for example, there is a need for transfer on such grounds.[37]

### The Disability Discrimination Act 1995

The Disability Discrimination Act 1995 already makes it unlawful to sell or let property in circumstances or on terms that discriminate against disabled people, including the maintenance of housing lists and priority for allocation of housing. Since October 1999 housing and service providers have been required to provide information in alternative formats and to review policies and practices that may have a discriminatory impact upon a disabled person. (See, for example, residence qualifications for eligibility for housing, above.)

### The local authority's duties to homeless people

The law relating to homelessness is a complicated area, and a disabled person wishing to apply to a local authority for housing under Part VII of the Housing Act 1996 should take advice from a housing aid centre or disability advice project.[38]

The initial obligation of each local authority to those who may be homeless or threatened with homelessness is to provide advice and information about homelessness and its prevention or to enable some other advisory service to do this, free of charge.[39] Where the premises used are inaccessible a home visit should be arranged.[40] In addition any information about the services of the local authority's homeless persons' unit should be available in Braille or on tape. What issues each advisory service should cover will be determined by local housing circumstances, although they must primarily be about homelessness and the prevention of homelessness. The Code of Guidance on Allocations and Homelessness[41] lists a very wide range of possible issues for advice in this context, some of which may arise as a consequence of disability, including local housing opportunities in both social housing and the private sector.[42] The Code does not, however, mention issues which are specific to the needs of disabled people such as disability housing registers, adaptation of existing accommodation, disabled facilities grants and home repair assistance, all of which could enable a disabled person to remain in her present accommodation when appropriately adapted and about which most housing advisory services should be able to provide information. The advice service is also available to those who may be otherwise disqualified from assistance under the homelessness provisions.

The accommodation ultimately provided – where an applicant does satisfy all the rigorous homelessness criteria imposed by the Act – may not be permanent, although those housed under the homelessness provisions may apply to be included on the housing register and so ultimately gain access to long-term social housing.

### The homelessness hurdles

In satisfying the local authority that they are homeless, or threatened with homelessness, applicants will have to overcome the 'homelessness hurdles' by providing satisfactory answers to the following questions:

> Is the applicant homeless or threatened with homelessness?[43]
>
> Is the applicant eligible?[44]
>
> Is the applicant in priority need?[45]
>
> Is the applicant unintentionally homeless?[46]
>
> Does the applicant have a local connection elsewhere?[47]

When, upon initial inquiry, the local authority has reason to believe that an applicant may be homeless, eligible and in priority need it has an interim duty to the applicant to provide accommodation while it makes further enquiries[48] but the final duty of the local authority will vary depending on all the answers to the questions above.

The law requires that the applicant for housing has the mental capacity to accept or reject an offer; a disabled child or an adult with a severe mental handicap will not be in a position to do this. In such cases an adult member of the household or a carer must make the application and satisfy the necessary homelessness criteria.[49]

## Is the applicant homeless or threatened with homelessness?

Homelessness is specifically defined by the Act[50] and includes:

> having nowhere to live at all;
>
> having accommodation which is not big enough for the all family unit and/or a carer to live there;[51]
>
> having accommodation but which it is not of a size or condition whereby it is reasonable to stay there (this criterion is relative in the sense that the accommodation is subject to comparison with prevailing accommodation conditions in the area);[52] and

living in emergency or crisis accommodation such as a refuge.[53]

Being threatened with homelessness is defined as having accommodation but likely to be homeless within 28 days. It is possible that an early referral to the housing advisory service may prevent homelessness by the initiation of preventive action.[54] The mere fact that accommodation is temporary, short-term or precarious will not of itself cause an applicant to be considered homeless.[55]

One of the definitions of homelessness refers to being unable to secure entry to accommodation.[56] This is explained in the Code[57] as referring to exclusion because of illegal eviction or occupation of the property by squatters, that is, it is the possession of the property, rather then denial of access due to physical constraints such as stairs which cannot be managed by someone with a disability, which is relevant here. As far as the definitions of homelessness which relate to 'reasonable' occupation, much will depend on size and physical condition and the number of people occupying the property;[58] it may also depend on access, internal arrangements and other physical characteristics of the accommodation which may make it unsuitable, for example, for elderly or long-term disabled applicants, or for people with HIV or AIDS. Where an applicant has care, health or support needs the Code of Guidance requires that the homelessness unit liaises with other bodies in establishing the homelessness status of an applicant.[59]

## Is the applicant 'eligible' for housing assistance?

As when determining who is a 'qualifying person' entitled to go on the housing register, the local authority must exclude anyone 'ineligible', that is subject to immigration control[60] unless they are persons from abroad who are specifically identified as qualifying persons by the relevant regulations.

## Is there a priority need?

Only categories of applicants who can be described as having 'priority need' are entitled to be assisted under the homelessness provisions.[61] These are:

a woman who is pregnant or the woman with whom the person is living or might reasonably be expected to live is pregnant;

a person with dependent children living with them or who might reasonably be expected to live with them;

a person, and anyone who might reasonably be expected to live with them, who is especially vulnerable because of age, mental illness or handicap, physical disability or other special reasons;

a person who is homeless through an emergency such as flood, fire or disaster.

Whereas a disabled person might fall into any or all of the categories above, it is likely that vulnerability will be a key issue. The Act does not define what is meant by the word 'vulnerable' but case law has produced tests which focus on whether the applicant is less able to fend for himself in the housing context and thereby make himself vulnerable in circumstances where a less vulnerable person would be able to cope without harmful effects.[62] Someone discharged from a psychiatric hospital or a local authority hostel for those with mental health problems is likely to be vulnerable; where there is physical disability or long-term acute illness, such as those defined by the Disability Discrimination Act 1995, which affect the applicant's housing situation and give rise to vulnerability, effective liaison between housing, social services and health authorities will be required.[63]

### Is the applicant intentionally homeless?

The Act defines intentional homelessness[64] in terms of an applicant deliberately doing or failing to do something, the result of which is that he has ceased to occupy accommodation which was available for occupation and which it would have been reasonable to continue to occupy.[65] Failure to take up suitable accommodation offered by a local authority may also be considered as intentional homelessness. Any collusion between a landlord and a tenant that the tenant be evicted in order to get rehoused by the local authority will be considered intentional homelessness.[66] It is up to the housing authority to establish the intentionality of an applicant's homelessness and it may take past events into account in reaching its decision. Applicants should always be given the opportunity to explain their actions; incapacity to manage affairs as a result of old age, mental illness or impairment, acts or omissions as a result of limited mental capacity or temporary aberration caused by mental illness or frailty should be taken into account.[67] It would normally be appropriate for social services to be involved in making such an assessment.

In addition, where an applicant is genuinely unaware of a fact, such as an entitlement to housing benefit in order to prevent rent arrears, any resultant homelessness may not be considered intentional.[68]

Decisions on intentionality must take all relevant matters into account and they must be reasonable. There has been a considerable amount of case law on what amounts to intentional homelessness and early cases made it quite clear that intentionality can be traced back beyond the immediate cause of homelessness.[69] The chain of causation can be broken by acquisition of a 'settled' residence but most property in the private sector is now let on a short-term basis only so other matters may need to be taken into account when considering whether the chain has been broken.[70] It could be argued that where a disability arises that causes the continued occupation of present, albeit not long-term, accommodation to become unreasonable, because of the needs to which the disability gives rise, then the chain could be broken.[71]

Where an applicant is considered to be intentionally homeless it is possible for a household member to apply instead, provided that they did not collude in the act or omission which gave rise to the intentional homelessness and they have capacity to be an applicant. Where a disabled child is a member of a homeless household, social services may have a responsibility for that child which includes the need to provide suitable accommodation under section 17 of the Children Act 1989. Social services may ask the housing authority[72] for assistance in obtaining suitable housing, but a housing authority need only comply with a request for assistance from social services if it is compatible with its own statutory functions. In the final analysis children remain the responsibility of social services which cannot 'get round' adverse findings of the housing authority, such as intentional homelessness, by the back door.[73]

## Does the applicant have a local connection?

Where a local authority is of the view that an applicant has a priority need and is not intentionally homeless it may refer the application to another local housing authority if that applicant has no local connection with the district to which he has applied and they, or someone with whom they might reasonably be expected to reside, do have a local connection with another local authority in England, Wales or Scotland.[74] The local connection provision will not apply to an applicant who fears domestic violence if returned to another area.[75] The local authority to whom the applicant is referred (the notified authority) is bound by the decision of the referring authority as to the housing obligation, even if the notified authority has previously rejected the applicant as intentionally homeless. It is possible to establish[76] local connection with another area by showing there is or was normal and voluntary residence in that area,[77] or by employment in the area or by having close family in the area or by any other special connections with the area.

### Duties of the local authority to the homeless

The extent of the local authority's duty will depend on the success of the applicant leaping the hurdles identified above. If the applicant is homeless, eligible, has a priority need and is not intentionally homeless, the local authority has a duty either:

> if satisfied that other suitable accommodation is available in its district, to provide such advice and assistance as to enable them to secure such accommodation[78]; or

to secure them accommodation[79] for a minimum of two years, after which the authority must satisfy itself that the person remains entitled under the legislation.[80]

The local authority may decide to refer the application to another local authority on the grounds of local connection. The level of advice and assistance offered should reflect the special needs that a disabled person might have in being able to find appropriate accommodation, particularly where private letting agents may not provide information in a format that is readily accessible. However, if there is someone who might reasonably be expected to live with the applicant, such as a carer, his or her ability to help secure accommodation will be taken into account. Where the applicant refuses an offer of accommodation which the local authority considers to be suitable the local authority's duty is discharged and they no longer have any obligations to the applicant. The critical issue in all cases, and particularly where disability is concerned, is whether the accommodation offered is suitable, not only for the applicant but also for anyone who might reasonably be expected to live with the applicant, including carers. The cases which deal with the issue of suitability suggest that the courts are reluctant to interfere with the local authority's discretion.[81] Applicants and advisers need, therefore, to be vigilant in ensuring that the local authority has properly taken into account the medical and other evidence submitted to support an application under the homelessness provisions. Otherwise the local housing authority duty is to give advice and help with finding accommodation and to provide temporary accommodation sufficient to give applicants time to make their own arrangements, after which no further duty is owed.

The local authority must notify applicants in writing of their decisions and, if the decision is adverse, reasons must be given.[82] The notification must also inform applicants of the right to request a review, which must be made within 21 days of notification of a decision. Reviews may be requested concerning decisions on the applicant's eligibility, the local authority's duty, a local connection referral and suitability and availability of accommodation offers. The applicant should be notified of the review decision within eight weeks and should be informed of his or her right of appeal to the county court on a point of law. Although local authorities have no duty to provide accommodation pending a review or an appeal,[83] they may choose to do so.

An applicant still dissatisfied after the review procedure has right of appeal to the county court on a point of law only (as opposed to a finding of fact). In addition, applications can be made for judicial review to challenge local authority decisions where the applicant wants to show that the local authority did not exercise its discretion properly, for example by not considering some important matter such as medical evidence. This is a complex legal process in the High

Court and only provides remedies at the discretion of the court. Since the review and appeals procedure was introduced after the 1996 Act came into force there has been a decline in the number of homelessness cases being judicially reviewed.

### Those who fall outside the housing authority's homelessness duty

The local authority's duties under the 1996 Act are limited and a number of the categories of people will be excluded and be forced to rely upon the powers and duties of social services for accommodation. Those who are 'ineligible' because of their immigration status, and who previously came within the scope of the local authority duties under section 21 of the National Assistance Act 1948, will no longer do so unless they are ill or disabled.[84] Those who are children or mentally impaired, and so not capable of deciding whether or not to accept accommodation, will also have to rely upon social service duties to accommodate them under the Children Act or the National Assistance Act. Someone who is not vulnerable under the rather narrow test adopted under the Housing Act[85] may nevertheless fall within the scope of NAA s.21 as in need of care and attention. Once it appears to a local authority that an applicant may be in need of a service which it may provide,[86] such as an accommodation need, it is under a duty to carry out that assessment[87] and to provide where appropriate, despite apparent reluctance, 'ordinary' housing.[88]

## ADAPTATION OF EXISTING ACCOMMODATION

Where a disabled person already occupies accommodation, either individually or as a member of a household, it may be possible to improve the facilities, internal arrangements and access to the property in order to increase the potential for independent living. This may be appropriate for both owner-occupied accommodation and rented accommodation in either the private or social housing sectors. The cost of such adaptations may be considerable but the Housing Grants, Construction and Regeneration Act 1996 (HGCR Act)[89] provides a number of sources of financial aid which include disabled facilities grants and home repair assistance.

Any disabled person,[90] whether or not on the local authority register of disabled persons, is entitled to apply for assistance which can be used, *inter alia*, for building extensions, widening doorways, constructing handrails, converting kitchens and installing stair lifts, special baths and lavatories. Owner-occupiers can apply and, where the applicant is a tenant, the application for a disabled facilities grant will have to be accompanied by written permission from the owner agreeing to the application.[91]

The grants are administered by the local authority and are means-tested, despite the fact that the grant is mandatory for some adaptations. The maximum amount for a mandatory grant is £20,000 [92] and the local authority has the power to make a discretionary grant[93] in addition if the cost of the adaptation is more than this. Also social services have duties[94] under the Chronically Sick and Disabled Persons Act 1970 section 2 to assist with provision of greater safety, comfort and convenience in the home, and may be able to provide additional loans or grants to 'top up' the disabled facilities grant. A disabled person should not be put off applying merely because of the estimated cost of adaptations.

Procedure for making applications will vary from area to area but the applicant should approach either social services or the housing authority, who may well make initial informal preliminary inquiries to inform both themselves and the applicant about extent of the adaptation, the likely financial contribution, if any, from the applicant and whether the accommodation is suitable for adaptation.

### Mandatory disabled facilities grants

Mandatory disabled facilities grants are available for a wide variety of adaptations[95] including:

> creating access for a disabled occupant to and from the dwelling;
>
> making the dwelling or building safe for the disabled occupant and other persons living with him;
>
> enabling access by the disabled occupant to a room used or usable as the principal family room;
>
> enabling access by the disabled occupant to a room used or usable for sleeping;
>
> providing access for the disabled occupant to a room in which there is a lavatory, a wash-hand basin and a room in which there is a bath or shower (or both);
>
> adaptations to a kitchen for the preparation and cooking of food by the disabled person;
>
> improving or installing a heating system;
>
> adapting the locations of light, heating and power switches to make them easier to use; improving access and movement by the disabled person around the accommodation in order to enable him to care for someone else who is living there.

Where the applicant is a tenant of the local authority, the authority may decide to carry out the adaptations itself without recourse to the disabled facilities grant system. Housing Association tenants may receive assistance from the Housing Association rather than applying for a disabled facilities grant. In both cases the disabled person should be provided with the same facility for adaptation. All applications must be submitted formally, including plans, planning permission, where relevant, building regulation approval, two estimates detailing the cost of the work and financial information for the means test.[96] Whether an owner occupier, tenant or landlord, the applicant will also be required to submit a certificate of intention that throughout the grant condition period, currently five years, or such shorter period as the applicant's health and circumstances permit, the disabled person will occupy the dwelling as his only or main residence.[97]

The main considerations for the local authority in deciding whether to make the grant or not are whether the work is necessary and appropriate and is reasonable and practicable.[98] In order to decide this it will first consult social services and an assessment of the need will be made by an occupational therapist or some other professional who can determine the extent to which the proposed adaptations will assist in enabling independent living and even reduce the need for care and support from social services. The guidance identifies the factors which should be considered, including:

> whether the adaptations and improvements are needed to provide for a care plan to be implemented which will enable the disabled occupant to remain living in the existing home as independently as possible;

> whether they would meet, as far as possible, the assessed needs of the disabled person, taking into account both medical and physical needs; and

> making a distinction between the desirable and possibly legitimate aspirations of the disabled person, and what is actually needed and for which grant support is fully justified.[99]

In addition the needs of the particular household group in which the disabled occupant resides should be considered so that adaptations do not cause strain on the household by, for example, interfering with the privacy of the disabled person or carer following completion of works.[100] Disabled facilities grants are designed to give the disabled person a degree of independence in the home and would not have achieved their objective within a care package if the disabled person does not gain an acceptable degree of independence, where possible, or, where the disabled person remains dependent upon the care of others, where the adaptation does not significantly ease the burden of the carer.[101] There may be alternative ways of meeting the needs of the disabled person which the local authority may wish to consider, particularly if there are cost implications.[102]

The property will also be assessed in order to see if the adaptations are practical, given its age and condition. Property which is in serious disrepair or lacking in some essential amenities such as piped water, internal sanitation or other defects which would make it statutorily 'unfit for human habitation'[103] may not be considered appropriate for a disabled facilities grant. If this is the case then a 'renovation grant' may be considered to remedy major defects,[104] although rehousing to more suitable accommodation may be the most acceptable alternative. A local housing authority is not entitled to have regard to its resources in determining whether or not to approve an application for a disabled facilities grant[105] for purposes of section 23(1) of the Act.

### Discretionary grants

Local authorities may also award discretionary grants to make the dwelling suitable for accommodation, welfare or employment of the disabled occupant in any other respect. This can include[106] extending a dwelling which is already suitable for the disabled occupant in all other respects, providing access to a garden or creating a safe play area for a disabled child, or adapting a room for the use of a disabled person who is housebound but able to work from home. These grants are subject to a means test. The means test[107] assesses the financial circumstances of not only the disabled person but also any other 'relevant persons', that is a spouse or partner or the parent of a disabled occupant under the age of 18. It ignores any savings or capital less than £5000. However any capital above £5000 will be assumed to generate an income of £1 per week for every £250 (or part of £250) above the £5000. (This the same assumption of income that is made for the purpose of assessment of means for housing benefit (see below, p178) and income support, even though the capital clearly will not be generating such income.) The average weekly (combined) income of the relevant persons is also assessed and, together with any notional or assumed income from savings, is set against an applicable amount (assumed on the same assessment of basic needs as housing benefit, and which are uprated annually). Details of these allowances can be obtained from the local authority or RADAR,[107A] among others. If the resources are less than the applicable amount plus a grant premium of £40 then the applicant will not normally have to make a contribution to the cost of the adaptation of the accommodation. If the applicant is on income support or income-based job seeker's allowance she will not normally have to make a contribution. However, if the resources are more than the applicable amount then a proportion of the income will be used to calculate the size of 'loan' that notionally could be afforded to help pay for the adaptations.[108] It does not matter that there will be no 'loan'; this is merely a device for working out the applicant's contribution to the total cost, which the disabled person may well have to pay from capital. Therefore, in practice, the amount of grant will be equal to the cost of the works minus the 'affordable loan'.

The local authority is required to give a decision in writing on the application within six months; this may seem a very long time to wait but it is very important that an applicant does not start work before the local authority approves the grant, otherwise she may find that no grant is payable at all. It is also important to get the application in as soon as possible so that the six months can begin to run. If the work is very urgent then it should only be undertaken in advance of the grant with the agreement of the local authority. The grant will only be paid by the local authority when the work has been completed by the builder to its satisfaction and in accordance with the grant specification. The grant will be paid when invoices or receipts are produced; however, if a relative or member of the family has done the work the local authority will only pay for materials and any services bought in. It is possible for the grant to be paid in instalments as the work progresses.

## Home repair assistance

In addition to disability facilities grants, local authorities have the power to give home repair assistance,[109] which is intended to pay for small-scale but essential repairs, improvements or adaptations in the homes of the elderly or disabled such as insulation, repairs to the drains or home security, a wheelchair ramp or grip rails. Work or repairs which are small but essential may make all the difference between enabling a disabled person to remain independent in his own home and having to move. The grant is discretionary and local authorities can set their own criteria for determining priority for what work will qualify for the assistance. The local authority should publish its local guidelines and may operate a means test to help determine priority. It will be important for an applicant to obtain advice on the possible options from either the local authority or other agencies, such as Care and Repair and Anchor Staying Put.[109A] The maximum grant is £2000 per application and £4000 in total in relation to a property over a period of three years.

Applications may be made by a carer of a disabled or elderly person; otherwise the applicant must be disabled, elderly (that is over 60) or infirm or in receipt of an income-related benefit (income support, income-based job seeker's allowance, working families tax credit, housing benefit or disabled persons tax credit). The grant is limited to owner occupiers and private tenants (not landlords) but it is available to those living in mobile homes and house boats. Applicants must normally have occupied the property for three years. Detailed information must be supplied with the application, including estimates and confirmation that an application for a disabled facilities grant has not been made.

Tenants of Housing Associations can apply directly to the Housing Association which will have considerable powers to make structural modifications specifically to meet the needs of the disabled, including widening doors, installing lifts and hoists and altering kitchens and bathrooms. Confirmation of the needs of the individual will be required from either social services, a doctor or another appropriate professional. The Housing Corporation can make grants to meet costs over £500 and the Housing Association should meet the costs up to £500.

### New property

Building regulations now require that new housing must be accessible for disabled people.[110] These regulations affect all housing developers, including all social housing landlords and local authorities, but will not apply to extensions or alterations to property.

The main features are:

> level or ramped approaches to a building, except where the plot is exceptionally steep where a stepped approach would be acceptable;

> the main entrance door should provide a minimum clear opening width of 775mm;

> corridors and hallways in the entrance storey should be sufficiently wide to allow convenient circulation by a wheelchair user;

> switches and socket outlets for lighting and other equipment should be between 450mm and 1200mm from the floor;

> a toilet should be provided in the entrance storey and wheelchair users should be able to access the toilet;

> the provisions which apply to dwellings also apply to the design of each flat;

> where a lift is provided it should meet specified access standards.

There are some exceptions: for example, where the gradient from the point where a disabled person would alight from a vehicle to the property is too steep to allow ramped access; where there is no front garden; where the property has a basement; or where the property is in a conservation area. There are also exceptions for town houses, where the toilet and other accommodation may not be at the entrance level, and flats on upper storeys where no lift is provided.

## OTHER FINANCIAL ASSISTANCE

### Housing benefit

Housing benefit (HB) is a means tested benefit for those with low incomes, whether that income is derived from work or benefits or a combination of both. It is paid to cover rent, not mortgage payments (disabled people with mortgages who claim income support or income-based job seeker's allowance must include this as a housing cost for assessment of the applicable amount for those benefits), irrespective of whether the claimant is available for or in full-time work. It is administered by local authorities.[111]

Housing benefit is paid in a variety of ways. Local authority tenants will receive it by way of a deduction in their rent, so, if housing benefit is paid to cover 100 per cent of the rent, local authority tenants will not pay any rent. Private and Housing Association tenants can receive their housing benefit directly from the local authority or it may be paid to the landlord directly. Payments for residential care and nursing homes are not normally covered by HB. Those who receive income-based jobseeker's allowance (IBJSA) or income support are automatically entitled to maximum housing benefit and claimants who are in low-paid work or receive other benefits, such as pensions, will need to have their incomes assessed for housing benefit purposes.

Those entitled to housing benefit include private tenants, local authority tenants, lodgers, boarders, licensees and occupants of houseboats, caravans, mobile homes and almshouses. Those not entitled include owner occupiers, most asylum seekers and those who fail the habitual residence test, people living with close relatives and most full-time students.

### Assessment and calculation

Although the process for claiming may seem complicated, the calculation can be broken down into stages – the calculation of the applicable amount, income (if not on IBJSA or income support), eligible rent and deductions for non-dependants (see below, p.182) living in the claimant's home.

### Applicable amount

The applicable amount for a housing benefit claimant is calculated by reference to personal allowances, which reflect the family composition of the claimant, together with any premiums to which the claimant, partner and dependants are entitled, for example, because of disability.

## Income

In most respects the calculation of income is the same as for IBJSA and income support (IS); it includes the income of a partner, earned income, other income and capital. The capital cut-off is, however, set at £16,000 and capital over £3000 will be taken to produce a 'notional' weekly income of £1 for every £250 over the £3000. Some income may be ignored (for example, £25 of earnings for a lone parent not claiming IS, £10 earnings disregard for a couple.) In addition, some social security benefits or credits are included in the assessment of income and some disregarded. For example, Disability Living Allowance (DLA) is disregarded but disabled person's tax credit (DPTC) will count as income, as will maintenance, but where the claimant is a single parent, or a couple with a child, there is a £15 disregard of maintenance. An allowance for childcare costs may also be deducted from earnings.

## Non-dependants

Regulations also provide a scale of deductions to be made to a claimant's housing benefit in respect of certain non-dependants who live in the same household. A non-dependant is someone who normally lives in the household, such as an adult son, daughter or other adult relative.[112] Someone who pays a proper rent on a commercial basis is a tenant or lodger. The local authority will assume that a close adult relative is a non-dependant and not a lodger or tenant. However if the claimant has a carer living with him, who is paid for by a voluntary organisation or a public body, he or she will not be considered as a non-dependant. Where the claimant or the claimant's partner is registered blind or receives attendance allowance, constant attendance allowance or the care component of disability living allowance, no non-dependant deductions will be made. Unless the claimant or the non-dependant is exempt a deduction will be made from the eligible rent (that is, the rent in respect of which the local authority will pay housing benefit) for every non-dependant irrespective of whether they actually contribute this amount to the rent or not. Deductions[113] for non-dependants aged 18 or over in full-time work are based upon gross income and the amounts deducted diminish the smaller the income.

## Eligible rent

The housing costs payable are the 'eligible rent' (this will not necessarily be the full rent) and some service charges in very limited circumstances, for example, cleaning of the claimant's own accommodation where there is no one else in the household to do it[114] or alarm systems in accommodation that is adapted or designed for the elderly or the disabled.[115] A number of housing costs are not eligible for housing benefit; these include water rates, mortgage interest and the interest on home improvement loans, payments under a co-ownership scheme and charges for fuel, meals and certain service charges, for example, nursing and personal care.

In addition to these restrictions on eligible rent, the local authority may decide that the rent paid is too much for the accommodation or that accommodation is too large for the claimant's needs. The local authority has the power, therefore, to restrict the amount of rent eligible for housing benefit for private tenants. The rent that will be eligible for housing benefit is calculated by a rent officer, not the local authority, and is known as the maximum rent. The calculation is made with reference to what is considered to be an appropriate rent in comparison with other rents locally for similar accommodation. This is a complicated assessment and advice should always be sought. Where the claimant is a single person under 25, the maximum rent is limited to a 'single room rent', which will be an amount determined as the midpoint of the range of rents for one-room accommodation in the area or less, if the actual rent is lower. However, single room rent does not apply where the applicant is a Housing Association tenant or has a severe disability premium as part of the applicable amount.[116]

Anyone who has claimed housing benefit since before 2 January 1996 is exempt from the application of the restricted rent for as long as housing benefit has been claimed on a continuous basis since that time and he or she continues to occupy the same dwelling, unless forced to leave as a result of fire, flood, explosion or natural catastrophe which has rendered the dwelling uninhabitable.[117] Accommodation which provides care, support or supervision to the occupants is also exempt from the current rules. In addition certain groups of claimants are 'protected', including those with young children or young persons, claimants aged 60 or more, and sick or disabled claimants whose rent must not be restricted unless suitable cheaper alternative accommodation is available and it is reasonable to expect them to move.[118]

## Review of housing benefit decisions

There is a standard housing benefit review procedure, whereby, on receipt of the decision in respect of a claim, a full statement, detailing how a particular housing benefit decision has been reached, may be sought by the claimant. The claimant can then require the authority to review its housing benefit decision, after which a written decision with reasons must be provided. The scope for challenging a rent restriction, however, is limited. If the challenge is to the amount of maximum rent payable, the claimant may have difficulty in proving that there are comparable properties with comparable rents.

Under the regulations the local authority has the power to pay extra benefit in exceptional circumstances.[119] These circumstances are not defined but do not have to be unique[120] and must take individual circumstances into account. It is up to the claimant to make known these circumstances, which may arise from disability or ill health, and anyone refused consideration should request a review. In addition to this discretion the local authority has the power to increase benefit where exceptional hardship would be caused by local reference rent restrictions. The local authority guidance on the exercise of its discretion includes consideration of ill health and disability.

The claimant has the right to a second review, or 'appeal', to be heard by a review board. The claimant has the right to be heard and may be represented, although legal aid is not available. The board must provide a written decision. There are no further appeal procedures but the decision of the review board may be challenged through an application for judicial review or by way of a complaint to the local government ombudsman if there is an allegation of maladministration.

## Housing Benefit calculation

Work out eligible or maximum rent

Subtract any non-dependant deductions

Work out earnings or income (net)

Work out applicable amount (AA)

If income is less than AA, then maximum housing benefit is payable

If income is more than applicable amount, then work out 65 per cent of excess income over AA and deduct this from eligible rent/maximum rent to get HB payable

Formula: HB = maximum rent − 65 per cent (income − applicable amount).

## Council tax benefit

Council Tax (CT) is payable by most occupiers of property. The amount paid is set by the local authority and varies from one area to another. It is based on an assumed valuation of property from year to year and all properties are put into one of eight bands (A–H), with A being the lowest. The higher the band, the greater the council tax. Disabled tenants and owner occupiers who have a low income can claim council tax benefit, which is payable by the local authority. In addition there are reductions for disability (to the valuation band below the one allocated to that property) claimable by the person liable to pay the CT if a disabled person resides in the home and the home has specially adapted facilities for that disabled person.[121]

CT is based on the assumption that two adults live in each property but, where the person liable to pay CT lives on his own, he will be entitled to a 25 per cent discount on the CT payable. Certain residents are ignored for this purpose, for example, students, but if all residents fall into the ignored category, a 50 per cent discount is made.

There are two types of benefit: main CTB and second adult rebate. Eligibility will depend on income and possession of capital in the same way as for housing benefit, and the number of people in the family or the household. Similarly certain benefits, such as attendance allowance and Disability Living Allowance, are disregarded totally, as are payments from charities and voluntary organisations, such as the Macfarlane Trust and the Independent Living Funds. Other payments, such as war disablement pensions, have £10 disregarded, although local authorities do have a discretion to disregard more or even the full amount.[122]

It is assumed, as with HB, that a non-dependant will be making a contribution towards the council tax, so a standard reduction will be made from CTB regardless of whether the non-dependant does actually contribute. The deductions[123] for non-dependants aged 18 or over in full-time work are based upon gross income.

A second adult rebate can be claimed if the claimant is the only person liable for CT in that home and there is another adult living with the claimant who is on a low income and does not pay rent; this would apply with an adult child claiming income support. A 'second adult' does not include a spouse or, for example, a joint tenant.

A claimant who is receiving IS/IBJSA can claim CTB through the Benefits Agency (combined HB/CTB form) and will be entitled to maximum CTB. Otherwise the claim form is obtainable from the local authority. For those not on IBJSA/IS, and therefore not entitled to the maximum CTB, there is a simple formula to work out entitlement.

The calculation procedure is as follows:

check capital limits

income – same as for HB

applicable amount – same as for HB

MaxCTB is net weekly liability (calculated by dividing annual council tax charge by 365 (or 366) and multiplying by seven) after disability reduction or discount and minus any non-dependent deductions

if income is equal to or less than AA, then MaxCBT

if income is greater than AA, calculate the difference

calculate 20 per cent of the difference and deduct from MaxCTB to get weekly amount of CTB payable

Formula: CTB = MaxCTB − 20%(income − applicable amount)

As with housing benefit the local authority has a discretion to increase CTB in exceptional circumstances.[124] Any claimant who feels that her individual circumstances are exceptional and that these have not been taken into account should ask for the decision to be reviewed.

## POSTSCRIPT: HUMAN RIGHTS ACT 1998

Local housing authorities are public authorities and will come within the scope of this Act. The issues that may be raised under the Act are likely to centre on Article 8 and the right to family life.[125]

## REFERENCES

Arden, A. and Hunter, C. (1997) *Homelessness and Allocations*. London: Legal Action Group.

Bradford, I., Bullock, T. and Duke, A. *In Good Repair*. London: Care and Repair/ Scope.

Disability Alliance (2000) *Disability Rights Handbook*. London: Disability Alliance.

George, C. *et al.* (2000) *Welfare Benefits Handbook, 2nd edn*. London: Child Poverty Action Group.

Shaw, V. (1999) *A Perfect Match? A Good Practice Guide to Disability Housing Registers*. York: The National Disabled Persons Housing Service.

## NOTES

1    Shelter's *Housing Rights Guide* provides useful information on these issues.

2    As defined by s.29 National Assistance Act 1948, that is permanent rather than temporary disability.

3    Housing Act 1996 s.179 (all statutory references hereafter are to this Act unless otherwise stated).

4    The Draft Code of Guidance on the Allocation of Accommodation and Homelessness para. 7.11 (1997/ 9.11). See the website www.housing.detr.gov.uk/local/guide/ for this draft published in April 1999. All references to the Code are initially to the draft and then to the 1997 version. It is understood that local authorities are being encouraged to have reference to the draft although the version of the Code in force was published in 1996 and revised in March 1997. See Arden and Hunter (1997).

5    s.162

6    s.161

7    s.159 (7)

8    s.167(1)

9    s.167(2)

10    The term 'reasonable preference' was considered in *R v Wolverhampton MBC ex p. Watters* (1997) 29 HLR 931.

11    It is important to remember that the Code is advisory only. All local authorities must have reference to it (see *L v Newham LBC, ex p. Ojuri* [1998] The Times, 29 August 1998) but they are not obliged to follow its advice.

12    Draft Code of Guidance para. 5.6 (5.18/1997).

13    Para. 5.9 (5.14/1997)

14    s.167(2) and para. 5.14 (5.9/1997)

15    Para. 5.15

16    *R v Port Talbot Borough Council and ors, ex p. Jones* [1988] 2 All ER 208 – individual allocation based on irrelevant considerations was *Wednesbury* unreasonable, '…was unfair to others on the housing list and was an abuse of power,' per Nolan J.

17    *R v Canterbury City Council, ex p. Gillespie* (1986) 19 HLR 7 where the challenge to the local authority's policy succeeded because 'it constitutes a rule which requires to be followed slavishly rather than a merely a stated general approach which is always subject to an exceptional case and which permits each application to be individually considered', per Simon Brown J. See also para 5.19 of the Code.

18    Draft Code Annex 3 (Annex A/1997).

19    s.168

20    Appendices 1–3 of Shaw 1999 describe the Gable Project in Liverpool, the categories used in classifying and matching disability and housing type in Waltham Forest and the application form used by Hull Accessible Housing.

21    s.166(1)

22    See *R v Lewisham LBC ex p. Pinzon* [1999] 2 CCLR 152 where an allegation that the council's allocation scheme was unlawful because it restricted the number of bedrooms allocated to a family and failed to give additional points for disability was rejected on the basis that the council had done its 'honest and reasonable best to measure and weigh the competing claims'.

23    Para. 5.23 (5.22/1997)

24    But note *R v Islington LBC, ex p. Aldabbagh* [1994] EGCS 156 where the local authority policy not to transfer existing tenants to new houses until they had cleared all arrears of rent, even where an applicant for transfer had an urgent medical need, was an unlawful fettering of its discretion. In *R v Forest Heath DC, ex p. West & Lucas* (1992) 24 HLR 85 the Court of Appeal took the view that it was an abuse of power to refuse to consider applicants for the housing waiting list until they had cleared any 'poll tax' liabilities.

25    See *R v Wolverhampton MBC ex p. Watters* (see note 10). Although the case related to s.22 Housing Act 1985 the same criterion of reasonable preference applied. Legatt LJ explained that 'reasonable preference envisages that other factors may weigh against and so diminish and even nullify preference'. The local authority obligation to consider the need to balance its housing revenue account could be brought into balance against the preference that the applicant in substantial rent arrears might otherwise be given.

26    Para 5.33

27    s.161(4)

28    A case study in Shaw 1999 illustrates how Liverpool City Council's owner/occupier rule was mitigated by the use of the Accessible Homes Register to match the applicant's need to provision of sheltered accommodation owned by a local Housing Association.

29    See s.161(2) and Chapter 20 of the Code of Guidance (Annex E3/1997).

30   See Regulations 4, 5 and 6, Allocation of Housing Regulations 1996 (SI 1996 No.2753 as amended by SI 1997 No.631, SI 1997 No. 2046 and SI 1999 No.2135).

31   s.166(1)(a)

32   Allocation of Housing Regulations 1996 (SI 1996 No. 2753 Reg 7).

33   s.164

34   Housing Act 1985, s.106(1)(b)

35   See, for example, *R v Wandsworth LBC, ex p. Lawries* (1997) 30 HLR 153 and *R v LB of Tower Hamlets, ex parte Spence* (1996) 29 HLR 64.

36   DoE Circular 10/92; DoHE in LAC (92) 12.

37   In *R v Wigan ex p. Tammadge* (1998) 1 CCLR 581 the court found that where a need for larger accommodation had been formally identified, in this case by a Social Services Review Panel for a family with severely mentally impaired members, the authority could not refuse to provide it because 'the potential benefits…do not justify the significant cost'; it had a duty to make provision for the need. However, in *R. v Lambeth LBC ex p. A1 and A2* (1998) 1 CCLR 336 the Court of Appeal held that it was not unreasonable, on the evidence, for the local authority not to exercise its discretion (s.9(5) Housing Act 1985) to acquire a four bedroom house for a family which included children aged 15, 12 and twins aged three. One of the children had cerebral palsy and a severe learning difficulty, many epileptic fits a day, was incontinent, unable to dress or feed himself or attend to his toilet needs.

38   RADAR has an *Information Guide on Homelessness*; see also Arden and Hunter (1997) for a full discussion on law.

39   s.179

40   Para. 7.15 (9.15/1997) of the Code of Guidance (see note 4).

41   See note 4.

42   Para. 7.11 (9.11/1997) of the Code of Guidance (see note 4).

43   s.179

44   s.185

45   s.189

46   s.191

47   s.198

48   s.188

49   See *Garlick v Oldham MBC* [1993] AC 509. In *R v Tower Hamlets LBC ex p. Begum* (1993) 25 HLR 319, HL, a 24-year-old woman with severe mental impairment purported to make an application for housing under the homelessness provisions after other members of her family had been rejected on the basis of intentional homelessness. The House of Lords held that an adult lacking mental capacity is not owed a duty under the provisions of the Act.

50   ss.175–177 for a full description of all the definitions of homelessness.

51   s.176

52   s.177 (2)

53   See *R v LB Ealing, ex p. Sidhu* (1983) 2 HLR 45.

54   See Code para. 8.16.

55   In *R v Brent LBC ex p. Awua* [1995] 3 All ER 493 at p.498a Hoffmann LJ commented: 'I find it hard to imagine circumstances in which a person who is not threatened with homelessness cannot be reasonably expected to continue to occupy his accommodation

simply because it is temporary.' He pointed out that if the tenure is so precarious that he is likely to have to leave within 28 days, then he will be threatened with homelessness.

56   s.175(2)(a)

57   Para. 11.10 (13.11/1997)

58   *R v Hillingdon LBC, ex p. Pulhofer* [1986] AC 484. See also The Homelessness (Suitability of Accommodation) Order 1996 (SI 1996 No. 3204).

59   Draft Code para. 9.7 and Chapter 18, which sets out a framework for co-operation between the various responsible agencies including the housing authority and other social landlords and social services.

60   See s.161(2) and Chapter 20 of the Draft Code.

61   s.189

62   *R v Waveney DC ex p. Bowers* (1983) 4 HLR 118, *R v LB Lambeth ex p. Carroll* (1987) 20 HLR 142.

63   Social services and the health authority have a joint duty to provide after care services under s.117 Mental Health Act 1983 – see *Clunis v Camden & Islington Health Authority* (1998) 1 CCLR 225. See also *R v Lewisham LBC ex p. Pinzon and Patino* (1999) 2 CCLR 152 which considered the meaning of s.47 (3) of National Health Services and Community Care Act 1990 and the nature of co-operation required between social services and the housing authority in assessing a need.

64   s.191

65   See *Devenport v Salford City Council* (1983) 8 HLR 54 for the meaning of 'deliberate'.

66   s.191(3)

67   Code para.13.6 (15.6/1997)

68   Code para.13.10 (15.9/1997)

69   See *Dyson v Kerrier DC* [1980] 1 WLR 1205 and *Din v Wandsworth LBCD* [1983] AC 657.

70   In *R v Brent LBC, ex parte Awua* (see note 55) at p.69, Lord Hoffmann said: 'I would wish to reserve the question of whether the occupation of a settled residence is the sole and exclusive method by which the causal link can be broken'.

71   It is arguable that incidence of disability could well fit into Lord Hoffmann's reservation (note 71).

72   s.27 Children Act 1989

73   *R v Northavon DC, ex p. Smith* [1994] 3 All ER 313.

74   s.198

75   s.198(2)(c)

76   s.199

77   But see *R v Eastleigh Council, ex parte Betts* [1983] 2 AC 613 where the House of Lords took the view that local connection meant more than normal residence which was only a subsidiary component of the formula to be applied and the Local Authorities Agreement on Procedures for the Referrals of the Homeless was guidance to be taken into account when making a decision on the facts of the individual cases.

78   s.197

79   s.193

80   s.194

81   See however, for example, *R v Ealing LBC ex p. Parkinson* (1997) 29 HLR 179, *R v Haringey ex p. Sampaio* (June 1998) *Legal Action* 16, *R v Kensington and Chelsea RLBC ex p. Campbell* (1996) 28 HLR 160.

82   s.184

83   *Ali v Westminster City Council* [1999] 1 All ER 450.

84   See Chapter Four and also ss.116 and 117 Immigration and Asylum Act 1999.

85   See *R v Waveney DC ex p Bowers* (note 62).

86   s.47 National Health Service and Community Care Act 1990.

87   See *R v Bristol CC ex p Penfold* (1998) 1 CCLR 315 where, *inter alia*, Scott Baker J held that a housing authority's discharge of its obligations did not preclude the need for a community care assessment and also that a local authority is empowered to provide 'normal' or ordinary accommodation provided the need for housing is a function of the need which would otherwise have to be met by community care services.

88   See *R v Newham LBC ex p. Medical Foundation for the Care of Victims of Torture and ors* (1998) 1 CCLR 227 and also *R v Newham LBC ex p. C* (unreported) where the authority had accepted that it had a duty to provide accommodation under s.21 NAA to a woman from Zambia who was HIV positive and destitute. It had provided bed and breakfast accommodation with shared cooking and toilet facilities, which were a risk to her health. Social services argued that it did not have access to 'ordinary' rented housing but it was held that there was nothing to stop the local authority from renting a self-contained flat in the same way that it rented bed and breakfast accommodation.

89   The Housing Renewal Grants Regulations 1996 (as amended) and DoE circular 17/96 contain detailed guidance on the Act.

90   See definition in s.100 HGCR Act 1996.

91   s.22 HGCR Act 1996

92   Disabled Facilities HGCR Act Grants and Home Repair Assistance (Maximum Amounts) Order 1996.

93   s.23(2) HGCR Act 1996

94   See guidance in LAC (90) 7 originally issued with DoE circular 10/90. However, while DoE circular has been withdrawn and superseded, LAC (90) 7 remains in force. See also Chapter Four.

95   s.23 HGCR Act 1996 and guidance in LAC (90) 7 Annex I.

96   See s.2 HGCR Act 1996

97   ss.21 and 22 HGCR 1996

98   s.24(3) HGCR 1996.

99   Annex I para. 47 LAC (90) 7

100  Annex I para. 48 LAC (90) 7

101  Annex I para. 49 LAC (90) 7

102  See *R v Kirklees MBC ex p. Daykin* (1996) 1 CCLR 512 where the choice was between installation of a stairlift or rehousing.

103  s.604 Housing Act 1985 (as amended)

104  See s.12 HGCR Act 1996.

105  *R v Birmingham CC ex p. Mohammed* [1998] 3 All ER 788.

106  Annex I paras 32–36

107  Housing Renewal Grants Regulations 1996.

107ᴬThe Royal Association for Disability and Rehabilitation, see www.radar.org.uk

108  Regulation 10, Housing Renewal Grants Regulations 1996.

109  s.77 HGCR Act 1996

109ᴬ See Bradford *et al.*, or www.careandrepair-england.org.uk

110  Approved document for Part M of the Building Regulations 1999.

111 See Social Security Contributions and Benefits Act 1992 and the Housing Benefit (General) Regulations 1987 (as amended). The rules are quite complicated since not all rent that is actually due to be paid by a tenant will automatically be paid as housing benefit. It is important for claimants to obtain advice from a housing advice agency.

112 Regulation 3(1) Housing Benefit Regulations.

113 See either Disability Alliance 2000 or George 2000 on housing benefit for current rates.

114 Schedule 1 para. 1(a) HB Regulations.

115 Schedule 1 para. 1(c) HB Regulations.

116 Regulation 10 (6) HB Regulations.

117 SI 1995/1644 Housing Benefit (General) Amendment Regulations. Schedule A1.

118 Regulation 11 (3) HB Regulations. Health reasons may mitigate against a move.

119 Regulation 61(2).

120 *R v Maidstone BC* (1994) 27 HLR 375.

121 Council Tax (Reductions for Disabilities) Regulations 1992 (SI 554).

122 SSAA 1992 ss.134(8) and 139(6); Regulations 7 and 8 Income-related Benefits Schemes (Amendment) (No 2) Regulations 1995.

123 Supra f.n. 113.

124 Regulation 54 (4) CTB Regulations.

125 See generally 'Housing and Human Rights', *Legal Action*, March 1998, 8.

CHAPTER EIGHT

# Disability and Mental Health Law

*Kate Harrison*

One in four people suffer with some mental health problem at some time in their lives. These may range from mild depression to conditions such as schizophrenia which are regarded as severe mental illnesses. A mental health problem may be invisible and for many will not, for that reason, connect to the notion of 'disability'. Some people reject the connection because they do not accept that anything about their mental health problem makes them less able than others. Others reject the disability label because their mental health problem is a fluctuating and not a permanent state.

The disability movement has also, at times, been reluctant to include people with mental health problems. The fear of mental illness which stalks society at large is shared by many who otherwise are active in challenging social exclusion and who argue, in other contexts, that disability resides in the attitudes of society rather than in physical or mental variations from the norm.

If the social model of disability is adopted (see Chapter One, p.13), that is, the idea that people are disabled primarily by society's prejudiced attitudes towards certain characteristics rather than by those characteristics themselves, then it is clear that people who have or have had a psychiatric diagnosis are disabled. False beliefs that people with a psychiatric diagnosis are inevitably incapable, irrational and likely to be violent are prevalent. People with a psychiatric diagnosis find, as a consequence, that they are discriminated against in most spheres of life.

One example of differential treatment is law which applies only to people with mental health problems. This chapter outlines the current law which permits forced detention and treatment of people with mental health problems (the Mental Health Act 1983) and proposals for its reform. It also considers the application to people with mental health problems of the law which prohibits less favourable treatment on the grounds of disability (Disability Discrimination Act 1995).

## TERMINOLOGY

Just as the notion of 'disability' is problematic and experienced as disparaging, so is the use of language to describe people with a psychiatric diagnosis.

There is still no agreement about what mental disorders or mental illnesses are. Some do not accept they are illnesses:

> Psychiatry is a house of cards, held up by nothing more, or less, than mass belief in the truth of its principles and the goodness of its practices. If this is so, then psychiatry is a religion, not a science, a system of social controls, not a system of treating illness (Szasz 1989, Preface p.ix).

Those who do believe that 'mental illness' is a physical or psychological disease disagree about its causes. Some think that mental illness is caused by chemical, hormonal or other physiological disorders, others that it is caused by genetic defects, others that it is caused by environmental factors such as early childhood problems and traumas and still others that it is caused by a combination of factors. With no agreement about what mental ill health is, it is not surprising that there is no consensus on how those with a psychiatric diagnosis should be treated – whether the treatment be by doctors, other professionals or society at large.

The current edition of the International Classification of Mental and Behavioural Disorders, published by the World Health Organisation, uses the term 'disorder':

> The term 'disorder' is used throughout the classification, so as to avoid even greater problems inherent in the use of terms such as 'disease' and 'illness'. 'Disorder' is not an exact term, but it is used here simply to imply the existence of a clinically recognisable set of symptoms or behaviour associated in most cases with distress and with interference with personal functions. Social deviance alone, without personal dysfunction, should not be included in mental disorder as defined here. (World Health Organization 1992)

The last sentence is a reminder that diagnosis, hospitalisation and forced treatment should not rest on social disapproval alone. It is not so long since the days when women were found insane and committed to mental institutions with no other symptom of mental illness than producing an illegitimate child.

The Mental Health Act 1983 uses the terms 'mental disorder' and sub-categories of 'mental illness', 'mental impairment', 'severe mental impairment' and 'psychopathic disorder'. The medical profession talks about 'mental illness' which includes specific forms of mental illness such as schizophrenia, depression, mania, dementia, post-traumatic stress syndrome and anorexia. 'Personality disorder' is applied to people with a fixed condition characterised by undesirable personality traits.

### Finding a new language

The growth of the civil rights movement in the US, its application to disabled people and parallel developments in the UK have brought with them increased scrutiny of the language used to describe people diagnosed with mental illness or with some other form of 'mental disorder'. Terms which suggest that a person with a diagnosis of mental illness should be identified only by that diagnosis – such as 'mental patient', 'the mentally ill', 'schizophrenic' and so on – are narrow in that they suggest that a psychiatric diagnosis is sufficient to describe a whole person. The disability movement in the US has adopted the word 'consumer' to denote the people who are treated by mental health law and services. This term is intended to focus on the needs and wishes of the people at the centre of the practice of psychiatry. In the UK the terms 'user of mental health services' or 'user' and 'survivor' are used to describe those who are or who have been treated in the mental health system.

It should be noted that many of the terms used by the legal and medical establishments can be found offensive and degrading by those who are labelled by them.

## MENTAL HEALTH AND LAW

What is the role of law in relation to mental health or ill health? Possible functions for law are many. Law could enforce rights on behalf of people with mental health problems – rights to services, such as medical treatment, housing or social support. Law could prohibit discrimination on grounds of mental illness. It could guarantee the safety of treatments, protect choice and/or provide for compulsory detention and/or treatment of people with mental health problems. It could do all or any of these things either as part of the general law which applies to everybody or only in respect of people with mental health problems.

The Department of Health recently commissioned an expert committee to advise on 'how mental health legislation should be shaped to reflect contemporary patterns of care within a framework which balances the need to protect the rights of individual patients and the need to ensure public safety.'[1] The Committee started its task by asking what the scope of mental health law should be.[2] Following consultation, their draft proposals answered the question by sticking to a narrow view of mental health legislation:

> The Committee considered extending the scope of the current legislation so as to embrace issues of service quality and provision for all those with a mental disorder. They favour instead proposing that new legislation should, as now, be primarily concerned with providing a framework for compulsion in respect of certain people who suffer from mental disorder.[3]

This chapter will focus on the primary concern of mental health law. Although not examined here, current law does provide some limited rights to services[4] and some safeguards.[5] Rights not to be discriminated against on grounds of mental disorder contained in the Disability Discrimination Act 1995 and possible implications of the Human Rights Act 1998 will also briefly be considered.

## THE COMMON LAW

Mental health law is to be understood against the background of the common law: the judge-made law that has grown up on a case by case basis.

The common law enshrines the principle of autonomy:

> An adult patient…has an absolute right to choose whether to consent to medical treatment, to refuse it or to choose one rather than another of the treatments being offered…This right of choice is not limited to decisions which others might regard as sensible. It exists, notwithstanding that the reasons for making the choice are rational, irrational, unknown or even non-existent.[6]

Thus the patient whose life could be saved by a simple medical procedure, such as a blood transfusion, is free to refuse that transfusion and to die. However painful it is for the medical practitioner to allow this to happen, knowing that a life could easily have been saved, treatment cannot be forced on an unwilling patient.

Under the common law a violation of this right to autonomy amounts to an assault or battery. For treatment to be lawful, consent by the patient is required. The consent must be 'informed', which means that a patient must be given relevant information before giving valid consent to a test, treatment or procedure. This enables an informed and voluntary decision whether or not to consent to treatment to be made. Informed consent can only be given if the patient has the capacity to make a reasoned decision. 'A legal incapacity arises whenever the law provides that a particular person is incapable of taking a particular decision, undertaking a particular juristic act, or engaging in a particular activity.'[7]

Although the current law is confused and unclear, it is safe to say that it takes the functional approach to deciding capacity. Capacity to make a particular decision is judged in relation to that decision. A person is considered incapable if they are not able to process the information and make the judgements and choices required for a particular decision. Thus, a person may have capacity in relation to one decision but not in relation to another. For example, the same person may be capable of deciding whether or not to buy food from a shop but not whether and how to invest a large sum of money. In the case of medical treatment, the capacity to make a decision about medical treatment means being able first, to comprehend and retain treatment information, second, to believe it and third, to weigh it in the balance to make a choice.[8]

If a person does not have the capacity to consent to treatment then the problem becomes who makes treatment decisions for her or him, and upon what basis. In this area the law has developed piecemeal. The common law defence of 'necessity' serves to convert what would otherwise be an unlawful battery into lawful medical treatment. Medical treatment falls within the defence of 'necessity' where it is in the patient's 'best interests' and the treatment is necessary to preserve life, health or well-being or to prevent deterioration or ensure improvement in physical or mental health.[9] 'Best interest' decisions can be complex and controversial. There may be disagreement among medical professionals, the family and the patient about what treatment is best and there is no systematic provision for legal safeguards. For this reason there has been a long campaign for the clarification, rationalisation and codification of the law in this area, culminating in the Lord Chancellor's proposals for new legislation on making decisions on behalf of mentally incapacitated adults (HMSO 1999a). However, there is no immediate prospect of the proposals being translated into law.

## THE MENTAL HEALTH ACT 1983

The Mental Health Act 1983 is a consolidation of the 1959 Mental Health Act and its 1982 amendment.[10] The principles behind the legislation are contained in the Royal Commission on the Law relating to Mental Illness and Mental Deficiency, chaired by Lord Percy (1957).[11] These included the view that compulsory powers of detention and treatment could be justified on the grounds that someone suffering from a mental disorder required care for their own benefit or for the protection of others and it was likely that unwillingness to accept care was linked to the mental disorder.[12]

The Mental Health Act 1983 represents a departure from both the common law principles outlined above and the principles of the Percy Commission in that it permits the compulsory detention and treatment of people who fall within its terms regardless of whether or not they have the legal capacity to make their own decisions and regardless of whether their refusal of treatment is linked to their mental disorder. It provides a code for the admission, detention, treatment and discharge of patients suffering from 'mental disorder' according to criteria which apply even if the patient is capable of making his or her own treatment decisions.[13] Its extensive provisions are further explained and enlarged upon in a Code of Practice.[14]

'Mental disorder' is given a wide and open-ended definition. It means 'mental illness, arrested or incomplete development of mind, psychopathic disorder and any other disorder or disability of mind.'[15] The concept of mental disorder is limited only by the provision that no one can be dealt with as suffering from mental disorder by reason only of promiscuity or other immoral conduct, sexual deviancy or dependency on alcohol or drugs.[16] The Act goes on to classify four forms of mental disorder: mental illness, severe mental impairment, mental impairment and psychopathic disorder.

'Mental illness' is not defined in the statute. In *W v L* [17] Lawton L J stated that the words 'mental illness' were ordinary words of the English language with no particular medical significance and that the courts should construe them in the way that ordinary sensible people would construe them.

> That being in my judgement the right test, then I ask myself, what would the ordinary sensible person have said about the patient's condition in this case if he had been informed of his behaviour…? In my judgement such a person would have said: 'Well, the fellow is obviously mentally ill.'

This test has been characterised as 'the man must be mad test' (Hoggett 1996). Its wholly arbitrary application is, however, limited by the fact that, for the operation of most of the compulsory powers contained in the Mental Health Act, the opinions of two doctors that 'mental illness' is present are required.

'Psychopathic disorder' is defined as 'a persistent disorder or disability of mind…which results in abnormally aggressive or seriously irresponsible conduct'.

'Severe mental impairment' means 'a state of arrested or incomplete development of mind which includes severe impairment of intelligence and social functioning and is associated with abnormally aggressive or seriously irresponsible conduct'.

'Mental impairment' means 'a state of arrested or incomplete development of mind which includes significant impairment of intelligence and social functioning and is associated with abnormally aggressive or seriously irresponsible conduct'.

Each of the last three definitions focuses not only on the state of mind but also on the behaviour which is associated with or results from the state of mind. There have been few cases about the standard required for the involuntary treatment or detention for people with mental impairment, severe or otherwise. In the recent case of *Re F* [18] the court referred to and applied the reasoning of Lord Elton who introduced the new term 'mental impairment' – replacing that of 'subnormality' – in the Mental Health (Amendment) Bill in 1982:[19]

> Having provided the substitute term, we had to ensure that it was not going to be used to describe any people other than the small group to whom we wished it to apply. We therefore attached to it the requirement that, where the Act is to have effect upon a mentally impaired or severely mentally impaired person, that impairment must be 'associated with abnormally aggressive or seriously irresponsible conduct'.

We have tried in this phrase not only to establish the requirement that the behaviour of the person to whom the Bill applies shall be aggressive or irresponsible but that it shall be aggressive or irresponsible to a marked degree.

Clinicians do not use the term 'psychopathy' and the legal term encompasses many forms of what psychiatrists refer to as 'personality disorder' or 'borderline personality disorder'. The legal definition requires a 'persistent disorder' but its existence is inferred from anti-social behaviour. The legal definition can and frequently is criticised on the basis that it posits a disorder on the basis of anti-social behaviour while, at the same time, suggesting that the anti-social behaviour is caused by the mental disorder. The danger of providing a circular definition for forms of mental disorder was acknowledged by the Percy Commission: 'If one concentrates on the patient's behaviour rather than on the mental condition which lies behind it, one comes very close to making certain forms of behaviour in themselves grounds for segregation from society, which almost amounts to the creation of new criminal offences'.[20]

The Act seeks to restrict the potential application of the powers of compulsory hospitalisation and medical treatment to anybody who might behave in a way which is persistently anti-social through the limiting provision that psychopathic and mentally impaired patients cannot be compulsorily admitted to hospital for treatment unless it can be shown that the medical treatment is likely to alleviate or prevent a deterioration of their condition.[21]

However, the meaning of 'medical treatment' which, although not precisely defined, includes 'nursing, and also includes care, habilitation and rehabilitation under medical supervision',[22] and its interpretation in case law, means that most cases which fit into the legal definition of 'psychopathic disorder' will also be treatable. In *Reid v Secretary of State for Scotland*[23] the House of Lords held that a patient whose anger management improved when he was in the structured setting of a hospital satisfied the 'treatability' test. The cases show that being contained, cared for or nursed or even assessed in hospital can amount to 'medical treatment' for the purposes of the Act.

Whether or not 'psychopathic disorder' or the conditions covered by the medical term 'personality disorder' ought to be included in a Mental Health Act is frequently debated. It is almost universally agreed that the term 'psychopathic disorder' should be removed from the Act (HMSO 1999b). Opinions are divided about whether personality disorder should be included at all. Many argue that, although personality disorders might be classified as mental disorders,[24] they are not treatable and should not therefore be subject to compulsion.

In practice, the use of the Act for people who could fit within the definition of 'psychopathic disorder' and could meet the criteria for admission is limited by the reluctance of psychiatrists to admit them for treatment. This in turn has led to the draconian proposals for reform of the law to enable the indefinite detention, without treatment, of those suffering from 'Dangerous, Severe Personality Disorder' [DSPS] [DOH 1999] (see below, p.209).

## ADMISSION TO HOSPITAL

Notwithstanding its proposals for the compulsion of people suffering from 'mental disorder', the Percy Commission wanted to approach mental illness by putting people with that diagnosis on the same footing as those being treated for physical illnesses. This is an early example of an attempt to approach people with mental illness on a non-discriminatory basis. The Commission wanted to do away with the idea that admission should follow bureaucratic and stigmatising processes of certification or proof of valid consent to admission. It recommended that the concept of 'informal admission' should replace the idea of 'voluntary admission'. The significance of this change was that admission to hospital did not need to be demonstrably voluntary and that the legal process should be resorted to only where someone was clearly involuntary. If they were passive, not protesting or, as recently decided, incapable of consent or refusal, then they could be treated without resorting to the mechanism of the Mental Health Act 1983.

This principle was translated into what is now section 131 of the Mental Health Act which provides:

> Nothing in this Act shall be construed as preventing a patient who requires treatment for mental disorder from being admitted to any hospital…in pursuance of arrangements made in that behalf and without any application, order or direction rendering him liable to be detained under this Act, or from remaining in any hospital or mental nursing home in pursuance of such arrangements after he has ceased to be liable to be so detained.

Although this attempt to put mental patients on the same footing as others was laudable in its intentions, the drawbacks of this approach were illustrated by the decision in *R v Bournewood Community and Mental Health Trust ex p. L.*[25] The House of Lords held that people admitted to hospital without detention formalities fell into two categories – those who had capacity and consented (voluntary patients) and those who lack capacity to consent but do not object (informal patients). The latter could be admitted without using the provisions of the Mental Health Act and could be treated on the common law basis of 'necessity'. This meant that the safeguards of the Act did not apply in his case.

It is estimated that about two thirds of psychiatric patients are informal. A large number of these are 'de facto' detained – that is, without capacity, but compliant and treated in hospital under the common law (HMSO 1999c).

## Compulsory admission to hospital

Part II of the Mental Health Act sets out the criteria for compulsory civil admission to hospital, guardianship and supervision after discharge.

Section 2 permits the compulsory admission for up to 28 days of someone suffering from mental disorder of a nature or degree which warrants their detention in hospital for 'assessment or for assessment followed by medical treatment' who 'ought to be so detained in the interests of their own health or safety or with a view to the protection of other persons'. The scope of 'mental disorder' has been held not to include individuals detained against their will merely because their thinking was considered unusual, bizarre, irrational or contrary to the views of the majority.[26]

Section 3 permits compulsory admission for six months, renewable for a further six months and then for periods of one year. The criteria are that the patient is suffering from one of the four categories of mental disorder, that the mental disorder is of a nature or degree which makes it appropriate for him or her to receive medical treatment in hospital and it is necessary for the health or safety of the patient or for the protection of others that he or she should receive such treatment and it cannot be provided unless he or she is detained under this section.

Further provisions enable a person to be admitted as an emergency for up to 72 hours (s.4) or, when already a patient in hospital, prevented for a limited period from leaving (s.5).

There has been much debate over what it means to say that someone 'is suffering' from mental illness. Can someone who has failed to take their medication, and who is symptom free but thought likely to deteriorate in the future, be someone who 'is suffering' from mental illness? The Department of Health thought not;[27] an influential committee of inquiry disagreed.[28] The point has not been tested in the courts, but an interpretation which allows a patient to be hospitalised simply on the basis that she has not taken her medication should be resisted. It would leave some people who do not need or want it condemned to accepting medication indefinitely. Neither the course of mental illness nor the response to medication is predictable. At least one third of those who suffer a serious episode of mental illness never do so again. Others suffer only intermittently. Not all respond to medication and of those who do, many prefer not to endure concomitant side effects which can be serious and permanent.

The provisions permit admission to hospital where there is no risk of harm either to the patient or to others. Admission can be justified simply in the interests of the patient's health. Here, the contrast between the common law protection of patient autonomy and the statutory provisions for overriding the treatment choices of patients with mental health problems is stark.

## USE OF THE MENTAL HEALTH ACT

The number of civil admissions under Part II of the Act has been steadily rising from 16,000 in 1984 to 22,000 in 1996–1997. The reasons for this rise are not clear, although the number of admissions increased when it was emphasised to mental health professionals that admission could be on the basis of the patient's health alone.[29] Research shows that males are more likely to be sectioned than females. There is a dramatic difference in the use of the Act for black people who are approximately twice as likely to be detained against their will as white people (Wall *et al.* 1999).

### Admission to hospital through the criminal justice system

> The medical label may protect the patient from punishment, only to submit him to interminable instruction, treatment, and discrimination, which are inflicted on him for his professionally presumed benefit (Illich 1976, p.98).

Although the existence of mental disorder may operate to exempt a person from criminal responsibility (if found not guilty by reason of insanity) or to prevent him or her standing trial (through being found unfit to plead) some people with a mental disorder will also be convicted of a crime. Others may develop a mental disorder in prison. In any case the Mental Health Act contains provisions for admission to hospital. Recent law has allowed the Court, in the case of psychopathic disorder, both to pass a sentence of imprisonment and to direct that the defendant start their sentence in hospital.[30]

Part III of the Mental Health Act enables any criminal court to remand a defendant to hospital for reports (s.35) and a crown court to remand for treatment (s.36).

A crown court or a magistrate's court may make a hospital order on the grounds that the defendant is suffering from one of the four forms of mental disorder of a nature or degree which makes it appropriate for him or her to be detained in hospital for medical treatment and the court thinks 'having regard to all the circumstances including the nature of the offence and the character and antecedents of the offender, and to the other available means of dealing with him' that the hospital order is the most suitable way of disposing of the case.[31]

A magistrates' court may make a hospital order without recording a conviction if the court is satisfied that the defendant did the act charged and he is classified as suffering from mental illness or severe mental impairment. A court cannot order the provision of a hospital bed, but must be satisfied that arrangements have been made for the defendant's admission to hospital within 28 days.

A restriction order may be made by the crown court if, 'having regard to the nature of the offence, the antecedents of the offender and the risk of his committing further offences if set at large...it is necessary for the protection of the public from serious harm'.[32] A restriction order may be made for a fixed period, but most are made 'without limit of time'.

The effect of the restriction order is to place major decisions about discharge, transfer or leave of absence in the hands of the Home Secretary. Only the Home Secretary or a Mental Health Review Tribunal may discharge a restricted patient.

The Home Secretary may transfer a convicted or unconvicted prisoner to hospital. In that case the Home Secretary may place restrictions on the patient's discharge and almost invariably does so. When a restriction direction is given it stays in force until the earliest date on which the person would have been discharged from prison without remission. The person then continues to be detained in hospital until discharged.[33]

### Medical treatment for mental disorder

> There's no discussion about it except the side-effects. I want to know what they're doing with my treatment. You have to sign a consent form and if you refuse, they get a second opinion but that only reinforces that you need to take it. So they force you to take it.

> If you don't take your medication, they force a depo on you. If you refuse the depo, they deck you and jab you. You get a cross if you refuse like you get ticks if your room is tidy. It affects the money you get (Parry-Crooke, Oliver and Newton 2000).

Patients compulsorily admitted to hospital under most sections of the Act may be given 'medical treatment for mental disorder' under the direction of the responsible medical officer without their consent.[34] As discussed above, 'medical treatment' covers a number of activities – such as restraint, seclusion or containment – not normally regarded as medical treatment.[35]

Some treatments fall into special provisions affording safeguards. Psychosurgery and implantation of hormones to reduce the male sex drive may only be given if the patient consents and if there is approval of a second opinion doctor appointed by the Mental Health Act Commission.[36]

Electro-convulsive therapy (ECT) and medication after three months may only be given if either the patient consents or a second opinion appointed doctor has given approval.[37] In practice, over 90 per cent of second opinion appointment doctors do approve (Fennell 1996).

The safeguards do not apply to any treatment to be administered without consent or a second opinion if it is urgent. Urgent treatment includes treatment which is immediately necessary to save the patient's life or not irreversible and immediately necessary to prevent a serious deterioration in his condition or not irreversible or hazardous, immediately necessary to alleviate serious suffering by the patient or immediately necessary and representing the minimum interference necessary to prevent the patient from behaving violently or being a danger to himself or others.[38] According to the Act 'treatment is irreversible if it has unfavourable irreversible physical or psychological consequences and hazardous if it entails significant physical hazard'.[39]

Evidence suggests that section 62 is most frequently used to administer ECT, a treatment about which opinions are sharply divided. Some psychiatrists argue that it saves lives, others that it is harmless, others that it is useless. No one knows if or how it works – its application has been likened to kicking a malfunctioning television set. Users and survivors have argued that it has permanent damaging effects, including trauma and memory loss. ECT administered with restraint and anaesthetic can be hazardous, particularly for the elderly.

Recent cases have expanded the meaning of 'medical treatment for mental disorder' to include forms of treatment which were not envisaged when the Act was passed. This means that no consideration has been given to whether special safeguards should apply. Force feeding has been permitted in the case of a patient diagnosed with anorexia nervosa[40] and in the case of a patient suffering from a personality disorder which made her want to harm herself through starvation.[41] The Court of Appeal decided that a range of acts ancillary to the core treatment that the patient is receiving fall into the term 'medical treatment', that treatment can be ancillary if it is nursing care 'concurrent with the core treatment or a necessary prerequisite to such treatment or to prevent the patient from causing harm to himself or to alleviate the consequences of the disorder' and that relieving the symptoms of the mental disorder is just as much a part of treatment as relieving its underlying cause.

This expansion of the notion of 'medical treatment for mental disorder' was applied in the case of a pregnant patient to enable the performing of a Caesarean section without her consent and to sanction the restraint necessary for the operation to take place.[42]

Since that case was decided the Courts have demonstrated a more restrictive approach. The Court of Appeal has decided that a person detained under the Mental Health Act cannot be forced into medical procedures unconnected with her mental condition [43] and it has been held that renal dialysis could not be treatment for mental disorder within s.63. [44] But s.63 now has a much wider application than was originally intended.

## Discharge from hospital

Under the Mental Health Act it is easier to get in to hospital than to get out. Patients detained under sections 2, 3 and 37 without a restriction order can be discharged by their responsible medical officer, the hospital managers, their nearest relative[45] or a Mental Health Review Tribunal. In the case of a patient detained under a restriction order, discharge can be by the Home Secretary (who rarely does this) or a Mental Health Review Tribunal. A Tribunal must discharge from s. 3 or s. 37 if it is satisfied that the patient is not suffering from one of the four forms of mental disorder, or that mental disorder is not of a nature or degree which makes it appropriate for him or her to be liable to be detained in a hospital for medical treatment, or that it is not necessary for the health or safety or the patient or for the protection of other persons that he or she should receive such treatment. Although the statutory discharge criteria do not precisely mirror those for hospital admission, recent cases have established that an applicant who satisfies the Tribunal that the entry criteria do not apply will be entitled to discharge.[46] The Mental Health Review Tribunal also has the discretion to discharge in the case of patients detained other than under a restriction order.

The provision that the MHRT must 'be satisfied' that one of the conditions applies means that the burden is on the patient to prove that he or she does not meet the statutory criteria for detention.

A recent case [47] has established that someone may be stable and symptom-free but still suffering from a condition which is of a 'nature' although not of a 'degree' which makes it appropriate for him to be liable to be detained:

> The patient was in a stable condition and it is quite clear that the illness was not of a degree which of itself made it appropriate for him to be liable to be detained. The reason for that was because he had a chronic condition that was static. However, the nature of the condition was that it might cease to be static... If one had simply to look at the degree it would have been right for the discharge to take place, but the nature of the condition was such that it was clear that he should not be discharged.

This decision, combined with the fact that the Tribunal must be 'satisfied' that the nature or degree of the mental illness does not require detention in hospital, presents an enormous hurdle for Tribunal applicants. If stability and lack of symptoms do not suffice to trigger mandatory discharge, how can the patient prove to the Tribunal that he or she does not need hospital treatment?

In practice, patients with a chronic mental illness are likely to satisfy the Tribunal of their entitlement to discharge only by convincing them that they will continue with their medical treatment without compulsion – whether by staying in hospital voluntarily or by accepting treatment and supervision in the community.

In this sense the existence of the Mental Health Act and the possibility of admission for treatment in hospital stands as an ever-present threat for those with a diagnosis of mental disorder. Many report accepting treatment which they would otherwise have refused because the alternative presented to them was admission and treatment under the Act.

### Control outside hospital

The current Mental Health Act also makes provision for some weaker controls outside hospital.

Under s.7–10 of the Mental Health Act patients who have reached the age of 16 can be 'received into guardianship' if they are suffering from one of the four forms of mental disorder and it is necessary in the interest of their welfare or for the protection of others that they be so received. The effect of guardianship is that the patient can be required to live in a specified place and to attend specified places for the purpose of medical treatment, occupation, education or training.

Similarly under s.25 a patient who is detained in hospital under s.3 or s.37 can be discharged subject to aftercare under supervision on the grounds that he or she is still suffering from one of the four forms of mental disorder and that there would be a substantial risk of serious harm:

> to the health or safety of the patient; or

> the safety of other persons or of the patient being seriously exploited if they were not to receive the aftercare services to be provided after they leave hospital;

> and being subject to aftercare under supervision is likely to help to secure that they receive the aftercare services.

Patients who are detained in hospital under a restriction order or direction may be given a conditional discharge. A conditional discharge will usually specify conditions, such as residence, or social supervision. A conditionally discharged patient can be recalled to hospital by the Home Secretary at any time, although such a recall must be subjected to speedy independent review and cannot be justified in the absence of mental disorder justifying hospitalisation.

Further provisions enable the police to detain for the purposes of assessment for up to 72 hours someone who appears to be suffering from mental disorder and in immediate need of care and control.[48] A constable with a warrant can enter a person's premises and remove them to a place of safety for up to 72 hours on the grounds that 'there is reasonable cause to suspect that a person believed to be suffering from mental disorder has been ill treated or neglected or not kept under proper control or is unable to care for themselves and is living alone'.[49]

None of the provisions for detention or control outside hospital allows compulsory treatment. This has been the subject of recent debate and is the driving force behind new proposals for reform.

## THE CURRENT DEBATE: COMMUNITY CARE AND COMPULSION IN THE COMMUNITY

In the early 1960s the then Minister for Health, Enoch Powell, announced:

> nothing less than the elimination of by far the greater part of this country's mental hospitals as they stand today. This is a colossal undertaking, not so much in the physical provision which it involves as in the sheer inertia of mind and matter which it requires to be overcome. There they stand, isolated, majestic, imperious, brooded over by the gigantic water tower and chimney combined, rising unmistakably and daunting out of the countryside – the asylums which our forefathers built with such solidity.[50]

The 1962 Hospital Plan launched the closure programme and 'community care' has remained government policy ever since.

It is a policy which has been much criticised. From those arguing for a return to institutional care[51] to those who saw community care policies as a liberal mask to save the money spent on institutions by dumping the vulnerable on intolerant or impoverished people (Scull 1984) a range of negative opinions combined to create the perception that the policy of community care is a failure. But the overwhelming evidence is that community care policies have brought real and lasting improvements to the lives of people diagnosed with mental health problems (Sayce 2000).

Two significant events – one a legal decision, the other a highly publicised tragedy – initially stoked the call for legal reform.

### The legal decision

The courts decided that the common psychiatric practice of admitting patients for a nominal period and immediately granting leave in order to activate the compulsory treatment powers in the Act was unlawful:

> There is no canon of construction which presumes that Parliament intended that people should, against their will, be subjected to treatment which others, however professionally competent, perceive, however sincerely and however correctly, to be in their best interests. What there is, is a canon of construction that Parliament is presumed not to enact legislation which interferes with the liberty of the subject without making it clear that this was its intention. It goes without saying that, unless clear statutory authority to the contrary exists, no one is to be detained in hospital or to undergo medical treatment or even to submit himself to

medical examination without his consent. That is as true of a mentally disordered person as of anyone else.[52]

This decision led the Royal College of Psychiatrists to campaign for a change in the law: first for Community Treatment Orders or Community Supervision orders which would allow compulsory admission to hospital on the basis only that a patient failed to take medication.[53] This firmly introduced the idea that the main problem with the policy of community care was the patients' refusal or failure to take medication. Measures to ensure medication outside hospital were to be the solution.

### The tragic event

The tragic event was the killing of Jonathan Zito by a person diagnosed with schizophrenia. The stabbing, in a London Underground station, was random and unprovoked and fuelled the belief that community care policies had failed and that the public were at risk from abandoned and inadequately controlled discharged psychiatric patients. This and other highly publicised tragedies led to a public enquiry (HMSO 1994) and a Department of Health 'ten point plan' for improved community care. The plan included a review of legal powers in the community, the introduction of 'supervision registers', and a requirement that all health authorities hold an enquiry into any homicide by any person who had been in touch with psychiatric services in the previous 12 months.

The review into legal powers rejected calls for compulsory treatment in the community, but as a compromise led to the introduction of aftercare under supervision.[54]

Supervision registers were introduced on 1 April 1994 and required NHS providers to set up registers to identify and provide information on patients who have a diagnosis of mental illness (including personality disorder); who are receiving treatment from a specialist psychiatric service; and who are known to be at significant risk or potentially significant risk of suicide, serious violence to others or severe self-neglect.[55] The stated aim of the registers was to ensure that people with a severe mental illness obtained effective care in the community. The registers imply no extra powers but have the potential to increase the stigma for patients included on it. Information that a patient is on the register or disclosure of the information on it also increases the likelihood that the confidentiality normally afforded to health information will be breached. Despite these civil rights implications of the register there is no statutory right of appeal. No administrative law cases challenging inclusion on a register have been reported.

The inquiries into homicides by people diagnosed mentally ill have proved hugely damaging for people with mental health problems. They ensure that any such killing is kept firmly in the public eye, reported when the event took place, during the subsequent trial, during the inquiry and when the inquiry team reports. The process and the reports strengthen the already firm public perception that mental illness is linked with violence, that killings by people with mental illness in the community are frequent and that all such killings are predictable and could be prevented if only psychiatrists and other mental health professionals would do their job properly. In fact, only a small proportion of people with mental disorder are violent, most violent crimes (over 90 per cent) are committed by people who are not mentally ill and the ability of psychiatrists to predict violence is limited.

This climate firmly influenced the policy of the incoming Labour Government in 1997 which signalled early on in its term its commitment to extending legal powers to enforce treatment in the community. The determination has persisted despite the research that supports neither the assumption that mental illness is linked to violence, nor that there has been an increase in homicides by people with mental disorder since the introduction of community care:

> One of the concerns of patient groups and others is the preoccupation in the press and elsewhere with violence committed by people with mental illness and the risk that the mentally ill pose to the general public. Critics of such publicity argue that most serious violence is not committed by the mentally ill, that the great majority of mentally ill people are not violent and that to focus on rare incidents of serious violence adds to the stigma that limits the rights and freedoms of the mentally ill. Our findings offer support to these views (DOH 1999, p.93).

The health minister announced a 'new vision':

> Modern patterns of treatment and care – particularly the growing realisation of the importance of social care interventions – mean that legislation that is largely about hospital based treatment is now out of date. Modern legislation must recognise the growing importance of life outside institutional settings for those who are mentally ill.[56]

The argument contains a fallacy which is often stated but rarely examined. It is certainly true that life outside institutions is of more importance for those with 'mental disorder'. A success of the community care policy has been the reduction in the number of people consigned to long-term institutional care and the waste of lives incarceration entails. But it does not follow that the compulsion that was experienced by so many as the worst feature of hospitalisation should follow the patient into the community. 'This is the real, awful secret of community control...that the same old experts have moved office into the community and are doing the same old things they have always done' (Cohen 1985).

## REFORM OF THE MENTAL HEALTH ACT 1983 – THE GREEN PAPER[57]

The proposals in the Green Paper demolish the hospital walls as the boundary which separates those who may be compulsorily treated from those who cannot. The essence of the proposals (which, having been out for consultation, are soon to form the basis of a White Paper) is the replacement of the current law on admission to and treatment in hospital with a new compulsory order, made by a new independent Tribunal. The compulsory order would be made on the following criteria:

1. the presence of a mental disorder which is of such seriousness that the patient requires care and treatment under the supervision of specialist mental health services; and

2. that the care and treatment proposed for the mental disorder, and for conditions resulting from it, is the least restrictive alternative available consistent with safe and effective care; and

3. that the proposed care and treatment cannot be implemented without use of compulsory powers; and

4. it is necessary for a. the health or safety of the patient; and/or b. for the protection of others from serious harm and/or c. for the protection of the patient from serious exploitation.

Nowhere does the word 'hospital' appear. Compulsion is no longer to be determined by deciding whether the mental disorder is bad enough to need hospital treatment.

This, combined with the proposed new and wide definition of 'mental disorder' to mean 'any disability or disorder of brain or mind, whether temporary or permanent, which results in an impairment or disturbance of the mental functioning' means that the range of the new compulsory order far outstrips the reach of the current Mental Health Act.

The Tribunal would have the power to make an order which would stipulate the place of residence, define the proposed care and treatment plan and oblige the patient to allow access to and attend appointments with case workers. It would include powers to enter premises, convey patients to a stipulated place for the care and treatment prescribed in the care plan and convey the patient to hospital.

Thus, the proposals are for a far-reaching power enabling the psychiatric services to locate, access, transport and force treatment on unwilling 'patients', whether inside or outside the hospital. Under the rubric of a 'modern, safe, sound and supportive' mental health service, control and compulsion of people with mental health problems is to be extended as never before.[58]

Even more draconian are the proposals for people with 'dangerous severe personality disorder' (DSPD), defined as a person with an 'identifiable personality disorder to a severe degree, who poses a high risk to other people because of serious anti-social behaviour resulting from their disorder' (Home Office/DOH 1999, p.9).

The proposal is that the requirement that a personality disorder be 'treatable' should be removed and indefinite detention of people with DSPD should be permitted solely on the ground of dangerousness. This liability to indefinite detention in a place which is neither a hospital nor a prison would apply whether or not the person with DSPD had committed an offence.

## THE EUROPEAN CONVENTION ON HUMAN RIGHTS AND THE HUMAN RIGHTS ACT 1998

Chapter Five has already referred to the Human Rights Act 1998 which came into force on 2 October 2000. Current law and any replacement law are now measured against the rights guaranteed by the Convention and to be incorporated in domestic law. Among those rights are those protecting liberty (Article 5), physical and moral integrity, privacy and family life (Article 8) and freedom from inhuman or degrading punishment or treatment (Article 3).

However, the convention, like domestic law, allows the deprivation of liberty on the grounds of 'unsound mind' if the patient is reliably shown, upon objective medical expertise, to be suffering from a true mental disorder and the disorder is of a kind or degree warranting compulsory confinement.[59] Interference with a person's life falling short of deprivation of liberty is covered by Article 8. Article 8 (2) permits interference with the rights protected by Article 8 in the interests of public safety, the prevention of disorder or crime and the protection of health. Moreover, European cases have shown the Convention to be weak in the protection of human rights if the treatment complained of is pursued as a matter of clinical judgement.[60]

Although subjection to a compulsory community order does not necessarily imply deprivation of liberty, conveying to a place for treatment or detention in hospital for failure to comply with the order do. The community order would affect people whose mental disorder is not of a kind or degree warranting compulsory confinement: detention in hospital for failing to comply with community treatment could be in breach of Article 5.

The impact of the Human Rights Act remains to be seen. What is certain is that current and future mental health law will be tested against the rights protected by the Convention. Cases involving the liberty and treatment of people with mental health problems are likely to be in the forefront of the development of the Human Rights Act.

## LIVING EQUALLY WITH OTHERS: THE DISABILITY DISCRIMINATION ACT 1995

The Mental Health Act 1983 permits differential treatment of people who fit into the class of people suffering from 'mental disorder'. Any successor legislation looks set to do the same. Such legislation is by its nature discriminatory, sanctioning, as it does, what most would agree is less favourable treatment[61] on grounds of mental disorder.

Other forms of discrimination are suffered by those who have or are thought to have a mental health problem. Common discrimination ranges from neighbourhood campaigns against the resettlement of people discharged from mental hospitals to insurance companies refusing cover to anyone with a psychiatric diagnosis; from verbal and physical abuse to refusal of employment or education; from curbs on travel to the refusal to serve a drink in a pub.

The Disability Discrimination Act (DDA) goes some way to providing redress, and is dealt with in more detail in Chapter Six. The Act includes provisions which mean that it could be unlawful to treat 'less favourably' someone who has or has had a disability, unless there is a reasonable justification for doing so. For the purposes of the Act a person has a disability if she or he has a physical or mental impairment which has a substantial and long-term adverse effect on her or his ability to carry out normal day-to-day activities.

Some people with mental health problems are included in the ambit of the DDA, albeit grudgingly. The Act provides that it does not include any impairment resulting from or consisting of a mental illness, unless that illness is a clinically well-recognised illness. Regulations prescribe that certain 'conditions', including alcohol dependency and some behaviour disorders such as pyromania and kleptomania, are not to be treated as amounting to impairments. Many people discriminated against because they are wrongly perceived as incapable do not fit within the definition.

Nonetheless, the DDA goes some way to demonstrating the possibility of a new and enabling role for law in relation to people with mental health problems.

## CONCLUSION

Law has a greater impact on the lives of people with a psychiatric diagnosis than on any other disabled person. Theoretically, state power to detain or force treatment on people is justified either because subjects lack the capacity to look after themselves or because 'policing' powers permit the state to protect society from harm. The Mental Health Act permits the state to intervene in the lives of people with 'mental disorder' whether or not they have the capacity to decide for themselves. Research shows that there is only a weak link between violence and mental disorder (Monahan *et al.* 1994) and psychiatrists' success in predicating future violence is only slightly better than chance (Monahan 1981). Despite this, the Act permits long detention on the grounds of risk to others.

Community care polices are progressive, favouring care outside hospitals for people with mental health problems. There has been no increase in violence by people with a psychiatric diagnosis since the introduction of community care policies. Yet recent policies and law reforms have been driven by the belief that mental illness and violent behaviour are strongly linked. The proposed new law is justified in relation to progressive ideals for community care, the irony is that it results in greater interference in the lives of people with mental health problems. Under the guise of ensuring treatment which represents 'the least restrictive alternative' the proposed new powers will become a means of forcing people to take antipsychotic medication or to participate in treatment programmes even though they do not meet the criteria for formal admission to hospital.

Against the background of unfavourable treatment by the state of people with mental health problems, it is not surprising that discrimination is rife. The Disability Discrimination Act 1995 represents a small but significant step towards outlawing such discrimination.

## REFERENCES

Blom-Cooper, L. Itally, H. and Murphy, E. (1995) *The Falling Shadow.* London: Duckworth.

Cohen, S. (1985) *Visions of Social Control.* Cambridge: Polity Press.

Crichton, J. (ed.) (1995) *Psychiatric Patient Violence.* London: Duckworth.

DOH (1999) *Safer Services: National Confidential Inquiry into Suicide and Homicide by People with Mental Illness.* London: Department of Health.

Fennell, P. (1996) *Treatment Without Consent: Law Psychiatry and the Treatment of Mentally Disordered People since 1845.* London: Routledge.

HMSO (1994) The Report of the Inquiry into the Care and NHS Management Executive Introduction of Supervision Registers for Mentally Ill People from 1 April 1994, HSG (94)5. Treatment of Christopher Clunis. London: National Health Service, HMSO.

HMSO (1999a) *Making Decisions.* October 1999, Cmnd. 4465. London: HMSO.

HMSO (1999b) *Report of the Committee of Inquiry into the Personality Disorder Unit, Ashworth Special Hospital.* Cmnd. 4194. London: HMSO.

HMSO (1999c) *Mental Health Act Commission Eighth Biennial Report (1997–9).* London: HMSO.

Hoggett, B. (1996) *Mental Health Law.* London: Sweet and Maxwell.

Home Office/DOH (1999) *Managing Dangerous People with Severe Personality Disorder.* London: Home Office/Department of Health.

Illich, I. (1976) The Limits to Medicine. Harmondsworth: Penguin.

Monahan, J. (1981) *Predicting Violent Behaviour.* Beverly Hills, CA: Sage Publications.

Monahan, J. et al. (1994) *Consensus Statement, Violence and Mental Disorder: Public Perceptions vs. Research Findings.* New York: National Stigma Clearinghouse and the MacArthur Research Network on Mental Health and the Law.

Parry-Crooke, G. Oliver, C. and Newton, J. (2000) *Good Girls: Surviving the Secure System.* London: University of North London.

Sayce, L. (2000) *From Psychiatric Patient to Citizen.* London: Macmillan.

Scull, A. *A Decarceration.* Cambridge: Polity Press.

Szasz, T. (1989) *Law, Liberty, and Psychiatry.* New York: Syracuse University Press.

Unzicker, R. (1989) 'On my own: a personal journey through madness and re-emergence.' *Psychological Journal 13,* 71.

Wall, S., Churchill, R., Hotopf, M., Buchanan, A. and Wessely, S. (1999) *A Systematic Review of Research Relating to the Mental Health Act 1983.* London: Department of Health.

World Health Organisation (1992) ICD-10 Classifications of Mental and Behavioural Disorders: Clinical Descriptions and Diagnostic Guidelines.

## NOTES

1     Department of Health press release, October 1998.

2     'Key Themes' document, circulated by the Department of Health in November 1998.

3     Draft Outline Proposals by Scoping Study Committee, April 1999, p.3.

4     For example, s.117 Mental Health Act 1983.

5     For example, as well as the treatment safeguards outlined below, The Mental Health Act Commission which has responsibilities towards detained patients.

6     *Re T* [1993] Fam 95 per Lord Donaldson.

7     Paragraph 2.10 Law Commission Consultation Paper No. 119.

8     *Re C (Mental Patient: Medical Treatment)* (1993) 15 BMLR 77.

9     *Re F* [1989] 3 WLR 103.

10     It has since been amended by the Police and Criminal Evidence Act 1984, the NHS and Community Care Act 1990, the Mental Health (Amendment) Act 1994, the Criminal Justice Act 1991, the Mental Health (Patients in the Community) Act 1995 and the Crime Sentences Act 1997.

11     Cmnd. 169 (1957)

12     Para. 317

13     The Act also provides for the management of property and affairs of a patient – in this context 'a person incapable, by reason of mental disorder, of managing and administering his property and affairs' – but those provisions are outside the context of this chapter.

14     Under s.118 Mental Health Act 1983. The third edition of the Mental Health Act Code of Practice came into force on 1 April 1999 (HMSO).

15     s.1(2)

16     s.1(3)

17     [1973] 3 All ER 884

18     [2000] 1 FLR 192

19     ibid

20     Para. 338. Percy Commission, 1954–57 Cmnd 169

21     s.3(2)(c)

22     s.145 Mental Health Act 1983

23     [1999] 1 All ER 481

24 ICD 10

25 [1999] AC 458

26 *R v Collins ex p. S* [1998] Fam. Law 662

27 Internal Review of Legal Powers on the Care of Mentally Ill People in the Community (1993, para.3.2).

28 Blom-Cooper *et al.* (1995).

29 Revised Code of Practice, August 1993, April 1999

30 Crime Sentences Act 1997

31 s.37

32 s.41

33 s.50

34 s.63

35 Supra pp. 199 *et.seq.*

36 s.57

37 s.58

38 s.62

39 s.62(3)

40 *R v Riverside NHS Mental Health Trust ex p. Carolyn Fox.* The Guardian, 26/10/93

41 *Tameside and Glossop Acute Services Trust v C.H.* [1996] 1 FLR 762.

42 *B v Croydon District Health Authority* [1995] 1 All ER 683.

43 *R v Collins ex p. S* [1998] Fam. Law 662.

44 *Re J.T. (Adult: Refusal of Medical Treatment)* [1988] 1 FLR 48.

45 The nearest relative's power to discharge can be barred if the patient is a danger to themselves or others – s.25.

46 *Reid v Secretary of State for Scotland* [1999] 1 All ER 481, *ex parte Moyle.*

47 *R v MHRT ex p. Moyle* [2000] Lloyd's Rep. Med. 143

48 s.136

49 s.135

50 Speech to National Association for Mental Health (MIND), 1962.

51 Notably by Marjorie Wallace, a campaigning journalist, in a series of articles for *The Times* in 1987. She subsequently founded the charity SANE – an acronym 'Schizophrenia a National Emergency'.

52 *R v Hallstrom ex p W (no. 2); R v Gardner ex p. L* [1986] 2 All ER 306.

53 *Royal College of Psychiatrists (1993) Community Supervision Orders.*

54 s.25, MHA, introduced by Mental Health (Patients in the Community) Act 1995.

55 Introduction of Supervision Registers from 1/4/94 HSG (94) 5.

56 Paul Boateng, September 1998, announcing appointment of expert committee to first phase review of MHA.

57 Reform of the Mental Health Act 1983 Proposals for Consulation 1999 Cmnd. 4480.

58 ibid, Foreword at p.5

59 *Winterwerp v Netherlands* (1979) 2 EHRR 387

60 *Herczegfalvy v Austria* (1992) 15 EHRR 437

61 Certainly it is less favourable treatment in terms of civil rights. Whether it is so in relation to health is more open to debate.

CHAPTER NINE

# Disabled Children: (Still) Invisible Under the Law

*Mairian Corker and John M Davis*

## INTRODUCTION

In this chapter, we argue that the way the law thinks about disabled children continues to be led by 'old' ideas about disability and childhood, particularly in the tendency to regard children and disabled children within separate categories. Thus although children, in law, may be viewed as occasional 'victims', 'witnesses', 'bundles of (human) needs' and 'bearers of rights' (King and Piper 1995, pp.64–82), in practice disabled children are more often regarded as perpetual victims, silent, voiceless witnesses, and bundles of 'special' needs. Their rights, or rather lack of rights, are usually in the hands of adult 'caretakers' (Archard 1993, p.51) who often 'see the disability, not the child', to reverse a somewhat well-worn phrase. Using examples from our own research with disabled children on the *Lives of Disabled Children* project, and from the research of others, we examine four core elements of children's rights – protection, prevention, provision and participation (Van Bueren 1993, 1995) as they are articulated in the experience of disabled children in a variety of contexts. Our own project was a two-year research project, co-ordinated by staff from the Universities of Edinburgh and Leeds, and funded by the Economic and Social Research Council.[1] The research was carried out in two locations, one in England and one in Scotland, in a variety of contexts. We worked with over 300 disabled young people aged 11–16 (165 in-depth), who had an enormous range of impairments and experiences of disability.

By reference to three key pieces of legislation in both England and Wales, and Scotland – the Education Act 1981 (as amended by the Education Act 1996); the Children Act 1989 and the Children (Scotland) Act 1995; and the Disability Discrimination Act 1995, we suggest that disabled children's voices remain invisible under the law. We consider what this invisibility means in the context of the 'globalisation' of children's rights through the medium of the United Nations Convention of the Rights of the Child, which has effectively transformed children's rights into international law.

## FROM 'OLD' TO 'NEW' UNDERSTANDINGS OF CHILDHOOD, DISABILITY AND THE LAW

Since the 1960s, there has been an enormous growth in the study of both childhood and disability, which has led to the emergence of 'new sociologies' that aim to reconstruct both childhood and disability in a way that emphasises disabled people and children as competent social actors who are an integral part of society. The new agenda for the study of childhood has challenged 'the dominant and dominating conceptual pair of socialization and development,' which 'represented childhood and children as natural, passive incompetent and incomplete' (James and Prout 1999, pp.ix–x). This agenda has drawn from both interactionist accounts that describe children as agents in, as well as products of, social processes and social constructionist accounts that emphasize the social, cultural and historical variability of childhood and its irreducibility to a given biological reality. James, Jenks and Prout (1998) describe the outcomes of this work in terms of four different positions which they call the 'socially constructed' child; the 'tribal' child; the 'minority group' child; and the 'social structural' child.

The new agenda for disability studies has concentrated on the development of the social model of disability (see Chapter One), which has emerged from within the disabled people's movement. The social model is based on a conceptual distinction between disability and (physical, sensory and/or cognitive) impairment. Disability is then located in the changing character of social and economic structure (Barnes, Mercer and Shakespeare 1999; Oliver 1996) where it is positioned alongside race, gender, age and sexuality as an important axis of social inequality. The social model therefore seeks to move away from approaches that focus on impairment and disability as an individual problem where the person with an impairment is viewed in terms of 'deviance', 'abnormality', 'incompetence', 'tragedy', dysfunction and so on. The application of the social model has been strongly grounded in showing how society can be restructured and social barriers removed to ensure the equal participation of disabled people in the main domains of social reproduction, such as work and administration (Oliver and Barnes 1998). However, as with the new sociology of childhood, a number of positions have emerged from this work which reflect different methods and approaches to disability studies (Corker 1998; Shakespeare 1999), and differing positions with respect to broader sociological questions of materialism/idealism, universalism/particularism (Priestley 1998a), structure/culture/agency (Davis 2000), and social inclusion/exclusion (Corker 1998).

Law, too, has seen similar changes. In the UK, increasing numbers of law students are being encouraged to understand the relationship between social systems and their environments as influenced by the ideas of Teubner (1988, 1993) and Luhmann (1988). Teubner and Luhmann make a clear distinction between social constructions of 'reality' and psychic constructions or 'mental maps', and emphasise the fragmentation of society into 'a multiplicity of closed communicative networks', that include the law itself (Teubner 1989). This means that the law cannot deal directly with 'the outside world', it can only 'construct that world in forms that are acceptable as legal communications accessible to other legal communications in the network of legal communications' (King and Piper 1995, p.27). In this kind of framework, people become 'role-bundles, character-masks, internal products of legal communication', who are reproduced in 'the social life of the law in which human actors are not elements but constructed social realities' (Teubner 1988, p.133 and 1989, p.741). This view has been supported by an increasing concern, both inside and outside the legal profession, for the tendency of the law to reproduce social inequalities in terms of gender (Kennedy 1992; Young 1990), race (McPherson 1999; van Dijk 1993), disability (Corker 1998; Jones and Basser Marks 1999; Silvers, Wasserman and Mahowald 1998), and childhood (Alderson 1995, 1999; Archard 1993; Franklin 1995).

These changes in how childhood, disability and the law are understood are echoed neither in the wording of the legislature nor in the practice of its implementation, however, which seems to support Teubner's perspective on what is 'wrong' with the law. We now turn to some specific examples in UK law which relate to disabled children.

## LEGAL 'WRONGS' AND LEGAL 'RIGHTS'

Hill and Tisdall (1997), writing about the influential Warnock Report, the prime motivator for the enactment of the Education Act 1981 and the Education (Scotland) Act 1981, note that the term 'special educational needs' (SEN) was intended to move away from medical categorisation and to underline the part played by the school environment in creating a child's 'special needs'. Though this seemed to indicate that it was the school's responsibility to adjust, many have argued that this responsibility has not been fulfilled (Clough and Barton 1995; Cook and Slee 1999; Corbett 1996; Fulcher 1989). Statements and Records of Needs are still used mainly to provide children with access to segregated schools, or for the provision of special assistance and yet, without a Statement or Record, meeting the child's SEN can be a matter of discretion. This is where the legal qualifier 'wherever possible' is used as a loophole in avoiding responsibilities or justifying a failure to meet responsibilities on the grounds of lack of or poor management of resources (Corker 1998). Further, although Section 29(2) of the Disability Discrimination Act 1995 amends the Education Act 1993 (information relating to pupils with SEN to be included in the school's annual report) so that the report must include details of the arrangements for the admission of disabled pupils, the steps taken to prevent disabled pupils from being treated less favourably than other pupils, and the facilities provided to assist access to the school by disabled pupils, there is still no concept of disabled children as bearers of rights with teeth – that is, enforceable. The 'annual report' remains a statement of intent that often translates into a discretionary practical reality or, as one of us has written elsewhere:

> the Act makes *special* provision for individual disabled children to experience capacity and opportunity to choose and enact choice in pursuit of their *special* personal needs and interests, as determined by the views of the child's parents and the 'expert' judgment of professionals who assess these needs. It also *protects* children who do *not* have learning difficulties from denial or infringment of their capacity and opportunity for experiencing…self-determination (Corker 1998, p.77).

The law does not require schools to alter their ethos, physical environment or policies, which research has proven can be extremely effective in removing many disabling barriers, and can therefore reduce financial costs in the long term. So, for example, one school that we visited as part of our research on the *Lives of Disabled Children* project was set in a beautiful new building that was fully accessible to wheelchair users, but all of the disabled children who attended the school had cognitive, intellectual or sensory impairments, not mobility impairments.

SEN remain firmly located in the individual child and not in their school or family environment (Armstrong, Galloway and Tomlinson 1993), in spite of the fact that some of the worst violations of children's rights take place in the family (Fottrell 1999). With respect to the latter, the much-celebrated Children Act 1989 and Children (Scotland) Act 1995 were considered to introduce important new provisions and protections for disabled children, particularly the right of children to be safeguarded when undergoing periods of 'care', the right to have their opinions sought with regard to matters and decisions concerning their welfare (Beresford 1997), and the replacement of parental rights with parental duties and responsibilities. Archard (1993) has looked at the question of 'future-orientated consent' in terms of a 'caretaker thesis' (pp.51–7). The suggestion is that 'the caretaker chooses for the child in the person of the adult which the child is not yet but will eventually be' (p.53), which means that adult choices may be linked with 'self-justifying' rather than 'future-orientated' consent. Although we would emphasise that not all adults make decisions in this way, these ideas become complicated in relation to disabled children and young people because, irrespective of where they are in the life course, they continue to be regarded by society's institutions as being in a state of 'perpetual childhood' (Priestley 1998b). In short, there is no future to orientate to other than one in which disabled adults remain 'dependent', 'vulnerable' and 'in need of care.'

Further, as Fottrell (1999) points out, in some cultures, 'the autonomou
an anathema and a perceived threat to the family, with the latter prio
both the foundation of that [culture] and a rights holder whose inte..
trump those of its individual members' (p.168).

As King and Piper (1995) note, lawyers still fight to assert the rights of
parents over those of their children and, in some cases, as we will see in the next
section, the rights of professionals over both. This seems to be saying that the
advocacy of children's rights is antipathetic to adults' rights and diminishes
adults' 'genuine' rights claims (Heartfield 1993, p.13). In these circumstances,
children's rights are simply demands for protection by adults. Indeed, although
children's rights to resources and protection are promoted far more than their
autonomy rights, resources and protection tend to be justified in terms of
children's best interests usually as defined by adults, in contrast to rights as
chosen and claimed by right-holders.

> Young people are often more concerned about their right, as they see it, to stay
> out late with their friends, than about their best interests as perceived by their
> parents to be safe at home. Experts' advice about child care which used to be
> framed in terms of 'what is right for children' is being re-written as 'your child's
> right to', for instance music lessons. If the child does not want or need these, such
> advice plays fashionable rights language and distorts its meaning. Rights can be
> claimed in the wrong context. When adults define children's rights, rights
> language can be more oppressive than other terminology if it suggests freedom
> and choice when these are actually missing (Alderson 1993, p.33).

What this means is that 'the best interests of the child' is a concept in transition
throughout childhood. Decisions motivated by best interests can mean at one
stage special protection, and at another involve respect for the individual's
autonomy. But this transition cannot be achieved if, as noted above, it is not
acknowledged. In recent research commissioned by the Who Cares? Trust and
carried out by Jenny Morris (1999), looking into how social services departments
in England and Wales are fulfilling their duties under the Children Act to disabled
children, there were a number of disturbing findings. For example:

> some disabled children were spending time away from home in
> short-term placements without any knowledge or involvement of the
> social services authority;
>
> some disabled children on long-term placements were not being
> accorded the protection of the Children Act;
>
> there was little evidence of disabled children's 'wishes and feelings'
> about their placements being 'ascertained' (as stipulated by the Act);

there was a lack of information about how many disabled children are spending time away from home in order to give their parents a break, and in what kind of service provision.

### Table 9.1: Article 23 of the UN Convention on the Rights of the Child

| Article 23, text | Unofficial summary of main provisions |
| --- | --- |
| 1. States Parties recognize that a mentally or physically disabled child should enjoy a full and decent life, in conditions which ensure dignity, promote self-reliance, and facilitate the child's active participation in the community. <br><br> 2. States Parties recognize the right of the disabled child to special care and shall encourage and ensure the extension, subject to available resources, to the eligible child and those responsible for his or her care, of assistance for which application is made and which is appropriate to the child's condition and to the circumstances of the parents or others caring for the child. <br><br> 3. Recognizing the special needs of a disabled child, assistance extended in accordance with paragraph 2 of the present article shall be provided free of charge, whenever possible, taking into account the financial resources of the parents or others caring for the child, and shall be designed to ensure that the disabled child has effective access to and receives education, training, health care services, rehabilitation services, preparation for employment and recreation opportunities in a manner conducive to the child's achieving the fullest possible social integration and individual development, including his or her cultural and spiritual development. <br><br> 4. States parties shall promote, in the spirit of international co-operation, the exchange of appropriate information in the field of preventative health care and of medical, psychological and functional treatment of disabled children, including dissemination of and access to information concerning methods of rehabilitation, education, and vocational services, with the aim of enabling States Parties to improve their capabilities and skills and to widen their experience in these areas. In this regard, particular account shall be taken of the needs of developing countries. | *Handicapped children* <br> The right of the handicapped child to special care, education and training designed to help them achieve greatest possible self-reliance and to lead a full and active life in society. |

It is perhaps because of the widespread failure of national policies to adopt approaches which regard disabled children as holders of rights that those who are concerned with promoting these rights are turning increasingly to 'globalised' notions of disabled children's rights, particularly as enshrined in the United Nations Convention on the Rights of the Child (hereafter referred to as the UN Convention). The aim of the UN Convention (see Chapter Three, p.67) is to bring together in a single instrument the full canon of human rights applicable to children – that is, the 'best interests of the child must be a primary consideration in all matters and decisions affecting the child' (Article 3) – and to assert the right of children to full equality in the enjoyment of these rights (Article 2). There is some indication, however, than not all children do have full equality in the enjoyment of these rights, and these children include disabled children. Article 23 of the UN Convention is therefore dedicated to the specific rights of disabled children, and is reproduced in Table 9.1.

The UN Convention Article 12 states that children not only have a right to articulate their concern with regard to issues that affect them but have the right to have these opinions heard (Morrow and Richards 1996). Article 13 declares that the child has a right to seek, receive and impart information and ideas of all kinds and Article 29 indicates children's education should respect the child's cultural identity, language and values (Alderson 1995). The message held in this legislation is that children's 'voices' should be listened to by adults who make decisions concerning children's lives (Davis 1998). The following section of this chapter therefore attempts to understand, in the context of the above discussion, whether, and if so, how, disabled children understand their rights, and whether they consider that they have the same rights as non-disabled children.

## WHAT DO DISABLED CHILDREN THINK ABOUT THEIR 'RIGHTS'?

The most fundamental of human rights is the right to life, and this is currently an important topic of discussion in the disabled people's movement in relation to genetic screening for disabled foetuses and gene therapy, for example. This raises a whole series of difficult questions about the quality of life, ethics and social justice which are beyond the scope of this chapter. But it is worth pointing out that decisions about the right to exist are frequently based on 'the widespread assumption that disabled people's lives are not worth living' (Morris 1991, p.12), and there is no research that has proven a link between 'type' and 'severity' of impairment and quality of life. Nevertheless, this is a topic that disabled children and their parents discuss, and their perspectives are varied. When asked about what they would do if their mother was pregnant with a deaf baby, Maria and Alan told us:

> *Maria*:     I would have it aborted, don't let it be born deaf. If it was mine I would, I'd want it to be hearing. Deaf people can't have the jobs we want, all we have is anything to do with Sign Language.

*Alan*: It is always difficult for deaf people to find work because we can't do everything. Really there should be more things for deaf people and not concentrate on who has hearing and who don't...

But Alan, as we will see below, also alluded to the fact that adults think deaf children are 'thick', 'won't allow' them to learn what they want, and so 'it's impossible to get jobs' (Corker 2000), which suggests that there is nothing intrinsically wrong with being disabled. It is the restricting characteristics of the social environment that create perceptions of quality of life. In another example, the right to life was briefly discussed by Bobby (who is unable to speak), his mother and his sister, Lisa:

*Mother*: Sometimes he watches the telly, or goes into his room. He likes *Neighbours, Home and Away, Coronation Street, Emmerdale, EastEnders*. He watched that last night – that wasn't very good last night, did you see it? Bianca got rid of the baby last night.

*Int*: But I thought she and Ricky were happy.

*Lisa*: They are but the baby was disabled inside so they got rid of it.

*Mother*: We werny happy with that, like getting rid o' disabled kids, were we [turns to her daughter].

*Lisa*: [shakes head]

*Bobby*: [shakes fist and head to indicate disapproval of the programme]

Van Bueren (1993, 1995) argues that children's rights can be reduced to four core elements identified as protection, prevention, provision and participation. The initial focus for children's rights activists was on the first three, reflecting a conceptualisation of the child as essentially weak and dependent which dominated relevant international instruments up to the late 1970s. Recently, however, as we saw above, a consensus emerged that in addition to enjoying certain rights associated with their status and their particular needs, children are autonomous beings, and, as we saw above, have been reconceptualised as participants in the wider society, independent of the family unit and, consequently, as holders of participatory rights not traditionally associated with childhood, including, for example, freedom of association, expression and religion (Fottrell 1999). We now move on to examine how the concept of children's rights itself operates in the lives of disabled children.

## THE RIGHT TO FREEDOM OF ASSOCIATION, EXPRESSION AND RELIGION

Disabled children find themselves in something of a double-bind. First, although the children in our study wanted to locate themselves within the world of children, there were various barriers to their full participation, and considerable infringements of their right to freedom of association. Some of the children complained that it was difficult to maintain friendships with non-disabled children when they were unable to access areas like some fast food outlets and other child-centred spaces. Many children did not attend their local school, either because they went to segregated schools some distance from their homes, or because the only accessible mainstream school also involved travelling. They therefore had few friends at home. In these cases, friendships outside the school day tended to be confined to family members. The way provision was delivered shaped the peer groups of disabled children. For example, some schools had a 'base' for children with particular impairments; in other schools, disabled children had to sit at a particular table in open plan classrooms or even had separate spaces in the dining hall and the school playground; often children associated with others as a result of shared transport facilities. This outcome was sometimes used by staff to reinforce their belief that disabled children preferred to associate with other disabled children, irrespective of the children's own preferences. Vanessa recognised the difficulties this created. She told us:

> I don't like school with hearing people. Because I'm separate from my deaf friends and it's like we learn separate but now I'm forced always with hearing people…some hearing people are awful and make me so angry. I have my friend in some lessons and sometimes he helps me in Chemistry when I'm on my own, but that's all…everyone else, I don't like. But, when people go away to deaf school it's OK because you can choose friends, lots of choice, but in my school you can't, it's not easy because not many to choose from… I can't choose because maybe 18 are deaf and 16 are not nice people and so many hearing are awful which means maybe only three or four people that I like. Nice people. So I have two good friends…both hearing…at school, both good friends. Most of the deaf people I like go to residential and they maybe have parties once a week and they make special friends there. Also I'm a bit older – most of them at my school are younger than me. I think it's because my birthday is a different time…so there's all younger and I don't meet people my age…they're like babies.

She suggests there is a right not to be associated with children who have similar impairments, and this is a theme we picked up in the situated narratives of other children (Davis, Priestley and Watson 1999). In another school we encountered two children, Irene and Maxine, who had similar impairments but whose requirements with regard to work were different. They complained that their teachers failed to recognise these different requirements because they were unable to separate them as people from their impairments. However, these girls had the confidence to express their concerns and change the teachers' practice. Nevertheless, these issues are clearly complex, as another child, Chick, explained:

*Int*: What about primary school?

*Chick*: I find that at the start, because everyone's so much younger, they didn't really realise that I had a problem. It didn't matter that I was disabled, 'cause there wasn't really that much difference. But then when I made friends, they didn't want to wait for me. I think they maybe felt that I was keeping them back. So they went on ahead and I was left on my own.

*Int*: What about this secondary school?

*Chick*: I mean, I've never really developed friends like other people do. It's not because I don't want to. I want to. I don't think it's because I'm a horrible person, although you can make your mind up about that, but I really have to do all the work. I have some friends who talk to me at break time, but that's as far as it goes. And I'm a bit scared, because I was let down before in the past. Once I wanted to go swimming with my friends at primary school and at the last minute they phoned up to say more or less go away. Also my parents have tried so hard to help me get friends, but it's not really worked out.

These experiences sound very negative. However, over the course of a number of weeks Chick's school carried out disability awareness days involving children from Chick's classes, and they also invited Chick's mother to come and speak. Chick himself carried out a question and answer session with his classmates as part of his curriculum requirements in language (Scottish Office Education Department 5–14 curriculum). Eventually a few months later Chick had started to develop closer friends:

*Chick*: Now people are more relaxed with me, they're beginning to chat. And, I've one close friend now, Shona. She's different because I talk to her and she talks back to me, instead of me having to ask questions all the time. We have been to cinema and she has come over, so that is good. The Friday that we finished for Christmas, me, Jason, James, Benny – 12 people, six boys, six girls – went up town so that was good.

But it is worth noting Chick's mother's experience of 'letting go': 'It was the most nerve-racking two and a half hours I have ever spent. Handing him over to kids I didn't know, in his wheelchair, in the dark, in the cold. He was fine. Oh I was pleased [he'd been invited]. I let him go, but behind the scenes, I was…' Chick's mother and Chick's school made a breakthrough in effecting structural and cultural changes which diminished Chick's experience of disability and recognised his right to associate with whom he wished, but many adults we met continued to put disability before the child and to create dependent children.

Other children talked about the conflict between adult perceptions of them as disabled children 'unable' to make decisions for themselves, and the cultural and religious expectations of their family. For example, Sabina, a disabled girl from a Muslim family, told us about a sporting event where the staff insisted that she changed into 'white' sports clothes, which she felt was contrary to her ethnic and religious background:

> *Sabina*: Well yeah they wanted me to change into a track suit and I didn't want to, I'm Asian and I enjoy wearing Asian clothes like the ones I'm wearing now. Like this, there are a lot of Asian girls who do wear trousers, I don't. All that changing all the time.

> *Int*: I wanted to ask you how you felt but there wasn't the opportunity at the time. Did the teacher actually tell you to change?

> *Sabina*: Well I was saying no and they were telling me that I had to and that if I didn't then I couldn't play. So I didn't join in, I had to.

> *Int*: The rest of the activities, did you enjoy them?

> *Sabina*: Mm, I enjoyed it but…

> *Int*: But…

> *Sabina*: They were forcing me to change and I didn't want to and there were lots of other [non-disabled] Asian girls there dressed like me and they hadn't been forced to get changed. It didn't feel fair on me at all.

Another disabled boy, of ethnic Chinese origin, Lee, said:

> I think it would be good to have a fellow Chinese student here because we think in similar ways and we could talk and laugh. I can feel stupid sometimes trying to understand English all the time. You know, it would feel good to see some Chinese again and have a chat with someone Chinese. Others here talk about *EastEnders*, *Neighbours* or *Emmerdale*, this doesn't interest me, I don't know what to talk about when they talk about these things. My parents watch Chinese television, I can find that boring too. I'm trying to understand Chinese programmes through subtitles … it's tough going but I'm trying to learn Chinese anyway. In China every Sunday you go to school and work for four hours. We don't do that here.

## PARTICIPATION RIGHTS

Children's claims to 'liberty' rights – the freedom to self-determine and to participate in decision making, for example – have always been fiercely contested by philosophers like John Stuart Mill, who argue that 'such rights require the capacities for reason, rationality, and autonomy and that therefore children are excluded from their possession – along with people who are mentally ill or brain damaged' (Franklin 1995, p.12). In the Who Cares? Report (Morris 1999) it was found that in only 12 out of the 66 cases studied had the social worker attempted to find out the child's views. In at least five cases, the social worker had not even seen the child. Typically, the section of the form headed 'Child's view' was left blank or the social worker had made comments such as, 'She is unable verbally to communicate and therefore her view is not available'; 'it is not possible to know what his views are owing to his level of disability'. This is in keeping with the common assumption that disabled children who are 'inarticulate' are also unable to consent, or to express views. But consider these views, expressed through an electronic voice synthesiser by Katie Caryer (1999), a member of the disabled children's group 'Young and Powerful':

> A lot of people think inclusive schooling consists of two things – lifts and ramps – wrong. That's integration. Inclusive education is where people have the right attitude towards disabled young people. It is based on the social model of disability, which I think all secondary schools should teach... In my English class, I was pleased that *My Left Foot* was included but the booklet introduced Christy Brown's piece with 'Christy Brown was born a victim of cerebral palsy'. Now I have cerebral palsy. I have often been the victim of other people's attitudes but I have never in my life felt myself to be a victim of cerebral palsy. When my English teacher found out how I felt about the word victim, the whole class had a discussion about it. This was good for the 30 teenagers in my class, but what about the other 1400 in my school – especially those who've called me a freak, invalid, retarded and other fantastic words.

As McDermott (1988) has written, inarticulateness might represent 'not a disability, but an invitation to listen in a new way' (p.40), and this requires a great deal of reflexivity (Davis 1998; Davis, Cunningham-Burley and Watson 2000). But although some disabled children we interviewed had equally clear ideas about what they wanted to learn (Corker 2000), they suggested that many of the adult teaching strategies they experienced were focused on the very things they didn't find helpful or useful:

*Int*: OK, where would you like to start?

*Maria [to Alan]*: Tell her what you think about learning.

*Alan*: Because I get so fed up with it. It feels like a waste of time what we learn here. I want to learn proper things, not what we learn here. Maybe things about what is happening in the world today, I don't know like problems people have, maybe moving house or something and what that's like.

*Int:* So you think that's not learning?

*Alan:* I just think that we could be learning other things like what is happening in this country, Britain and the things that this country does. We could be learning so much more. We could be learning about how to vote for the banning of global warming... I want to have proper English, reading and things like that. We don't get that and I hate it.

*Int:* Would anyone like to add to that?

*Maria:* I didn't understand what he was talking about.

*Int:* You don't understand what he has just said? – Right, you want me explain again? OK, erm – Alan said that he thought that what you learn was not like proper learning, just useless information. [*To Alan*] But maybe because it is not linked to your experience?

*Maria:* No, he means [names teacher] is just crap.

*Alan:* It's just too fast, really that is all it is, it's too fast.

*Maria:* He thinks we are all thick anyway. He once asked us all what 'as well' means. We all know what 'as well' means!

*Alan:* Yeah, he thinks that we don't understand...

*Int:* ...OK...

*Alan:* ...he thinks we don't know what 'turn up' means and we do. He thinks we're thick. He made us write down what it meant. So then we had to write longer and longer lists of what words meant. It's such a waste of time.

Alan's comments hark back to the Alderson quote in the previous section about the discrepancy between what kind of things young people want to have the right to and what kind of things are perceived by adults to be in their best interests. When it was suggested to Alan that he might be able to change things, his response was telling: 'How can I change things, *they* won't! Like, if a new rule is introduced, it then stays. It doesn't mean that if everyone behaves, we have fewer rules. No it doesn't work the other way does it?'

It is also important to understand that participation often requires information, knowledge and language and communication skills. As Vanessa continued, disabled children are often prevented from accessing information and/or are dependent on informal channels for this information:

*Int:* Do you know about something called human rights? Like...children have the right to language and the right to be safe... Have you learnt about that at school?

*Vanessa*: No…but sometimes I watch TV or read newspapers or teletext or something and they say… umm… something like… umm… maybe deaf person … I don't know just an example about some deaf people, but I don't understand because it's all oral, so I don't know the law, the rules really… only [indistinct].

*Int*: For a long time there's been a law abroad, but it's not included in the law here in Britain but the government is trying to include it in the law here now so in future things like children's right to language will be included…

*Vanessa*: Uh-huh [thinks] Umm, I know about disabled rights and how disabled people should be allowed to work because I read newspapers and watch TV… that's where I get it.

## PROTECTION RIGHTS AND THE ABUSE OF DISABLED CHILDREN

The sexual abuse experienced by disabled children is well documented and we will not attempt to repeat it here (see for example, Corker 1996; Cross 1994; Kennedy 1996). However, we will highlight one area of abuse which was very significant in our project. Disabled children, according to many of our respondents, have one thing in common: as one of the children told us when asked what disability meant, 'we all get picked on'. Children told us about their experience of bullying, which ranged from being called names such as 'spastic' or 'deaf bastard', as Katy described above, to being excluded from peer groups or being kicked and hit, and we observed all these processes in action in many different contexts. In one school there were security cameras in communal areas, and notices relating to the school's anti-bullying policy posted throughout the school, but disabled children reported to us that they still experienced systematic bullying.

Very often, school responses to bullying appeared to us to punish the individual child more than the bully. For example in one school we visited a disabled girl, Beth, who was kept inside school during break times 'for her own safety'. Beth had her own view of what should be happening:

*Beth*: I think the head or the other head teachers should go to them and tell them to stop it or if they don't they'd get excluded for it.

*Int*: And if they excluded these children?

*Beth*: I would be back outside again in the playground.

Further, disabled children often learnt that this was acceptable behaviour – one child described how he 'gave the left hook and booted them' after he had been insulted. Neither of these solutions do anything to close the social space between bully and bullied. It would appear that a more nuanced response is required if protection or self defence is not to lead to reduced participation (Davis and

Watson 2001). It is also the case that when disabled children misbehaved, adults often attributed this to the effects of their impairment. Any resistance displayed by the children was thus neutralised or diagnosed as indicative of abnormality. For example, a disabled boy displaying age-appropriate 'naughtiness' was labelled as having ADHD (attention deficit hyperactivity disorder). Because his behaviour could not be explained away by the existing impairment, some adults actively sought a diagnosis of ADHD, and he was prescribed the drug Ritalin. Before the additional diagnosis, he was very much in the thick of things and 'in' with the bullies. Although his concentration did appear to improve after the drug had been prescribed, and his parents described the change as liberating, his day became more structured around the times when he needed his doses of the drug. As a result, he lost all his friends and was bullied mercilessly. The only solution was a change of school (see Corker and Davis 2000 for more details), and indeed, many of the children in special schools explained to us that bullying was the reason for them leaving mainstream provision.

There were, however, more subtle examples which are part of the normalising process of rehabilitation. We observed totally blind children being taught to restrict their everyday 'blind behaviour' such as failing to make eye contact, rocking and poking their eyes. The children were sometimes told that if they didn't learn the 'normal' way or were not 'polite to normal people', sighted people 'wouldn't give money to blind charities, or to the school' and 'wouldn't help them or other blind people if they needed help outside in the street'. We believe that such 'blindisms' are different from teaching blind children to use a white cane in a responsible way. These issues have been explored in great depth by Michalko (1998).

## THE RIGHTS OF PROFESSIONALS OVER PARENTS AND DISABLED CHILDREN

There are numerous examples of adults being no more competent to make decisions than children are. Adults repeatedly behave in certain ways and do certain things which children have been taught are wrong or ill-advised (Dworkin 1977). Not only did we observe this in our fieldwork, but disabled children highlighted this.

*Sarah*: ... I don't get angry at teachers...well sometimes...

*Int*: What's that about?

*Sarah*: ... They will shout at you to 'sit down', 'stop talking and listen to me'. That sort of thing can make me angry.

*Int*: Is it just the way they talk? Or what they ask you to do?

*Sarah*: Yeah when they ask me what to do like... [names teacher]? I remember once I was sitting and [teacher] was talking to another teacher and I began talking and he told me to shut up. I thought what I was saying was important. That made me angry. You know that teacher?

*Int*: Yeah, I wonder sometimes... do you think all the teachers are like that or just some?

*Sarah*: Some.

*Int*: Some, yeah.

*Sarah*: That teacher's is the worst of all of them...talks such rubbish all the time. For example in the mainstream setting all the other students have started working and that teacher is still talking...that makes me late and then I have to rush.

However, sometimes the double standards of adults who behave badly or act in an abusive fashion receive legal backing. Our final example is one which we believe shows what can happen when disabled children are not accorded rights of any kind, and where the law acts to reinforce this absence of rights. In a November 1999 edition of the BBC TV programme *Panorama* an appalling catalogue of abuses of the law was uncovered in relation to the treatment of disabled children with chronic fatigue syndrome (ME), based on research in over 700 families. In one situation, a doctor went to the High Court, in conjunction with Social Services, to enforce the doctor's view that he should treat a 16-year-old boy against the wishes of the boy and his parents. The boy was made a ward of court, and when the parents took their son to Europe to escape from this legal ruling, Interpol was alerted and forced their return. The boy was immediately placed in the treatment centre, where another young person with ME had this to say:

When I arrived he'd already been there for a couple of months, and obviously was very unhappy about the situation. But doctors weren't listening to him and weren't taking his views into account that [ME] wasn't a psychological illness, he wasn't depressed. He was perfectly happy at home and they weren't listening to him and wouldn't take into account his physical problems and wouldn't believe he wasn't making them up... He'd been very into sports, academically a high flyer, good social group, good friends, enjoyed school, and was very much the same as me in those respects. Then everything has gone and it was very obvious that if he'd been able to get up and walk he would have done. But the nurses didn't see that. They saw him as being awkward and stubborn... He was put on a Zimmer frame to try and help him because when he went in he was able to walk. As he was in he got worse and worse and worse and they put him in a Zimmer frame and as he was sort of totally exhausted, his knees scraping the floor, his chin sort of touching the bar, when the consultant said to him 'Do you know how much your bed is costing us?'

When this boy was finally released from the unit another doctor found that he was 'suffering from severe ME and post-traumatic stress disorder as a result of his experiences in that hospital, and he has lost total faith in the medical profession'.

## CONCLUDING REMARKS

It seems that what has been achieved through the law is effectively a split between a theoretical movement from concepts of individual children's needs to 'globalised' notions of children's rights, and the individualising and largely reactive practice of implementing the law. In spite of the similar patterns in change of the approach to understanding disability, childhood and the law, it remains the case that the dominant discourse of law in relation to disabled children is one that sees disability or children, but not disabled children, and views disability itself in terms of dependency. Thus the duty to 'care' or to provide 'reasonable accommodation' is put before a notion of disabled children's rights. This is in part because, as Priestley (1998b) explains:

> There has been relatively little work that explores the intersection between these new perspectives on childhood and disability. Research on contemporary childhoods has marginalized the experience of disability, while social model research on disability has marginalized the experience of childhood...the vast majority of studies that address the lives of disabled children remain poorly informed in one or both of these areas (p.208).

But it is also because the law itself has made disabled children an exemplar of all that is 'old' in legal discourses about rights, particularly in how the law is applied in an individualising and reductionist way very effectively to transform complex moral and social policy concerns relating to disabled children into simplistic interpretations of legal rights and wrongs, villains and victims, and rights-transgressors and the rights-transgressed. In short, the law offers society a version of social reality which substitutes normative expectations for those derived from experience. In doing so, the law not only simplifies and reduces social issues, but also absorbs and neutralises them. Jones and Basser Marks (1999) suggest that the law achieves this 'by categorising, isolating, ostracising, dehumanising, rather than by just punishing identifiable acts of wrong doing' (pp.3–4). We think that this is Luhmann's notion of 'fragmentation' in practice, as described by Teubner (1989): '[the] fragmentation of society into a plurality of autonomous discourses. The crucial feature of modern society is the loss of a unifying mode of cognition. Society is seen as a multiplicity of closed communicative networks' (p.738).

How this translates in the application of the law to disabled children operates at both the service level and at the level of the child. When communicative networks – and we must emphasise that the law itself is one such network – are closed, this prevents dialogue, whilst also creating a situation where some networks are more privileged than others. At the level of services, law, medicine, education and science are privileged over both the social and the individual disabled child. This means that the law often includes tasks which it performs for medicine, education and science, including dealing with and 'resolving' some of the contentious disputes we described above. At the level of the individual disabled child, the different networks within the law, for example, networks relating to race, gender and disability, are similarly hierarchically organised. This means that the child's difference tends to be simplistically described in terms of disability first or race first or gender first, for example. At the level of practice, and in terms of the interaction of services and disabled children, what this means is that service resources are generally poured into disability at the expense of, for example, race or gender. It also means, as we saw above, that the law, because its function is to stabilise, impose order and resolve disputes, imposes the notion of the 'fragmented' child at the expense of the attempt to legislate for the systemic forces that lead to fragmentation. It is for this reason that we argue that the law, as a largely reactive structure, is ineffective when dealing with forms of discrimination that are institutionalised. It could be argued of course that challenging systemic, structural and cultural factors are better placed in the domains of education, social policy and overarching policies on human rights such as the UN Convention. We agree. But if this is to be the case, there has to be dialogue between these domains and the law as it now stands.

This is why we want to emphasise that we do not think that approaches which fragment the individual and the social, privileging one or the other, can resolve the issues that face disabled children, or disabled adults for that matter. With respect to children's right to education, for example, we continue to feel that the law could demarcate distinctions and differences that matter and are experientially relevant in the children's terms, rather than in the terms of adults. So, for example, we could make a distinction between the disabled child – that is, the child for whom educational success hinges on systemic factors such as the physical or attitudinal environment, access to technology and adaptive aids, and access to the full curriculum offer – and the child who has an impairment and/or chronic illness such that 'special' resources and time for learning are necessary. Most disabled children will experience elements of both, but since we are dealing with the educational system in this instance it is important that we remember what the function of education is meant to be, and to create the conditions that enable this function to be extended to all children. As Cook and Slee (1999) write:

Inclusive education demands new forms of 'knowing' disability and disablement, it demands a politics of discourse and recognition. The language of the law, and its interpretations, must become a part of that discourse which shapes the epistemic preconditions for enablement and the struggle against discrimination. In other words…inclusive education is more than the relocation of disabled students from segregated to mainstream schools (p.327).

Similarly, if we focus on health and social services, it has to be legally possible to distinguish between impairment – or a state of physical, sensory or cognitive difference which does not have health implications – and chronic illness, which has 'care' implications, whilst recognising that the boundaries between the two can become blurred. This is true particularly in the arena of mental health, as the examples of young people with ME showed. And finally, the law could ensure that disabled children's advocates follow the recommendations of the Reference Group of disabled young people for the Who Cares? Project, namely that advocates should:

be independent

find out what the child needs

have the sole aim of supporting the child

treat the child as an equal

have the power to sort out problems.

We believe that this kind of approach would enable the law to be more responsive to, and give equal credence to, both the systemic and the individual aspects of disability. This has to be better than the current legal framework, which allows an exponential growth of local interpretations of policy that are being increasingly led by the availability of 'appropriate' resources and/or by schisms in professional ideologies that make it very difficult to build a holistic picture of the disabled child in her or his social context. This continues to add to widespread abuses of the human and civil rights of disabled children, and the silencing of their voices, rendering them 'invisible under the law'.

## REFERENCES

Alderson, P. (1993) *Children's Consent to Surgery.* Buckingham: Open University Press.

Alderson, P. (1995) *Listening to Children: Children, Ethics and Social Research.* London: Barnardos.

Alderson, P. (1999) *Civil Rights in Schools Project Report.* London: Social Science Research Unit, Institute of Education (Research Briefing, October, No 1, available from the Economic and Social Research Council).

Archard, D. (1993) *Children: Rights and Childhood.* London: Routledge.

Armstrong, D.K., Galloway, D. and Tomlinson, S. (1993) 'Assessing special educational needs: the child's contribution.' *British Educational Research Journal 19*, 2, 121.

Barnes, C., Mercer, G. and Shakespeare, T. (1999) *Exploring Disability: A Sociological Introduction.* Cambridge: Polity.

Beresford, B. (1997) *Personal Accounts: Involving Disabled Children in Research.* York: Social Policy Research Unit.

Caryer, K. (1999) *How My School Would Benefit From Disability Equality Training.* Paper given at the launch of the Disability Equality in Education Trainers' Network, Department for Education and Employment, December 1999.

Clough, P. and Barton, L. (1995) *Making Difficulties: Research and the Construction of SEN.* London: Paul Chapman Publishing.

Cook, S. and Slee, R. (1999) 'Struggling with the fabric of disablement: picking up the threads of law and education.' In M. Jones and L.A. Basser Marks (eds) *Disability, Divers-ability and Legal Change.* The Hague: Martinus Nijhoff.

Corbett, J. (1996) *Bad Mouthing: The Language of Special Education.* London: The Falmer Press.

Corker, M. (1996) *Deaf Transitions.* London: Jessica Kingsley Publishers.

Corker, M. (1998) *Deaf and Disabled or Deafness Disabled.* Buckingham: Open University Press.

Corker, M. (2000) ' "They don't know what they don't know" – disability research as an emancipatory site of learning.' In A. James, P. Christensen, A. Prout and S. McNamee (eds) *Sites of Learning.* London: Falmer.

Corker, M. and Davis, J.M. (2000) 'Portrait of Callum: the disabling of a childhood?' In R. Edwards (ed) *Children, Home and School: Autonomy, Connection or Regulation.* London: Falmer.

Cross, M. (1994) 'Abuse.' In L. Keith (ed) *Mustn't Grumble: Writing by Disabled Women.* London: The Women's Press.

Davis, J.M. (1998) 'Understanding the meanings of children: a reflexive process.' *Children & Society 12,* 325.

Davis, J.M., Priestley, M. and Watson, N. (1999) 'Dilemmas of the field: what can the study of disabled childhoods tell us about contemporary sociology?' Paper presented to the British Sociology Association, University of Glasgow, 7 April 1999.

Davis, J.M (2000) 'Disability Studies as ethnographic research and text: research strategies and roles for promoting social change.' *Disability and Society, 15,* 2, 191–206.

Davis, J.M., Cunningham-Burley, S. and Watson, N.(2000) 'Learning the lives of disabled children: developing a reflexive approach.' In P. Christensen and A. James (eds) *Conducting Research with Children.* London: Falmer.

Davis, J.M. and Watson, N. (2001, forthcoming) 'Countering stereotypes of disability: disabled children and resistance.' In M. Corker and T. Shakespeare (eds) *Disability and Postmodernity.* London: Continuum.

Dworkin, R. (1977) *Taking Rights Seriously.* Cambridge, MA: Harvard University Press.

Fottrell, D. (1999) 'Children's Rights.' In A. Hegarty and S. Leonard (eds) *Human Rights: An Agenda for the 21st Century.* London: Cavendish Publishing.

Franklin, B. (1995) (ed) *The Handbook of Children's Rights.* London: Routledge.

Fulcher, G. (1989) *Disabling Policies? A Comparative Approach to Education Policy and Disability.* London: The Falmer Press.

Heartfield, J. (1993) 'Why children's rights are wrong.' *Living Marxism,* October 1993, 13.

Hill, M. and Tisdall, K. (1997) *Children and Society.* London: Longman.

James, A., Jenks, C. and Prout, A. (1998) *Theorising Childhood.* Cambridge: Polity.

James, A. and Prout, A. (1999) *Constructing and Re-constructing Childhood.* Second edition. London: Falmer.

Jones, M. and Basser Marks, L.A. (1999) 'Law and the social construction of disability.' In M. Jones and L.A. Basser Marks (eds) *Disability, Divers-ability and Legal Change.* The Hague: Martinus Nijhoff.

Kennedy, H. (1992) *Eve was Framed: Women and British Justice.* London: Chatto and Windus.

Kennedy, M. (1995) 'Rights for children who are disabled.' In B. Franklin (ed) *The Handbook of Children's Rights.* London: Routledge.

Kennedy, M. (1996) 'Sexual abuse and disabled children.' In J. Morris (ed) *Encounters with Strangers: Feminism and Disability.* London: The Women's Press.

King, M. and Piper, C. (1995) *How the Law Thinks about Children.* Second edition. Aldershot: Arena.

Luhmann, N. (1988) 'Closure and openness: on reality in the world of law.' In G. Teubner (ed) *Autopoietic Law: A New Approach to Law and Society.* Berlin: De Gruyter.

McDermott, R. (1988) 'Inarticulateness.' In D. Tannen (ed) *Linguistics in Context: Connecting Observation and Understanding.* Baltimore: Ablex.

McPherson, Sir W. (1999) *The Stephen Lawrence Enquiry: Report of an Inquiry by Sir William MacPherson of Cluny.* London: HMSO Cmnd 4262–1.

Michalko, R. (1998) *The Mystery of the Eye and the Shadow of Blindness.* Toronto: University of Toronto Press.

Morris, J. (1991) *Pride Against Prejudice: Transforming Attitudes to Disability.* London: The Women's Press.

Morris, J. (1999) *Disabled Children and the Children Act.* London: The Who Cares? Trust.

Morrow, V. and Richards, M. (1996) 'The ethics of social research with children: an overview.' *Children and Society 10,* 28.

Oliver, M. (1996) *Understanding Disability: From Theory to Practice.* Basingstoke: Macmillan.

Oliver, M. and Barnes, C. (1998) *Disabled People and Social Policy.* London: Longman.

Priestley, M. (1998a) 'Constructions and creations: idealism, materialism and disability theory.' *Disability & Society 13,* 1, 75.

Priestley, M. (1998b) 'Childhood disability and disabled childhoods: agendas for research.' *Childhood 5,* 2, 207.

Shakespeare, T. (1999) 'What is a disabled person?' In M. Jones and L.A. Basser Marks (eds) *Disability, Divers-ability and Legal Change.* The Hague: Martinus Nijhoff.

Shakespeare, T. and Watson, N. (1998) 'Theoretical perspectives on childhood research.' In C. Robinson and K. Stalker (eds) *Growing Up with Disability.* London: Jessica Kingsley Publishers.

Silvers, A., Wasserman, D. and Mahowald, M.B. (1998) *Disability, Difference, Discrimination: Perspectives on Justice in Bioethics and Public Policy.* Lanham: Rowman and Littlefield.

Teubner, G. (ed) (1988) *Autopoietic Law: A New Approach to Law Society.* Berlin/New York: De Gruyter.

Teubner, G. (1989) 'How the law thinks: towards a constructivist epistemology of law.' *Law and Society Review 23,* 5, 727.

Teubner, G. (1993) *Law as an Autopoietic System.* Oxford: Blackwell.

Van Bueren, G. (1993) 'The struggle for empowerment: the emerging civil and political rights of children.' In *Selected Essays on International Children's Rights.* Geneva: Defence for Children International, Volume 1.

Van Bueren, G. (1995) *The International Law on the Rights of the Child.* Dordrecht: Kluwer.

van Dijk, T.A. (1993) *Elite Discourse and Racism.* Newbury Park, CA: Sage.

Young, I. M. (1990) *Justice and the Politics of Difference*. Princeton: Princeton University Press.

## NOTE

1　　*Childhood 5–16 Programme* (award number L129251047). Further information on the project, including copies of the final project report, can be obtained from Mick Watson, Department of Nursing Studies, Adam Ferguson Building, University of Edinburgh, 40 George Square, Edinburgh EH8 9LL. Email: Nick.Watson@ed.ac.uk

# CHAPTER TEN

# Disabled Children and Social Care

## Law and Practice

*Suzy Braye*

## INTRODUCTION

Disabled children are children first, and the legal framework for services to meet their social care needs is dominated by the Children Act 1989. This legislation is not the whole story, however, for there are aspects of disability law that apply to children, providing sometimes stronger mandates for needs assessment and service provision. In addition to legal complexity, differing conceptual models and value perspectives inform social care practice, incorporating images of childhood and of disability that affect disabled children's position in society. These factors pose challenges to the legal framework, exposing shortcomings and inconsistencies in both structure and implementation.

Disabled children were notable by their absence from mainstream childcare policy for most of the twentieth century (Baldwin and Carlisle 1994). Emphasis on health and education provision, often in institutional settings, obscured their social care needs. An absence of clear statutory responsibility has contributed to services remaining fragmented. Macdonald (1991) notes 'a brief glance at the past fifty years of legislative duties and voluntary effort in the field of disability shows a lack of inter-departmental cohesion and accountability which may be unequalled in all our health, education and welfare services' (p.7).

Only a small proportion (1.5 per cent) of disabled children do not live in a family home (OPCS 1989). Developments in medical care have improved survival rates and extended life expectancy of children with complex and multiple needs, whilst care is now less likely to be undertaken in long-stay hospital or other health institutions (Russell 1996). Significant numbers of families care for more than one disabled child, often where siblings are severely disabled (Ball 1998). Yet there are concerns about community-based social care provision. Services to support families have not been extensively developed and, where they exist, have not been child-centred, predominantly focusing on needs arising from medical conditions rather than on disabled children's needs as children. The Children Act 1989 offered the opportunity to change this.

The Act has been described as 'the most comprehensive piece of legislation which Parliament has ever enacted about children' (DoH 1989a). Implemented in October 1991, it replaced much of the fragmented legal framework relating to public authorities' involvement in families' lives and to private arrangements for the care of children. Disabled children were not at the centre of debates during its development. More prominent were catalogues of concern about failures of social services departments to protect children (Beckford Report 1985; Carlile Report 1987) and over-zealous attempts to do so (Butler-Sloss 1988). The Act's integrative and unifying intentions, however, provided an opportunity to address the invisibility of disabled children in childcare services and to resolve some of the inconsistencies in the legal framework. It did this by locating them more explicitly as children first, benefiting like all children from the provisions of the Act in its entirety, and by creating additional specific requirements of the local authority as the agency responsible for taking a holistic view of their needs.

One early impact of the Act was to change the organisational context for disabled children's services, then commonly located within adult disability teams bringing specialist knowledge and expertise to issues of impairment but less able to respond to children's broader developmental needs. Responsibility for services has been relocated within children's services, with associated dangers of expertise being diluted and disability neglected in teams dominated by crisis-oriented child protection work. The Audit Commission (1994) advocates locating disability specialists within childcare teams, a model which enables the focus to be maintained whilst keeping abreast of important generic developments in childcare practice (Goodinge 1998).

## PRINCIPLES IN THE LEGAL FRAMEWORK FOR SOCIAL CARE FOR DISABLED CHILDREN

The Children Act 1989 incorporates two key beliefs that are fundamental to its whole structure and purpose: that the best place for children is with their families (DoH 1989a, para.1.3; 1989b, p.8) and that state intervention is sometimes warranted to support and protect (DoH 1989a, para.1.7; para.1.20). There is recognition that harm may occur to children both by remaining within their families and by being removed from them (DoH 1989a, para.1.31). Faced with the tension between these alternatives, Bedingfield (1998) argues that the extent of the state's duty of care is located on a continuum, increasing proportionally to the extent of potential harm to the child.

The emphasis on family autonomy and freedom from intervention is consistent with human rights declarations, for example Article 16(3) of the Universal Declaration on Human Rights 1948, identifying the family as the natural and fundamental group unit of society, and Article 8 of the European Convention on Human Rights on the right to respect for private and family life. Although the European Commission on Human Rights has taken the view that where interests conflict, those of the child prevail, it has implied that benefits to a child have to be of a high order before they outweigh parents' rights to bring a child up (O'Donnell 1995). This view is reflected in English court judgements.[1]

The Act's definition of family is a broad one, including 'any person who has parental responsibility... and any other person with whom he has been living'.[2] Parental responsibility 'means all the rights, duties, powers, responsibilities and authority which by law a parent...has in relation to the child'.[3] Parental responsibility endures even when parents do not have care of the child, and may be acquired by people who are not biological parents. Diversity in families is recognised and where state intervention is necessary it should reflect an understanding of culture, class and community differences, avoiding value judgements and stereotyping (DoH 1989b, p.7). Building on provisions under section 20 and section 71 of the Race Relations Act 1976, the Children Act provides an enhanced mandate for social care practice to avoid and challenge race discrimination in services.

Where intervention in family life is necessary, a further core principle applies – that of partnership between parents and professionals as the most effective way of supporting families (DoH 1989b, p.8). It is expected that children will be consulted too (DoH 1989b, p.12). The emphasis is upon intervention that is negotiated and agreed between the local authority and families. Partnership, however, should not be an end in itself – children's welfare must remain the objective (DoH/SSI 1995, p.11).

Guidance to the Children Act (DoH 1991a, para.1.6) provides additional principles relating specifically to disabled children, stating unequivocally that disabled children should have access to the same range of services. This emphasis reflects rights identified in the United Nations Convention on the Rights of the Child, in particular Article 23 – disabled children's right to achieve the fullest possible social integration and individual development (Morris 1998a). Disabled children's views are important and should be actively sought (DoH 1991a, para.6.7). These principles are strengthened by the Disability Discrimination Act 1995 making it unlawful to discriminate in access to and provision of goods and services[4] by unjustifiable refusal of a service or less favourable treatment.

Important principles relating to court interventions in family life are found in the Act itself: the child's welfare shall be the paramount consideration;[5] delay in decision-making is likely to be detrimental;[6] and an order should only be made if it is better for the child than making no order[7]. The court must also have regard to welfare factors listed in section 1(3). Although the welfare principle[8] is widely endorsed and promoted in social care practice with children, local authorities are not bound by it when supporting families without court involvement[9].

There is evidence that principles underpinning the Act are less likely to be observed in relation to disabled children than to others. Disabled children are more likely to be raised away from their homes, separated from their siblings and by multiple carers (Middleton 1996). Parental needs sometimes override children's welfare. Children's wishes and feelings are often not apparent (Goodinge 1998). Many children living away from home do not have access to a suitable communication system or to people who understand their communication (Morris 1998b). Whilst the Act promotes children's rights both as participants in decision making and as legal actors themselves, these rights are less exercised by disabled children (Roche 1995).

## DEFINING CHILDREN'S NEEDS

Social care arranged by social services is not a universal service. Whilst there is increasing recognition in government policy of the benefits of widespread, supportive early years services, social services' involvement is selective, reserved for higher levels of need (Home Office 1998). The Children Act 1989 facilitates targeting by creating a category of children who have greater entitlement to family support services through being defined as 'children in need'. Section 17(10) defines a child as in need if their health or development is not achieving a reasonable standard, or is being impaired, or they are disabled. This encompasses physical or mental health and physical, intellectual, emotional, social or behavioural development[10]. Disabled children are thus children in need merely by virtue of being disabled. During the development of the legislation this was both welcomed as evidence of positive action and resisted as stigmatising. Inclusion in the definition is nonetheless important, for whereas local authorities have powers in relation to all children, they have duties in respect of children in need.

Local authorities themselves determine the level and scale of services for children in need, although they cannot change the definition in section 17(10) or exclude children in any one of the three categories (DoH 1991b, para.2.4). Having identified the extent of need, they must make decisions about priorities and eligibility (DoH 1991b, para.2.11). Aldgate and Tunstill (1995), in a study of local authority policy-making for section 17 implementation, comment that the definition encompasses a wide range of greater and lesser risks. The range of factors seen as contributing to children's health and development is also very broad (Colton, Drury and Williams 1995) and can include structural and environmental factors such as poverty, homelessness and racism as well as stress within the family. Policy guidance on the assessment of children in need (DoH/DfEE/Home Office 2000) identifies the impact of environmental conditions in rendering children vulnerable but regards support for parental coping as the key factor in protecting children's health and development rather than environmental factors in themselves. So of a child population of 11 million, whilst four million children might be vulnerable due to poverty, only 300,000–400,000 might be deemed children in need.

The Children Act offers a definition of disability[11]: 'a child is disabled if he is blind, deaf or dumb or suffers from mental disorder of any kind or is substantially and permanently handicapped by illness, injury or congenital deformity or such other disability as may be prescribed'. The definition is narrow, and arguably excludes some disabled children. Like the Disability Discrimination Act 1995 it emphasises the medical condition or impairment as the defining feature of the individual and implies negativity about the lives and abilities of disabled children. This negative stereotyping is compounded by the requirement (Schedule 2, para.6) for local authorities to 'provide services designed to minimise the effect on disabled children within their area of their disabilities and to give such children the opportunity to lead lives which are as normal as possible'.

These expectations are located within a medical model of disability, focusing on the assumed functional limitations experienced by children as a result of their diagnosed impairments, which are seen as the source of abnormality or disadvantage. Services replace or compensate for the individual's impaired functions. An alternative, social model of disability (Oliver 1983) defines disability as the exclusion of people with impairments from the mainstream of society, and focuses on removing the environmental and social barriers to participation. Exclusion both results from and reinforces the stigma attached to people perceived as different through their impairments, evidenced for example by enduring images of disabled children as tragedies at birth, objects of pity and charity, and a burden on others (Middleton 1996). Such attitudes are used as justification for disabled people's location in segregated facilities, denied opportunity for full citizenship (Hirst and Baldwin 1994), and mean that 'to be a disabled person means to experience a particular and pervasive form of social oppression or institutional discrimination' (Barnes 1998, p.103).

Morris (1998a) points out that the Children Act 1989 uses the term disability to mean impairment and that the terminology of its guidance, referring to 'children with disabilities', defines them by reference to what their bodies or minds cannot do. The term 'disabled children' is a more accurate reflection of what society does to children with impairments, and is more compatible with the philosophy and practice of social inclusion.

Definitions are crucial in shaping service responses (Baldwin and Carlisle 1994). Recent government publications (Ball 1998; Goodinge 1998) reflect changes of terminology, if not a departure from the medical model. The Social Services Inspectorate rejects medical classifications as an insensitive basis for planning services (Ball 1998). The emphasis remains, however, on compensatory services and family coping rather than upon tackling the barriers to integration.

## TARGET DUTIES TO DISABLED CHILDREN

Section 17(1) of the Children Act 1989 requires local authorities to safeguard and promote the welfare of children in need and to promote their upbringing by their families by providing a range and level of services appropriate to their needs. This is a broad, target duty owed to the group in general rather than to any individual child. Policy guidance (DoH/DfEE/Home Office 2000) explains that 'safeguarding' includes duties to protect from maltreatment and prevent impairment. 'Promoting' means 'creating opportunities to enable children to have maximum life chances in adulthood as well as ensuring they are growing up in circumstances consistent with the provision of safe and effective care' (p.5).

There are a number of broad functions that the local authority must perform in order to support its duty, some relating to all children in need and some solely to disabled children.

### Identification of need

Local authorities must identify the extent to which there are children in need within their area (Schedule 2, para.1(1)). This is similar to the duty under section 1(1) of the Chronically Sick and Disabled Persons Act 1970 for the local authority to inform itself of the numbers of disabled people in its area and of the need to make arrangements for them. It is a necessary precursor to determining what range and level of services are appropriate.

### Registration

Local authorities must maintain a register of disabled children within their area (Schedule 2, para.2(1)). Again this parallels the requirement under section 29(4)(g) of the National Assistance Act 1948 and LAC(93)10 for local authorities to maintain a register of disabled people. Registration is not a prerequisite to receiving services, but local authorities should encourage registration by emphasising its usefulness in planning and monitoring services (DoH 1991b, para.2.19). Social services are encouraged to create registers jointly with education and health authorities (DoH 1991a, para.4.3).

## Publication of information

Local authorities must publish information about family support services, provided by themselves and by other agencies (in particular voluntary organisations) (Schedule 2, para.2(a)) and ensure it is received by those who might benefit (Schedule 2, para.2(b)). Published materials should take account of cultural and linguistic needs and are intended to help parents make informed choices about services (DoH 1991b, para.2.36–2.37). Under section 19(6), local authorities must publish reviews of day-care facilities, including playgroups, nurseries and childminders as well as statutory agency provision. Under section 1(2) of the Chronically Sick and Disabled Persons Act 1970 also, disabled children must be informed of services provided by the local authority or any other agency.

## Planning

The key purpose of identifying need is to assist in planning the range and level of services appropriate to children's needs required by section 17(1). In the early days of Children Act implementation many local authorities developed plans for children's services in the absence of a legal requirement to do so, and such plans were variable in content and effectiveness (DoH/SSI 1994). Services for disabled children in particular lacked strategic direction, due to unclear managerial responsibility for their development (Audit Commission 1994). Aldgate and Tunstill (1995) found that local authorities made planning decisions on the basis of problems already known or accepted as high risk, regardless of research evidence or empirical data.

The Children Act 1989 (Amendment) (Children's Services Planning) Order (SI 1996 No. 785) makes children's services plans mandatory. It requires local authorities to assess the need for provision to children in need, consult with various organisations in planning how that need will be met and publish the resulting plans. Guidance (DoH/DfEE 1996) promotes plans as giving an opportunity to view children and families in the broader context of a range of agencies. In relation to disabled children, it requires plans to specify how agencies will collaborate over the assessment and identification of special educational needs, how services for disabled children can be provided in non-segregated settings and how day-care serves young disabled children.

## Inter-agency collaboration

Inter-agency collaboration is a key feature of social care for children, particularly for disabled children, whose needs will routinely involve responses from a range of agencies. Many of the local authority's duties to children in need will require effective collaboration, for example:

providing information about services from voluntary organisations (Schedule 2, para.1(a)(ii))

encouraging children not to commit criminal offences (Schedule 2, para.7(b))

having regard to the different racial groups to which children in need belong when making arrangements for day-care and for recruiting foster carers (Schedule 2, para.11).

In addition, the Children Act contains specific requirements and powers relating to other agencies and organisations:

duty to facilitate family support provision by others (in particular voluntary organisations)[12]

duty to undertake together with the local education authority reviews of local day-care services[13]

power[14] to request the help of other authorities in supporting children and families and the duty[15] of such authorities to comply with the request provided it is compatible with and does not prejudice their statutory duties

duty to assist local education authorities with the provision of services for any child with special educational needs[16]

duty of education, housing and health authorities to assist with child protection enquiries.[17]

Guidance emphasises the importance of corporate, authority-wide policy for responding to children in need (DoH 1991b, para.1.8). Collaboration with voluntary organisations is particularly important due to their long and pioneering involvement with disabled children (DoH 1991a, para.7.4). Particularly relevant to disabled children are a number of consultation and notification duties, where health or education authorities and residential or nursing homes are accommodating children[18] and where a child is to receive residential education[19]. There are similar duties in education legislation[20] for the local authority to assist the education authority where a child has special educational needs.

### Commentary

In practice, ascertaining the numbers of children in need and the extent of their needs has posed major challenges for local authorities. Aldgate and Tunstill (1995) found that authorities experienced problems gathering data from their own and other agencies' records, finding the shift from a reactive approach (using referral data) to a proactive focus on demographic data very difficult. In addition, they struggled to relate their information to the categories of need specified in the section 17(10) definition. Misunderstandings of the definition have led to disabled children being overlooked as children in need unless they are not achieving a reasonable standard of health or development or are at risk.

Registers initially had a slow start. Even in 1997 one out of eight authorities inspected did not have one, only 50 per cent were held jointly and, whilst they were useful for disseminating information to parents, they were not integrated with planning mechanisms (Goodinge 1998). They have by no means been positively viewed by all. Middleton (1996) speaks for many in viewing them as an infringement of civil liberties that would be unthinkable for other oppressed groups.

Disabled children are perhaps more registered than any other group (AMA 1994) but differing definitions between health, education and social services have made comparability of information difficult to establish. There have also been bureaucratic arguments between agencies about confidentiality, and particular problems of co-ordination between education and social services where staff well placed to identify eligibility often remain in ignorance of the social services register (Preston and Russell 1997). Their use in planning remains potential rather than actual.

The dissemination of information has also run into difficulty. A recent inspection (Goodinge 1998) found a lack of co-ordinated, formalised approaches to the publication and distribution of information about services.

It appears that the planning function itself still has some way to go in respect of disabled children. SSI inspectors (Goodinge 1998) found that disabled children's services are still not firmly located at senior level within the management structure of social services departments, and there is limited progress in collaborative planning and joint commissioning of services. Poor management information on costs also inhibits strategic planning, and sound developments that do occur are not always the result of systematic analysis of need and supply. A lack of measurable objectives impedes monitoring. A recent inspection of generic children's services planning (DoH 1999a) found that plans were rarely perceived as the driving force for service development.

Collaboration between agencies has been notoriously poor. The Audit Commission (1994) was critical of fragmentation, duplication and lack of clarity between agencies, and noted the absence of a strong legal mandate to co-operate. Colton et al. (1995) report that inter-agency collaboration features poorly in policy documents, whilst recognising it may be better in practice. Health and education are the most likely partners for social services in meeting the needs of children in need. Least likely are housing, social security and the youth service. Barriers include differences of attitude and priorities. Aldgate and Tunstill (1995) report a low level of consultation on strategic issues, but observe better collaboration on specific issues such as the Register. They note that the Act acted as a catalyst for relationships to develop, particularly between statutory bodies.

Efforts made by local authorities to identify and understand the social care needs of disabled children can draw upon a large volume of established research evidence, although more is known about the needs of parents and carers than about the needs of children. Indeed, services are often provided initially to meet parental need, with children making of them the best that they can (Morris 1998c).

The care of disabled children has been described as going beyond the bounds of ordinary parenting (Beresford 1995). Its impact has been well documented. Studies conducted since the 1970s consistently find families experiencing financial and practical problems, lowering of living standards, lifestyle restriction, high levels of parental anxiety, worries about the future and negative effects on partnership relationships (Baldwin and Carlisle 1994). The enduring and unremitting nature of responsibility for a disabled child is sometimes all-consuming (Glendinning 1983). Parents report being physically and emotionally drained by care tasks that leave little opportunity for spontaneous family activity (Mittler 1994). Stalker (1990) found high stress levels associated with double incontinence and the need for constant supervision. Relatives and friends are often reluctant to assist (Wynn 1994; Morris 1998c), and thus the informal support systems available to other parents are more difficult to find (DoH 2000).

Family income and expenditure patterns undergo major transformation as a result of childhood disability. Baldwin's (1985) study found incomes were lower and were less likely to undergo lifetime progression and that women in particular experienced very different employment and earning patterns. By contrast, family living costs were higher. These findings are repeated in a more recent national survey of families caring for severely disabled children (Beresford 1995). Chamba et al. (1999) found families from black and minority ethnic groups were even more financially disadvantaged than the predominantly white families in Beresford's survey, with low levels of employment, particularly for mothers, and lower receipt of benefits. A recent study of working parents (Kagan, Lewis and Heaton 1998) found considerable barriers to employment from both lack of suitable childcare and workplace inflexibility.

Disabled children face additional challenges at the point of transition to adulthood. Hirst and Baldwin (1994) found disability prolonging or limiting transition to adulthood. Young people with multiple needs have few choices beyond residential accommodation (Morris 1999). The siblings of disabled children present their own needs, feeling ignored by their parents, or blamed and punished unfairly, and are often invisible to the disabled child's professional network (Newson and Davies 1994).

Despite such high levels of need, families are reticent about using services (Robinson 1991), not wanting to be seen as different, suspicious of the quality of care on offer, concerned that using external services will undermine their family relationships and feeling they should be able to cope. Agency responses are unco-ordinated, with resulting gaps and duplication (Audit Commission 1994). Beresford's (1995) study found a significant proportion of families had experienced poor understanding and little support from agencies, having to fight for services. In half the families, children's needs remained unmet in significant ways and the majority of parents reported shortfalls in responses to their own needs.

Chamba *et al.* (1999) report even poorer responses to the needs of black and minority ethnic families. This study confirms earlier work by Shah (1995) which catalogues a range of problems experienced by Asian families at the hands of service providers: stereotypical assumptions held by white professionals; service responses that are deeply discriminatory; barriers of language and attitude; poor information and access; failure to attend to other disadvantaging factors in families' lives; and tokenistic attempts to remedy deep-rooted exclusion.

Some conceptual models underpinning service delivery have also been criticised as failing to recognise racial diversity. Normalisation, as a philosophy promoting disabled people's access to socially valued roles and experiences, can mean compliance by black families with white Eurocentric norms, and integration can mean black children fitting in with mainstream services dominated by majority (that is, white) needs (Baxter *et al.* 1990). There are cumulative effects from disability and race oppression in a society dominated by white, non-disabled norms (Begum 1991).

Beresford *et al.* (1996), reviewing the literature on parental expectations of services, report seven key priorities: information, material resources, breaks from care, domiciliary support, parenting skills, social support and co-ordinated services. Morris (1998c) finds that routine and low-key services are as important as good crisis responses, parents wanting a flexible mix of services within their own control, especially in services coming to their home.

Research about families' needs has sometimes been conducted from a disablist standpoint, focusing on negative experiences, stress and burden (Phillips 1994). The negative characteristics of children's impairments are emphasised by professionals (Mittler 1994) working to what Dale (1996) calls the 'pathological/sick family model', dominated by assumptions that the family itself is disabled by the child's condition and that all family problems are attributable to abnormality in the child. More recent studies have seen the development of a strengths-based model. McConachie (1994) for example identifies cognitive coping strategies that promote resilience. Beresford (1994) found parents deriving pleasure and satisfaction from relationships with their disabled children, seeing themselves as parents, not as carers, and valuing services that promoted ordinary patterns of family life. Whilst not minimising the challenges of caring for a disabled child, services must recognise and build upon families' own strengths.

## DUTIES TO INDIVIDUAL CHILDREN

### Assessment of need

Assessment is a key function in relation to disabled children. Indeed, it is the route to basic entitlements such as housing, education, play and leisure which are available to non-disabled children without such gate-keeping mechanisms (DoH 2000).

There are a number of legal routes to assessment of disabled children's social care needs, more than for non-disabled children in need. Notable by its absence is any individual assessment duty in the Children Act itself. Mandates in disability law are more specific. The assessment duty in section 4 of the Disabled Persons (Services, Consultation and Representation) Act 1986 applies to disabled children. This requires the local authority, when requested to do so by a disabled person or their carer, to decide whether the needs of the disabled person call for the provision of services under section 2(1) of the Chronically Sick and Disabled Persons Act (CSDPA) 1970. (The Children Act 1989 specifically amended CSDPA 1970 to apply to children.)

Local authorities cannot avoid their responsibilities to children by arguing that no duty to assess exists under the Children Act and no request has been made under the Disabled Persons (SCR) Act: provision under CSDPA 1970 is dependent merely on the local authority being satisfied it is necessary, a condition which could be met without a formal request for assessment.[21]

Clements (1997) argues that the assessment duty in section 47(1) of the NHS and Community Care Act 1990 (NHSCCA) can apply to children. Here the duty to assess is triggered when it appears that a person eligible for community care services may be in need of them. Disabled children are eligible for home help services under paragraph 3 of the NHS Act 1977, which falls within the definition of community care services in section 46 of NHSCCA 1990. Thus if a child appears to need such services, the duty to assess applies.

The Disabled Persons (SCR) Act 1986 contains an additional assessment mandate in relation to older disabled children. Section 5 requires local education authorities to notify social services departments of children with statements of special educational need, at the first review following their fourteenth birthday. Social services must determine which of these children are disabled and help plan for those children a smooth transition between education and adult life. The education authority (or college of further education if the young person attends one) must notify social services again prior to a young disabled person leaving full-time education. Social services must assess their need for services and give advice about other matters affecting their welfare, such as employment, further education, health and benefits (LAC(88)2). This liaison duty between education and social services has been strengthened by requirements for social services' contributions to formal transition plans for disabled young people (DfEE 1994).

Returning to the Children Act, whilst there is no duty, there does exist a power (Schedule 2, para.3) to assess the needs of a child who appears to be a child in need at the same time as making an assessment under CSDPA 1970, the Education Act 1996, the Disabled Persons (SCR) Act 1986, or any other enactment. Thus a range of needs may be assessed concurrently. It may be the case that the courts are not too concerned with which precise legal mandate is used for assessment, provided the problems are addressed.[22]

Explicit provision is made in law for the assessment of carers of disabled children. Section 1(2) of the Carers (Recognition and Services) Act 1995 provides that where a local authority is assessing the needs of a disabled child, a carer providing substantial and regular care may request an assessment of their ability to provide that care. The local authority must take the results into account when deciding whether the child's needs call for provision of services. Guidance (LAC(96)7) indicates that carers should be informed of their right to make this request. The assessment duty is not accompanied by any mandate for service provision direct to the carer, but family support services under the Children Act may in any event be provided to family members as well as to children, thus making possible a direct service to a child's carer. The Carers and Disabled Children's Act 2000, if implemented, will alter this position. It gives carers a right to assessment even if the person they are caring for refuses an assessment of their own needs. It will give local authorities the power to provide services to help the carer fulfil their caring role, and extends the facility for direct payments to carers.

The Children Act does contain significant individual assessment duties in circumstances where it is suspected a child may be abused. Section 47(1)(b) requires the local authority to make enquiries to help it decide whether action is necessary to safeguard or promote the welfare of a child where significant harm is suspected. Significant harm is not defined in the Act but is described in guidance (DoH/Home Office/DfEE 1999) as 'a compilation of significant events, both acute and longstanding, which interrupt, change or damage the child's physical and psychological development'.

It is now widely believed that disabled children are both more vulnerable to abuse and less well protected by the child protection system than are non-disabled children. This is hard to quantify because disability is not identified as a factor in UK statistics, but a North American study (Crosse, Kaye and

Ratnofsky 1993) found the incidence of abuse of disabled children to be 1.7 times higher, with a rate twice as high for emotional neglect and physical abuse. Vulnerability factors include relative isolation, intimate care received from multiple carers and possible incapacity to resist, avoid or report abuse (DoH/Home Office/DfEE 1999). Disabled children are invisible and relatively powerless in their social context, and aspects of their care such as force-feeding and restraint may constitute abuse (Westcott and Cross 1996). Abusers may consider detection of abuse less likely (Westcott 1993).

Despite this vulnerability, a number of myths about disabled children abound, combining to make vigilance and protection less effective (Marchant and Page 1993). Black disabled children are likely to endure additional failures of the system through misplaced cultural assumptions (Macdonald 1991). Even if abuse is detected, investigative requirements designed to ensure criminal prosecutions (Home Office/DoH 1992) may fail disabled children. In theory, the facility to submit video evidence might offer a better opportunity for disabled children's evidence to be heard, but in practice, videos involving disabled children are less likely to reach court and, even if they do, the expertise for live cross-examination is often not available (Davies *et al.* 1995).

Guidance sets out how agencies and professionals should work together to protect children from abuse and neglect. The most recent version (DoH/Home Office/DfEE 1999) recognises the risks to disabled children and sets out proactive measures to improve their protection.

### The conduct of assessment

Assessment should be an open process, undertaken with the participation of the child and their carers (DoH 1991b, para. 2.7), and use communication techniques appropriate to the needs of disabled children (para. 2.8). The outcome of assessment should be a holistic and realistic picture of the individual and family, incorporating strengths as well as difficulties, acknowledging their expressed views and preferences (DoH 1991a, para. 5.4).

Assessments should not be limited in scope. For example, in failing to consider a family's need for re-housing under section 17 of the Children Act, a local authority's assessment was found to be fundamentally flawed.[23]

Policy guidance on assessment has been issued (DoH/DfEE/Home Office 2000). This defines assessment as 'a systematic way of understanding, analysing and recording what is happening to children and young people within their families and the wider context of the community in which they live' (p.viii). It sets out the key principles to underpin assessment and proposes a three-dimensional framework incorporating the child's developmental needs, the capacity of care-givers to respond and factors in the wider family and environmental context.

Time targets are set, and whilst emphasis is placed on the use of standardised assessment tools and measures, the process is seen as requiring finely balanced professional judgement. The intended outcomes of assessment are an analysis of needs and parenting capacity, identification of what intervention is required to secure well-being and a realistic plan of action.

Practice guidance on the assessment framework (DoH 2000) gives more detailed attention to assessing the needs of disabled children, noting that in addition to the core elements in the framework, assessment must also consider the direct impact of a child's impairment, the disabling barriers faced and the means of overcoming these. There is recognition that disabled children may progress through developmental dimensions at differing rates from those without impairments and the impact of the child's impairment must be differentiated from the impact of their experiences. The stated purpose of assessment is to assess the child's situation rather than the child, who is an essential member of the assessment team rather than the passive focus of attention.

One significant aspect of the new assessment framework is the degree to which it is intended to integrate family support with child protection. A trend noted in the early 1990s was the disjunction between social care services for children in need and investigative activity for protecting children (DoH 1995). Many children subject to section 47 investigations received no family support services as a result of professionals' involvement. Enquiries were narrowly focused on whether abuse or neglect had occurred rather than on the family's wider needs and circumstances. Yet child protection often becomes the all-absorbing focus in social services departments, leaving few resources for broader supportive provision to promote welfare. This trend has left disabled children neglected where they do not trigger the significant harm threshold. Policy guidance (DoH/Home Office/DfEE 1999) makes it clear that the children in need assessment framework (DoH/DfEE/Home Office 2000) is for use also in child protection investigations, creating a bridge between the two strands of local authority activity.

Whilst assessment is preferably conducted in partnership with families, there is provision in the Children Act for parental objection to be overruled. A court may make a child assessment order[24] for a maximum of seven days if satisfied there is reasonable cause to suspect significant harm but assessment will be impeded without an order. The court may make directions about the assessment, including for the child to be kept away from home.[25] The child, however, may refuse to submit to the assessment (including to medical examination) if she or he is of sufficient understanding to make an informed decision.[26]

### Service provision

To provide services to individual children, local authorities can draw on both the Children Act 1989 and disability legislation. Under the Children Act the range of services is, in theory at least, almost unlimited (Clements 1997), although there is no individual entitlement to any specific form of service. Local authorities have wide discretion about what to provide to whom, provided the services are in general appropriate to the needs of children in their area (Schedule 2, para.8). Bainham (1998) comments that it is difficult if not impossible to argue that children have legal rights to any particular service, and that enforcement of local authority duties is highly problematic. Case law reflects this: 'an assessment of a disabled child's needs pursuant to paragraph 3 of Schedule 2 to the Act does not appear to give rise to any specific duty pursuant to the Act itself'.[27]

Whilst the types of service might vary, they fall broadly into two categories: services to children in their own homes and services that involve children being looked after elsewhere, such as in residential or foster care, for short or long periods. In addition, significant numbers of disabled children are placed for adoption (Argent 1998).

The balance of investment historically has been towards looking after disabled children away from home. Berridge and Brodie (1998) found significant numbers of disabled children in short-term residential placements. Accommodation must be provided to children in need under section 20 of the Children Act, where it is needed as a result of no one having parental responsibility, the child being lost or abandoned, or his or her carer being unable to accommodate them. Such arrangements are voluntary, and may not be made if objected to by a person with parental responsibility, who can themselves arrange for the child's care,[28] or by the child if 16 or over.[29]

In accommodating a child the local authority must:

> ascertain and give due consideration to the child's wishes and feelings[30] and to those of the parents, others with parental responsibility and other relevant people[31]

> give due consideration to the child's religious persuasion, racial origin and cultural and linguistic background[32]

> explore possibilities for placement within the child's family and friendship networks[33]

> place the child near to home and with siblings[34]

> advise, assist and befriend a child when they cease to be looked after,[35] including a power to give financial assistance.[36]

Where a disabled child is being looked after, the local authority must 'so far as is reasonably practicable secure that the accommodation is not unsuitable to his particular needs'.[37] This may include making suitable adaptations to a foster carer's home (DoH 1991a, para. 11.1).

The placement of children is subject to the Arrangements for Placement of Children (General) Regulations 1991 (SI 890) and the Review of Children's Cases Regulations 1991 (SI 895). A series of short-term placements, such as may be provided to disabled children as part of an arrangement for regular breaks, can in certain circumstances (LAC(95)14) be regarded as one placement and reviewed accordingly. Placements are subject also to either the Foster Placement (Children) Regulations 1991 (SI 910) or the Children's Homes Regulations 1991 (SI 1506).

In relation to provision to children living with their own families, the Children Act stipulates that certain services must form part of the range available for children in need:

day-care for children under five not attending school[38]

activities out of school hours and during school holidays[39]

advice, guidance and counselling, occupational, social, cultural or recreational activities, home help, assistance with travel to services, holiday assistance (Schedule 2, para.8)

family centres (Schedule 2, para.9).

The services may include giving assistance in kind or, in exceptional circumstances, in cash.[40] This can include contributing towards the cost of living accommodation for a family not eligible for housing authority assistance[41], although section 17 does not impose an absolute duty to house homeless children together with their families.[42] The local authority may not refuse or make assistance conditional on parents pursuing a particular course of action.[43]

Also relevant for disabled children living at home is the Chronically Sick and Disabled Persons Act 1970, section 2(1) of which specifies a range of services the local authority must provide to individuals if satisfied it is necessary to do so: practical assistance in the home, recreational and educational facilities, travel, adaptations and equipment, holidays, meals and telephones. Arguably this legislation gives greater entitlement to individual disabled children for some of the services from which they stand to gain most (Morris 1998a). Local authorities cannot avoid their responsibilities here by choosing to make decisions about services under less binding legislation such as the Children Act.[44] For adaptations to housing, families of disabled children may also apply to housing authorities for disabled facilities grants under the Housing Grants, Construction and Regeneration Act 1996. The duty contained in the National Health Services Act 1977, Schedule 8, para.3, to provide home help, and the power to provide laundry services, also applies to disabled children (Clements 1997). The Carers and Disabled Children's Act 2000 empowers local authorities to extend eligibility for direct payments, as an alternative to direct service provision, to families with disabled children, to meet both carers' and children's needs.

Social care services for disabled children at home have started from a low base. Developments have often prioritised services providing 'respite', defined as 'regular complementary care as a form of on-going support to parents' (Stalker 1990, p.158) (although there are concerns about the negative connotations of this term, implying that parental roles are burdensome, and 'short-term breaks' has come to be preferred (AMA 1994)). Support arrangements commonly combine periods away from home with other forms of provision. In link family schemes children stay for a few days regularly with the same foster carers. Sitting services provide carers to look after children at home for short periods of a few hours while a parent goes out. Befriending schemes provide facilitators to support disabled children accessing mainstream recreational and leisure facilities. Some of these examples have the advantage of taking the service to the child rather than the child to the service (Westcott and Cross 1996). Whilst much provision is located in the voluntary sector, local authority childcare services have undertaken a degree of 'refocusing' and are now seen to be providing a wide range of innovative services including outreach work in families' homes, parenting skills and support groups (DoH/SSI 1999a).

There are problems, however, with both domiciliary and residential services. Disabled children's services lack a clear sense of direction and are often isolated from the mainstream of local authority childcare. Prewett (1999) found significant marginalisation of shared care services within the structure and investment patterns of social services departments. In particular, disabled children over eight are poorly served, and there are difficulties over continuing care for children with complex healthcare needs (DoH/SSI 1999b). Argent and Kerrane (1997) note that disabled children's services have a different culture from mainstream childcare, more likely involving partnership with parents and focusing on their needs, rather than being child centred. Indeed this focus is endorsed by policy guidance: 'providing services which meet the needs of parents is often the most effective means of promoting the welfare of children, in particular disabled children' (DoH/DfEE/Home Office 2000, p.9).

The philosophy of disabled children's integration into mainstream social care provision has been influential but in fact leaves them excluded because that provision is inaccessible or unsuitable (Morris 1998c). Scope (1998) reports that families struggle to obtain equipment, delays and mistakes resulting in equipment being outgrown by the time it arrives. Whilst the benefits of short-term breaks are widely accepted, both for parents and for children (Robinson 1991), link families can rarely meet the intensity of need that arises when coping strategies have all but broken down (Stalker 1990). Whilst significant numbers of disabled children do receive a link service, half as many again are on waiting lists (Prewett 1999).

Often such arrangements are not well-linked to a structured support plan for the family (Goodinge 1998). Older children and those with complex healthcare needs or challenging behaviour are less likely to be placed. There are problems securing equipment and adaptations in link carers' homes, local and health authorities refusing to duplicate provision (Morris 1998c). Health and social services commonly fail to agree protocols for the care of children needing invasive clinical procedures as part of their daily care. Whilst parents routinely undertake such tasks, short-term care is often blocked through insurance problems or fear of litigation about negligence or abuse (Rhodes 1999).

Disabled children are often placed geographically distant from their own families, separated from siblings (Morris 1998c). They may be placed in residential education settings because of social care rather than educational needs (Morris 1995). For many there is no statutory monitoring and review of their general welfare and social care needs, either because social services are not aware of a placement arranged by education or health, or because they misunderstand the status of children receiving short-term breaks and do not consider them 'looked after' (Morris 1998c). This may account for the finding (Beckford and Robinson 1993; Prewett 1999) that local authorities struggle to implement the Placement and Review Regulations for link family placements.

### Compulsory measures

The principle of partnership requires services provided to be by agreement where possible. There are, however, a number of ways in which local authorities can intervene if parental agreement is lacking and the need or risk is sufficiently high to warrant compulsion. In extreme circumstances a local authority is among those who may apply to court for an emergency protection order under section 44 of the Children Act. Such an order, which lasts for eight days, renewable for a further seven, may be made if the court is satisfied that there is reasonable cause to believe the child is likely to suffer significant harm if not removed and accommodated elsewhere. The police have powers[45] to remove a child to suitable accommodation in similar circumstances. A local authority may, alternatively, make a care or supervision application to the court, which may place the child in the authority's care or under its supervision if satisfied[46] that the child is suffering, or is likely to suffer, significant harm as a result of inadequate parental care. Along with a care order the local authority acquires parental responsibility for the child, and will make decisions about, among other matters, where and by whom the child will be looked after. The Family Law Act 1996 amends the Children Act to offer the court, when making an emergency protection order or an interim care order, the option of excluding someone from the family home, if doing so will remove the risk to the child.

## Charges for services

Charges may be made for any service arranged under sections 17 and 18 of the Children Act, other than for advice, guidance and counselling.[47] Those liable are the child's parents or the child him or herself once aged 16 or over. Family members may be charged if provided with services. Charges must be reasonable and not beyond what it is practicable for the individual to pay. People receiving certain state benefits will not be charged. Local authorities may also request contributions to the costs of looking after children (Schedule 2, part III). Services provided under the National Health Services Act (NHSA) 1977 and the Chronically Sick and Disabled Persons Act 1970 (CSDPA) may be charged for under section 17 of the Health and Social Services and Social Security Adjudications Act 1983.[48] Services to carers, established through the Carers and Disabled Children's Act 2000, may also be charged for.

## Representations and complaints

Section 26(3) of the Children Act requires local authorities to establish procedures for receiving representations and complaints about family support services provided under the Act. These may be accessed by looked-after children and children in need, their parents, anyone with parental authority, foster carers and others with an interest in the child's welfare. The Representations Procedure (Children) Regulations 1991 (SI 894) contain more detailed requirements. These procedures complement complaints procedures set up under the Complaints Procedure Directions 1990, which may be accessed by children in relation to provision under CSDPA 1970 and NHSA 1977.

# FUTURE DIRECTIONS

## The modernisation agenda

There is renewed interest in social care for children. Concerns about inconsistency in definitions of need and thresholds for services have led to the setting of national objectives and detailed performance indicators against which local authorities will be judged (DoH 1999b). The objectives for children's services (DoH 1999c) include the aim 'to ensure that children with specific social needs arising out of disability or a health condition are living in families or other appropriate settings in the community where their assessed needs are adequately met and reviewed' (para. 6.0). Priorities are accurate identification, increased volume of support, increased use of inclusive play and leisure services and ensuring families receive information.

Standards for disabled children's services have been identified and are used as benchmarks in service inspections (Goodinge 1998). They address familiar themes of inclusion, choice, information, equality of opportunity, collaboration and co-ordination. Improvements to assessment and care planning are sought under the Quality Protects programme, monitoring of which shows local authorities seeking to improve consultation, information and transition planning for disabled children (DoH 1999d). Significant barriers to integration and participation are likely to remain, however, whilst awareness of the Disability Discrimination Act's implications for disabled children remains at the currently low level observed (Council for Disabled Children 1999). Government policy itself effectively discriminates. Proposals in the Children (Leaving Care) Bill 1999 to strengthen local authorities' aftercare responsibilities to looked-after children will exclude children who have been in a series of short-term placements (DoH 1999e). Breaking down inter-agency barriers remains a key theme, with a strengthened statutory duty of partnership under the Health Act 1999 and opportunities for the transfer of funding to improve service integration.

Despite the grand aims, all services are subject to the duty to deliver by the most economic, efficient and effective means available (Audit Commission 1999). Managerialist cultures within agencies prioritise budget efficiency and this can mean establishing restrictive eligibility criteria. Much attention is given to screening by 'referral and assessment processes (that) discriminate effectively between different types and levels of need' (DoH/DfEE/Home Office 2000, p.xi). Local authorities may take resources into account when determining and responding to the needs of disabled people.[49] Whilst other judgements relating to education[50] and disabled facilities grants[51] have come to the opposite conclusion, the *Gloucestershire* judgement (see note 49) is significant for social care in that it relates to services provided under the Chronically Sick and Disabled Persons Act 1970. Thus, organisational cultures and the law may together conspire against progress on service users' terms. LASSL(97)13, however, warns that local authorities do not have licence to take decisions on the basis of resources alone. They must still take account of all other relevant factors, and must not act in an arbitrary or unreasonable way.

### Parental partnership or children's rights?

There is an inherent tension in the legal framework between the sometimes competing interests of parents and children. In work with disabled children a child-centred perspective is arguably not compatible with the Children Act's focus on partnership with parents and a service culture that prioritises responses to parents' needs. Even when partnership may legitimately be abandoned in the interests of a child, it remains the professionals' judgement as to what those interests are. Freeman (1998/1999) notes that the Children Act qualifies its emphasis on the child's wishes and feelings by requiring them to be heard in the light of the child's age and understanding. He contends that 'Gillick competency', requiring sufficient understanding and intelligence before a child may make up their own mind[52] is interpreted too narrowly in relation to many children whose understanding is compromised by adult failures of communication. His view that children's experiential knowledge of their own interests should be more actively sought has a direct relevance for many disabled children whose views might otherwise be unelicited. It is not uncommon to find disabled children presented in guidance (for example, DoH/SSI 1995) as needing to be protected from the stress and conflict of participating in decisions rather than as social actors in their own right. This equivocation sits uneasily with the 'practical rights-oriented con-sciousness' which is growing in response to the impact of international human rights conventions (Fortin 1998, p.58). Reviewing UK progress on the United Nations Convention on the Rights of the Child, Lansdown (1997) notes changes of attitude to children and developing strategies for their participation, but is critical of the rate of progress and of the limited legal backing. The Human Rights Act 1998, whilst much anticipated as strengthening civil and political rights, may have limited impact on social, economic and cultural rights important to those receiving social care (Preston-Shoot, Roberts and Vernon 2001) and particularly for children growing up in the relatively sheltered home and school environment (Fortin 1999).

There thus remain some key challenges in social care for disabled children. In the light of extensive knowledge about needs and shortcomings in services it is hard not to conclude that higher priority investment would make a difference. But volume of provision is not the whole story. Future developments must reflect the clear requirements of a social model of disability in tackling the barriers to disabled children's participation. Social care must have as its aim the empowerment of children, where possible through the provision of effective support to their families, in ways promoting the achievement of their own potential and determined with their active participation.

## REFERENCES

Aldgate, J. and Tunstill, J. (1995) *Making Sense of Section 17. Implementing Services for Children in Need Within The 1989 Children Act.* London: HMSO.

AMA (1994) *Special Child: Special Needs. Services for Disabled Children.* London: Association of Metropolitan Authorities.

Argent, H. (1998) 'Who wants George? Recruiting alternative families for children with disabilities.' *Adoption and Fostering 22*, 1, 40–45.

Argent, H. and Kerrane, A. (1997) *Taking Extra Care. Respite, Shared and Permanent Care for Children with Disabilities.* London: British Agencies for Adoption and Fostering.

Audit Commission (1994) *Seen But Not Heard.* London: HMSO.

Audit Commission (1999) *Best Value and the Audit Commission. Frequently Asked Questions.* London: Audit Commission.

Bainham, A. (1998) *Children, The Modern Law.* Second Edition. Bristol: Family Law.

Baldwin, S. (1985) *The Costs of Caring. Families with Disabled Children.* London: Routledge.

Baldwin, S. and Carlisle, J. (1994) *Social Support for Disabled Children and Their Families – A Review of the Literature.* York: Social Policy Research Unit.

Ball, M. (1998) *Disabled Children: Directions For Their Future Care.* London: DOH/SSI.

Barnes, C. (1998) 'Disability, disabled people, advocacy and counselling.' In Y. Craig (ed) *Advocacy, Counselling and Mediation in Casework.* London: Jessica Kingsley Publishers.

Baxter, C., Poonia, K., Ward, L. and Nadirshaw, Z. (1990) *Double Discrimination: Issues and Services for People with Learning Disabilities from Black and Ethnic Minority Communities.* London: Kings Fund Centre.

Beckford Report (1985) *A Child in Trust.* London: London Borough of Brent.

Beckford, V. and Robinson, C. (1993) *Consolidation or Change? A Second Survey of Family Based Respite Care Services in the UK.* Bristol: Norah Fry Research Centre.

Bedingfield, D. (1998) *The Child in Need. Children, The State and The Law.* Bristol: Family Law.

Begum, N. (1991) 'Setting the context – disability and the Children Act 1989.' In S. Macdonald (ed) *All Equal Under The Act?* London: NISW/REU.

Beresford, B. (1994) *Positively Parents. Caring for a Severely Disabled Child.* London: HMSO.

Beresford, B. (1995) *Expert Opinions: A Survey of Parents Caring for a Severely Disabled Child.* Bristol: Policy Press.

Beresford, B., Sloper, P., Baldwin, S. and Newman, T. (1996) *What Works in Services for Families with Disabled Children?* Ilford: Barnados.

Berridge, D. and Brodie, D (1998) *Children's Homes Revisited.* London: Jessica Kingsley Publishers.

Butler-Sloss, E. (1988) *Report of the Inquiry into Child Abuse in Cleveland.* London: HMSO.

Carlile Report (1987) *A Child in Mind. Report of the Commission of Inquiry into the Circumstances Surrounding the Death of Kimberly Carlile.* London: London Borough of Greenwich.

Chamba, R., Ahmad, W., Hirst, M., Lawton, D. and Beresford, B. (1999) *On The Edge. Minority Ethnic Families Caring for a Severely Disabled Child.* Bristol: Policy Press.

Clements, L. (1997) *Community Care and The Law, Revised Edition.* London: Legal Action Group.

Colton, M., Drury, C. and Williams, M. (1995) *Children In Need. Family Support Under The Children Act 1989.* Aldershot: Avebury.

Council for Disabled Children (1999) *Quality Protects: First analysis of management action plans with reference to disabled children and families.* London: Council for Disabled Children.

Crosse, S., Kaye, E. and Ratnofsky, A. (1993) *A Report on the Maltreatment of Children with Disabilities.* Washington, DC: National Center on Child Abuse and Neglect.

Dale, N. (1996) *Working with Families of Children with Special Needs: Partnership and Practice.* London: Routledge.

Davies, G., Wilson, J., Mitchell, R. and Milsom, J. (1995) *Videotaping Children's Evidence. An Evaluation.* London: Home Office.

DfEE (1994) *Code of Practice on the Identification and Assessment of Special Educational Needs.* London: Department for Education and Employment.

DoH (1989a) *An Introduction to The Children Act 1989.* London: Department of Health/HMSO.

DoH (1989b) *The Care of Children. Principles and Practice in Regulations and Guidance.* London: Department of Health/HMSO.

DoH (1991a) *The Children Act 1989 Guidance and Regulations. Volume 6. Children With Disabilities.* London: Department of Health/HMSO.

DoH (1991b) *The Children Act 1989 Guidance and Regulations. Volume 2. Family Support, Day Care and Educational Provision for Young Children.* London: Department of Health/HMSO.

DoH (1995) *Messages From Research.* London: Department of Health/HMSO.

DoH (1999a) *Planning For Change.* London: Department of Health.

DoH (1999b) *Performance Assessment Framework.* London: Department of Health.

DoH (1999c) *The Government's Objectives for Children's Services.* London: Department of Health.

DoH (1999d) *Mapping Quality in Children's Services: An Evaluation of Local Responses to the Quality Protects Programme.* London: Department of Health.

DoH (1999e) *Me, Survive Out There? New Arrangements for Young People Living In and Leaving Care.* London: Department of Health.

DoH (2000) *Assessing Children in Need and Their Families. Practice Guidance.* London: The Stationery Office.

DoH/DfEE (1996) *Children's Services Planning Guidance.* London: Department of Health/Department for Education and Employment.

DoH/DfEE/Home Office (2000) *Framework for the Assessment of Children In Need and their Families.* London: The Stationery Office.

DoH/Home Office/DfEE (1999) *Working Together to Safeguard Children.* London: Department of Health.

DoH/SSI (1994) *Report on the National Survey of Children's Services Plans.* London: Department of Health/Social Services Inspectorate.

DoH/SSI (1995) *The Challenge of Partnership in Child Protection: Practice Guide.* London: Department of Health.

DoH/SSI (1999a) *Getting Family Support Right. Inspection of the Delivery of Family Support Services.* London: Department of Health/Social Services Inspectorate.

DoH/SSI (1999b) *Modern Social Services. A Commitment to Improve. The 8th Annual Report of the Chief Inspector of Social Services. 1998/1999.* London: Department of Health/Social Services Inspectorate.

Fortin, J. (1998) *Children's Rights and the Developing Law.* London: Butterworths.

Fortin, J. (1999) 'The Human Rights Act 1998: how will it help children?' *Young Minds 40,* 9–10.

Freeman, M. (1998/99) 'The right to be heard.' *Adoption and Fostering 22,* 4, 50–59.

Glendinning, C. (1983) *Unshared Care: Parents and Their Disabled Children.* London: Routledge and Kegan Paul.

Goodinge, S. (1998) *Removing Barriers for Disabled Children. Inspection of Services to Disabled Children and their Families.* London: Department of Health/Social Services Inspectorate.

Hirst, M. and Baldwin, S. (1994) *Unequal Opportunities. Growing Up Disabled.* York: Social Policy Research Unit.

Home Office (1998) *Supporting Families: A Consultation Document.* London: Home Office.

Home Office/DoH (1992) *Memorandum of Good Practice on Video Recorded Interviews with Child Witnesses for Criminal Proceedings.* London: HMSO.

Kagan, C., Lewis, S. and Heaton, P. (1998) *Caring To Work: Accounts of Working Parents of Disabled Children.* London: Family Policy Studies Centre/JRF.

Lansdown, G. (1997) 'Children's rights and the law'. *Representing Children 10,* 4, 213–224.

Macdonald, S. (1991) *All Equal Under the Act?* London: NISW/REU.

Mandelstam, M. (1999) *Community Care Practice and The Law, 2nd Edition.* London: Jessica Kingsley Publishers.

Marchant, R. and Page, M. (1993) *Bridging the Gap: Child Protection Work with Children with Multiple Disabilities.* London: NSPCC.

McConachie, H. (1994) 'Changes in family roles.' In P. Mittler and H. Mittler (eds) *Innovations in Family Support for People with Learning Disabilities.* Chorley: Lisieux Hall.

Middleton, L. (1996) *Making A Difference. Social Work with Disabled Children.* Birmingham: Venture Press.

Mittler, H. (1994) 'International initiatives in supporting families with a member with learning disabilities.' In P. Mittler and H. Mittler (eds) *Innovations in Family Support for People with Learning Disabilities.* Chorley: Lisieux Hall.

Morris, J. (1995) *Gone Missing? A Research and Policy Review of Disabled Children Living Away From Their Families.* London: Who Cares? Trust.

Morris, J. (1998a) *Accessing Human Rights: Disabled Children and The Children Act.* Ilford: Barnados.

Morris, J. (1998b) *Still Missing. Volume 1. The Experiences of Disabled Children and Young People Living Away From their Families.* London: Who Cares Trust.

Morris, J. (1998c) *Still Missing. Volume 2. Disabled Children and The Children Act.* London: Who Cares Trust.

Morris, J. (1999) *'Hurtling Into A Void': Transition to Adulthood for Young People with Complex Health and Support Needs.* Brighton: Pavilion Publishing.

Newson, E. and Davies, J. (1994) 'Supporting the siblings of children with autism and related developmental disorders.' In P. Mittler and H. Mittler (eds) *Innovations in Family Support for People with Learning Disabilities.* Chorley: Lisieux Hall.

O'Donnell, K. (1995) 'Protection of family life: positive approaches and the ECHR.' *Journal of Social Welfare and Family Law 17,* 3, 261–280.

OPCS (1989) *Office of Population Censuses and Surveys. Surveys of Disability in the UK.* London: HMSO.

Oliver, M. (1983) *Social Work with Disabled People.* London: Macmillan.

Phillips, J. (1994) 'Family centres.' In P. Mittler and H. Mittler (eds) *Innovations in Family Support for People with Learning Disabilities.* Chorley: Lisieux Hall.

Preston, L. and Russell, P. (1997) *Positive Partnerships in Developing Registers of Children with Disabilities. Interim Report.* London: Council for Disabled Children.

Preston-Shoot, M., Roberts, G. and Vernon, S. (2001) 'Values in social work law – strained relations or sustaining relationships?' *Journal of Social Welfare and Family Law 23,* 1.

Prewett, B. (1999) *Short-Term Break, Long Term Benefit.* Sheffield: Joint Unit for Social Services Research/Community Care.

Rhodes, A. (1999) *Promoting Partnership. Supporting Disabled Children Who Need Invasive Clinical Procedures. A Barnados' Guide to Good Practice for Family Support Services.* Ilford: Barnados.

Robinson, C. (1991) *Home and Away: Respite Care in the Community.* Birmingham: Venture Press.

Roche, J. (1995) 'Children's rights: in the name of the child.' *Journal of Social Welfare and Family Law 17*, 3, 281–300.

Russell, P. (1996) 'Looking after children with disabilities.' In S. Jackson and S. Kilroe (eds) *Looking After Children. Good Parenting, Good Outcomes. Reader.* London: HMSO.

Scope (1998) *Equipped for Equality.* London: Scope.

Shah, R. (1995) *The Silent Minority. Children with Disabilities in Asian Families.* London: National Children's Bureau.

Stalker, K. (1990) *'Share the Care'. An Evaluation of a Family Based Respite Care Service.* London: Jessica Kingsley Publishers.

Westcott, H. (1993) *The Abuse of Disabled Children and Adults with Disabilities.* London: NSPCC.

Westcott, H. and Cross, M. (1996) *This Far and No Further: Towards Ending the Abuse of Disabled Children.* Birmingham: Venture Press.

Wynn, A. (1994) 'Lend-a-hand. A community-based project for children and young people with learning disabilities and their families.' In P. Mittler and H. Mittler (eds) *Innovations in Family Support for People with Learning Disabilities.* Chorley: Lisieux Hall.

## NOTES

1   For example *Re T* (a minor) (wardship: medical treatment)[1997] 1 All ER 906 and *Re C* (a child)(HIV test) [1999] Family Division 3 FCR 289.

2   s.17(10)

3   s.3(1)

4   s.20

5   s.1(1)

6   s.1(2)

7   s.1(5)

8   s.1(1)

9   *Re M* (Secure Accommodation Order) [1995] 1 FLR 418

10   s.17(11)

11   s.17(11)

12   s.17(5)(a)

13   s.19(2)(a)

14   s.27(1)

15   s.27(2)

16   s.27(4)

17   s.47(9)

18   s.85(1) and s.86(1)

19   s.28

20   s.322, Education Act 1996

21   *R v Bexley London Borough Council, ex parte B* [1995] CL 3225 (QBD)

22   *R v Lambeth Borough Council, ex parte A* [1997] 10 ALR 209 (CA)

23   *R v Tower Hamlets London Borough Council, ex parte Bradford* [1997] 29 HLR 756 (QBD)

24   s.43(1)

25   s.43(9)

26    s.43(8)

27    *R v Bexley LBC ex parte B* [1995] CL 3225 (QBD)

28    s.20(7)

29    s.20(11)

30    s.20(6)

31    s.22(4) and (5)

32    s.22(5)(c)

33    s.23(6)

34    s.23(7)

35    s.24(1) (provided the child was being looked after at age 16, s.24(2))

36    s.24(7)-(8)

37    s.23(8)

38    s.18(1)

39    s.18(5)

40    s.17(6)

41    *R v Northavon DC ex parte Smith* [1994] 3 All ER 313 (HL)

42    *R v Barnet LBC ex parte Foran* [1998] 2 CCLR 329 (CA)

43    *R v Hammersmith and Fulham LBC ex parte Damoah* [1998] 2 CCLR 18 (QBD)

44    *R v Bexley LBC ex parte B* [1995] CL 3225 (QBD)

45    s.46(1)

46    s.31(2)

47    s.29(1)–(5)

48    Confirmed in respect of CSDPA 1970 by *R v Powys County Council ex parte Hambidge* [1998] 1 CCLR 458 (CA).

49    *R v Gloucestershire County Council, ex parte Barry* [1997] 2 All ER 1

50    In *Re T* (a minor)[1998] 1 CCLR 352 HL

51    *R v Birmingham City Council ex parte Taj Mohammed* [1998] 1 CCLR 441

52    *Gillick v West Norfolk and Wisbech Area Health Authority* [1986] AC 112

# CHAPTER ELEVEN

# Clear Voices for Change

## Messages from Disability Research for Law, Policy and Practice

*Michael Preston-Shoot*

## INTRODUCTION

Volumes of literature have been published on community care, much reporting the experiences of disabled people and their carers. This chapter reviews these reported experiences against the key elements of community care law and policy. Through this review emerges a critical analysis of law, policy guidance and practice, and signposts for how they might be developed.

One of several contradictions in community care policy centres on user opinion. Their opinion on need, and the services required to meet need, is subordinate to the view of the assessing practitioner (DoH 1990). Users and carers are, nonetheless, portrayed as the people in the best position to assess service quality (SSI 1993a). Moreover, 'client'[1] studies have a long history since Mayer and Timms (1970) surprised the social work world by uncovering a clash of perspective between users and professionals about problem definition and targets for intervention. That clash in perspective remains relevant, for accounts of practice given by users, carers and agencies show marked variations (Buckley, Preston-Shoot and Smith 1995; Warner 1995). This points to the value of seeing services from the position of users and carers, for a perception audit may both support and challenge assumptions upon which policy and practice are built.

## EXPECTATIONS

Low expectations of services have been found with disabled people (Baldock and Ungerson 1994), mentally distressed people (Donnelly and Mays 1995), learning disabled people (Day 1994) and carers (Warner 1995). These appear linked with lack of information (McFarland, Dalton and Walsh 1989), seeing others in greater need coupled with a lack of faith in services (Pilgrim, Todhunter and Pearson 1997) and with awareness of local authority budgets. Users often appear to have little concept of their rights (Caldock and Nolan 1994). How disabled people are told, therefore, about the implications for them of the Human Rights Act 1998 will be one key to its effectiveness.

The picture may be changing because of the existence of pressure groups and voluntary organisations. However, low expectations may lead to people self-defining needs accordingly, and to missing opportunities to engage in partnership and to exercise choice that community care policy is meant to offer. It may also mean that expectations held by practitioners, for example that people move from hospital through day services to independent living, clash with those held by service users. Assessment should, therefore, explore any clash of perspective and, in relation to expectations, focus on people's knowledge of alternatives and of their rights, their experiences of services to date, and their preferences for future provision.

## INVOLVEMENT AND CHOICE

Meaningful involvement and consultation requires power sharing. It requires a willingness by practitioners and managers to open up ways of working for reappraisal. As a minimum this means involvement in planning from the outset, with agendas open rather than predetermined. Different methods of involvement and consultation should be used in order to integrate perspectives from those groups which often find themselves excluded. Financial support, time, transport, information, training, and care back-up should be provided in order to maximise people's participation. Tangible goals and plans which reflect user and carer concerns and priorities encourage participation, as do positive messages that service users' experiences and perspectives are valued and that they can take effective action. Important too is feedback on what has happened to their contribution (Bewley and Glendinning 1994; Harding and Oldman 1996; Read and Wallcraft 1992).

These dimensions parallel administrative law principles concerning consultation and involvement. Where local authorities plan to meet need in a different way from previously, they must consult with users at a time when proposals are still at a formative stage. Authorities must present clearly the reasons behind the proposals, consider all relevant matters, and ensure that individual needs and views are properly taken into account. Authorities must give users reasonable time to put their views, and must provide reasons for their decisions which, themselves, must be reasonable. This applies to both community care and residential care provision, to local authorities and to health authorities.[2]

The duty to consult with users and carers in relation to service planning derives from the Disabled Persons (Services, Consultation and Representation) Act 1986[3] which requires consultation with organisations of disabled people when co-opting people to committees and advisory bodies. It receives further legislative endorsement from the NHS and Community Care Act 1990[4]which requires, in relation to community care plans, consultation with voluntary organisations which represent users and carers. Nonetheless, both the above judicial review cases and research findings illustrate the vulnerability to distortion of consultation and involvement.

Users appear sceptical about the value for them of consultations regarding community care plans (Bewley and Glendinning 1994), sceptical about whether a change from residual welfare services is possible in the current climate. They express cynicism about whether their experiences are valued and research fatigue (Hardwick, Kershaw and Preston-Shoot 1999; Lankshear and Giarchi 1995; Nocon and Qureshi 1996; Shaw 1995) because of the absence of feedback which demonstrates clear benefits from having engaged in consultation. They are more likely to be asked about their experiences of services than to be involved in service planning, defining quality or setting standards and outcomes against which services are to be evaluated. Agencies may define the agenda beforehand and consult with limited numbers of hand-picked 'clients' or even with carers on behalf of service users.

Willetts (1994) found little effective consultation with visually disabled service users, or translation of unmet needs into the planning process. Less than one quarter of local authority community care plans gave specific attention to meeting the needs of visually disabled people (Lovelock, Powell and Craggs 1995). The Social Services Inspectorate (SSI 1998) found that some local authorities were consulting systematically with visually disabled people about the planning and quality of services but that others were doing little.

A survey of community mental health teams (Onyett, Standen and Peck 1997) found inadequate service user participation in their management. Only 8 per cent of teams had routine user attendance in a decision making role; 23 per cent had user attendance in an advisory role, whilst 43 per cent regularly surveyed users or collected information on their views. Moreover, Wells (1997) cautions that consulting service users and carers can give the appearance of including them in decision making whilst also shaping their perceptions to match available resources. How involvement is approached is, therefore, crucial.

Involvement in, for example, the Care Programme Approach (Sbaraini and Carpenter 1996) does appear to promote choice, to lead to 'clients' being better informed about services and their rights, and to increase participation in planning their own care. These researchers also found service users being involved in training on the Care Programme Approach and in research. However, the SSI (1996a) found little significant involvement from user and carer organisations in developing policy and strategy relating to the Care Programme Approach. Individual involvement was especially limited after hospital discharge. Many users and carers felt disadvantaged, unaware of their entitlements and of services that might have enabled them to make better choices within their care plans.

Researchers into housing and support for people with mental health problems (Warner *et al.* 1998) found examples of good consultation procedures but stressed the need for participation and involvement in the running, management and monitoring of all settings and services. Morgan (1998) found that service users were keen to forge alliances and partnerships with professionals, and were ready to acknowledge their skills and experience. However, in turn they wanted professionals to acknowledge their unique skills and understanding, and to assist them in having a greater say in how services are run.

A review of home care services (SSI 1997a) found a need to involve service users and carers in service planning. It appeared unusual to give copies of care plans to them; carers' needs were not routinely taken into account, and there were few formal arrangements for review. A review of services for physically disabled people (SSI 1996b) found that physical disability did not have a high profile and that service users were not regularly and actively involved in planning services for the community or for themselves. Community care plans did not routinely illustrate a co-ordinated inter-agency strategy for service development. Lack of effective consultation has also been the experience of deaf people (SSI 1997b).

Empowering people to exercise a stronger voice and to secure greater involvement is easier to promise than achieve. Guidance makes clear that the goal is user and carer empowerment (DoH 1991). Their wishes should not be subordinated to those of service providers. They should have a widening choice of service options. However, people often feel unable to participate and report a lack of involvement in assessment. They are critical of intermittent or insufficient contact with social workers. They are not knowledgeable or well-informed, and feel disempowered and oppressed by professional language and power. They have difficulty gaining access to information. Feedback brings accounts of limited choice, ignored preferences, and inadequate services (for instance, DoH 1993; Harding and Oldman 1996; Robbins 1993; SSI 1991, 1993b; Twigg and Atkin 1994). Users and carers have not always been routinely involved in assessment and review meetings (SSI 1993a) and may not even know that they have been assessed. Disabled people feel disabled by their environment and believe their views are not taken into account by those planning and providing services (Lloyd *et al.* 1996).

In a study of 76 cases, 39 per cent of service users and 50 per cent of carers said that the former had no choice about the provision of services (Buckley *et al.* 1995). Forty eight per cent of carers said that they had no choice about services for themselves. Social workers thought that this was the case for only 8 per cent of service users and 9 per cent of carers. Service users and carers complained that they did not know what services were available and were, therefore, unable to

make informed choices about which options would best meet thei.
also complained about hurried interviews. This same study found enc
levels of satisfaction with overall contact with social services but muc.
satisfaction with levels of involvement. However, whereas over one fifth of use.
and carers felt that their level of involvement had been unsatisfactory, social
workers were almost unanimous in being satisfied, at least to some extent, with
the level of involvement achieved. Studies of mentally distressed service users
(Harrison, Mayhew and Preston-Shoot 1999) and visually disabled people
(Hardwick *et al.* 1999) found similar levels of dissatisfaction with involvement
and with the absence of choice. There were complaints about limited options,
about poor knowledge and skills shown by assessors and providers, and about
the lack of co-ordination between different service agencies. Some respondents
did not know that they had been assessed.

Research with people with multiple disabilities (SSI 1993b) and changing
physical conditions (SSI 1996b) found evidence of limited choice, sometimes
rooted in restricted information about resources, and services that did not match
people's needs. Research with people with dual impairments (learning disability
and dementia) (Stalker, Duckett and Downs 1999) found that most were able to
express clear preferences but that the opportunities available to exercise choice
varied widely. Others usually limited choice, whether concerned with everyday
matters, choice of living location or of carers, future planning or daily activities.
Barriers to choice included other people's anxiety about risk-taking, inadequate
resources, information being withheld and inadequate communication. Stanley
(1999) also found that choice was limited to the services available. It was also
affected by the level of competence attributed by assessors to 'clients' and
whether the latter's choice corresponded with professional judgement. Stanley
concludes that, with limited time available to assessors, only those 'clients' who
are able to articulate their own needs forcefully are likely to be able to exercise
choice. Those whose voices are more difficult to hear, who are confused, who
have low expectations and/or are dependent on carers, are likely to have their
needs defined by others. These findings highlight the importance of advocacy or
authorised representative schemes and of the continuing need to implement
sections 1–3 of the Disabled Persons (Services, Consultation and Representation)
Act 1986.

Day (1994) found that learning disabled people believed that their views
would have little impact. Their low expectations and lack of experience of
'partnership' activities, coupled with the culture of health and welfare agencies,
affected involvement in a way which would need time, with individuals and
groups, to overcome. Similarly, Jahoda and Cattermole (1995) found that
learning disabled people could participate in major decisions about their lives.
They are often denied this opportunity because of images about their

competence, or because their experiences of segregation and exclusion combine to deny them the knowledge about what choices are available, and the confidence to express opinions. Images about competence have been features of several judicial review cases, where learning disabled people and their carers have successfully challenged their exclusion from decision making.[5]

## INFORMATION

A prerequisite to effective involvement and exercise of choice is information. Law (Disabled Persons (Services, Consultation and Representation) Act 1986)[6] and policy guidance (DoH 1990) provide the necessary mandate. However, the provision of information brings the prospect of increased demand, raised expectations that are difficult to meet, and further pressure on budgets. Thus, whilst policy guidance requires that information is accessible, monitoring across different 'client' groups (DoH 1993; SSI 1991, 1993b, 1996a, 1996b, 1997b) continues to find:

> that service users have insufficient information on the range of services available, and are unsure where to find information or who to approach;

> a failure to provide users and carers with copies of assessment and care plans;

> information in different languages and forms remains inadequate;

> that local authorities need to provide more detailed information on services available from different agencies and on people's rights, on service standards and procedures, having consulted with users and carers on what they want information about, from where, and in what form;

> that local authorities should use different types of outlets for information and provide training for staff in offering information in a manner which is easy to retain.

A study (Fryer 1998) of eight social services departments found that only three had an information policy. Priorities and a structure for planning information services, and strategies for the assessment, development and distribution of information, were often lacking as a result. Whilst there were excellent examples of producing information for service users through agency collaboration, the information that was produced did not always follow an assessment of what was needed. Nor was targeting and distribution always efficient. Similarly, information strategies appear rare in home care services (SSI 1997a).

Given the bewildering range and complexity of services (Fryer 1998), information helps people to understand what is available and from where, and therefore assists them to retain control, maintain their independence, and pursue their legal entitlements confidently. However, service users and carers can become confused by information and the health and welfare systems to which it seeks to introduce people (Twigg and Atkin 1994). Professionals may expect service users to be proactive in seeking information, or may assume that others will provide it (Pilgrim *et al.* 1997). They may, of course, not be aware of everything to which service users and carers are legally entitled. Poor communication systems and constantly changing policies make it difficult for service users and carers to keep up to date. People require clear, reliable and comprehensive information about a wide range of issues (Coombs with Sedgwick 1998), including eligibility for provision and different types of services, and how to challenge assessments if dissatisfied. The reality often appears to be the opposite (SSI 1997a).

In one study of disabled people (Lloyd *et al.* 1996) many were uncertain of their entitlements, for example to daily living equipment and adaptations. People who said that they needed a high level of support, for example with household tasks or personal assistance, were often not receiving any information about what care services were available. People receiving services from statutory agencies were more likely to know about and use a range of services than people who needed similar amounts of care but received it from informal carers. A lack of information, about rights, service availability and decision making, is linked to dissatisfaction (Cullen *et al.* 1997; Harrison *et al.* 1999; Lamb and Layzell 1995) and contributes to feelings of powerlessness. Warner (1995) found that carers' knowledge of available services remains poor, with literature specifically relevant to their needs much needed. He further found that the majority of carers interviewed did not know that they could ask for a separate assessment of their own needs, or that people to be discharged from hospital could ask for a care plan. A significant minority of carers did not know how to access an assessment.

The provision of information to visually disabled people mirrors the above findings. Information is not widely publicised and not regularly available in Braille or on tape, making it difficult for visually disabled people to overcome barriers (French, Gillman and Swain 1997; Hardwick *et al.* 1999; SSI 1998). Too many visually disabled people are offered no information about their rights, how their needs will be assessed and decisions made, about the availability of health, voluntary and social services, or about the nature of their visual disability (Coles, Willetts and Winyard 1997; Hardwick *et al.* 1999). This can create disappointment, anger and distress.

Social workers are much more likely to be satisfied with the information they provide than users and carers are with the information they receive about how needs are assessed, how decisions are made, and about their rights (Buckley *et al.* 1995). In this study, which compared the views of 76 users, carers and social workers in individual cases, users and carers wanted more information. Carers were less satisfied than users but both groups found information too brief and confusing and bemoaned the absence of leaflets. Users and carers were concerned with how information was given, highlighting the importance of professional skills in checking that information has been understood and retained. Information-giving should be a process over time, not a one-off procedure.

Arguably, studies will continue to report difficulties in relation to information provision until the tension between needs and resources in community care policy is adequately addressed in a manner which openly negotiates policy objectives and empowers practitioners to practise.

## ASSESSMENT AND DECISION MAKING

The passport to services is assessment. However, users and carers continue to feel that their needs are not understood, and that services are often not based on a coherent plan (SSI 1991). They report difficulty in expressing need (Ellis 1993) and are not always aware that an assessment has been completed (Baldock and Ungerson 1994; DoH 1993). Decision making can reflect provider preferences and resources rather than user needs and wishes, with people reporting that assessment is subordinated to agency policy needs and procedures, where professionals determine the goals (Day 1994). Assessment retains a problem-focused and resource-focused approach that does not fully meet people's needs (Ellis 1993; Nocon and Qureshi 1996; Robbins 1993; SSI 1997a), for example for emotional support. Narrow eligibility criteria, a focus on deficits rather than abilities, and insensitive and patronising attitudes are sources of complaint (Lamb and Layzell 1995).

In a study of stroke victims, Baldock and Ungerson (1994) found that many had no clear idea of why some services had been offered, and had not experienced decision making as involving negotiation and consultation. Uncertainty about for how long services would be provided was a source of anxiety and stress. People appeared confused about the boundaries between health and social care, and had few ideas about what could or should be done. This pointed not just to the provision of information but also to social workers recognising and attending to the emotional distress and crisis involved, the process of adjustment to increased dependency, and the 'map' people have of services.

Visually disabled people have reported that assessment is rationed by delay. Some local authorities are providing screening rather than comprehensive assessments if there are no other indicators of need, although this is unlawful

(DoH 1990). There is some evidence of practitioners helping people to identify what they need and planning care packages with them. However, visually disabled people also report a lack of systematic assessment of social care and sight loss needs and having to fit into existing services (Coles *et al.* 1997; Hardwick *et al.* 1999; Lovelock *et al.* 1995; SSI 1998). The story is similar with deaf people (SSI 1997b) – poorly developed assessment, which too often focuses on equipment rather than wider social needs. Here, despite an absolute duty,[7] young deaf people's needs were not always assessed.

Evidence suggests that practitioners under-estimate people's needs (Buckley *et al.* 1995). This study, focusing on 13 practical needs and five social or emotional needs, found that carers were more likely to suggest that service users needed a lot of help than were service users themselves. This mismatch was especially striking with depression, managing medication and managing finance. Service users were more likely than carers to say that they needed some help. Social workers underestimated the numbers of 'clients' who required a lot of help, particularly relating to mobility outside the home, household tasks, managing money, managing medication, claiming benefits and feeling depressed. They compensated for this by suggesting that a greater number of 'clients' needed some help. Even so, they still underestimated need concerning mobility at home, help with communication, difficulties seeing and hearing, housing problems and depression. If the categories of needing a lot of help and needing some help are aggregated, social workers still identified fewer 'clients' as needing help in seven categories of need compared to service users – mobility at home, household tasks, communication, difficulties in seeing or hearing, housing problems, claiming benefits and feeling depressed.

Social workers similarly underestimated the number of carers who thought that service users needed help in 11 categories of need. Carers were more likely to have an accurate perception of users' needs than social workers in 16 of the 18 categories of need, the two exceptions being difficulties in seeing or hearing and feeling depressed. There were significant levels of disagreement between 'clients' and social workers about the former's need for help, particularly concerning loneliness, claiming benefits, worries about health or disability, family relationship problems and housing.

Mental health service users frame their problems differently from care managers (Rogers and Pilgrim 1995). The Rogers and Pilgrim study concluded that distress has many meanings in addition to those implied by a psychiatric diagnosis, and that what people receive from mental health services is not necessarily what they want. Carpenter and Sbaraini (1997), however, found that the majority of service users they interviewed agreed with their care programmes, and thought that they were clear, comprehensive and appropriate to their needs. Nonetheless, this study found evidence of the difficulty in moving away from a diagnosis and service-led approach. Moreover, survivors are critical of the conceptual models that underpin professional responses to distress and particularly of assumptions that mental illness prevents people from understanding what is best for them (Plumb 1999). Whilst mental health services may aim for inclusion, professional responses may actually promote segregation rather than integration. Assessment must not focus just on symptoms but also on the social, psychological and environmental aspects of distress.

Learning disabled people report (Jahoda and Cattermole 1995) that professionals overlook their worldview but rather focus on assessing deficits. The familiar clash of perspective re-emerges. For example, staff may emphasise training skills for independence whilst learning disabled people emphasise greater freedoms, improved social life, a sense of belonging and foundations on which to build a meaningful, not isolated future. Staff concentration on domestic or living skills may obscure the importance of community integration and of wider emotional and practical experiences, which provide a better quality of life and a more successful outcome to independent living.

Studies have also criticised the process of assessment for disabled people (Davis, Ellis and Rummery 1998; Ellis 1993; Lamb and Layzell 1995; Nocon and Qureshi 1996; Pilgrim et al. 1997; SSI 1993b, 1996a; Twigg and Atkin 1994), particularly:

> a lack of understanding of cultural issues;
>
> a failure to provide written confirmation of assessments and decisions;
>
> focusing on incapacity rather than ability;
>
> irregular contact with assessors, with assessments being experienced as slow, confusing, incremental, reactive, fragmentary and often irrelevant to service users' own concerns and priorities;
>
> off-hand attitudes and insensitivity;
>
> different interpretations between teams of eligibility criteria for assessment, and a failure to acknowledge disabled people's entitlement to a comprehensive assessment;
>
> priority systems not in place to identify effectively potential service users with the highest priority needs;
>
> denying access to assessment when need cannot be related to available services or when 'clients' are not considered at risk;
>
> a lack of time, producing stereotyped responses to need and a feeling among service users that their needs are not understood;
>
> social worker decisions about risk being narrower than those held by disabled people and their carers;

a failure by workers to explain their role;

a neglect of emotional needs and of people's wider needs, such as for leisure, transport and employment;

a neglect of carers' needs and of the complex and changing patterns of caring relationships;

treating users and carers as separate units of assessment rather than as an inter-related whole, thereby accentuating conflicts between those involved and running counter to how disabled people experience caring in their lives.

The picture that emerges is that assessment can be experienced as thorough and sensitive. Good experiences of assessment are likely to be reported when 'clients' feel that workers are interested in them, take time to establish relationships, offer choice and are able to provide services that are wanted and suitable. Poor experiences of assessment are likely when 'clients' and carers feel that they have to fight for assistance, that they are not listened to, and that assessors make assumptions about what help is required (Lloyd *et al.* 1996).

However, an alternative picture also emerges, one of managing and controlling demand by delaying or refusing to assess, or by undertaking less comprehensive assessments than required. Assessment and decision making are compromised (Salter 1994; Wells 1997). Indeed, judicial review cases have criticised a refusal to assess,[8] the narrow scope of assessment[9] and the inappropriateness of care plans.[10]

## NEEDS AND SERVICES

Users and carers have criticised the range and scope of community care provision, the skills of paid carers and the restrictions imposed on lifestyle by inadequate, inflexible and limited services. They are concerned about the relevance, continuity and reliability of provision (Buckley *et al.* 1995; Harrison *et al.* 1999; Wilson 1995). Services can be perceived as off-the-shelf rather than tailor-made, with domiciliary care, for example, not providing the help that people regard as needed, and with simple needs remaining unmet (Baldock and Ungerson 1994; Twigg and Atkin 1994). Counselling and emotional support services have been criticised as unavailable (Hoyes *et al.* 1994). It is significant that the barriers that people encounter are attitudinal, institutional and environmental (Nocon and Qureshi 1996). Since the focus of provision often does not address these barriers, opportunities for integration into the community and for social inclusion are seriously restricted.

Eligibility criteria and a narrow interpretation of care management appear prioritised above relationships with 'clients' (Morgan 1998; Onyett 1992). Thus, not only are there concerns about whether proper support and care are available (Goodwin 1997), but also a recognition that the move from hospital to community care on its own does not transform the social lives of people who have spent long periods in institutions. More attention needs to be given to the conditions necessary for community presence and participation. Otherwise community care, like institutional care, can become a metaphor for neglect rather than progress (Sullivan 1998).

Moreover, local authorities are left with responsibilities without the necessary means to fulfill them. To protect supply, they restrict services through eligibility criteria, block contracts and the removal of care support (Hoyes et al. 1994; Salter 1994; Tanner 1998). Resource constraints also influence professionals who (have to) prioritise their accountability to their employing organisations. This is likely to encourage defensive practice and to reduce the quality of care offered (Wells 1997). Indeed, the outcome has sometimes been decisions that are inhumane, unlawful and/or in contravention of policy guidance.[11]

### Collaboration

Users and carers continue to criticise levels of co-ordination and collaboration between services (Barnes 1997; Coombs with Sedgwick 1998; Lamb and Layzell 1995; Lloyd et al. 1996; SSI 1993b, 1996b, 1998). Inquiries too (Sheppard 1996) regularly report inadequate liaison and information exchange between agencies. When professionals work in isolation, each unilaterally determining their level of involvement, the wider needs of individuals are neglected, with consequent impact on integration and independence. What is required for effective inter-agency working (DoH 1995) is the development of a strategic perspective between partner agencies, commitment to joint working at all levels of the agencies involved, commitment to user and carer involvement, and using available resources to develop appropriate services in responding to individual needs. Particular efforts must be made to include agencies whose primary purpose is not community care, such as transport, further education and leisure services. Quality of life will often depend on services other than those provided by the NHS and by social services departments (Lloyd et al. 1996; Nocon and Qureshi 1996). Poverty, difficulty finding affordable and accessible transport, lack of employment opportunities and of services to enable people to retain jobs, and unsuitable housing all impact on social exclusion. If these needs are not met, those services that are offered may well appear irrelevant.

### Minority groups

There has been little research on community care for people from ethnic minority communities (Ahmad and Atkin 1996). In research and in practice, black disabled people are often excluded and forgotten (Begum, Hill and Stevens 1994). Minority groups criticise the failure to address their specific needs (Boneham *et al.* 1997; Mirza 1991; DoH 1998). Local authorities demonstrate commitment to meeting their needs but only some have made links with communities and developed culturally sensitive services (SSI 1996b). This is despite several requirements: to recognise the circumstances of minority communities; to be sensitive to their needs; and to plan community care in consultation with them (DoH 1990); to eliminate unlawful racial discrimination and to promote equal opportunities (Race Relations Act 1976, section 71); and to encourage the development of appropriate provision.[12] Black disabled people are, moreover, likely to have significantly higher levels of unmet need (Lloyd *et al.* 1996). Barriers to service use include:

> lack of knowledge, including unfamiliarity with concepts underpinning services;
>
> a tendency to homogenise the experiences of all disabled people (Begum *et al.* 1994; Stuart 1996), which privileges white perspectives on disability;
>
> culturally inappropriate assessments and services, and experienced racism;
>
> access barriers – information, transport, cost, language, stigma, fear;
>
> over-reliance on families to provide care;
>
> racist attitudes and stereotypes, and misrepresentation of people's needs;
>
> under-developed policies;
>
> short-term or inadequately funded specialist provision;
>
> marginalisation in community care planning and provisions.

There remains an urgent need for purchasers and providers to reflect on their treatment of and interaction with black disabled people, on their limited awareness and understanding of the potentially devastating effects of race and disability combined (Begum *et al.* 1994).

### Disabled people

Even when disabled people report satisfaction with health and welfare services (Lamb and Layzell 1995), they criticise patronising and dismissive attitudes, charges, lack of choice and access barriers (cost and transport especially), and inadequate and delayed provision. In one study that compared the views of service users, carers and social workers in individual cases (Buckley *et al.* 1995), 'clients' were sometimes confused about who was providing services, especially the distinction between social services, voluntary agencies and private organisations. Whilst levels of service were generally thought to be sufficient, the highest levels of dissatisfaction with sufficiency concerned domiciliary care, aids and adaptations, chiropody and respite care. The most often mentioned 'missing' services were counselling provided by social workers, informal visitors, and chiropody, followed by respite care, transport, recreational services, day-care, and aids and adaptations. Service users and carers were more likely to identify missing services than social workers, and carers more likely than service users. Night sitters and day-carers were criticised for their lack of skill and experience.

Disabled people commonly identify gaps in provision (Evans 1998b; Lloyd *et al.* 1996; Nocon and Qureshi 1996) – adequate transport, affordable domestic help, relevant information, suitable housing, telephones, contact with social workers, emotional support, and opportunities to develop and maintain skills and to engage in social activities. In a study of 607 disabled people (Lloyd *et al.* 1996), their assessment of how far their needs were being met was encouraging. However, significant levels of unmet need did emerge, for example concerning daily living equipment, personal assistance, communicating, mobility and household tasks. Informal carers rather than agency services met a significant level of need. This accords with government policy but begs questions (see below) about support for carers. High levels of unmet need were reported concerning public transport and specialist transport services, which affected their use of public and leisure facilities, with an obvious impact on community presence and integration. Younger disabled people were especially likely to feel that employment and training opportunities were poor, whilst disabled people generally wanted more social support and counselling services. Barriers affecting service use, especially among respondents from ethnic minority groups, included lack of staff awareness, lack of co-ordination, long waits for assessment and workers to whom they could not relate.

Stroke survivors (Pound, Gompertz and Ebrahim 1995) were highly satisfied with most aspects of their in-patient care but were less satisfied with the degree of their recovery and with most of the domiciliary services received. They were most satisfied with the type of therapy received but not with the amount offered or with the ease and speed with which it could be arranged.

Service providers may be more responsive to individual need and undertaking some innovative work, but reliable and consistent services are not always available (SSI 1996b). Independent living schemes give people more control but there can also be long delays for services such as occupational therapy. Direct payments do promote independence. However, disabled people must first surmount the hurdles of lack of information, of having had historically to think of their needs in terms of services, and lack of confidence that results from prolonged experiences of disempowerment (Evans 1998a). Few learning disabled people know anything about direct payments (Holman with Bewley 1999) and are often unnecessarily excluded from local authority schemes, which have been slow to develop. That decisions on direct payments are dependent on the exercise of professional judgement can add to the tension between assessor and assessed.

Local authorities and disabled people may have different views about what constitutes a valued service, for example concerning respite care, highlighting again the clash of perspective. However, innovative services are characterised by involving learning disabled people in planning, promoting choice by learning from disabled people, and creating new opportunities, for instance through supported employment schemes and befriending services that offer a real increase in purposeful activity (JRF 1996a, 1996b).

One study of 50 visually disabled people (Hardwick *et al.* 1999) found a clear majority of respondents identified some level of practical need concerning basic living skills, mobility outside the home, managing money and claiming benefits. One third identified housing needs. Again, about half identified some level of social or emotional needs concerning loneliness, isolation, worries about health or disability and feeling depressed. However, some respondents felt that service providers did not identify emotional needs. Others seemed frightened and anxious about their disability, and/or deterred from going out, seeking work or accessing leisure and community facilities because of societal attitudes. There was evidence of:

> 'missing' services, particularly counselling, social work support, advocacy, aids and adaptations, home visits and education opportunities;
>
> 'insufficient' services, for example restrictions on time and content of domiciliary care, delays in adaptations, irrelevant activities in day centres;
>
> a loss of skills and confidence following completion of rehabilitation because of the absence of employment or other opportunities;
>
> barriers to service take-up, especially the absence of locally based provision, travelling distance, difficulty accessing transport, and the lack of co-ordination between services.

Three themes were prominent in this study, namely: resignation (taking what comes); co-ordination (no central place for service provision and a lack of collaboration between providers); and partnership (not being listened to). Other studies have found, for instance, that help with housework, daily living tasks and mobility is being steadily eroded (Inman 1998), and that home help services are being lost if people are 'just' blind, notwithstanding their likely difficulties with, for example, sell-by dates. Services are being rationed through the loss of lower levels of home care and tighter eligibility criteria (Coles *et al.* 1997). Charging policies are causing hardship and leading some visually disabled people to cancel services. Substantial social, economic and environmental barriers remain, for instance in housing, access to community buildings and employment. The SSI (1998) concluded that, of eight authorities surveyed, only half were providing services effectively. The rest had a haphazard approach to supporting service users. It reported that low vision services, variously provided by social services departments, voluntary organisations and health authorities, would benefit from greater co-ordination and coherence. It did note more positively, however, that a range of services was meeting different types of sight loss needs.

### Mental health

Practical help appears highly valued, together with support in going out (Cullen *et al.* 1997). 'Clients' expressed dissatisfaction in this study with the difficulty of obtaining help out of hours, which resulted in contact with unfamiliar people and settings and a consequent avoidance of contact with needed services. The researchers stressed the importance to 'clients' of seeing someone regularly, although the required frequency would vary between individuals, and of having contact with someone who was liked and trusted. Godfrey and Wistow (1997) similarly have argued that regularity of contact and the existence of a relationship of trust assist entry into services with a worker who hears, listens and responds. Facilitating reintegration into everyday life requires not just symptom management but understanding the origin of ill health and distress in the context of an individual relationship. Godfrey and Wistow (1997) argue the importance of placing a high value on the quality of relationship with practitioners, highlighting its therapeutic value for devalued people with low self-esteem. In similar vein, Onyett (1992) talks of the need for care managers to be 'travel guides' or companions rather than 'travel agents', with evidence that such involvement can promote engagement with services and user satisfaction. Staff attitudes and understanding, together with an emphasis on relationships, emerge, therefore, as crucial.

Carpenter and Sbaraini (1997) also found a lack of evening and weekend services. Such provision can enable situations to be contained where previously 'clients' might have been sectioned. Quilgars (1998), observing that living independently can sometimes cause isolation, reports on a home-link scheme that involves the provision of secure tenancies; flexible, low-intensity, practical and emotional support from a support worker; and group support. Service users positively assessed the combination of practical (budgeting, bills and household matters) and emotional support. Warner *et al.* (1998) report on a scheme of adult placements, in which landlords or landladies provided support as well as rented rooms. This provided a flexible and non-stigmatising approach and appeared to facilitate integration of residents into the community. The same study, however, found that nearly a quarter of those in supported housing had no identified health or social services key worker, and nearly one fifth were receiving housing and support services inappropriate to their current needs. The researchers argue the need to develop effective strategies to help people move on, and to allow the level of support provided to be changed as needs alter.

The effects of mental distress can be wide-ranging and devastating (Harrison *et al.* 1999), with some level of need particularly likely concerning loneliness, worries about mental health and depression. People may also need help with basic living skills, mobility outside the home, claiming benefits, getting people to understand what they want or need, housing and accessing employment and education opportunities. What helps to counteract isolation and to rebuild confidence is having people available who offer time, understanding, and support. This study of 59 mental health service users found evidence of 'missing' services – counselling, advocacy, night and weekend services, assistance with holidays, informal visitors providing contact and support – and of 'insufficient' services – counselling, education opportunities, informal visitors, restricted time at day centres and night services. A clash of perspective emerged again, with providers seeing day centres as temporary stepping stones and users as permanent opportunities. Respondents stressed the importance of continuing supportive relationships, especially with support workers who helped to counteract loneliness. Barriers to accessing provision included having to travel, the location of services in areas felt to be unsafe, lack of service co-ordination, the irrelevance of activities, lack of time with staff and not being visited at home.

Inquiries (Sheppard 1996) mirror these findings. Finding services to be inadequate or unacceptable, they suggest that a low priority is accorded to mentally ill people, including inappropriate closure of cases and reliance on contact with duty social workers for assistance. Missing services include an adequate range of accommodation, appropriate placements outwith hospital, and a lack of planning and monitoring of aftercare.

A common complaint (Rogers and Pilgrim 1995; Cullen *et al.* 1997) concerns lack of contact with psychiatrists and dissatisfaction with its content. In general, service users want a range of options outside hospital and object to a predominantly medicalised approach to their problems, treatment and care. In this vein, Godfrey and Wistow (1997) identify that outcomes in mental health are linked to employment, housing and social support systems. A quality service should be based on participation, respect, information, choice and individuality, and address a diverse range of needs – income, accommodation, information, practical help, emotional support and access to services (Perring, Willmot and

Wilson 1995). However, as Morgan (1998) identifies, whilst 'clients' do recount good experiences, common themes emerge of being treated with disrespect, of powerlessness and fear, and of 'office hours' services when more extensive crisis services are needed.

## CARERS

Warner (1995) found some improvements in agencies' awareness of carers' needs and in the delivery of support services to meet these needs. However, he also found that the majority of carers believed that community care developments had made no difference and that services had deteriorated. They reported that it was no easier to have their own needs met.

Godfrey and Wistow (1997) found that professionals tended not to demonstrate awareness of the fluidity and complexity of the carer/cared-for relationship, or to appreciate carers' knowledge and expertise concerning the shifting manifestations of a person's illness. Barnes (1997), reviewing Mental Illness Specific Grant spending, found examples of services for carers – sitting services, respite care, including at weekends and evenings, support workers and groups.

Carers' needs often appear to be overlooked, especially if they are living with the person being cared for, despite the fragility of some support arrangements (Hardwick *et al.* 1999; Lloyd *et al.* 1996). Users and carers comment on the need for respite care, domiciliary care, flexible cover, mobility assistance and counselling. Carers do not feel valued and yet can feel unable to admit that they cannot cope, because that would imply that they had 'failed'.

In another study (Buckley *et al.* 1995) social workers overestimated the number of carers who needed a lot or some help with practical needs compared to carers' own views. However, they underestimated their need for help with social or emotional needs, especially depression, worries about the 'client's' disability, and worries about their ability to continue to care. As with service users (reported earlier), social workers underestimated the number of carers needing a lot of help but overestimated the number requiring some help with social/emotional needs. This can have an eroding effect on carers' willingness and ability to care. Where carers perceived themselves as needing no help, there was a relatively high level of agreement with social workers' perceptions. This was less and less the case as carers expressed a need for help. Agreement was not reached in 50 per cent of cases across different practical and social or emotional needs except for management of money and relationship problems with family and friends. Evidence suggests that practitioners' ability to provide practical services may (be used to) deflect attention from carers' social or emotional needs. Support, understanding, and time to discuss their worries and fears were important for carers, who also prioritised different needs, dependent on whether they are caring for an older and/or disabled person. However, social workers did not identify these same emphases.

Social workers overestimated the number of carers who had received services that met their needs. They also thought that fewer carers required a service, which they were not receiving, than did carers themselves, for example transport, night sitting, respite care, domiciliary care, or counselling. Sixty-six per cent of carers said that caring had affected their health but only 40 per cent felt that services had assisted here.

Few carers appear to ask for an assessment, and then usually only when they have reached breaking point or are finding it difficult to cope. A significant number appear unaware of their rights, for example to specific help, and are dissatisfied with their own assessments in terms of process and outcome – lack of thoroughness, and a failure to meet such needs as home care, respite and night care (CNA 1997; Warner 1995). Indeed, care plans often do not involve carers, or consider them only in terms of what support they can offer to the service user (Sheppard 1996; SSI 1996b). These findings confirm the variable outcome of the Carers (Recognition and Services) Act 1995, notwithstanding government policy (DoH 1991) that carers' contributions should be recognised and that, where necessary, they should be offered a separate assessment of their needs. They resonate with concerns about the exploitation of women as carers, paid and unpaid (Barnes and Walker 1996).

Research on carers has tended to neglect the experience of black carers (Atkin and Rollings 1996), an invisibility exacerbated by racist stereotypes and policies that rarely move beyond principles about the importance of supporting carers. Yet their experiences of the physical, financial and emotional effects of caring are similar, and their needs may be compounded by isolation, inequality in income and employment, non-recognition of need and inappropriate support services.

## COMPLAINTS

Evidence from across the range of community care service user groups has pointed to a lack of knowledge about complaints procedures and, where details of how to complain are known, a reluctance to access them. This reluctance appears to be related to the possibility of adverse consequences – a loss of services and/or relationships with professionals, concern about how the complainant will be perceived and feeling daunted by the procedures – and to low expectations and felt subordination in power relations (Braye and Preston-Shoot 1999). Some service users have expressed doubt that their complaints will be taken seriously because of the limited independent element within the procedures. Users perceive that they are not always encouraged to assert their views. Ellis (1993) found that agency practitioners see people who are knowledgeable and claim their rights as fussy and demanding. Moreover, people who have spent considerable time in rule-bound institutions may be reluctant to voice negative opinions about their environment and care received.

Studies of mentally distressed people and disabled people and of carers have reported similar findings, highlighting for example poor knowledge of procedures and disappointing outcomes (Buckley *et al.* 1995; Sbaraini and Carpenter 1996; SSI 1996a, 1997a). Holland (1996), in her study of 60 visually disabled service users, found that only 53 per cent knew how to make a complaint. In one survey of carers (CNA 1997), just over half had not been informed of their rights. The Social Services Inspectorate (SSI 1993b) similarly found that few people knew of complaints procedures and no one remembered having information in writing or other accessible formats. These findings suggest, perhaps, defensive practice by professionals.

A greater proportion of users and carers want to complain than actually do so (Buckley *et al.* 1995; Hardwick *et al.* 1999). These findings, once again, point to the value and necessity of advocacy and authorised representative schemes.

## IMPLICATIONS

User and carer experiences seriously challenge how authorities approach assessment and provision but will not, alone, guarantee the future appropriateness or legality of services. Moreover, assessors hold pessimistic views about the outcome of care management systems (Stanley 1999). They regard core elements of community care policy – needs-led assessments, user choice and enabling 'clients' to live within their own homes – as undermined by resource constraints. A commitment to 'something different' is needed to change a system characterised by ambiguity, meanness and contradiction.

### Law

Quite clearly, discretionary duties are interpreted restrictively. Disabled people and carers are denied assessments because discretion to determine apparent 'need'[13] and 'regular and substantial amount of care'[14] encourages resource-led decisions. Once assessed, the emphasis is reactive, meeting current need, rather than proactive, planning for future possible need.[15] Duties to consult and to involve disabled people in service planning are undermined by the absence of sanctions if agencies choose to interpret this requirement narrowly, emphasising professional dominance rather than any transfer of power.

Policy guidance[16] is more honoured in the breach than observance, its significance often unknown to practitioners and managers ( and Preston-Shoot 1999). Disabled people are not receiving comprehensive assessments required by policy guidance (DoH 1990). Services are being withdrawn without reassessments and/or when needs have not diminished.[17] Policy guidance on charging for residential care has been widely ignored.[18] Proper assessment of need may be the cornerstone of high quality care (DoH 1990), to be designed according to individual needs and preferences. However, assessments are not covering all the areas of need outlined in policy guidance and are more often an application of eligibility criteria than an exploration of needs.[19] As a regulator of practice, policy guidance is too distant and its usefulness, as currently constituted, therefore questionable. This point has, perhaps, been conceded by central government after the Sefton case (see note 18), when policy guidance was confirmed in primary legislation.[20]

Accountability is too weak. Success against one authority in judicial review does not remove the need to instigate proceedings against any other authority acting similarly. This point was influential in the government's decision to reinforce policy guidance on charging for residential care in primary legislation. Moreover, the availability of redress through judicial review and the Commission for Local Administration lies at the discretion of the courts and Ombudsman respectively and does not prevent authorities from disregarding their statutory duties. The legal mandate, therefore, does not prevent either abuse of power or a collusion between organisations and their employees that sometimes overrules professional values and knowledge.

Partly this is because entitlement to services, and to standards of provision, is not transparent. The argument, then, is that rights, which would give rise to public law duties on authorities, should replace a model of welfare based on discretionary duties and powers (Morris 1998). This has found support in proposals for reform of the Mental Health Act 1983 (DoH 1999a). In response, the government (DoH 1999b) has been more equivocal in legislating new rights to assessment, information about treatment and care, independent legal advice and authorised representatives, and an adequate level of service. The government's reasoning, the need to balance different interests, misses the point. Every area of social care, affecting every 'client' group, is a contested area involving competing perspectives and conflicting imperatives. Nonetheless, there are basic social rights that should be guaranteed to ensure meaningful citizenship (Barton 1993) and an optimal satisfaction of basic needs or, where need outstretches resources, a constrained optimum – the highest level of satisfaction possible (Doyal and Gough 1991).

The Human Rights Act 1998 will force rights more centrally onto the agenda. Health and local authorities have, as discussed above, already been criticised for consultation practices that obfuscate the right to a fair and public hearing. The right to an effective remedy is relevant to the preceding discussion of the availability and effectiveness of complaints procedures and judicial review. The right to respect for private and family life has already been successfully invoked in a case involving the proposed closure of a nursing home.[21] However, this Act is concerned only with civil and political rights. One essential accompaniment, then, is primary legislation that provides rights to information and to advocacy and authorised representatives; to define one's own needs and to participate in decisions about how these needs might be best met. The legislation would define rights to quality through the use of standards for every aspect of service, and would delineate how such policy principles as independence, community presence and participation, choice and partnership are to be understood. A second essential accompaniment is to broaden anti-discriminatory legislation to include statutes concerning sexuality and age, and to strengthen existing requirements in relation to health and welfare provision concerning 'race', gender and disability, by means of primary legislation, in order to counteract barriers to social inclusion and community presence.

### Policy

The (arguably deliberate) contradictions and ambiguities in community care policy have been fully analysed elsewhere (Braye and Preston-Shoot 1995). They remain unacknowledged in policy guidance (DoH 1990) with the result that clashes in perspective should not surprise. Inquiries (Ritchie, Dick and Lingham 1994) and judges[22] have criticised government guidance for its lack of clarity. Moreover, because key principles, such as empowerment, need, partnership and choice remain vaguely defined, they encapsulate rather than resolve practice dilemmas. Co-opted by different stakeholders for different agendas, they are likely to confuse and disappoint rather than realise their (radical) potential.

For example, practitioners and managers predominantly utilise a normative (standards defined by professionals) and comparative (eligibility; individual need relative to others) definition of need. Users and carers articulate felt need, altogether a broader concept that expresses what they value in their lives and how they experience their situation. The predominant paradigm is assessment that focuses on existing services, with integration a by-product. There has yet to be a fundamental paradigm shift, which embraces fully a social model of disability, and which takes as its starting point a reduction in exclusion, inequality and disabling features of the social, economic and political environment.

The different paradigms are illustrated quite clearly in different models of partnership. For agencies partnership might mean involvement in pre-set agendas within a listening culture that focuses on individual needs. Users and carers might want greater control over their lives and a focus on collective needs. Similarly in relation to choice, agencies may adopt a narrow market-oriented philosophy (Barnes and Walker 1996), which users may experience as offering neither exit from services to alternatives nor an effective voice, that policy purports to promise. Indeed, expression of choice is heavily influenced by who agrees or disagrees with whom, the view of risk taken by practitioners involved, and the degree to which workers act as arbiters between 'clients' and others or as advocates for service users (Myers and MacDonald 1996).

Judicial review has highlighted the wretched position in which central government has placed local authorities,[23] confirming the myth of needs-led assessments. Resource constraints affect what is discussed during assessment (Stanley 1999). Increasingly, a bureaucratic model appears to have replaced one based on human relations skills, mutuality and exchange, even though the latter is what users and carers say they find empowering and valuable.

Resources have been the preoccupation for government rather than defining and securing the most appropriate form of care for disabled people. Resources have, arguably, become a stronger pull for authorities and individual practitioners than legality. Good practice has become synonymous with procedurally correct practice. Struggling with irreconcilable demands, perhaps it is not acquiescence to the erosion of professional values and knowledge that should surprise, but the survival of sensitive and innovative practice. In the short term this highlights the importance of developing comprehensive advocacy and authorised representative schemes. In the longer term, it illustrates the need for a debate about the purposes and goals of community care, which results in an honest policy that articulates rather than fudges the balance between needs and resources, autonomy (rights) and paternalism (risks), consumerism and citizenship.

### Practice

Skills for empowering practice in social care have been described elsewhere (Braye and Preston-Shoot 1995). What this review highlights is the importance of practice which:

> challenges policies and procedures that are unlawful, unfair and/or counter to professional knowledge and values, as they are expressed generally or imposed in individual cases;

> recognises accountability to employing authorities but which refuses to prioritise this above what is lawful (in statute and in policy guidance) and/or good practice;

> counters the narrowness of the legal and service mandate by having equality at its core and, therefore, addresses social and environmental barriers to inclusion and integration.

### The modernising agenda

The government has accepted that serious problems affect services for adults (DoH 1998). Eligibility criteria exclude severely disabled people who need help. Decisions are service-driven rather than needs-led. Reviews and services for carers are patchy. Its proposals aim to provide needs-led services that are characterised by flexibility and consistent quality, an integrated system of care, and standards and regulation that safeguard users from abuse and poor practice. Five key principles underpin the proposals, namely:

1. care should support people's independence and respect their dignity;

2. services should meet people's specific needs;

3. people should have a voice in what is provided and how;

4. staff should be adequately trained;

5. services should be underpinned by clear and accountable standards that are enforceable.

Some developments derived from the modernising proposals are welcome, such as the extension of direct payments schemes, strengthening the requirement for reviews, providing greater support for carers, and developing employment and rehabilitation services. Arguably, however, they do not overcome the barriers to partnership between different agencies and with users and carers. Nor do they address concerns about the sufficiency of service provision. Whilst clear and accountable standards are long overdue, they will have little meaning if users and carers have not been involved in their creation and if they do not guarantee levels of provision that are desirable or essential (Darvill 1998). The ambiguities and contradictions in policy remain, for example about funding for local authorities and about whose perspective, ultimately, guides assessment decisions. The modernising proposals do not change the traditional paradigm. They retain faith in a system of duties, powers and guidance, rather than guaranteeing rights. The focus remains on welfare, on provision to meet need, rather than extending the emphasis to challenging barriers to inclusion and participation.

## CONCLUSION

The clear voices for change, to which this chapter has given space, have yet to have a major impact on cultures, structures, processes and, most fundamentally, ourselves as practitioners and managers. They call out not so much for modernisation of services as for a fundamental reappraisal of what law, policy and practice are attempting to achieve.

# REFERENCES

Ahmad, W. and Atkin, K. (1996) (eds) *'Race' and Community Care*. Buckingham: Open University Press.

Atkin, K. and Rollings, J. (1996) 'Looking after their own? Family care-giving among Asian and Afro-Caribbean communities.' In W. Ahmad and K. Atkin (eds) *'Race' and Community Care*. Buckingham: Open University Press.

Baldock, J. and Ungerson, C. (1994) *Becoming Consumers of Community Care: Households within the Mixed Economy of Welfare*. York: Joseph Rowntree Foundation.

Barnes, D. (1997) *Monitoring the Use of the Mental Illness Specific Grant in 1994/95 and 1995/96*. London: Department of Health/Social Services Inspectorate.

Barnes, M. and Walker, A. (1996) 'Consumerism versus empowerment: a principled approach to the involvement of older service users.' *Policy and Politics 24*, 4, 375.

Barton, L. (1993) 'The struggle for citizenship: the case of disabled people.' *Disability, Handicap and Society 8*, 3, 235.

Begum, N., Hill, M. and Stevens, A. (1994) (eds) *Reflections. Views of Black Disabled People on their Lives and Community Care*. London: CCETSW.

Bewley, C. and Glendinning, C. (1994) *Involving Disabled People in Community Care Planning*. York: Joseph Rowntree Foundation.

Boneham, M., Williams, K., Copeland, J., McKibbin, P., Wilson, K., Scott, A. and Saunders, P. (1997) 'Elderly people from ethnic minorities in Liverpool: mental illness, unmet need and barriers to service use.' *Health and Social Care in the Community 5*, 3, 173.

Braye, S. and Preston-Shoot, M. (1995) *Empowering Practice in Social Care*. Buckingham: Open University Press.

Braye, S. and Preston-Shoot, M. (1999) 'Accountability, administrative law and social work practice: redressing or reinforcing the power imbalance?' *Journal of Social Welfare and Family Law 21*, 3, 235.

Buckley, J., Preston-Shoot, M. and Smith, C. (1995) *Community Care Reforms: The Views of Users and Carers – Research Findings*. Manchester: University of Manchester School of Social Work.

Caldock, K. and Nolan, M. (1994) 'Assessment and community care: are the reforms working?' *Generations Review 4*, 4, 2.

Carpenter, J. and Sbaraini, S. (1997) 'A healthy approach.' *Community Care*, 23–29 October, 32.

CNA (1997) *Still Battling? The Carers Act One Year On*. London: Carers National Association/Association of Directors of Social Services.

Coles, D., Willetts, G. and Winyard, S. (1997) *A Question of Risk. Community Care for Older Visually Impaired People in England and Wales*. London: Royal National Institute for the Blind.

Coombs, M. with Sedgwick, A (1998) *Right to Challenge. The Oxfordshire Community Care Rights Project*. Bristol: Joseph Rowntree Foundation/The Policy Press.

Cullen, D., Waite, A., Oliver, N., Carson, J. and Holloway, F. (1997) 'Case management for the mentally ill: a comparative evaluation of client satisfaction.' *Health and Social Care in the Community 5*, 2, 106.

Darvill, G. (1998) *Organisation, People and Standards*. London: National Institute for Social Work.

Davis, A., Ellis, K. and Rummery, K. (1998) *Access to Assessment: Perspectives of Practitioners, Disabled People and Carers*. Bristol: Joseph Rowntree Foundation/Policy Press.

Day, P. (1994) 'Ambiguity and user involvement: issues arising in assessments for young people and their carers.' *British Journal of Social Work 24*, 5,577.

DoH (1990) *Community Care in the Next Decade and Beyond. Policy Guidance*. London: HMSO.

DoH (1991) *Care Management and Assessment: Practitioners' Guide*. London: HMSO.

DoH (1993) *Informing Users and Carers*. London: HMSO.

DoH (1995) *Building Bridges: Guide to Arrangement for Inter Agency Working for the Care and Protection of Severely Mentally Ill People*. London: HMSO.

DoH (1998) *Modernising Social Services*. London: The Stationery Office.

DoH (1999a) *Draft Outline Proposals by Scoping Study Committee. Review of the Mental Health Act 1983*. London: Department of Health.

DoH (1999b) *Reform of the Mental Health Act 1983. Proposals for Consultation*. London: HMSO.

Donnelly, M. and Mays, N. (1995) 'Users' views of care in the community 6 months after discharge from long-stay psychiatric care.' In G. Wilson (ed) *Community Care. Asking the User*. London: Chapman and Hall.

Doyal, L. and Gough, I. (1991) *A Theory of Human Need*. London: Macmillan.

Ellis, K. (1993) *Squaring the Circle. User and Carer Participation in Needs Assessment*. York: Joseph Rowntree Foundation.

Evans, C. (1998a) 'User empowerment and direct payments.' In S. Balloch (ed) *Outcomes of Social Care. A Question of Quality?* London: National Institute for Social Work.

Evans, C. (1998b) 'Personal social services acceptable to users.' In A. O'Neil and D. Statham (eds) *Shaping Futures. Rights, Welfare and Personal Social Services*. London: National Institute for Social Work.

French, S., Gillman, M. and Swain, J. (1997) *Working with Visually Disabled People: Bridging Theory and Practice*. Birmingham: Venture Press.

Fryer, R. (1998) *Signposts to Services: Inspection of Social Services Information to the Public*. London: DoH/SSI.

Godfrey, M. and Wistow, G. (1997) 'The user perspective on managing for health outcomes: the case of mental health.' *Health and Social Care in the Community 5*, 5, 325.

Goodwin, S. (1997) 'Independence, risk and compulsion: conflicts in mental health policy.' *Social Policy and Administration 31*, 3, 260.

Harding, T. and Oldman, H. (1996) *Involving Service Users and Carers in Local Services*. London: NISW/Surrey Social Services Department.

Hardwick, L., Kershaw, S. and Preston-Shoot, M. (1999) *'Focus on the Future.' A Survey of Visually Disabled People and their Experiences of Service Provision*. Liverpool John Moores University School of Law and Applied Social Studies.

Harrison, P., Mayhew, J. and Preston-Shoot, M. (1999) *'Like Walking in the Wind.' User Perspectives on Developing Mental Health Provision in Liverpool*. Liverpool: Liverpool John Moores University School of Law and Applied Social Studies.

Holland, P. (1996) *The Accessibility of Local Authority Services in Liverpool: The Views of Visually Impaired Users*. Unpublished MA Thesis.

Holman, A. with Bewley, C. (1999) *Funding Freedom 2000: People with Learning Difficulties using Direct Payments*. London: Values into Action.

Hoyes, L., Lart, R., Means, R. and Taylor, M. (1994) *Community Care in Transition*. York: Joseph Rowntree Foundation.

Inman, K. (1998) 'Out of sight.' *Community Care*, 17–23 September, 21.

Jahoda, A. and Cattermole, M. (1995) 'Leaving home: a real choice for people with learning difficulties?' In G. Wilson (ed) *Community Care. Asking the User.* London: Chapman and Hall.

JRF (1996a) *Respite Services for Adults with Learning Difficulties. Social Care Research 82.* York: Joseph Rowntree Foundation.

JRF (1996b) *Supported Employment for People with Learning Difficulties. Social Care Research 86.* York: Joseph Rowntree Foundation.

Lamb, B. and Layzell, S. (1995) *Disabled in Britain: Counting on Community Care.* London: Scope.

Lankshear, G. and Giarchi, G. (1995) 'Finding out about consumer views: an experiment in the group method.' In G. Wilson (ed) *Community Care. Asking the User.* London: Chapman and Hall.

Lloyd, M., Preston-Shoot, M., Temple, B. and , R. (1996) 'Whose project is it anyway? Sharing and shaping the research and development agenda.' *Disability and Society 11,* 3, 301.

Lovelock, R., Powell, J. and Craggs, S. (1995) *Shared Territory: Assessing the Social Support Needs of Visually Impaired People.* York: Joseph Rowntree Foundation.

Mayer, J. and Timms, N. (1970) *The Client Speaks.* London: RKP.

McFarland, E., Dalton, M. and Walsh, D. (1989) 'Ethnic minority needs and service delivery: the barriers to access in a Glasgow inner-city area.' *New Community 15,* 3, 405.

Mirza, K. (1991) 'Community care for the black community – waiting for guidance.' In CCETSW (ed) *One Small Step Towards Racial Justice.* London: CCETSW.

Morgan, H. (1998) 'Looking for the crevices. Consulting with users of mental health services.' *Soundings 8,* Spring, 171.

Morris, J. (1998) 'The personal social services: identifying the problem.' In A. O'Neil and D. Statham (eds) *Shaping Futures. Rights, Welfare and Personal Social Services.* London: NISW.

Myers, F. and MacDonald, C. (1996) 'Power to the people? Involving users and carers in needs assessments and care planning – views from the practitioner.' *Health and Social Care in the Community 4,* 2, 86.

Nocon, A. and Qureshi, H. (1996) *Outcomes of Community Care for Users and Carers.* Buckingham: Open University Press.

Onyett, S. (1992) *Case Management in Mental Health.* London: Chapman and Hall.

Onyett, S., Standen, R. and Peck, E. (1997) 'The challenge of managing community mental health teams.' *Health and Social Care in the Community 5,* 1, 40.

Perring, C., Willmot, J. and Wilson, M. (1995) *Reshaping the Future.* London: MIND.

Pilgrim, D., Todhunter, C. and Pearson, M. (1997) 'Accounting for disability: customer feedback or citizen complaints?' *Disability and Society 12,* 1, 3.

Plumb, A. (1999) 'New mental health legislation. A lifesaver? Changing paradigm and practice.' *Social Work Education 18,* 4, 459.

Pound, P., Gompertz, P. and Ebrahim, S. (1995) 'Stroke survivors' evaluations of their health care.' In G. Wilson (ed) *Community Care. Asking the User.* London: Chapman and Hall.

Quilgars, D. (1998) 'Going it alone.' *Community Care,* 17–23 September, 24.

Read, J. and Wallcraft, J. (1992) *Guidelines for Empowering Users of Mental Health Services.* London: Mind/COHSE.

Ritchie, J., Dick, D. and Lingham, R. (1994) *Report of the Inquiry into the Care and Treatment of Christopher Clunis.* London: HMSO.

Robbins, D. (1993) (ed) *Community Care. Findings from DoH Funded Research 1988–1992.* London: HMSO.

Rogers, A. and Pilgrim, D. (1995) 'Experiencing psychiatry: an example of emancipatory research.' In G. Wilson (ed) *Community Care. Asking the User.* London: Chapman and Hall.

Salter, B. (1994) 'The politics of community care: social rights and welfare limits.' *Policy and Politics 22,* 2, 119.

Sbaraini, S. and Carpenter, J. (1996) 'Barriers to complaints: a survey of mental health service users.' *Journal of Management in Medicine 10,* 6, 36.

Shaw, R. (1995) 'User involvement in hostel accommodation: overcoming apathy.' In G. Wilson (ed) *Community Care. Asking the User.* London: Chapman and Hall.

Sheppard, D. (1996) *Learning the Lessons.* Second edition. London: The Zito Trust.

SSI (1991) *Hear Me: See Me. An Inspection of Services from Three Agencies to Disabled People in Gloucestershire.* London: DoH.

SSI (1993a) *Social Services for Hospital Patients III: Users and Carers Perspective.* London: DoH.

SSI (1993b) *Whose Life is it, Anyway? A Report of an Inspection of Services for People with Multiple Impairments.* London: DoH.

SSI (1996a) *Social Services Departments and the Care Programme Approach: An Inspection.* London: DoH.

SSI (1996b) *Progressing Services with Physically Disabled People.* London: DoH.

SSI (1997a) *Caring for People at Home. An Overview of the National Inspection of Social Services Department Arrangements for the Assessment and Delivery of Home Care Services.* London: DoH.

SSI (1997b) *A Service on the Edge. Services for People who are Deaf or Hard of Hearing.* London: DoH.

SSI (1998) *A Sharper Focus. Inspection of Services for Adults who are Visually Impaired or Blind.* London: DoH.

Stalker, K., Duckett, P. and Downs, M. (1999) *Going with the Flow: Choice, Dementia and People with Learning Difficulties.* Brighton: Pavilion Publishing.

Stanley, N. (1999) 'User-practitioner transactions in the new culture of community care.' *British Journal of Social Work 29,* 3, 417.

Stuart, O. (1996) ' "Yes, we mean black disabled people too": thoughts on community care and disabled people from black and minority ethnic communities'. In W. Ahmad and K. Atkin (eds) *'Race' and Community Care.* Buckingham: Open University Press.

Sullivan, P. (1998) 'Progress or neglect? Reviewing the impact of care in the community for the severely mentally ill.' *Critical Social Policy 55,* 193.

Tanner, D. (1998) 'Empowerment and care management: swimming against the tide.' *Health and Social Care in the Community 6,* 6, 447.

Twigg, J. and Atkin, K. (1994) *Carers Perceived. Policy and Practice in Informal Care.* Buckingham: Open University Press.

Warner, N. (1995) *Better Tomorrows? Report of a National Study of Carers and the Community Care Changes.* London: Carers National Association.

Warner, L., Ford, R., Holmshaw, J. and Sathyamoorthy, G. (1998) 'Homing in on need.' *Community Care,* 30 July–5 August, 20.

Wells, J. (1997) 'Priorities, "street level bureaucracy" and the community mental health team.' *Health and Social Care in the Community 5,* 5, 333.

Willetts, G. (1994) 'Community care for the one in sixty.' *British Journal of Visual Impairment 12,* 2, 47.

Wilson, G. (1995) (ed) *Community Care. Asking the User.* London: Chapman and Hall.

# NOTES

1   Quotation marks are used throughout to denote the contested nature of this term.

2   *R v Devon County Council, ex p. Baker* [1995] Ac. 1 ALL ER 72; *R v North and East Devon Health Authority and North Devon Healthcare NHS Trust, ex p. POW and Others*; *R v Same, ex p. Metcalfe* [1999] 1 CCLR 280.

3   s.10

4   s.46

5   *R v Avon County Council, ex p. M* [1995] Fam Law 66; *R v North Yorkshire County Council, ex p. Hargreaves* [1997] 1 CCLR 104.

6   ss.9–10

7   Disabled Persons (Services, Consultation and Representation) Act 1986 s.4.

8   *R v Bristol County Council, ex p. Penfold* [1998] 1 CCLR 117.

9   *R v Berkshire County Council, ex p. P* [1998] 1 CCLR 141; *R v Haringey LBC, ex p. Norton* [1998] 1 CCLR 169.

10  *R v Staffordshire County Council, ex parte Farley* [1997] Current Year Law Book, 1678.

11  *R v Gloucestershire County Council, ex p. Mahfood and Others* [1995] 160 LGR 321; *R v Staffordshire County Council, ex p. Farley* [1997] Current Year Law Book, 1678; *R v Sefton MBC, ex. P. Help the Aged and Charlotte Blanchard* [1997] 1 CCLR 57.

12  s.35

13  NHS and Community Care Act 1990, s.47.

14  Carers (Recognition and Services) Act 1995, s.1.

15  *R v Mid Glamorgan County Council, ex p. Miles* [1993] Legal Action, January 1994; Stalker *et al.* 1999.

16  Local Authority Social Services Act 1970, s.7.

17  *R v Gloucestershire County Council, ex p. Mahfood and Others* [1995] 160 LGR 321.

18  *R v Sefton MBC, ex p. Help the Aged and Charlotte Blanchard* [1997] 1 CCLR 57.

19  *R v Haringey LBC, ex p. Norton* [1998] 1 CCLR 169.

20  Community Care (Residential Accommodation) Act 1998.

21  *R v North and East Devon Health Authority, ex p. Coughlan* [1999] 2 CCLR 285.

22  *R v Gloucestershire County Council, ex p. RADAR* [1995] CO/2764/95.

23  *R v Gloucestershire County Council, ex p. Barry* [1997] 2 WLR 459.

# The Contributors

**Suzy Braye** is a Reader in Social Work in the School of Law and Social Work at Staffordshire University.

**Catherine Casserley** is a qualified barrister working as Legal Officer for the Royal National Institute for the Blind, and specialising in the Disability Discrimination Act.

**Jeremy Cooper** is Professor of Law at Middlesex University where he is also Director of the Disability Law Research Unit.

**Mairian Corker** is Senior Research Fellow in the Department of Education and Social Science at the University of Central Lancashire.

**John Davis** is a Research Fellow in the Research Unit, Department of Health and Behavioural Change, at the University of Edinburgh.

**Kate Harrison** is a freelance solicitor specialising in mental health law.

**Mary Holmes** is a Principal Lecturer in the School of Law at Kingston University.

**Clare Picking** is an occupational therapist in private practice.

**Michael Preston-Shoot** is Professor of Social Work and Social Care at Liverpool John Moores University.

**Belinda Schwehr** is a solicitor in private practice specialising in training local government managers in community care and social services law.

**Lisa Waddington** is a senior lecturer in European Union Law at Maastricht University.

# Subject Index

# Author Index